DEEPLY DAMAGED

An Explanation For
The Profound Problems Arising From
Infant Abortion and Child Abuse

Mount Joy College
Victoria, BC Canada
For Counselor Training, Seminars and Research

Philip G. Ney MD, FRCP (C) MA, RPsych

First Printing: November 1997

Printed and Bound in Canada ISBN: 0-920952-10-0

Third Edition

TABLE OF CONTENTS

8. REQUIREMENTS FOR THE GROUP TREATMENT OF ABORTION WOUNDED PEOPLE

9. SOME KEY CONCEPTS OF THE TREATMENT PROGRAM ...299

INDEX OF FIGURES AND TABLES

Figures

Tables

INTRODUCTION
TO THE THIRD EDITION

1. DOWN IN THE DARK VALLEY OF DESPAIR

A man and a woman came puffing up the hill, looking tired and very worried. They began shouting. “You have got to help us. It is terrible down there. There is a huge battle going on. Millions of people are being killed and hundreds of thousands of people are wandering around in the darkness with deep wounds looking for somebody to treat them. Please help us.” A few curious people stopped their leisurely picnics or joyful recreation or intense but meaningless work.

Most people responded to their urgent pleas with, **‘7** *do not see anything. All I see is a valley covered in a blanket of fog. I am sure it will soon lift and we will see the beautiful river down there.”*

“No. Can you not hear the screams? It is terrible down there. There are dead babies lying all over the place and mothers and fathers walking around with open wounds. People are randomly killing each other and others are hiding in fear. Many are drinking or drugging themselves to death trying to ameliorate their pain. Do not be fooled by the fog. It is dark and desperate down there. Please help.”

The majority wandered away. Some stopped long enough to learn more and a few of them volunteered to help, but the situation posed a deep dilemma. The wounds were sufficiently deep that extensive training would be required before they could do a proper job. There would never be enough professionals. Since there were so many people, even the most superficial first aid for a lot of people might be better than nothing. Trainees had to understand it was a difficult, tiring and dangerous job. Maybe there was some way to properly train people from so many walks of life, if only they were sufficiently brave and determined.

2. THE OVERWHELMING NEED

Deeply Damaged is the first of a two-part book, the second part being the training manual, Hope Alive. It is designed for those who are engaging in a training program to learn the theory behind the techniques of Hope Alive group counselling. This is not a program to learn psychotherapy or counselling in general, but a specific type of group counselling for those damaged by childhood mistreatment, pregnancy loss and being a pregnancy loss survivor. Although reasonably well described in the second part, the techniques are difficult to do properly. No one should try to carry out this program without training.

Now that we are developing a network of trainees, it becomes increasingly possible for people in many countries to make contact with an area director or an affiliated organisation and obtain training. The International Institute for Pregnancy Loss and Child Abuse Research & Recovery (IIPLCARR) provides training for qualifying people who desire to become group counsellors. We are training people as fast and as carefully as we can because there is an urgent need.

There are literally millions of people who are suffering the effects of unresolved pregnancy losses, past childhood mistreatment and being a survivor in a family where there has been a pregnancy loss, usually by abortion. This overwhelming need may not be readily apparent. Yet, careful, clinical observation and research indicate there are many thousands of people in every country who are deeply wounded by confusing conflicts, intense emotions, personality handicaps and progressive dehumanisation resulting from unresolved losses and abuses. Many people are able to keep up a facade of health, but they quickly decompensate with physical complaints or psychiatric disturbances in times of relatively minor crisis. If you are able and interested in a unique counselling program with proven effectiveness, you are invited to explore training with us.

Our purpose is to train as many people as quickly and carefully as possible given the desperate situation. The Hope Alive method is for counsellees suffering from the effects of pregnancy loss, particularly abortion and/or child abuse and neglect, and being a pregnancy loss survivor. The training includes experience both as counsellee and counsellor.
Trainees will study to understand the basic pathology, how the treatment works and the techniques that facilitate healing. This includes 1) Psychology of Created Humanity, 2) The elaboration of False Faces, 3) Causes of psychological splits in a person, 4) Triangles of abuse and neglect, 5) Reasons for pregnancy loss, 6) Trans generational Tragedy, 7) A person's Blueprint, 8) The Original and Alternative Plan for humanity, 9) The Universal Ethic of Mutual Benefit, 10) The process of scapegoating, 11) Understanding Abnormal Grief, 12) Ten types of Post-Abortion Survivor Syndrome, 13) Progressive Dehumanisation and 14) Practical Reconciliation.

Treatment techniques include a basic working knowledge of insight oriented group counselling, operant conditioning, role-playing, safe re-enactment, psychodrama, modeling, grief facilitation, visual parables and decision-making. Treatment is designed to facilitate 1) remembering traumatic events, 2) understanding the roots of psychological conflict, 3) controlling fear, withdrawal and rage, 4) learning assertion, 5) dealing with guilt, 6) discarding false faces, 7) passing through despair, 8) mourning the loss of the Person I Should Have Become, 9) grieving pregnancy losses, 10) negotiating realistic expectations, 11) reconciliation with perpetrator, observer and victims, 12) learning to utilize a painful past for the benefit of others, 13) finding ways to rejoice and 14) saying good good-byes.

3. WHY THE URGENCY?

The problem of pregnancy loss and child mistreatment is both intensive and extensive, deep, widespread and with myriad ramifications. It is extensive because there are approximately 200 million new patients a year as a consequence of induced abortions. There are approximately 60 million abortions each year in the world. Subtracting repeat abortions, this means that there are approximately 50 million fathers and 50 million mothers and 100 million siblings and the same number of grandparents who are deeply damaged annually. In addition, there are millions of children throughout the world who are being neglected and abused. In most instances, people suffer from the effects of both childhood mistreatment and pregnancy loss. In at least 70% of the cases we see, people are suffering the combined effects of abuse, neglect and abortion.

The problems are deep. Abortion, abuse, neglect and surviving cut at the very roots of our humanity. Neglect makes a person vulnerable to hurt and susceptible to seduction. Abuse destroys the person the child is building. Abortion completes the dehumanisation. It is very difficult to rebuild a whole human.

The difficulties that come from these combined problems are generally denied by experts and ignored by authorities. For most people it is like sitting on a hilltop looking at the top of the fog that shrouds the valley of death below. They may hear muffled cries, but unless they descend into the valley they will not see the millions of walking, wounded, and dying people who lay scattered about the battlefield. When those who have seen the enormity of the problem ascend the hill and try to inform the rest of the world what is going on, they are met with denial, self-imposed ignorance, or rationalizations for not becoming involved.

In the tradition of medicine, whenever there is an epidemic and there are insufficient medical personnel or resources, people who feel responsible go into the towns and countryside to recruit anybody who is willing and in anyway able.

In this way, blacksmiths have found themselves burying bodies, carpenters building coffins, housewives feeding sick people, town clerks looking for resources, farmers digging ditches and latrines, and daintily bred ladies bandaging ugly wounds. In that tradition, and because we are facing the largest, most destructive epidemic in the whole history of humanity, we are recruiting mature people from many backgrounds; anyone who is eager to learn and prepared to have a professional attitude. Of course, we welcome professionals and experienced counsellors with a keen interest to learn this type of group counselling.

We are continually looking for good people to train, particularly those who are prepared to go to areas of high need such as Eastern Europe. The people who come for training must be, upon application, screened and interviewed. There is also a certain amount of self-selection of trainees. Some people who apply soon realize they are not that interested or motivated or suitable. Some people may not complete the training as they find it too arduous. Some may not do all the work. Some who complete the intensive residential training course are invited to write the examination. Those who pass the examination must agree to the Commitment to Professional Conduct. Then they must spend time as a co-therapist and continue with group supervision. Some may not continue because they realize it is too demanding of their personal resources.

We believe the whole process of writing this book (and setting up the research and training) has been prodded along by God. We have been and continue to be directed, guided and blessed in large and small ways. Though there are now some very competent, talented people providing Hope Alive group counselling, the need is still enormous. It is high time that people leave their comforts and pleasures to devote themselves to healing the people injured in this huge plague caused by abuse and abortion.

4. THE PURPOSE AND BACKGROUND OF DEEPLY DAMAGED

Child abuse and infant abortion have many terrible aspects in common. We have evidence to show that one leads to another in a complex cycle of cause and effect. Both create very deep damage and profound conflicts that are not easy to resolve. Any attempt to rectify and treat one without the other will probably be ineffective.

Because child abuse and infant abortion so often go together we felt it was necessary to discover a theoretical framework to explain the process and a detailed treatment plan to offer healing those who are damaged. Although initially we felt that it was possible to put these two components together in one book, it now appears one comprehensive book is less than ideal. There are many people who would like to read about the reasons for the extensive damage who have no particular interest in counselling people. Others who would like to treat people and accept the need for proper training must also understand the theoretical and scientific basis for the treatment techniques we use.

Too often people believe that they can counsel after reading techniques from a manual. They cannot. There is no proper clinical training without clinical experience and supervision. To avoid having untrained people harming patients, we insist that counsellees obtain training in the techniques described in Hope Alive. For this reason, only those who have done the training have access to and a right to use the treatment manual. This may appear rather rigid. However, as two well-experienced clinicians and teachers of medical students, we believe that the therapist's first responsibility is to do no harm. Without proper training, well meaning, but untrained therapists attempting to use this manual can harm patients more than they help them.

Deeply Damaged describes the Hope Alive approach to the understanding of child abuse and infant abortion. The mistreatment of children not only damages children, but also the people who are doing the mistreating. In the first section we describe the Psychology of Created Humanity, which attempts to take the development of a child's inner problems back to their most basic roots. Section 2 looks at the psychopathology, which necessitated the development of the Hope Alive treatment program. We devote Section 3 to the Post-Pregnancy Loss and Post Abortion Syndromes, which describes possible after-effects of pregnancy loss and/or abortion on the parents of the aborted or miscarried baby. In Section 4 we describe the theory behind Post-Abortion Survivor Syndrome - the helpless cry, scapegoating, and the "wanted child" versus the welcomed child. Section 5 examines the impact of abortion on euthanasia and eugenics. We present our response, the Universal Ethic of Mutual Benefit. Section 6 describes the philosophy and characteristics of the Hope Alive healing process. Section 7 reviews the "hypothesis testing" counselling method. Section 8 looks at some of the requirements for treatment in depth. Section 9 defines and summarizes the Hope Alive treatment methods. Finally, Section 10 gives a summary of our research findings related to child abuse and abortion.

Since Deeply Damaged and the Hope Alive program are continually being revised and updated, it is recommended that interested persons not only read this book but also obtain the references of the scientific literature included in the resource section. Any feedback, advice, correction, criticism and helpful comments are always appreciated.

PURPOSE

Infant abortion and child abuse are the most profound and most extensive tragedies of our time. Both are an expression of deep and difficult unresolved conflicts in the world. Both demonstrate humanity's perpetual ambivalence toward children. Children are seen both as the cause and the solution to family difficulties. They are both a family's most treasured possession and its most disposable irritant.

Abuse and Abortion are symptomatic of hopelessness in the world. Both are an expression of how the child has always been scapegoated for the sins of humankind. The massive destruction of unborn children is a recent phenomenon. That amount of child scapegoating indicates the extent of unresolved conflict and selfishness present in the world. Much of that is the mistreatment of children. Thus, both infant abortion and child abuse are the result and the expression of scapegoating.

Mistreating and killing children causes deep, often irreparable, harm in families. The harm is always reciprocal. Damage done to children always affects those who harm them. We are tightly bound together in the bundle of life. One cannot hurt without being hurt. One cannot kill another without destroying something inside oneself. Because the family unit is the basic component of society, when the family is hurt, society is damaged and civilization begins to crumble. When the smallest and the most innocent humans are mistreated, there is no basis for a civilized society. With rampant abuse and abortion no one can remain safe or sane.

Abuse and abortion are intimately connected. They are both cause and effect. They are so intertwined that it is impossible to heal the effects of one without treating the other. Men or women who have been abused and/or neglected are more likely to abort their unborn children. Abortion interferes with sensitive parenting mechanisms and increases the tendency of all those involved to mistreat their children.

The purpose of the Hope Alive program is to provide a new approach to the treatment of Child Abuse and Neglect (CAN), Post Abortion Syndrome (PAS), Post Abortion Survivor Syndrome (PASS), and Lack of Partner Support (LOPS). We must treat both the symptoms and the root causes, otherwise all these tragedies will repeat from one generation to the next. Abortion kills both the innocent infant in the mother and the mother's childlike innocence, which is an important part of the person she "should have become." Part of the treatment process requires engaging in a number of difficult griefs. Out of the dust of death a wholesome, authentic, if somewhat damaged, person may grow. Wholeness cannot even begin unless grieving is initiated.

We have observed that abortion is usually tied to conflicts stemming from the mistreatment of children in the present family or past generations. It can also be occasioned by family or government coercion, fetal abnormality, famine or war. All of these circumstances are a part of the cause and effect of child mistreatment.

Treatment must try to correct the harm done during their childhood, both to the aborting mothers and to their partners. It must deal with the broken relationships in the family and in the world. It must treat the surviving children. There must be reconciliation of wounded with wounding before anyone can let go of the painful past and stop tragic history from repeating from one generation to the next.

The Hope Alive treatment program is designed not just for those with psychological sophistication, but also for those who have a variety of professional backgrounds, e.g. teachers, priests, pastors, and others who are professional in their approach to treatment. We believe that if counsellors ensure that the counsellees participate in the group process, carry out the group exercises and do all their assignments, then they will benefit whether the counsellor is absolutely convinced of the theory or not.

This third edition includes some clinical examples that come out of the training we have done. We have had the opportunity and privilege of conducting training seminars in Bosnia, Canada, Denmark, Eire, England, France, Germany, Hungary, Northern Ireland, Norway, Poland, Romania, Scotland, Switzerland, the Ukraine, and the USA. Although the trainees were very different and came from diverse backgrounds, the common factors were a deep appreciation for the need for training and a quick ability to learn. Out of those training experiences we have made some important additions to the technique. God continues to teach us, so there is further elaboration on the basic theory. The treatment is addressed as if to women, mainly because more women then men are seeking treatment. However, the program also works for groups for men or for both sexes.

This book describes a different approach to the psychology of human development, which is the theoretical basis for Hope Alive group counselling. The treatment manual outlines a progression of events and specific techniques in sufficient detail that it can be used as a guide to treatment. We do not recommend that anyone attempt to carry out this program of treatment without completing a proper training seminar and passing the examination. There are too many critical nuances of communication and practice, which cannot be learned by just reading this book. This edition is only the third of more to come. Both theory & practice keep developing. We praise God and thank our trainees and patients for fresh insights.

BACKGROUND

The authors come from different cultures and different perspectives but have a similar view of the destructive way that the world is treating children.

Philip Ney was raised in Canada, graduated in medicine from the University of British Columbia and trained as a child psychiatrist and child psychologist at McGill University, University of London and the University of Illinois. He is an academic and clinician of thirty years. He has taught in five medical schools, been full professor three times, served as hospital and academic department chairman, and established three child psychiatric units. He has done research into child abuse for twenty years and has had published more than twenty-five papers and books on this subject. In his early research he became increasingly aware of the connection between child abuse and abortion. More recently he has studied children who are the survivors of abortion. From his experience conducting therapeutic groups for men and women suffering from the effects of child abuse and/or abortion, the book, "Ending the Cycle of Abuse," was recently published (Brunner/Mazel, New York).

Contributing author Marie Peeters-Ney was born in the USA and is from Belgium. She obtained her medical training in Belgium and her pediatric specialty training in Boston and Toronto. She most recently worked in France with the world famous geneticist Jerome Lejeune. She won a prestigious Academy of Medicine (Paris) award for her research into the biochemical causes of mental retardation. She has been long associated with L'Arche, where she worked with handicapped people. She is deeply concerned about the ideology regarding eugenics and the vulnerability of disabled people. She sees a desperate need for healing the abortion-and-abuse trauma in Europe. She believes that unless these are dealt with, the consequences will be a totally disrupted society.

Both Dr. Ney and Dr. Peeters-Ney have a deep desire to protect children and encourage parents by treating the roots of the problems that make children such vulnerable scapegoats. They are now lecturing in a variety of countries and conducting training seminars in the treatment of Child Abuse and Neglect

(CAN), Post-Abortion Syndrome (PAS), Post-Abortion Survivor Syndrome PASS) and Loss of Partner Support (LOPS). The authors are both Christians, one from a Roman Catholic tradition and one from a Protestant background. They have used fundamental Christian tenets in their construction and elaboration of the basic psychology behind this treatment program. In theory and practice they want God to be praised as the source of all knowledge and healing.

The International Institute for Pregnancy Loss and Child Abuse Research and Recovery (IIPLC ARR) is a group of counsellors who are devoted to effective treatment of and research into the effects of all types of pregnancy loss - not only on a woman's health, but also on men, grandparents, and children. Our agreed purpose is to do careful research, publish findings in scientific journals, investigate the effective types of treatment, train therapists and encourage each other's endeavours. The association is supported through donations, membership dues, book sales, and lecture fees. The directors are scientists and clinicians from various countries.

5. BASIC ASSUMPTIONS

There are basic assumptions to every approach. While everyone claims to be objective, his or her assumptions are seldom stated. As with any science, it is important to state what these assumptions are, and to try very hard to perceive where these assumptions affect the observations and bias the conclusions. Some of our underlying suppositions are:

TRUTH

There is only one truth and only one source of truth. Scripture and science must agree. So far as our research has shown, they do agree. Without being inconsistent, we can write as scientists and physicians, and as children of God, followers of Jesus Christ and taught by His Spirit. There is nothing true in us or what we say that does not come from God.

TRAGIC TRIANGLES

All tragedies involve a Perpetrator, Victim and Observer. These tragic triangles rotate with time and circumstances. In matters of life and death, particularly abortion, there are no innocent bystanders. Because the pain and confusion affect the perpetrator and victim more, the observer has a greater responsibility, even though it appears they have a less important contribution.

DAMAGE

From our scientific and clinical observations, we conclude that abortion results in the deepest and most extensive damage to a family of any phenomena known to humankind. Unfortunately, because abortions are done by medical personnel with government approval and the apparent support by the majority of people, the damage is not taken seriously. There are approximately 60 million abortions each year. Thus, discounting the number of repeat abortions, there are 60 million unnecessary deaths of innocent children, approximately 50 million deeply damaged women, 50 million confused and angry men, 100 million siblings of the aborted child who are guilt ridden and anxious, and 70-80 million grandparents who are fearful of their increasing frailty and dependency. This results in approximately 250 million new patients each year. This is an epidemic greater than any other - past or present.

The damage is also deep, cutting at the very roots of our humanity by affecting the sensitive, ecological, biologically based mechanisms that sustain human relationships.

MUTUAL HARM OR BENEFIT

We are tightly bound together in the bundle of life. It is not possible to benefit at the expense of another. When we hurt somebody we harm ourselves. When we contribute to another's death, something of our humanity dies. When we love others we are loving ourselves.

ECOLOGY

Although humans assume that they are immune to any destructive force, which might threaten the human species, it is evident that the human species is endangered. There are many ways to show this. For example, the birth rate is dropping in every part of the world except Africa. Monetary incentives, e.g. East Germany, or restrictive laws, e.g. Romania, have been ineffective in stopping the escalating decline in the ratio of children to adults. The declining population is adversely affecting the economy of these countries. The sensitive balance that maintains the relationship between mother and father and between parents and children is being distorted in such a way that people have considerably less concern for one another, especially for the weak and poor, thus costs of social services and medical care increase.

INTENTION TO KILL

There is a continuum of the intention to kill unborn babies. This goes all the way from the extreme in which the parents hate the unborn baby and, with no other apparent thought, want it killed as soon as possible. Near the other extreme are parents who lovingly anticipate the appearance of an unborn baby but, due to factors beyond which they have any control, the baby is miscarried or born dead. In between, there are women who are forced to abort babies they desire and women who miscarry babies they do not welcome.

TRANSGENERATIONAL TRAGEDY

From history and from our studies on transgenerational child abuse, it is apparent that humans will repeat history until they learn from the essential components of its tragedy. Truth will always prevail. Eventually we will have to understand the essential conflicts, even if that painful experience must be repeated to the third and fourth generation of a family. We can learn from our history. The most useful lessons are in our painful history. Because it is painful, it is deeply buried. It takes courage to examine deeply buried, painful history, especially when there are so many diversions and rationalizations that give one the impression there are many painless shortcuts.

1
A PSYCHOLOGY OF CREATED HUMANITY

1. THE ORIGINAL PLAN

God's intention was that humans would become His friends. As friends, He desired interesting, mature persons. In God's Original Plan, these people are eager to learn so that they can know and be known. They are able to choose for themselves and judge for others. They are loving and accept love. They procreate, happily assisting God in making a beautiful world with more of the plants, animals and children that He originally created. They enjoy this world and spontaneously praise and thank God. They defend the weak and the wounded and serve God in helping and healing His creation. They do not avoid responsibilities. They co-operatively organize other people. They are happy to teach what they may know and work hard to reconcile warring or conflicted parts of God's creation, particularly His humans.

We would all recognize these people as beautiful, mature individuals. The difficulty is that humans were seduced and lost their way. Now they are immersed in problems and enmeshed in constant conflicts. The degree to which humans differ from their individual designs in the Original Plan is a measure of their unwellness. The units of measurement of sickness and sorrow are griefs and kilogriefs (see Section 3.1).

Although it may appear that these measures apply only to psychological functioning, they also relate to physical and spiritual wellness. The purpose of counselling is to reduce the number of kilogriefs. That is, to restore the person and the family as much as possible to the Creator's original intentions, e.g. to fully and consistently enjoy God. In counselling, part of our effort is devoted to removing the persistent sorrows by initiating and guiding the process of grief and mourning that should have been completed long ago.

The Original Plan for each infant coming into the world is that:

- he/she is welcomed into a family with two happy, healthy parents.
- all his/her needs will be met.
- he/she will grow into full maturity.
- he/she will develop a mature relationship with his/her family, neighbours and friends, and with God.

2. GOD'S PURPOSES FOR HUMANITY

Humans are born to know and to be known. Though many choose ignorance, those who insist on knowing are travelling together. No one has arrived. No one but God can claim to know anymore than a small portion of the truth. This attempt to explain core human psychology, we hope, is a step in the right direction to knowing and being known.

With humans, as with machines, the best way to understand damage to one's form and function is to know the designer's intention. This purposeful view of humanity is in direct opposition to a mechanistic, evolutionary point of view which asserts that designs grow out of function and are selected by environmental contingencies.

It is possible to determine part of God's purposes for humanity by examining human design - how we are constructed and how we function. A better way is to know the Designer and His intentions. It appears that some of God the Creator's intentions for the humans He made are:

FRIENDSHIP

God designed us to be His friend and friends with His friends (of many different kinds). Communication and intimacy are the goals. This implies that humans should be mature, knowledgeable, interesting, honest and able to communicate. All of these functions were built into a natural tendency for men and women to mature, learn and express themselves honestly. Every human regardless of size, shape or intelligence can be a friend of God. Handicapped people can become good friends with God, for God is not impressed with human qualities. However, it was never God's intention that anyone become handicapped, feeble, insane or limited in any way. God's purpose was for the best in humanity, and His purposes will all be accomplished.

TO BE, TO BECOME AND TO BE HERE

Humans were created indestructible. We were to be the permanent apex of God's earthly creation, graciously and generously in charge of all He made. We were given great potential to grow and to become wiser and brighter throughout our whole existence.

In creation, God did not just want us for Himself, but desired us to be ourselves. He allowed us to choose to not become what He desired us to be. There was a relatively large risk in creating us. It is a little bit like creating a machine that has a 50% chance of killing you. However, God took the chance and lost out on His Original Plan. The Alternative Plan will not fail.

To KNOW AND BE KNOWN

We were created to know God, each other, ourselves, the world and the universe, and to be known. Knowledge and wisdom are the goals. Humans were created with an immense curiosity and an amazing capacity to understand. We use only a small percentage of our brain power. We were created with the ability to know ourselves and to know God. Unfortunately, Adam and Eve chose what appeared to be the quick route to be like gods with the knowledge of good and evil. They chose not to know God patiently, quietly walking with Him in the garden. Yet, God is constantly making Himself known. We could leam so much if we patiently and carefully observed.

We could be very angry at Adam and Eve for ruining everything, except we know that we would have chosen the same thing. We know this because we continue to choose the quick fixes rather than quietly fellowshipping with God throughout the day. We are created with the sufficient capacity that makes it possible to get to know God, who He is and how He operates, but mind you, it will take an eternity to do so.

TO DECIDE

We were designed with the capacity to choose God, love and life. Freedom is our goal. We were given the opportunity to choose for ourselves and for others: to be free and to free others. Thus we are to be judges. We have an ability to choose, though limited by who and where we are. Only God has a free will. With God-given wisdom, and practise, we can expand our freedom to choose. We can limit our freedom to choose by not choosing or making wrong choices.

TO LOVE AND TO BE LOVED

Using faith, hope and joy, we are to love by meeting the needs of all creation - through loving God first, humans second. The goal is that all may develop as God intended. Men and women are happiest and healthiest when they are as loving as God created them and commanded them to be. Humans who have God's spirit are given the capacity to love and then commanded to love.

TO PROCREATE AND CO-CREATE We have the honour to join with God in producing beauty, harmony and life that we all can enjoy. New life and loveliness are the goals. God created us with the ability to create alongside the Creator. He has given us all strong desires to procreate for the benefit of others.

If we ignore or obstruct or use those desires for selfish purposes, we are not part of God's creating. The first command, chronologically, in Scripture is to procreate. As loving procreators, our intentions grow in agreement with God's intentions. We co-create when we join with

God in completing the construction of the beautiful "building" He designed us to be.

TO ENJOY AND EXPRESS JOY

To worship and praise Him for who He is and everything He created is God's expressed intention for us. Joy is the goal. We are created with a capacity to experience God directly. We know Him in His self-declaring activities and in His creation. From those experiences, we have a natural tendency to praise God and thank Him for all the wonderful things He created for our enjoyment. He has given us many senses with which to see, hear, taste, smell, feel and emotionally sense Him and this beautiful world.

TO DEFEND

It is our joyful duty to overcome the evil that disables, defaces or destroys ourselves and the lives of others. Victory is the goal. We are equipped with brains, muscles, canine teeth, nails, etc. which make it possible for us to be aggressive in defence of the weak and wounded, the children and the created world.

TO ADMINISTRATE

This is the opportunity and skill of helping others by organising their opportunities and skills so that everyone can benefit (individually and collectively) more often and more deeply. Administration does not mean power, dictatorship or control. It should vary with the circumstances and depend upon each individual's ability within different context. Perhaps one of the solutions is that administrative positions should rotate and be renewable every third to fifth year. The administrator's primary task is to co-ordinate and facilitate the service and development of others.

TO SERVE

We are created to care for others, to serve God by helping and healing His creation (especially His children), and to obey His command to be loving in all we do. We are to bum out in service, not to wimp out, cop out or rust out being "kind to ourselves."

TO TEACH

People, depending upon their abilities, are given the responsibility of sharing what they have learned so others may learn, enjoy and praise the Lord. Since everybody has learned some valuable lessons, and painfully, these should be passed on to others; if to nobody else, at least to their own children. The teaching ability has to do with one's ability to analyze, conceptualise and express. It may be an innate ability, but it can also be honed.

TO RECONCILE

This is the task of bringing people together and helping them deal with unresolved conflicts within and between them so that they can enjoy each other and gain from each other's experience. The process of reconciliation can be, and perhaps should be, initiated by the Victim. It begins with a confrontation, asking the Perpetrator and Observer to apologise for their part of the tragedy so that they may be forgiven. Although the forgiveness can happen quickly, the reconciliation may take many years while an individual learns to trust and appreciate somebody who has deeply wounded them. In situations where individuals will not recognize what they have done or apologise, it may be necessary to accept that the reconciliation will never take place in this earthly life, and good-byes should be said so there is no false relationship.

3. SUMMARY TABLE

The table on the following pages attempts to summarise God's intentions for humanity and the environment. The goals listed serve to explain the purposes. A description of the normal and abnormal responses of humans and how the environment affects them is given.

God's Intention	Human Attributes	Goals for Design	Environment Factors	Normal	Abnormal
• **Friendship (Friend)**	Languages of body, mind, spirit	Communion as Individual with God, self, others, creation	Challenging alternatives	Reverent camaraderie Spectrum of friendships	Isolation Loneliness Fusion
• **To be, to be here, to become (Pilgrim)**	Indestructible Eternity conscious Intrinsic worth	Welcoming Always present but knowing past and future	Changing Apparently limiting	Confident Trusting Always becoming integrated	Survivor guilt "Wanted" Self-destruction killing, rejecting
• **To know and be known, discern and understand (Wise student. Investigator)**	Intelligence and curiosity	To know and keep investigating with determination	Fears, confusion False information Knowable order in the Universe	Scientific mindset Curiosity Discernment	Willful ignorance Unquestionable tradition Mindful of distortions
• **To decide. Action Freedom (Pioneer)**	Ability to choose and recognize mistakes Anticipate consequences	Freedom within Royal Law of Love	Always alluring alternatives	Accepting challenge of hard choices	Lack of choice or choice according to circumstance Self-censored Arbitrary restriction

Table 1.1 Summary of God's Intentions for Humanity and the Environment

God's Intention	Human Attributes	Goals for Design	Environment Factors	Normal	Abnormal
• **To love and be loved (Lover)**	Empathy ability Capacity to know, meet and have needs	Fulfilled by being other focused	Sufficient resources Selfish Pleasures	Many loved and being loved by many	Selfish, self-centered Hedonistic Unloved
• **To Procreate and Co-create (Parent)**	Artistic senses Genitalia Fine co-ordination	Families Painting Composing	Filled with God's loveliness and constant creation	As many children as capable of parenting	Barren and bitter Distorted music, etc.
• **To Enjoy and Express joy** **(Choir member)**	Sensations, laughter Desire to share	Praise Worship Gratitude Enjoyment of people and environment	Some screening God out, but still able to see great beauty Pollution	Happy and sad when necessary Daily joy and praise	Sorrow filled Morbid Church routine
• **To Defend (Warrior)**	Strength Canine teeth Territorial Empathy Anger Feel **threa**tened	Defend life and love and creation Defeat the evil one	Hostile Acquisitive Scapegoating	UEMB Lots of partner support	Passive, Passive-aggressive or Aggressive-covetous

Table 1.1 Summary of God's Intentions for Humanity and the Environment

God's Intention	Human Attributes	Goals for Design	Environment Factors	Normal	Abnormal
• **To administrate (King)**	Concern for the running of things - an ability to organise and facilitate	Benign Theocracy Honour others	Appeal of power or passivity	Loving leadership, sharing	Dictatorship Love or fear of power
• **To Serve, help, heal, facilitate. (Servant)**	Desire to obey and please parent and potentate and God Ability to give even when not getting	Obedience to death in service to God, family and neighbour	Apparent pleasure of self-serving Animals willing to obey	Growth in serving even while dying	Demanding victim Manipulating
• **To Teach (Prophet**	Desire and language to systematise and explain	Careful researcher and explainer by word and example	Those who delude and confuse vs. wise teachers and searchers	Teacher who answers questions	Those who must be teachers and must
• **To Reconcile (Priest)**	Ability and desire to mediate, forgive and be forgiven	Mature, developing relationship	Wars Abuse Abortion Neglect	Peace with all through Christ	Hate Enmity Alienation Boundaries

Table 1.1 Summary of God's Intentions for Humanity and the Environment

We are all human to the extent we are fulfilling our designed purpose and carrying out God's intentions for us generally and jointly and individually.

In this life we have a jump start on the process of knowing and growing which will continue throughout eternity with no limit in sight. Eventually humans can become somewhat like God, but this time it is by His method and by His will, instead of the short cut tried in Eden.

4. The Child as Builder and Building

As with other difficult concepts, often the most clear way to explain what is happening is with a metaphor. The metaphor the Hope Alive treatment program uses is that of the construction of a lovely building. The architect is the Creator. The Blueprint is given to the contractor, who, in this model, is the child. He/she is both builder and building. The parents are the building supplier and the world is the resource that the suppliers order from.

Regardless of their genetic endowment, each child is a unique creation. He is becoming a castle with its own layout and particular beauty. In this building metaphor, the carpenter is also the child who is able to scan his own Blueprint (an accurate, intuitive awareness of what he/she is to become). The sentient aspect of every human is to understand what he is becoming and, because of that, to know what he needs.

It is essential that each child be recognised for his/her uniqueness and be welcomed for who he/she is, wherever he/she is, and whenever he/she is. To be a wanted child implies that the child has to meet some other person's prerequisites of what he/she should be. If the first right of every child is to be wanted, as some suggest, then if the child is not wanted, he/she has no right to be. It is an obvious corollary that is not lost on children. As wanted children, they feel they have to stay wantable to stay alive.

Though children have every desire to please their parents, trying to stay wantable distorts who they are. They begin to misread their own Blueprints and try hard to be what others expect them to be. The more uncertain their existence, the more dependent they are on being wanted and the more distortions they will read into their Blueprints. Thus the little castle becomes an unstable composite of who the child is and whom people expect him/her to be.

The child, as both castle and carpenter, constantly scans his own Blueprint. He feels intense inner pressure to obtain the right materials in the right order to create his structure. Obviously the first things he needs are a good building site, a firm foundation and plenty of reinforced concrete (security, acceptance and early nurturing).

The little contracting carpenter, having studied his Blueprint, goes to the nearest building supplier, i.e. his parents. Hopefully they will welcome him, go over the drawings with him, agree that he needs certain materials and provide him amply with what he needs. Unfortunately, too often the child arrives and is not particularly welcome. It may be that the suppliers want his business, i.e. want the child, but have preconceptions about what kind of building this little carpenter should construct or want his business only for certain purposes of their own. They may not know that, because the blueprint is embedded in the mind of the little carpenter, he can provide the most accurate description of what is needed. Too often, parents cannot see or hear the child expressing his needs. It may be that they cannot listen because they were never heard.

Parents who are able to welcome the child as she is, where she is and when she is, are more likely to be able to see that blueprint through the eyes of the builder. The little contractor requests certain building materials with cries and gestures. She provides corrective feedback with frowns or smiles. The supplier (primarily parents) may respond in one of four ways. 1) "That is not really what you need. What you need is this instead." 2) "We do not have any of what you need, so why are you asking you foolish little contractor?" 3) "We have it, but we are not giving it to you because we want it for ourselves. You had better go elsewhere." 4) "We have what you need, but we won't give it to you until you are a better builder and behave yourself."

The child is able to give the parents good correcting feedback about how clearly they are reading his Blueprint and providing him with what he needs. Unfortunately, parents are too often preoccupied with their own struggles to hear the child's correcting feedback or appreciate it for what it is. Because the Designer built such reserves and resilience into a child, it is not necessary for child development that parents are perfect, but they have to be adequate. They have to be capable of restraining themselves from imposing their own Blueprint on the child. They must provide sufficient affirmation to build into a child the sense that what he needs is legitimate.

Obviously, very few building suppliers have enough stock in hand to meet all the requirements, and therefore they have to order elsewhere. The world at large should provide materials for the parents with a modicum of effort on their part. Parents should not have to take from the essential time they must spend with the child. If all went well, when the building suppliers run out they should be able to put in an order, buy what is necessary and supply what is needed at exactly the right time the little contractor needs it.

It is now an almost worldwide phenomenon that parents are abandoning, neglecting or attacking and killing their own children. It creates an enigma that is difficult to explain. Why would parents of any species seek to damage or destroy their own young? It must surely indicate some significant ecological dis-equilibrium.

Neglect is defined in this metaphor as "not providing enough of, or the right building materials," and/or, "with the right timing for the construction." Because the little contractor is so determined to complete the construction, it is impossible for him to wait. He tends to go on with the construction regardless of whether he has the right materials and he may use scrap or leave off parts of the castle when the right materials are not available. When this happens, the little contractor becomes increasingly angry because he constantly scans his Blueprint and has in mind what he could be. Because of neglect or lack of welcome, he sees the castle he is building does not have a good foundation, is lop-sided and, consequently, everything else is out of square.

It is hard to remember a non-event, but neglect makes a deep impression. People tend to remember something dramatic rather than some continuous phenomena. They are more likely to remember an episode of molestation than they are a long period of being neglected. Yet it is the neglect that does the greater damage.

Too often, the child convinces him/herself that he/she did not need what he/she was desperately desiring. We all tend to not want something we know we will never get. It is a little bit like crawling across a desert and trying to stop your distress by saying to yourself "I am not thirsty ...I am not thirsty." It is easier to hope and to live if you can convince yourself that you do not need an essential ingredient, than it is to acknowledge you will never get what you need from the persons who are supposed to be caring for you.

Free from the misdirection of some parents and the coercion by the media to desire certain products, children know what they need and when they need it. Given the chance, they will pick out healthy foods.[1] They will initiate or terminate contact with their parents according to their individual needs.[2]

No one really knows how much of the building materials left out at an early stage of child development can be used at later stages of development. Yet, it is obvious that a child that was not breast fed has missed physical contact, psychological stimulation, essential fatty acids, anti-bodies and many other things that only breast feeding can supply. No amount of breast-feeding later on would make up for the deficit in brain-building materials breast-feeding provides. Unfortunately, the little contractor, having been neglected, still cannot understand why he could not find the building materials. He will search high and low, even obtaining material that is toxic or detrimental to the construction of his little castle. Thus a deep resentment for being neglected develops, coupled with a deep yearning that never seems to go away.

In an adequate world, the best building supplier is the one that knows the child's needs. The parents, having a similar Blueprint, should best be able to understand and read the child's Blueprint accurately. Strangers, day-care personnel, etc., may be well motivated, but they do not have the same intuitive ability to understand what and when the little contractor needs essential ingredients.

The suppliers also may not provide the child with what is necessary because:

- they do not know what good material is and give the contractor the wrong stuff.
- they consider themselves the wrong supplier and the child should go elsewhere.
- they consider the child is the wrong builder, just a poor replacement of the one who preceded him/her but who died or was killed before birth.

Abuse is defined as partially wrecking the little castle under construction. Infanticide is destroying the castle just started. This may occur as a result of malice or forethought, but more frequently it is stupidity and immaturity. Our studies have found that, given a variety of options, even small children are more likely to pick immaturity of parents as a cause of their mistreatment than they are choosing alcoholism, unemployment, etc. Children seem to perceive that their parents might be able to provide them with what they need, except that the parents are immature and have few provisions in their stock room.

When neglect or abuse occurs, it creates a conflict. The conflict increases the unnecessary expenditure of energy, delays construction (development) and smudges the blueprint. Children must resolve conflicts or die. In their early lives they seldom have the opportunity to understand because they are so desperately trying to construct their castle and because they have so few people who realize what occurred. Therefore the conflict is carried on into their adult life where they attempt to resolve it by either 1) thinking deeply about it, 2) discussing it with friend or counselor or 3) re-enacting it. It is the determined re-enactment of conflicts that result in most of the tragedies child psychiatrists see.

It is almost impossible to stop the contractor from building or repairing his castle. It may be possible to slow the child, but he is amazingly determined to do his best to follow the Blueprint. Abuse may destroy part of his little castle, but if he was not also neglected he will pick up the pieces and try very hard to put them together again. It is only after many occasions of partial destruction that the child tends to give up. It is for this reason that verbal abuse is more destructive. It convinces the little contractor that he is doing it all wrong and that he should not have even been trying. Moreover, he is told that rather than reading his own blueprint he should be listening to the orders given by the suppliers.

In their desperate search for building materials, children may develop false faces, the Dancer and Urchin (see Section 2.7.b. Two False Faces). The Dancer hopes that if he/she is good enough, for long enough, the supplier will eventually provide the right materials. The Urchin slinks into a corner, miserably considering his/her situation but, still hoping that somebody, out of pity, will give him/ her enough of what he/she needs.

Because of the inveterate order of building, and the determination whereby children keep trying, many little castles, for lack of materials, end up lop-sided with leaky roofs, holes in the floor and broken windows. It may be possible to repair some of these, but the foundation still is inadequate. Part of Hope Alive counseling is helping an individual realize that it is not possible for them to become the castle they were designed to be. If they can do that, they are less disappointed with what they are offered and more appreciative of what they get. When they are more appreciative of what they get, it is easier to give to them and consequently they get more.

5. THE BLUEPRINT

The Blueprint is a person's self-awareness of whom he or she was designed to be. This sentient aspect makes humans very different from animals. With their ability to scan and understand the Blueprint of whom they were intended to be, children can begin searching the environment for the things that they need. It is children's intuitive awareness of their Blueprint that tells them what they need and when they need it. Experts know what children need in general, but we recognize only each child knows what activities, experiences, people, knowledge, food, rest, etc. he or she needs to become the person God intended him or her to be.

Children are genetically and spiritually endowed with:

- a drive to develop.
- the basic building blocks for their development.
- a Blueprint, which is an intuitive awareness of their potential. This tells them what they should become and therefore the building blocks for which they should be searching, and in what order the project should be completed.

A child, like a builder, is given the Blueprint and a contract to build a beautiful castle. Joyfully he or she sets out to find a building supplier. The closest, best stocked building suppliers should be his parents. Others should be too far away. So he goes to the closest building supplier and attempts to get all the materials he needs to construct this beautiful building. Ideally, his suppliers should welcome him in the door, carefully read and analyze his Blueprint and freely offer him exactly the right materials. The child's responsibility is to help the suppliers understand the blueprint and provide feedback on whether the materials really do fit correctly.

Children who were neglected quickly realize the suppliers (parents) do not or will not give them what they need. Deficient or immature building suppliers react in one of three ways 1) "Go away. We do not have the materials. We cannot welcome you." 2) "We have the materials, but we will not give them to you unless you do exactly what we say and become the person we want you to be." 3) "You have misread your Blueprint. What you need are 2" X 6"s, not ***2"*** X 8"s." Too often the child is convinced the parents do have everything somewhere in the back of the store, but because they are inadequate contractors, have a bad reputation or bad credit (an unlovable child) they will not give the materials to them. Thus they try to make themselves more pleasing and elaborate False Faces (see Section 2.7.b).

The parents may have the child's building supplies but use everything up on their own interests, e.g. a holiday cottage. They may realize they have insufficient resources, but do not know where they can obtain these from other suppliers or are too lazy or too selfish or too proud to look for materials they do not have. If they cannot welcome the child into their supply warehouse, they may insist the child to be forcibly removed (abortion).

It is easier for the child to believe the parents have the materials and will not give them to him because he is bad then to believe the parents just do not have the material. If the child believes that he is bad, he can vainly hope that if he works hard at rectifying his deficiencies and becomes a really good child he will get what the parents have available for him. When children are neglected, their hope increases paradoxically. After all, it is their hope that helps them persist in seeking when the chance of finding what they need is so slim.

Children become confused when parents:

- misread their children's Blueprints because of their own mistreatment experience or because of selfishness.
- insist their children try to construct a home according to their preconception.
- try to build a house that they always wanted built for themselves.

Sometimes the supplier is almost sold (worn) out. Sometimes suppliers are keeping the building materials for themselves and resent rather than welcome every new customer.

A child may give up attempting to understand his own Blueprint in favor of accepting his parents' appraisal, but more often he retains a glimmer of the Blueprint in the back of his mind. He avoids scanning it because as he becomes older it becomes increasingly obvious that he is not being built according to his blueprint. The greater the discrepancy, the harder it is to look at the Blueprint and the fainter in his mind the Blueprint becomes. Many people, particularly abortion survivors, have never properly examined their Blueprints. They do not want to know what they could be if they feel guilty about existing.

Some building suppliers (parents) not only do not supply the right materials, but now and then come along and destroy the child's building that is half completed with verbal, physical or sexual abuse. Verbal abuse is particularly devastating because it makes the contractor very critical of his own work and makes him hesitate to continue building or try reconstruction. So often, a verbally abused child is like a building contractor who has all sorts of material lying around that he could use but will not build because he is afraid of his own building capacity and making mistakes.

Children lose the ability to know who they should have become because:

- the parents, through ignorance or indolence, misread their blueprint.
- they cannot get the right materials.
- the media lies about what are really good materials.
- they are so desperately coping just to survive and develop deliberately slowly.
- their perception of the Blueprint is twisted by having their desires for the right materials changed to a hunger for harmful materials, e.g. pornography.

- their parents force their own Blueprint on the child, e.g. "Be like me."
- they feel so guilty about existing they cannot even think of becoming themselves.
- they cannot believe they deserve good things, so they refuse many resources.
- they will not listen to God, who is trying to tell them who they really are.

Children must remain hopeful in order to keep trying to get what they need. For this reason, they tend to see their parents and the world at large as good or innocent; believing someday, somehow, someone will give them what they need. Even after repeated hurts and disappointments, they hope against the odds. It is amazing how often a dog will return wagging its tail, hoping to get a pat when so often it has been beaten. Children are even more persistent. If they give up, they tend to become cynical and manipulative.

It would be much healthier for the child's self esteem to get angry at the parent, e.g. "You have what I need. I know you have it. You are just keeping it for yourself." or "You don't have all my requirements. Why do you not just face the fact. Take a course on parenting or get some counseling or let me live with someone who is a good parent." Usually they get angry at themselves, e.g. "I am no good. That is why they do not give me what I need. I'll first try harder to please them (dancing) and, if that doesn't work, I'll be sick (urching) and they make take pity on me."

When children do not get the right building materials, they tend to fantasize an ideal parent and family. The more the deprivation children experience the greater their fantasy becomes. This is one of the reasons why they must say goodbye to the parent they should have had. If they can do so, it will allow them to better appreciate the parent they do have.

A child too often has to learn to try and impress the supplier or grovel to get the things that should come to him freely. He should be able to stand in front of the building supplier and have the supplier say, "Back up your truck. I now know exactly what you need and I have got plenty of it. When you are finished constructing this part of your house, come back for more."

Part of the reason for the elaboration of false faces is an effort to retain the Pilgrim (see Glossary) and the Blueprint, and part is to retain an innocent view of the world. There are many ways in which one can help people retain some perception of their Blueprint. One way is to ask them what they would do when they get to heaven, a place where they will have plenty of time and any amount of materials to become whom they were designed to be. The Blueprint shows the Original Plan. The Original Plan depicts all those God-given attributes the person will have an opportunity to develop throughout eternity, and only in eternity will there be enough time.

Children, when naturally conceived, live the first nine months in the beautiful environment of their mother's womb. All the child's earliest development takes place rapidly and almost automatically because she usually gets everything she needs in the womb. The baby has almost all that is needed and development unfolds beautifully if her mother is; reasonably well fed, well supported by her spouse, not exposed to undue stress or anxiety producing situations, not smoking, drinking or taking drugs, talking to, playing with and praying for her. Once the child is born, however, she immediately requires a great deal of conscious and intuitive wise parental nurture, guidance, and protection. The child's nurture by parents produces the energy that sustains her drive to develop. The secure holding environment and the parental affirmation of who she is, help her keep her Blueprint clear. The building blocks are supplied by nutrition, good experiences and appropriate instruction. Once the child is born, he/she becomes a co-creator with God in completing the "Person I Should Be." This implies a real freedom and real options in choosing whom we become.

No parent is perfect. Therefore no child has the optimal environment in which to develop. Yet, most children are given enough of what they need so that there is a continued unfolding of their development. This maintains the hope that they will continue to grow and be loved. Under these conditions their personality holds together. They can sustain and even benefit from life's traumas. However, her development is hampered if she is exposed to neglect or abuse or a combination thereof. Yet, her Blueprint stays reasonably clear so she will continually search for what she needs.

Sexual abuse and/or physical abuse is (are) often written about, but there are also less obvious forms. Verbal abuse is usually more damaging. Many forms of mistreatment are subtle and subconscious. Being a PASS child may be one of the most damaging. Sometimes the impoverished environment makes it impossible for even the best parents to meet their children's needs. Sometimes the government interferes or traumatizes the family.

After much neglect, a child begins to despair. However, before she gives up searching for a good home or the things she needs, she will attempt a major defensive adaptation. Under conditions of neglect or repeated abuse, a child automatically produces false faces, Dancer and Urchin. If the child is neglected, she does not have the necessary building blocks for her mental, physical and spiritual development.

Children who watch television while both parents are working try to recreate a proper childhood from fantasy. Without affirmation their Blueprint either begins to fade or becomes distorted by the impact of the world about them. Television and comic books tend to make them feel they could be anybody they want. If the neglect continues, they do not have the energy that maintains the drive to promote their development.

If a child is abused, there is a repeated partial destruction of the wonderful small creature or building that she was becoming. Verbal, physical and sexual traumas tend to take apart the little castle just as it was beginning to take shape. Moreover, abuse results in self-deprecation. The mistreated child is not only traumatized by others, but she works at destroying herself, especially if she is verbally abused. The things that are said to and about a child are the things she will say about herself for the rest of her life. Thus verbal abuse never stops, which is one reason it is the most damaging form of abuse.

If there are both neglect and abuse, the child's development is even more badly truncated and her vision of herself is corroded. Our evidence shows that when neglect precedes abuse, the child is both more susceptible and more vulnerable to the effects of the abuse. Both abuse and neglect tend to create either unrealistic hopefulness, or cynicism, or both. Yet, the Blueprint never entirely fades. There is greater pain, sorrow and rage associated with neglect because it creates greater damage. Hurts can heal but nothing can replace a lost childhood or remove the scars from the wounds that neglect inflicts.

The adult mistreated as a child is plagued by sorrow that invariably arises because they often compare the image of what they are with the Blueprint of what they might have become. The yearning to be better is always there, although it may be ignored or covered with an aggressive striving to promote one's self- interest. That yearning, plus feelings of hopelessness, creates a selfishness that is eventually self-destructive. Under these circumstances, it is not hard to abort the child in one's womb because the "Person I Should Have Become" has already died or is about to die. It is almost as if a woman says "I was killed, so I will kill. If I can't be what I should have become, I will destroy the baby inside me."

Jesus, on the cross, spoke to His Father, asking God to forgive those insulting and killing Him because they did not know what they were doing.[1] They were angry, bitter, and frustrated because Jesus had badly disappointed them in their hopes for a new kingdom of Israel, which would allow them to become the "Person I Should Have Become (PISHB)." They could not see His kingdom was and is everything they hoped for. To enter His way was too simple and too painful to their pride.

6. HOW CAN I READ MY BLUEPRINT?

- Some of the ways in which to know the absolute standards of the Designer are:

- to know the designer and his intentions for the machine.

- to analyze the machine, its components, and deduce for what they were designed and built.

- to ask the machine what is its design, i.e. Blueprint.

How does a person recognize his/her own design? Some ways are:

- resonance. "It feels right. What I am doing and what I am becoming really seem to agree."
- discovery. "I never realized before what kind of a person I could be. I never understood how well I could do this. I always suspected I had a bit of a talent, but now I am doing it I see how well I can do it."
- efficiency. "Now I am no longer struggling within myself. I am functioning so much better and feel so much more vigorous."
- full utilization. "I am using all my abilities and have a definite sense of fulfillment."
- hopes and dreams. "This is like what I have always dreamed of doing, even when I was a child."
- joy. "I feel so happy when I am like this, even though I am very tired."
- effectiveness. "I did not realize how well I could help people and now that I am doing it they are really grateful."
- blessing. "I feel God approves of what I am becoming, even though no one else does. There is a sense of peace even while I am struggling. I think this is right, even though I have not gained financially."
- growth. "I am really changing, even though I realize I am getting old."
- children. "My children are so much happier being themselves when they see I am more myself."
- childhood. "These are just like the kinds of things I did when I was a child - the things I made, the things that I thought, wrote, or fantasized."

- input. “This is like the kinds of books and movies that really interested me when I was young. This is the kind of country that I have always wanted to go to.”
- prayer. “When I pray for help and guidance, this is what God shows me I should pursue in becoming.”
- school. “I really enjoyed this subject.” “I really felt this lesson (piano) was fulfilling, but not art or dancing.”
- frustration. “I feel so trapped in this job or lifestyle.”
- regrets. “If only I had chosen the path of... e.g. being a mother, instead of a career.”

7. THE JOY AND RESPONSIBILITY OF PARENTING

A parent is not just being a passive need supplier to the child who is trying hard to build his little castle. Parents have vital responsibilities. Their ability to parent depends upon their maturity and their courage. They must keep changing as their child pushes them toward maturity. This is a short list of parental responsibilities:

Models

Parents, individually and as a couple, must provide the little castle carpenter with models of both what should be built and how to proceed. They must show him what a mature person is through their behaviour, expressions and interactions. They must illuminate the way for the child’s attempts to build his little castle. They must model how to love, serve and communicate with God.

Clarifying

The parents must interact with the child and help him learn more precisely who he is and whom he is becoming. They can do this by providing a smorgasbord of possible lesson, i.e. “We can only afford one type of lesson. What would you choose? Music lessons, sewing lessons, art lessons, elocution lessons, etc. Children are seldom able to verbalise their choices, but they can pick what best fits them by having a short experience with a variety of opportunity. Thus, through trial and error both parents and child have a clear picture of the blueprint. The parents must be able to read their own blueprints clearly and to make comparisons so that they see the similarities and differences with the child’s blueprint.

Explanations

Parents need to provide a child’s thinking process with words that help the child conceptualize his development and guide his development. They need to encourage a child to explore and investigate, then try to explain and replicate his discoveries. Children are intuitively little scientists and should have their research techniques encouraged and refined.

Protection

A child needs the security of protection to experiment and make choices. He must always know that his parents will welcome, accept, support and guide him, even though they do not always agree with his behaviour and will show their disapproval. They must protect him from dangerous activity and evil information.

Provide materials

Parents need to provide the ingredients necessary for a child's development. These include basic ingredients of food, good medical care, adequate housing, heat and water, etc. If they are unable to provide these, parents must be able to show the children that they are trying very hard on their behalf. Parents must also provide the child with an education that suits his Blueprint and experience from which he can best learn. Parents must advocate obtaining resources for the child from places outside the family when they are not available within the family. They must speak for the child, demanding resources from the community or government that are suitable for the children.

Affirmation

A child needs to be welcomed then affirmed for who he is as he develops. Children's experiences should encourage and challenge them. If overwhelmed, they know their parents will sustain and guard them. They must speak to God on their children's behalf.

8.THE MYSTERY OF MY UNFORMED BODY

There is a beautiful phrase in the Bible that states "you saw my unformed body."4 That one fertilized cell is the body that belongs to you. You were in that body. You entered that body at conception.

We find evidence for this mystery in the stories of many women we interviewed, spoke to, or trained. They state, "I felt a little presence enter me at the time of conception." "I knew I was pregnant right away." This sensation cannot be explained scientifically, at least not yet. There are no hormonal changes, there is no quickening, but somehow a mother can sense that a baby has arrived. Some women have even stated, "I knew I was going to conceive that night. Somehow I opened myself up all the way when we had intercourse."

So far, this is an amazing mystery. How could the huge spirit of a person reside within one cell? It is like the mystery of the fullness of God in Christ Jesus, a human. How could God, who is so amazing, magnificent and powerful, reside in a human body? We have no explanation, except we have a clue in an understanding of anti-matter, that kind of matter which can exist in the space of other matter, but in a much different form.

We know that as long as the spirit lives within a body that body is a person. When the spirit enters the "unformed body" he/she becomes fully human and stays human until their spirit leaves. The spirit leaves at some point during death. For Christians, there is an opportunity to dismiss their spirit, as Jesus did, and possibly avoid the final agonies of death. Once the spirit is dismissed, Christians can then confidently wait for God to take their spirit at a time God so chooses. Then there is no struggle of the body hanging onto the spirit as in most deaths.

9. LIFE IS LOANED, NOT GIVEN

God creates human life. He makes the body and then breathes into the body the breath of life, the spirit of the human. The life was made by God. The spirit belongs to God. Thus, a life is loaned, not given. Life is created. It is not an accident. Life has to be sustained. God is constantly pouring growing and healing energies into the world and into humanity.

It is great arrogance on the part of humans to feel that life was given to them. In pride, most people think humans can make life, sustain life, and therefore, that they can take life. Since life is loaned, it can never be given or taken without reference to God, who made that life. We have the privilege, the honour, the blessing of having children loaned to us, but they will always belong to God and will always go back to Him. These children are loaned to us, not given. We must also recognize that they are not possessions or chattel in the least way. As Christians, they are our brothers and sisters and are to be respected and treated as so.

Life is loaned specifically, not haphazardly. Certain couples get certain babies and God knows precisely what He is doing, even though sometimes it appears most cruel or most inconsiderate on the part of God. Parents must act responsibly. God did not plan on chromosomal abnormalities or the effects of smoking during pregnancy. Yet, every child is an opportunity to understand yourself through knowing that child. Raising a child is an opportunity to become a mature friend of God.

10. THE PURPOSE OF EVIL

The purpose of evil was to frustrate the intentions of God. Since evil cannot destroy the human, who is essentially an indestructible spirit, it seeks to dehumanize people. Instead of becoming like God, people may choose to become like the devil. Evil is able to:

- keep a person immature.
- confuse the truth with deceit.
- bind and enslave with fear.
- rob the person of joy and praise.
- persuade humans to destroy themselves, especially to destroy new human life, i.e. unborn babies.
- convince humans to give up and let evil and entropy reign.
- encourage selfishness, which inevitably leads to self-defeating and self-destructive behaviour.

Thus, evil seeks to deface, debilitate and disable the person God intended him/her to be.

God achieves His purpose by creating humans with:

- the essential building blocks of a whole person.
- the motivation to build the person God intended.
- a Blueprint of what we are supposed to become.
- opportunities in the world He created to progressively test our construction, both for the completed self and for the benefit of others.

God made sure that humans had to make maturity promoting choices. Every human must choose between truth and error, love and hate, freedom and enslavement, joy and grief, maturity and immaturity, trust and fear. God created a wonderful garden and a simple choice between being His friend or becoming like "God, knowing everything, both good and evil."[5] Adam and Eve were greedy and impatient. They wanted it all and now. Since that fateful mistake, all our knowledge is both good and evil.

More sadly, we lost the opportunity to really know; to know God, each other, ourselves and the universe created for our joy and a challenge to our curiosity. We nearly lost it all. Yet God provided an Alternative Plan when the Original Plan in the Garden of Eden was frustrated. Nothing can frustrate God's purposes for long. He still wants us to know and to grow. He will guide our quest even though it is now through pain. He continually sustains the universe and provides His Spirit of Truth. God protects our ability to choose by:

- allowing evil.
- not intervening as much as He would like to when we fail or fall.
- veiling His majesty.
- restraining His might
- restraining His righteous anger.

Evil attempts to achieve its purpose by:

- distorting Truth.
- making people distrust God and His love.
- creating destructive conflicts between men and women, parent and child, individual and state, humans and their environment.

Unwittingly, evil inadvertently promotes God's intention by continually posing choices. Having choices actually promotes the freedom and maturity of all those who will accept the opportunity to choose.

If evil could destroy human relationships, people would kill themselves and each other. Hoping to frustrate God's intentions, evil uses an effective ploy: to undermine the basic, God given instinctive bonding mechanisms between husbands and wives, parents and children. It now appears humans are on the brink of extinguishing themselves. They have so wittingly bought the lie about the relative value of human lives and effectively destroyed their instinctually determined relationships. Consequently, human ecology is very unbalanced. Human ecological dis-equilibrium is seen in people's lack of desire to have children or respond with nurture to their helpless cries. In some parts of the world, e.g. Eastern Europe, these balances seem irreparably damaged. In many countries the birth rates are well below population replacement rates and keep dropping. All kinds of incentives are unable to reverse the trend. People do not want to have children.

When parents destroy their young, no species can survive. When the young turn against their parents, they are left without guidance and will soon destroy each other. There are approximately sixty million abortions in the world, i.e. 60 x 10^6 unborn infants are killed at the request of the parents each year. Discounting repeat abortions, forty to fifty million mothers each year have broken the instinctual barriers of aggression against their own young. An equal number of male partners have broken the bond with their mates, by coercion or lack of support. They have given up their responsibility to protect their helpless offspring, thus promoting abortions. Approximately one hundred and twenty million children each year are being deprived of a sibling. As survivors, they distrust their parents and question their own existence. Ninety to one hundred million grandparents have begun to fear for safety in their old age. They realize their young people may treat them as callously in their infirmity as they were treated when they were unborn and helpless. For each of these approximately sixty million "terminations" of unborn babies, there are millions more being deeply damaged. The net effect is a program of unprecedented destruction and damage to people, which is defeating God's loving purposes.

11. EVIL DESIGNS TO DESTROY HUMANITY

There are many methods by which evil invents to destroy the apex of God's humanity, he could laugh at God. It seems from the book of Job that the devil cannot kill people directly. He can only destroy humanity by enticing humans to kill one another. However, God has always had an alternative plan. Frequently, what the evil one sees as triumph over God because humans suffer and die, God uses as an opportunity to promote beauty, truth and growth.

God never enjoys watching people suffer. He always wanted humans to gradually become His friends, quietly wandering in a garden. Since they chose evil, God will use that as an opportunity for man to get to know God again. When God is present in suffering and death, what looks to be tragedy is triumph. When God's wonderful only Son was cruelly killed on a cross and covered with sin so deeply that even God had to look away, God never abandoned His Son. It was the beginning of the most wonderful alternative plan, eternal joyful life as a gift from God for all who will accept Jesus as Saviour and Lord.

The effect of abortion, child abuse, child neglect and being an abortion survivor plays a large part in all the following destructive factors. This is not intended to be an exhaustive list, but to demonstrate the pervasive impact of abortion on many areas of human dysfunction.

DIMINISHED HOPE

Hope is essential for life. Children, prisoners, the infirm and the unwell die when hope is absent. Humans do not give up hope very easily because to give up hope means not to seek for what they need. Not trying to find what they need for life, they would surely die. Rather than see their parents for what hopeless models and providers they really are, children will continually burnish their parents' tarnished images so there is some reason to hope parents will somehow someday meet their needs.

Children create hope. When adults have children, they are more likely to maintain a committed relationship, plan for the future, conserve their resources, forgo personal gratification and mature as their children grow. Without children, people become narcissistic, hedonistic and materialistic. After all, "Why not eat, drink and be merry because there is no one else than ourselves to be concerned with?"

Without children there is declining hope in the world. When there is declining hope, people are less likely to have children. They argue when the world is coming apart, "Who would want to bring a child into such a global catastrophe?"

Without an increasing population of children and young parents, a free market economy cannot work. A good example of this is the Ukraine, which is a country well blessed with expansive wheat fields, oil, coal and other natural resources. However, they have a rapidly declining population, mainly because of abortion, and consequently there is no employment for a large percentage of people who would otherwise be teachers, home-builders, pediatricians and city planners. As a result of 80-90% of women having had abortions, approximately 8-9 per woman, about 30% of the child bearing population is sterile. Even if they were forced to have children as they were in Romania, the instinctual heart desire for children has been broken. In Romania, the police made sure women did not abort their children, but they put their children into orphanages.

The situation is so different in Ireland. Ireland, with almost no resources at all, but with many bright-eyed, tousled-haired children, has one of the best economies in the European Economic Community. Because eager workers are plentiful, many industries are settling in Ireland.

DIMINISHED MEANING IN LIFE AND DESIRE FOR LIVING

Suicide is very rare when women are pregnant. Depressed men and women state "I could never kill myself or commit a major offence because I have my children to think about. I would not want to leave them with that burdensome legacy and I know they would have to desperately struggle without parents." From a biological point of view, the most important thing a person will do is to have children to carry on their genes. Without children, people lose meaning in life and a desire for living. Without the desire to have children and learn how best to nurture, guide, educate and encourage them with advances in science and technology, humans gradually lose interest in all types of endeavours.

One effect of abortion is to take away the meaning and desire for life, and so culture and science spiral downwards. People become hedonistic, not caring how damaging they are to their minds or bodies, what kind of pollution they put into their brain and how recklessly they live. After all, they have no children to whom they could leave the sum of their efforts. Though suicide is thirty-five times less common in pregnant women[6], and abortion increases suicide by a factor of three to ten,[7] suicidal threats have been used to justify abortion. Pregnancy is the best condition for a suicidal woman and abortion is definitely contra-indicated in depressed people.

WAR BETWEEN MEN AND WOMEN

It should be apparent that increasing rates of marital violence, family break-up and parental irresponsibility indicate that the age-old tension between men and women has been fuelled and fanned. With the false idea that gross national product increases if both members of a couple work, women are encouraged to become part of the "work force." There they have to compete with men. Because men got there first, feminists feel equality can only be gained by "affirmative action," which means that, regardless of how well people are qualified, women get first opportunity. This sidelines and galls many male family providers.

Taking away the male partners right to determine the fate of his unborn child has made men hate women in a very deep and almost irreconcilable way. Because there is physical and sexual abuse by men, too many women feel free to taunt men, trap them with words, belittle them with innuendoes and then appeal for protection by the police. Women are manipulating male guilt. Men are pressuring women to have abortions with threats of abandonment. The protective instincts of men have been undermined.

Men's natural assertiveness has been discouraged in church. Their desire to explore and pioneer, dismissed. Most jobs are becoming sedentary and men cooped up in offices are feeling increasingly restless. Women are angry that men abandoned them to parent their offspring alone. Too often that anger is taken out on the children.

The net effects of this escalating war between men and women are a diminished desire to mate, propagate and nurture children. As always, children suffer most during adult altercations. Many more children are aborted as scapegoats, but this only increases the war between men and women, escalating in a vicious cycle.

DEVALUED PARENTING

So much of modem economics depends on consuming. One can only consume if one makes money. That requires paid work. Because parenting is unpaid, parents are discouraged by the media. Advertisements showing people having fun playing beach volleyball while drinking cola, show no evidence of children. The media clearly portrays parenting as a less enjoyable, less fulfilling activity than lounging on a beach among the palm trees.

The net effect of the declining number of people who want to parent their children is an increasing demand for day-care. The bill for this is picked up primarily by the government, which increases the taxes, which forces both parents to work. In some countries the taxes are so high it is almost impossible for one parent to stay at home. Attempts by some organizations, e.g. Kids First,[8] to change the tax laws so that double income families are not rewarded with relatively lower income tax, has met with little success. There is immense and subtle pressure to consume, to buy, to earn and to relegate your children to the care of somebody else. After all, a professional is seen to do a much better job than the average parent.

Abortion and being an abortion survivor has undermined parent confidence. The common view is, "It is best that you earn the money to buy nice things for you and your children, while they are cared for by a professionally trained child care worker." There is considerable evidence to show that day-care is damaging.[9] It increases competition between children, which might be good in the short run, e.g. trying to get good school grades. There is increased anxious attachment to parents and frequent depressions. Depression interferes with the child's immune system, increasing the number of intercurrent infections, so much that there are now pediatricians that specialize in day cares.

The net effect of day-care is to reduce a person's ability to make commitments, provide for family and nurture children. Another untoward effect of day-care is the high level of staff turnover. This arises partly from the fact that it is stressful working with children who are constantly crying out for their parents. At the same time, it is not hard to find mothers in offices gazing out the window, hearing the cries of their child echoing in their heads and longing to be with them, but feeling they are doing the right thing by helping to earn money to support the family and pay the taxes.

INCREASED IMMATURITY

Children are the most civilizing, maturing influence in the world. People are forced to go through a whole series of crises that demand they mature and learn to love as the child grows. With increased numbers of abortions and the increased number of parents who reject having any children, there is not the same vital push to make hedonistic young people into mature adults, loving parents, and wise grandparents. Childless couples have more funds to spend upon themselves. When they buy each new big "toy," there is a short period of exhilaration followed by a sense of boredom and meaninglessness that they try to replace with the excitement of more shopping.

The merchandising media constantly blares the sad but seductive message, "Blessed are the barren for they will have more pleasure." The net effect is that many people cannot postpone gratification. They resent a pregnancy for they know the baby will interfere with their pursuit of pleasure. Too often, the baby is not welcome and they quickly place the child in a day-care. The ensuing neglect undermines a child's inner stability. As an adult, they are less inclined to have and nurture children of their own.

Both pregnancy losses and being a pregnancy loss survivor interfere with the maturing process, but some women claim there is a sense of relief after an abortion, "Oh my, I am glad we got rid of that problem." Although people are depressed and guilt-ridden (men in particular), they cover these affects with a more desperate pursuit of fun, fun, fun, or travel, travel, travel or work, work, work. Thus abortion interferes with maturation and increases hedonism.

DEHUMANIZING THE HELPLESS

Governments in every country are trying to economies on the costs of their medical and social programs. To do this they cut back on welfare, education and medical care to "high risk" people, namely, the handicapped, the elderly, the infirm and the pre-born. To justify cutting back funds, governments, the media, the legal and medical professions are describing helpless people in dehumanizing terms. The unborn are not babies, they are "fetuses" or "tissue." The handicapped are not people, they are "special needs." The old and infirm are not sources of wisdom and stability, they are the "dependent aged."

When it is possible to term people as less than human, it is then easier to treat them as less than human. In war, the enemy is called by derogatory terms, e.g. Jap, Hun, Gook, that enables people to dehumanize them, then kill them. The enemy are no longer fathers or brothers, they are just the enemy. The only interest our brave soldier has, is to kill them and count their bodies. To kill the beautiful but helpless, voiceless and voteless unborn, they have to be termed "a piece of tissue" or "conceptus." No one should forget that the process of de-humanizing is always reciprocal.

DISTORT INSTINCTUAL NURTURING RESPONSE

The parents of every species respond to the helpless cry of their young with and protection. Abortion has badly distorted this instinctual response in humans. We found that parents who have had an unresolved pregnancy loss are more likely to feel helplessness and/or irritation in response to an infant's helpless cry. These feelings often result in neglect, frustration or rage.

The instinctual nurturing and protecting response to the helpless cry is, to a great extent, cross-species. Humans are upset when a puppy whimpers or a kitten mews. Bitches look very distressed when infants cry. The helpless cry triggers alertness and, if it persists, anxiety in the parent. Parents must be sufficiently mature to control their anger, frustration or anxiety, calm the child and provide him/her with what he/she needs. Since almost every human will be helpless at some stage of his/her life, if the response to the helpless cry of children is distorted, everybody is endangered.

The nurturing, protecting response to the helpless cry is necessary for the survival of our species. If that response is distorted or weakened, major human ecological distortions will occur. In Romania, many years of abortion were followed by a desperate attempt to increase the population by having police prevent abortions. Parents would bear their children, but there was no instinctual desire to care for them and large numbers were put in orphanages.

BREAK THE INSTINCTUAL RESTRAINT TO AGGESSION

It is not easy for a human to kill another human. One study has shown that a small percentage of the soldiers at the Battle of Gettysburg were intent on killing another soldier.[10] Most soldiers went about looking after supplies or the wounded or shooting their rifles at the air. Training techniques now encourage live ammunition exercises that almost kill, and sometimes accidentally do so. It has been found that if a soldier is able to kill once it is much easier for him to kill again. Soldiers know that something has radically changed in them once they have killed another human.

The strongest instinctual restraint to aggression in humans is against killing a helpless infant. Thus, the strongest repugnance is expressed at the idea of killing a child and the greatest popular outrage and dismay if a parent kills a child. Yet, the first human those 50-70% of the population kill, or agree to have killed, is a helpless human infant. Once they have broken through their instinctual restraint to kill an innocent baby, they are dangerous. They know that they are less able to restrain their aggression after an abortion. Thus they tend to be very cautious with their anger and careful with their children. Having had one abortion, it is much easier to have another.

Our research has shown that the outcome of the first pregnancy is the best predictor of the outcome of the second. If a woman has a full-term first pregnancy, she has the best chance of having a full-term pregnancy the second time. If she has an abortion in the first pregnancy, the second pregnancy is much more likely to also be aborted. Doctors should note this and spend more time helping a woman have a successful first pregnancy.

Because abortion breaks the instinctual restraint to aggression, it is not surprising that, with increasing abortions, there is an increase in child abuse, neglect and fatal child abuse, i.e. infanticide. In the United States, the most common cause of death to children six years and younger is not infections, cancers or accidents, it is being killed by their own parents." In many other countries, the rate of infanticide is escalating and people wonder why. If society allows, approves and often applauds killing an unborn infant, which breaks that instinctual restraint to aggression, it should be no surprise that more parents kill babies after they are born. After all, babies can be much more irritating outside the womb than they are inside the womb.

MYTH OF OVERPOPULATION AS AN ENVIRONMENTAL DISASTER

The United Nations is consciously promoting the idea (patently untrue) that the world population is escalating so rapidly that there will soon be no way to control global warming, ozone depletion, tree destruction and water pollution. Most serious demographers are more concerned about under-population. The only place in the world where the birth-rate is growing is Africa. In every other part of the world the birth-rate is declining rapidly. Food shortage is not a valid reason to limit population. During the 1980's, world cereals production increased 2.1% per annum while population grew by 1.7%.[12]

The first command in the Bible is "be fruitful and multiply."[1]-* It can be argued that this command was limited to the first few centuries of human existence and then the Lord withdrew that idea, but there is no evidence in the Bible that this occurred. Humans are, in fact, most happy when they are procreating, protecting, nurturing, guiding children and providing children a future. Why limit human population growth when the resources of the universe

are limitless? Is it not time we started colonizing the other planets, then remote space?
It is not lost on children that they are unwanted because they are a threat to the environment. Too many parents feel it is legitimate to abort children because of overpopulation. The best evidence shows that the most effective control of fertility is not contraception or abortion, it is proper perinatal care. When children are well cared for before and after birth, parents instinctually do not have large numbers. When infant mortality is high, people have many children, hoping that at least one will survive to look after them in their old age.

In North America and Europe the birth rate has declined to an average of 1.3 to 1.7 children per couple. This is an exponential decrement where fewer people produce fewer children. Attempts by governments to induce higher fertility have not worked. East Germany, which at one point offered a 10,000 D.M. interest free loan for each child, could not stimulate an increase in the birth rate. Countries who want their economies to flourish, import workers and consumers. Canada and the United States, with highly desirable environments and economies, attract wealthy, educated, intelligent people - draining many countries of their best resources. While North American economies grow because of increasing population, other economies decline. North America is a parasite on many developing countries.

The UN is consciously creating a panic about overpopulation, thereby increasing a demand for population, monetary, pollution and industrial control that, for those whom are promoting it, can only be obtained by world government.

INCREASED SEXUAL STIMULATION

To sell a product, many advertisers use innuendoes of sex or violence to gain attention. There is a growing industry in pornography and sexual titillation. The media also promotes the idea that you cannot have good sex if you have children. The net effect is that people seek to have sex in any way that does not result in pregnancy. This increases the amount of anal intercourse, which increases AIDS.

Men, not trusting their partners to not abort an unborn baby and finding it difficult to have intimacy, are more frequently resorting to all sorts of sexual activity that cannot result in a baby. This means there is a rapid increase in the amount of voyeurism, pornography, prostitution, "massage" and homosexuality.

Paradoxically, even though there is much more sexual stimulation, there is diminished intimacy and potency. Men, knowing that their erect penis and their ecstatic orgasm results in the death of a baby through abortion, feel ashamed of their manliness and their male organ.

Knowing that at any point their female partner could abort their baby without the knowledge or consent, they hesitate to attach to the unborn baby and therefore they are less likely to support their partner. Women who are not well supported during their pregnancy are more likely to have both miscarriages and abortions and thus ensues a vicious cycle.

DEVALUATION OF CHILDREN

At most times in human history, children were the most valuable asset of any family. People were considered blessed when they were about to give birth. Today it is more often said, "blessed are the barren." Children are seen as an impediment to the pursuit of pleasure, education and power. Consequently, there has been a progressive decline in the percentage of the GNP spent on children's health, welfare and education.[14] More and more children are living below the poverty line. As children are devalued, so they devalue themselves. Being considered an impediment to their parents' progress, a threat to the environment and a drain on the economy, children devalue themselves. Partly for this reason, there is a rapidly increasing suicide rate among adolescents, particularly young men.

Much of the monetary devaluation of children occurs because people are more concerned about looking after their parents than their children. After all, they will have to spend a larger percentage of their lives looking after their parents. In addition, old people vote. Since babies, children and adolescents do not have votes, they cannot demand their own services. As another indication of the declining value of children, there is a growing discrepancy between the sentences given to those who kill adults and those who kill children.[15]

As the birth rate declines and the population ages, there are fewer taxpayers to provide the services for older people. The young people then resent the old people who are a drain on their attempts to save. The old people fear the young people, thus producing a growing hostility between the old and the youngest generation.

INCREASING THOUGHT CONTROL

In most countries there is a growing demand for universal, government paid day-care centers. There have been many reports of abuse of children in day-care, so state and federal agencies are now demanding governments supervise the programs and control the selection and training of staff. With fewer models of thought and behaviour for young children, there is greater uniformity. These models are now selected by agents of the state.

As it becomes increasingly apparent that monetary systems prey upon each other and quickly run wild, there is an increasing demand for world-wide monetary control. This would eventually require a world bank with access to the computers of all the individual banks and their branches throughout the world. This places economic control in the hands of very few individuals. Although there is resistance by many because of the awesome implications, people are led to believe that to avoid economic chaos there has to be world-wide control.

To make the whole process work more efficiently, there is greater reliance upon electronic transmission of information and transactions so that currencies become increasingly less important and credit cards and numbers more important. Since people lose, steal or forget credit cards, it is understandable why individuals would agree to have their numbers encoded into microchips imbedded in hands or foreheads to be read by checkout scanners.

To introduce such ideas requires a subtle molding of human thought and behavior. At one end, children are placed in day-care and molded by state approved counselors. The fewer adult models children have the more likely they will think in a similar fashion. On the other end, there are mega media corporations that are able to control the slant of information and news. Gradually, people are being taught to accept control as necessary and beneficial.

Cultures and languages are dying as people become more immersed in the popular image and music culture. More modeling of thought and behavior is done in schools. There is a diminishing parental influence on educational curriculum and teacher selection.

It is widely reported by the media that medicine believes abortions are therapeutic, even when there is no scientific evidence to show abortion is good or safe treatment for any psychological or social condition. In a similar way, people believe the world is overpopulated and the environment dying, without questioning the media's accuracy.

INCREASING GUILT

With approximately 60 million unborn children being killed by induced abortion each year, and many dying by spontaneous abortion in situations where their parents do not welcome them, there is a vast increase in the amount of deep guilt. At a biological level, every species understands that they cannot destroy their own young and survive. Therefore, every species has an in-built instinctual restraint, with a warning sensation of tension if an individual is about to harm the young. There is also an alarm of guilt that sounds if any member of the species kills its infants. Humans also have a biologically based guilt that is unavoidable and universal. It is one of the deepest guilts and now affects about 50 million more women and 50 million more men annually. There are also 100 million children who have a survivor guilt from knowing a sibling was aborted. There are many millions of grandparents, counselors, medical professionals who contributed to abortion. There are millions of God-fearing people who know they are not doing as much as they could be to prevent abortions.

This immense amount of guilt is mostly denied. To deal with it requires acknowledging the existence of the destroyed baby and engaging in the painful process of mourning. Most people both deny that a real, living, unique child died and distract themselves from thinking about it. The distraction requires an immense amount of pleasure and excitement. People become immersed in fun, fun, fun, travel, travel, travel travel, sex, sex, sex, work, work, work - all to the detriment of children who are born. Thus, abortion leads to increasing amounts of hedonism, immaturity and neglected children, which leads to greater immaturity in adults. The media has to portray increasing levels of explicit sex and random violence on the television because otherwise people become bored. Eventually, nothing is exciting enough for some people except snuff films, real movies of real murders.

SELF-FOCUSED COUNSELLING

As the amount of deep guilt, intrapersonal conflict and intrapsychic turmoil increase that results from contributing to an abortion and being an abortion survivor, so there is an increasing demand for counselors. Since there are never enough properly trained and qualified counselors, all kinds of self-styled counselors are offering help. Some help is honest and some, e.g. that offered by International Planned Parenthood, is cynical and exploitative. Many counselors are telling people they should not feel guilty about the abortion. This only increases the amount of conflict, increasing the demand for more counselors.

Most unqualified counselors promote introspection that never ends. The idea of an "inner child" has been particularly destructive for millions of people, who can never stop trying to nurture a non-existent child, but indulge themselves in an attempt to do so. Much of this could be avoided by reconciliation, but that would undercut the counselor's source of income. Thus most counselors avoid or resist reconciliation between perpetrator, victim and observer. Self-focused counseling leaves people untreated, fearful and often constantly looking for someone else to blame.

DISCREDITING SCIENCE

In 1927, Heisenberg enunciated the principle of uncertainty. It states that there is a limit to our ability to know what is real. Quantum mechanics suggests there are parallel realities. Therefore, it is not possible to be objective. As a result, people have given up the idea of a real reality and have promoted their perspective as legitimate in qualifying reality, e.g. the feminist perspective. As a result, there is a major bias introduced in evaluating grant applications, journal articles and scientific meeting programs.

Medicine has never bothered to objectively evaluate the effectiveness and safety of so-called therapeutic abortions. It would be extraordinarily easy to do animal studies. Five hundred pregnant guinea pigs could be randomly selected and aborted at different stages to determine physiological and psychological damage. Although it is so obviously easy and absolutely necessary, nobody has tried. Longitudinal studies could be done on large numbers of teenagers to determine the eventual outcome of those who have or do not have abortions. None of this basic research has ever been done or even attempted.[16] When we and others sympathetic to unborn babies have done some research, it is extraordinarily hard to find funding, and even more difficult to have the findings published.

DEBUNKING ETHICS

If there are parallel realities, it is argued there are parallel moralities. Anyone's moral perspective is as good as another's. Eventually this means you may do in medicine anything that you can do technologically. Since technical prowess, rather than wisdom, determines what is done in medicine, law, business, banking, etc., there is no longer any attempt to adhere to a universal ethic. The Hippocratic Oath is no longer sworn by any medical graduating classes to our knowledge. Modem ethics increasingly require the doctor be guided by is what the patient desires, rather than by what is good for the patient in the longterm.

WEAKENED PROFESSIONS

The pillars of society for many centuries have been the ancient professions that adhered to careful rules of conduct and clearly delineated ethics such as the Hippocratic Oath. Medicine has discarded both ethics and science. What a doctor • does now is less determined by his/her clinical acumen and scientific credibility than it is by his/her popularity. To maintain a practice, doctors have to be liked by their patients. Since it appears that most patients approve of abortion, the doctor, in order to be liked, tries to maintain a "pro-choice" stance even when he/ she knows that abortion is harmful to the patient.

Since abortion increases the number of nightmares, many patients are complaining they cannot sleep. Their doctors are prescribing REM (dream sleep) suppressing hypnotics that interfere with necessary dreaming. Patients become increasingly anxious because of the lack of dream sleep and too often take more dream suppressing sleeping pills. Because abortion increases nightmares and the demand for hypnotics, the pharmaceutical industry is quietly supporting abortions, which is indirectly making millions of dollars for them.

The legal profession is also coming apart. Lawyers are now suing on a contingency basis in any situation in which they think they can make money, rather than worrying about if it is legal or ethical. Many lawyers do not concern themselves with whether abortion is destructive. It may be partly because both lawyers and judges have never dealt with their own guilt regarding abortion, that they cannot see the guilt arising from abortion in others. Consequently, quietly praying pro-life picketers are sentenced to increasingly long prison terms.

Many pastors and priests who realise their congregations are declining, become desperately determined to please their congregations. Therefore, they avoid dealing with many difficult subjects such as abortion. Unfortunately, being congregation pleasers only undermines their credibility and their courage so that eventually they are not able to speak out on any significant matter.

MATERIALISM

It becomes increasingly apparent to many people that good times come with expensive toys and wonderful trips. Credit makes it possible for people to have instant gratification. The media increases people's expectations of what is required for a normal lifestyle and advertising increases people's dissatisfaction with what they have. Men and women are more likely to spend money on each other with the prospect of having a good time. Once they are married and stable, they do not spend as much money on each other. Therefore, it is in the interest of consumer industry and the advertising media to break up marriages and promote new relationships.

THE LYING MEDIA

The media has difficulty telling the whole truth. Television can never provide the awful smells that accompany poverty or the pitiful anguish that accompanies killing. Since media is always distorting reality, people eventually become careless about real reality and accept the reality that is promoted by articles, movies and television. Since it appears that it is impossible to check out the facts, partly because they may be so far away, people become complacent and too lazy to determine whether it really happened as it was described. Not bothering to discriminate truth from lie, most people accept such myths as "abortion is therapeutic," "the world is overpopulated," and "pro-lifers are militant anti-abortionists."

CONDITIONED PASSIVITY

It has been found that most American teenagers, by the age of 17, have seen approximately 18,000 violent situations including rape, murder, etc. The human instinct would be to jump up and run to the rescue of someone about to be attacked, but since it is happening on television the only possible response is to sit and watch. This becomes such a conditioned response that many people are not able to do anything other than sit and watch in a really dangerous situation. Even in church, people who are stirred to do something about starvation or abortion find it very easy to rationalise away their concern. After all, they have been conditioned to sit and listen and watch situations that call for desperate action. They may be determined to act sacrificially while hearing sad stories, but by the time they sit down to Sunday dinner their earnest resolve has become, "Of course, I will go or give, but some other day. Can't you see I am having quality time with my family?"

If you were to ask an average church-going individual what they would do if the police were about to line up twenty Jews in the city square and shoot them, they would say, "Of course I would get down there and do everything I could to prevent that, even interposing my own body." You can with great confidence say that it is very unlikely they would do so because they are doing nothing while twenty Jewish unborn babies are being killed in abortion clinics and hospitals.

INCREASING INFECTIOUS DISEASES

The World Health Organisation has prided itself on the ability to control many infectious diseases. Yet, they are rapidly losing the control of measles, sleeping sickness, malaria, AIDS and many others. Part of the reason for this is that people are not concerned about problems world-wide, but only in their own niche, and partly because with the increasing desire to live one's life as fun-filled as possible, people do not want to spend money on something that may not affect them. With increasing interest in sexual stimulation and sex without having children, there has been, in many parts of the world, increasing amounts of anal intercourse. The semen is made for the vagina where it is absorbed and benefits a woman. In the anus, seminal plasma interferes with the local immune system so the AIDS virus can get a hold.

The millions of young people who are abortion survivors are increasingly pessimistic about their future. They are determined to live a fast or fascinating life. Too often this means selling their bodies to buy things. Many young professional and volunteer prostitutes get AIDS, which they transmit to others. Having children would settle down most of this frantic sexual promiscuity, but, because it is now easy to get rid of a baby, there is an increasing demand for abortion. Unfortunately, abortion produces guilt, increased narcissism and hedonism, which increases the amount of anal intercourse, etc.

INCREASING SUICIDES

There is an increasing rate of suicide, particularly among teenagers, in most countries. In North America, the suicide rate of teenage boys is four times that of teenage girls. The increasing hopelessness, anger, helplessness and alienation that comes as a result of being an abortion survivor increases rates of suicide. Most teenagers are not given the opportunity to talk about their survivor guilt, despair, existential anxiety, etc. with parents or counselors because nobody wants to hear their anguish, knowing that they themselves are implicated. No program to date has been successful in reducing suicides, although many have been tried. Abortions are both the cause and effect of suicidal ideation.

INCREASING KILLINGS

Although there are now no global wars, there are increasing numbers of tribal, internecine and religious wars going on that result in as many war deaths per year as there were during World War I and World War II combined.

Because of abortion, both men and women are more willing to kill - especially to kill a member of the other sex. Killing has become easier because: many parents have already killed a child.

- the media depicts violence as thrilling and a legitimate option to solve interpersonal problems.
- technology makes killing easier, swifter and less personal.
- people are de-humanized and de-humanize through abuse and abortion.
- abortion has weakened the instinctual restraint to aggression in many millions of people.
- watching on television killing and being stalked is a common way people distract themselves from the deep guilt following an abortion.

Technology has increased the efficiency of killing at a distance. In the old days, when you killed a man with your sword or spear you saw him die. His anguish restrained you from killing again. There is immense wealth coming from the sales of arms. Recently, the citizens of a town in Germany were bemoaning the lack of war because people in the nearby Messerschmitt armament factory were being laid off work.

INCREASING STARVATION

There is an obvious growing resource inequality, but no need for hunger. Only 11 % of the world's land surface is currently used for agricultural crops and could be double. The World Bank's index of food commodity prices fell by 78% from 1950-1992.[17] Those people who can afford it buy and consume a higher proportion of available resources at the expense of others. Developing countries plant crops, not according to their local nutritional needs, but according to what can be exported. Much of the media suggests the solution is to give money for food, but more for the full range of abortion services. The genocidal implications are not lost on Africans and Chinese.

Starvation thus becomes the lever that the UN and the media use to promote abortions as the long-term solution to problems of child abuse, reproductive health and starvation. There is no evidence to support this idea. The only measurable result is an increase in the number of aborted children. As more people abort children, their desire to consume and be distracted from feelings of guilt and despair increases.

One industry feeds on the other and promotes the other's business. Consuming promotes abortion and abortion encourages consuming. Similarly, the food industry promotes the idea of eating as much as you want when you can while the fitness industry counts on you spending more money to get back in shape. Both take advantage of human weakness.

SCAPEGOATING

Instead of people dealing with their problems, they tend to pass them on to the succeeding generation. In addition, problem promoters attempt to gain innocence by shortcuts. They pretend to be good, but scapegoat innocent people. There is a symbolic transfer of guilt and innocence. In ancient times, the High Priest, having heard the confessions of all the people, put his hands on the head of the goat, which was led into the wilderness to die. Thus, the goat was laden with guilt and the people blessed with its innocence.

The scapegoat now a days is usually the unborn child. The child is innocent, helpless and voiceless. If the abortion is done in a clinic or hospital, the child is never seen to suffer and therefore the mother believes she is not guilty, especially when the "termination" is done by somebody else. However, her guilt will not go away with scapegoating. Although for a brief period the mother and father feel relieved and even innocent because the baby carried their guilt from promiscuity, selfishness, etc., their guilt is accentuated by knowing they killed a baby. Eventually they will tend to abort another child. Because the guilt increases in an exponential parallel curve, the demand for abortion escalates.

Summary

All these mechanisms are used to destroy humans. Abortions and being an abortion survivor are at the root of them all. Abortion is one of the most effective ways evil has ever thought of to entice humans to destroy each other. What would stop evil is courageous surrogate scapegoating. This means standing in for the innocent, unborn baby so that the family conflicts and the anger at the innocent baby are directed at the surrogate scapegoat. People who have counseled outside abortion clinics know what it is like to allow themselves to vicariously experience some of the violence that is about to be perpetrated on a small, loving child. Those who have lost jobs and been imprisoned for their peaceful pro-life activities know what it is like to be a surrogate scapegoat.

As always, it is only the surrogate scapegoat that can stop tragic history from repeating. Then there has to be an ambassador of reconciliation so that once the cycle of tragedy is stopped, the reconciler can bring people to love each other and to seek God's forgiveness and love.

12. THE ALTERNATIVE PLAN

One of the most basic tenets of Christian theology and of biology is that "unless a grain of wheat falls into the ground and dies, it remains alone."[18] This tenet is true physically, psychologically and spiritually. Unless people die physically, they cannot be reunited with their loved ones in heaven. Unless they identify with Christ in His death and die spiritually, they remain alienated from God. Unless they recognize the death of the PISHB, they cannot have real relationships with other people and tragic history will repeat.

Unless an individual, in dealing with the conflicts engendered by confusion and trauma, can understand and significantly change, his/her personal and interpersonal history of tragedy must repeat. He/she will remain isolated from other people and from God. If all tragedy repeats, then there is no hope for humanity. Everyone would soon die despite the securely protected blueprint of

"My Name" (see Glossary). The process of acknowledging death and allowing for rebirth through the Alternative Plan is an integral part of this counseling program. It is an essential component of the way God uses the original Blueprint to recreate the person from the inside.

The Alternative Plan is that the person who has been mistreated by abuse or abortion will be able to heal some of his wounds, use his handicaps, learn from his misfortunes, and become as mature as possible. Then he can have an adult relationship with somebody, if not his parents. Included with the alternative plan is the hope that his spirit be made alive by God's Spirit, so that someday he will have a fresh start to developing the person he should have become (PISHB) under the Original Plan.

God's Original Plan for the children of Israel was that they would march directly out of slavery in Egypt and triumphantly into the Promised Land, confident God would destroy their enemies and give them all the good things He had in mind. It did not take much to discourage them. When they refused to believe God's promises, God told Moses to go the long way around. This was God's Alternative Plan - forty years of wandering in a hot, dusty wilderness with boring scenery, tedious food, painful blisters and various temptations. The nation of Israel eventually got to the Promised Land flowing with milk and honey as a group of believing lean and mean warriors, but not before everybody of military age and upwards, except for two individuals, left their bodies buried under the shifting sands.

Though abused, neglected, aborting or surviving people will always have scars and/or the handicaps of personality defects, warts and wounds, God can start the rebuilding from the inside. These changes in the core person eventually begin to show on the outside. The Alternative Plan is not the "second best" but a different, pain-filled route. With God, nothing is lost or destroyed, unless He destroys it Himself. His purposes are never thwarted. He takes every discarded piece of one's past and reorders it, so that, although the outside of the house looks very dilapidated, the interior becomes beautiful.

When people get to heaven they will see both the inside and the outside as God had originally designed them. The design was kept safe, as encoded in the spirit and genes, and the Blueprint kept by the Pilgrim for My Name. Now God uses that Blueprint to show that what was tragic can be triumphant.

The worst point in human history (when we killed God's only Son) was both the darkest and the brightest day for humanity. The man/God Jesus Christ, as the model Pilgrim, became a scapegoat for all of us. He was killed, died, buried and mourned. He came to life again with a new body. He was given a name above every name. Yet, even Christ's new body has the scars indicating the pain He went through to fulfill God's alternative plan. These scars will always be part of His makeup, but they will not hurt or hinder Him.

While the evil one is trying to destroy God's children and attempting to ruin God's Original Plan for humankind, God is reworking the discarded material and producing a new structure from within. Through His plan of salvation, first the spirit is renewed, then his/her psychology, and finally his/her body. In the process of renewing all three aspects of a human, it is important to lie to rest what was and what should have become so what God intended may grow. When an individual gives his/her life to Christ, God makes his/her spirit alive by infusing him/her with His Holy Spirit. Before resurrection and re-creation can take place, he/she must recognize the pain, evil and disobedience in his/her life and identify with Christ in His death and burial. Salvation is the spiritual process. These counseling groups are part of the psychological healing, maturing process.

The men and women who become counselees in Hope Alive groups are scapegoats and commit themselves to be surrogate scapegoats. In a very real way, they were loaded with the sins and griefs of their family of past and present generations. That is why they are suffering so much. In Hope Alive, they must consciously accept their role in counseling - to suffer the pain for the mistreatment of many in their family - even while everyone else is comfortably going on with their lives. By changing, they change the tragic transactions in their families. Because they are different, others must change, attack them or hide. If they patiently persist in growing and loving, many others in their family will begin to see the benefit and engage in the process. When counselees relinquish false faces, mourn the childhood they should have had, grieve the person they should have become, and reconcile with those who have injured them and those they have injured, other family members will often seek counseling for themselves. Seeing changes in a brother or niece, they realize that they, too, can heal and stop scapegoating.

Healing is not just getting rid of pain. It begins with a real, earnest, child-like desire to change in as many ways as possible. As Jesus said, to enter the Kingdom one must be child-like. Using the Hope Alive analogy, this is like a newly discovered Pilgrim.

Therapy is analogous to dealing with an infected wound. Before proceeding, the surgeon must have the patient's consent and the patient must be determined to get to the root of the infection regardless of the pain. "I have got to know what is at the root of my problem." There is the incision, "You hurt me when..." and other techniques used in the Hope Alive program to uncover the source of the problem. At that point, there is expression of pain and grief. The surgeon is not content with what flows out of the wound naturally. He cleans it all out, puts in antibiotics and sutures it up.

Many hurts, fears and confusion often arise from disappointed hopes. These hopes arise from unmet needs. Needs arise during the development of the person who is attempting to become whom they would have become according to their blueprint. There would be no disappointment if there were no hopes, and no hopes if there were no needs. The only person who has no earthly needs is a dead person. One cannot stop hoping, but those hopes must be realistic.

The figure on the following page charts God's Original Plan for humankind, Adam and Eve's choice, the Alternative Plan, humanity's choices and the two end results of those choices.

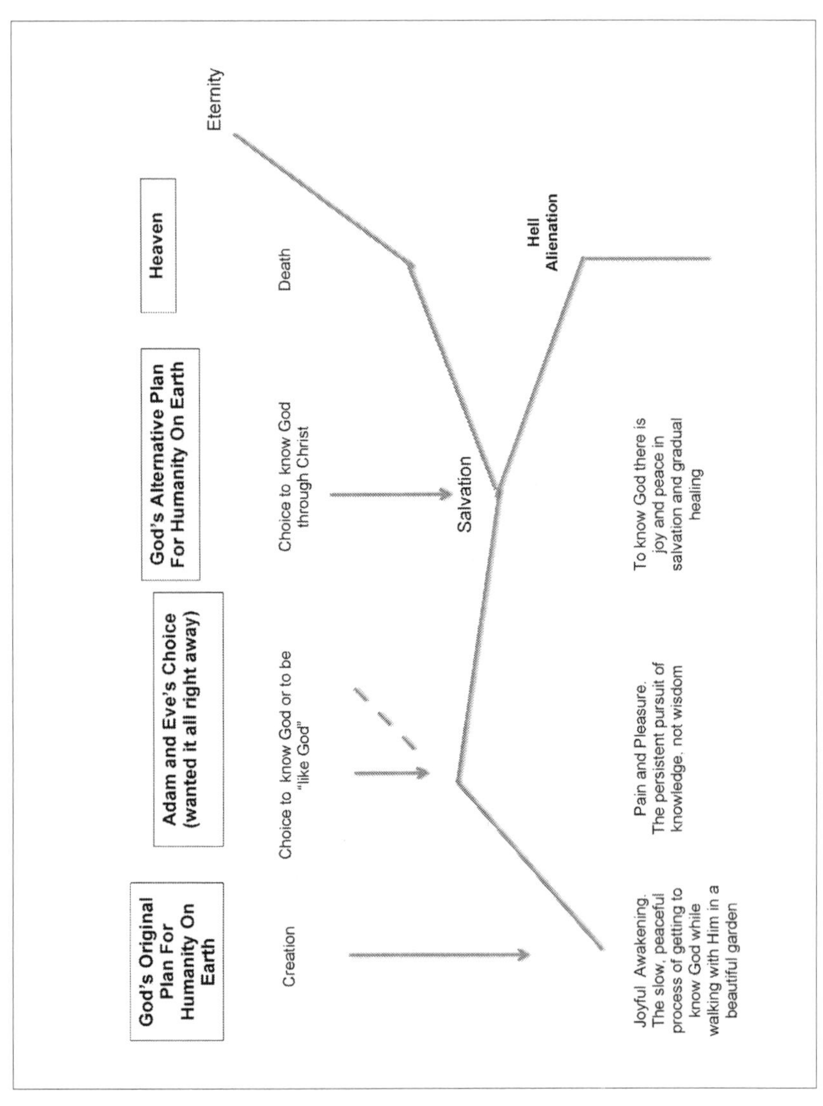

Figure 1.1 God's Original Plan for Humanity on Earth

13. SOME KEY CONCEPTS FOR UNDERSTANDING GOD'S PURPOSES FOR HUMANITY

This is a short list and brief description of the basic assumptions for the following chapters.

CHOICE

God wanted to be loved by humans, not because He was so powerful or beautiful, but because man had chosen to get to know Him even when it was not easy to do so. Any real choice has a fifty-fifty probability. God has always ensured that for mankind collectively, choices were real. He never abandoned man, nor did He overpower him with His majesty. He patiently preserved our (collective) choices.

For each individual the choice is obviously not fifty-fifty. Some are raised in evil ridden "party-houses" where degradation and death abound. Others are brought up in God-loving homes where it is easy to see and desire the love of Christ. In God's design, the inequality of individual freedom to choose what is good, but at the same time there being a collective choice fifty-fifty, forces a shared responsibility on humanity. Those who have a better chance of choosing Truth and Joy because of the circumstances into which they were born, must share that privilege with those who have considerably less chance because of the benighted situation into which they were placed. The choice is always between doing good or evil, killing or curing, not between right and wrong.[19] Jesus made it very clear there are no un-involved observers. You are either contributing to the problem or to the solution.

TRUTH

Truth describes reality. Reality is everything that is permanent. Because humans have been designed to have a strong curiosity, a desire to fill their needs, and a phenomenal capability of learning, they have an intuitive awareness of what is truth and what is error. When they make a mistake they know it by the guilt they feel.

CONFLICT

Humans were designed to be conflict free, but because they choose to be "like God" immediately and selfishly, they have been filled with personal and interpersonal divisiveness. What was originally a conflict with an external evil became a conflict within and between each other. Almost every external conflict eventually became internalized. Internalized conflicts result in humans using energy inefficiently. To survive, humans were designed to have self-correcting mechanisms. These mechanisms seek to resolve the conflict so humans can function more efficiently and live as long as possible. All too frequently and all too painfully, people seek to understand the how and why of their initial tragedy by re-enacting it. And when they still do not learn, they scapegoat. Because scapegoating resolved nothing, they pass their sins and griefs onto their children and grandchildren for at least three generations.

PAIN

The primary experience of humans in the conflict that is attempting to frustrate their intended purpose is pain. Pain - physical, psychological and spiritual - is an indication that damage is occurring to some aspect of their person. The damage probably is the result of abuse, neglect, or being a pregnancy-loss survivor. Usually, the more intense the pain the more serious the damage.

FEAR

Fear is the anticipation of damage, of further damage, or of death. Fears may be triggered by internal or external threats. Fears arise from:

- alienation. People are afraid of being alienated from God; they recognize this as hell. As children, they were afraid of being alienated from their parents because this meant they would not survive. They fear being alienated from their selves. They do not want their Blueprint effaced or the beautiful person God intended them to be destroyed or distorted. They fear they becoming insane, and wearing False Faces (see Section 2.7.b). People who are afflicted with Post Abortion Survivor Syndrome (PASS) do not often seek to know themselves because they feel there may be no self to be known. Unlike the existentialists, the authors do not believe that humans have a fear of non-being. At some level everyone is aware that they were built to last an eternity. Thus, the deeper human fear is that one may always be alienated from God, which is death and hell.
- a threat to survival. People fear their body will be killed, their mind will become split and their spirit will be entrapped by Satan.
- not being the person God intended them to be. If they cannot become the person they were intended to be they are afraid that they will be a shell, deformed, false or dehumanized.
- not being known. If one is not known, needs cannot be met.
- not being remembered. A history not read is as having no history. Having no history is like not ever existing.
- not having children to "carry on one's name."
- having a meaningless existence. Living is only real living to the extent one is becoming the person one is designed to be.

- **further pain.** The sensation of pain is there to alert people that damage is happening to some part of them. There are some constructive pains, indications one is stretching and growing.
- **one's own impulses.** E.g. aggression and lust. Humans all know that, under certain conditions, everyone could destroy oneself or others, even those one loves.
- **that the species, nation, clan, or family will die.** Without that fear, there would be little or no defensive aggression.
- **that one will have no joy, peace or praise.** Without these, a person cannot develop an essential part of his/her being.
- **that all our efforts will amount to nothing;** our best work will rust or bust. Without some continuing evidence of our efforts it is hard to know if we lived.
- **that God will not acknowledge we belong to Him.** That we will not gain His protection, and thus be vulnerable to evil and alienation from Life.

Guilt

Guilt is an individual's instinctive and/or rational awareness he/she has made choices that placed him/herself or others in danger of damage. He/she would like to undo that mistake, but realizes it is difficult, if not impossible. He/she knows he/she will soon feel the consequence of his/her wrong choice.

Maladaptive coping

Humans, not being able to deal with the threats to the frustration of their purpose on their own, adopt maladaptive coping mechanisms. These are:

- embracing death in order to avoid being powerless to prevent death being imposed on them.
- bargaining or swapping more intense fears for lesser ones, e.g. accepting pain if one can have a family. God wants people to be fearless, and to reverently respect Him.
- distorting reality, either with lies, drama or drugs.
- denying humanness, e.g.- embracing a mechanistic evolution.
- desperately looking for and trying quick fixes.
- relying on human intelligence and effort instead of God's good grace and power.
- trying to be God.

Survival

God built humans to last for eternity. Their spirit cannot be destroyed. Their minds are capable of enduring an incredible amount of assault and insult.

Their bodies are very durable. To make sure that the species did not die out, God encoded most survival mechanisms in the genes. Thus, human survival is guided by powerful instincts that, even in the worst circumstances, propel humans to procreate, co-create and care for their young. Because survival is so deeply encoded in human biology, it could not easily be tampered with, at least until recently. Because it is in biology, humans can trust their instincts more than their philosophy. Genes are now being manipulated by "genetic engineers" so human survival is not as safe as it once was. Now that human survival is not so secure, maybe only God's full-scale intervention will keep humanity from self-destruction.

SURVIVAL GUILT

If children for any reason are chosen to live when their siblings or neighbors are chosen to be aborted, they have a great sense they are not worthy to be alive. As small children, they might even believe that they somehow contributed to the death of their siblings. The survival guilt is so great that even though they are alive they cannot believe they will be allowed to continue to live. They anticipate that circumstances might change and that at any moment they also would be terminated. They cannot trust being alive, and therefore they do not participate in their own development or in the intense interactions with siblings and peers that is necessary for their maturation. Since the future is so uncertain, they do not plan for it and have enormous difficulty making decisions. They realize they are not utilizing their talents and opportunities, so they feel a further guilt for not developing the person they should have become.

CAIN COMPLEX

After killing his brother, Cain felt so much guilt that he believed everyone in the world would attack him.[20] He knew he deserved to die. He was much like those with survival guilt. Children born because they were wanted before an "unwanted" sibling was aborted have this Cain Complex. They believe their existence, neediness, or bad behavior made their mothers decide she could not cope with another child and therefore chose to abort him or her. They believe, with some justification, a brother or sister died because of them.

God forgave and reassured Cain. He placed on Cain a mark that said, "You cannot kill this man. He belongs to me." In the Hope Alive treatment program, abortion survivors with this kind of survival guilt are given an understanding of what is happening to them and are welcomed in the name of Christ. This is like giving them a protective mark. With the welcome goes the statement, "You do not deserve to die, so do not act like you do. Assert your God-given right to exist and acknowledge Christ's welcome and you will live." "In Christ's name and in my name I have welcomed you, granting you hospitality and protection."

Mutual benefit

We are so tightly bound in the bundle of life that what we do to others we do to ourselves. It is not possible to benefit at the expense of another. If we do them harm, we ourselves are harmed and become less human. If we deafen our ears to their helpless cry, we lose the ability to hear the very quiet but vital voices from inside us that tell us how we should develop, where we should go to have our needs met, and when we are being threatened or damaged. If we kill another, our humanity dies. If we ignore anyone's plight, we become more vulnerable ourselves. When we love another, we are loved accordingly. When we forgive others, we are forgiven, partly because we too are guilty for what happens to us. This Universal Ethic of Mutual Benefit applies to medicine, business, law, etc. By it we love and live.

SURROGATE SCAPEGOAT

In addition to temporarily accepting their role as family scapegoat and pioneer of change, counselees agree to be surrogate scapegoats, standing in for others, blamed and hurt by the community. As they work at preventing the mistreatment of others, especially children who suffer like they did as children, they learn to love and their rehabilitation is completed.

14. The Vicious Cycle of Dehumanization

God was not ashamed to become a human being. Humans are the apex of His creation. Originally God wanted to enjoy human company and created a lovely garden where they could walk and chat. In their pride and rebellion, humans tried to take a short cut to gradually getting to know God. Instead they chose to become "like God." Alas, instead of becoming like God, they became much less than they were intended to be. Yet, God's purposes are not frustrated for long. Humans can still become God's friends.

The process of dehumanization begins even before the infant is born. Babies are not considered a human, but a fetus. Though "fetus" is accurate Latin for the unborn child, the term is used in a derogatory fashion. A fetus is almost universally accorded lesser rights than every other human. Many people believe that a threat to the mother's life is a legitimate reason to kill the unborn infant. In this way they are systematically discriminating against the smaller human in favor of the larger one.

After children are born, they have to emit appealing or alarming signals to indicate their needs. These needs should be met by parents. Unfortunately, the signal "Please listen to me" frequently falls on deaf ears. Thus, a child not only learns to mute his call to others, he loses the ability to be sensitive to his own needs and distress. Thus, a child's ability to check his progressive development against his blueprint is hindered. When a child is hurt or threatened he needs to indicate that distress. The cry, "You hurt me" is easily suppressed, and so a child learns to repress his hurt, much to his detriment.

The process of dehumanization is progressive and cyclic. It is transmitted from one generation to the other. It manifests itself in various forms. A woman who is dehumanized during her childhood is much more likely to dehumanize the unborn infant and, therefore, more likely to have him/her murdered *in utero.* In so doing, she further dehumanizes herself and all her other children. In some respects, it is impossible to undo the damage, yet considerable healing is possible. That is why this manual was written. It is well worth the effort group counselors make to help heal the damages, illuminate the blueprint and reinstate God's intentions for anyone hurt by childhood mistreatment and pregnancy loss.

There is urgency to this task. With the progressive transgenerational cyclic dehumanization, our species is endangered. Parents are turned against children, and children against themselves and their parents. That vicious cycle is accelerating.

Evil seeks to reshape humans in its image, to become minions of darkness rather than friends of God in light. People learn to dehumanize themselves and each other. Once a person can be seen as an object they can be treated as an object of more or less value. Once value is debatable, so is the way the person is treated.

Evil sought to put humans in conflict with themselves and with each other. Males and females in conflict lead to derogatory discrimination, marital violence, rape, dishonor and abandonment. Parents turned against children destroy their young (abortion) or mistreat those who are born (abuse and neglect). To provide some justification they engage in eugenics to improve the race or to end the "suffering" of those whose lives are deemed to have "no value to them." When the young turn against each other it creates sibling rivalry and warfare. When the young turn against their parents it is euthanasia. Humans, in their wanton selfishness, are progressively destroying their environment so that their environment eventually becomes hostile to humans.

Though evil cannot destroy humanity, it can get humanity to destroy itself. For this reason, evil has created conflict; between men and women so they do not mate or propagate, between parents and children so they do not care for their young and either do not survive or do not develop, and between children and their peers or against their parents, resulting in euthanasia. These intertwining cycles are described later in the book.

13. SUMMARY

God created humans for His purposes. That is not the same as being made for His use. His purposes were for their greatest benefit. He is not benefiting at the expense of humans, but benefits with their benefit. This is not to say that God needs humans, being self-sufficient. It does imply that God, because of His personality, just wanted somebody to share His joy.

Humans are the highest order in God's creation. They were created with insatiable curiosity, remarkable perceptions and an immense ability to understand. Interestingly enough, they are approximately the middle-sized object halfway between the largest and the smallest parts of His creation. This gives humans the best position to view both the largest and the smallest objects.

The human was created with the challenge of co-creation - to create with God the person God designed each individual to be. Thus God does not leave the person to unfold. His designs allowed considerable plasticity, so each person has a major responsibility in molding him/herself. In order to help create themselves with God, God provides them with the ability to see themselves as they are and whom they should become. In the Hope Alive treatment program, a person's ability to discern whom he/she is becoming is termed "Viewing My Blueprint." Because the child can see his design, he can know what he needs to develop himself according to his Blueprint.

It would be hard, if not impossible, to change the floor plan, but the great Architect is happy to discuss and accept some fairly major modifications suggested by the individual builder. For example, a man's design may have impelled him to the be the father of a big family. After much prayer and counseling, God allows and blesses those who choose to be celibate so they can serve Him.

God created humans with the fifty-fifty chance of becoming all He hoped for them. His desire was that they would quietly get to know Him and get to know themselves as they chatted in the garden, naming animals and tending creation. When the humans ruined that opportunity, God provided an Alternative Plan. They can still become the person He planned, but it is by walking a much more difficult pathway.

Even children have choices in deciding what they become. If they are able and enabled to see their Blueprint, they will make good choices for what they need. They might choose to repair broken clocks rather than sit passively watching television. Though the child has limited choices, he/she is not passive. As children grow, their range of choices widens, but their ability to choose diminishes so that the amount of freedom is a constant.[21] If they choose the right ingredient they will feel the glow of maturing, they will sense they are fulfilling what they were intended to be and their ability to choose will gradually increase, i.e. He/she soon realizes that, "To him that has will more be given."[22] The person who chooses well what they are given, matures faster and better realizes what he/ she needs and what is noxious.

Parents have similar genetic constitution to their children and should be able to read their child's Blueprint more clearly than anybody else. They should constantly help the child make right choices in the materials for the construction of whom he/she is becoming. Too often, the parents are selfish and take what is available for themselves. In this way they are hating the child, adding to his/her frustration and destruction. As they love the child and give him what he/she needs, he grows and their joy in watching him/her mature increases, thus reinforcing their desire to meet his/her needs.

The parent's ability to see the child's Blueprint as opposed to their own, helps them more clearly discern what they are attempting to get for themselves and what they are providing the child. The child is not a *tableau erasa,* a blank page on which other people are writing either with conditioning, environmental contingencies or conflicts. The child is involved in the act of searching for what he needs. He is able to guide his parents, indicating his disapproval of things that he does not need, or that are imposed upon him, with a cry of distress. He indicates what is good for him with a smile and coos.

It is important to recognize that the child is created with enormous potential. People are admonished to get to know God, which implies that they have the capacity to know God. It is amazing to think that the child is a spirit given a body. That is not to say the spirit lives in a body that does not have any impact on the spirit. It does mean that the child is essentially a spirit and, though the body will die, he/she will remain. Made in the image of God, a child's spirit, mind and body interact, each part having a permanent impact on the other's parts.

The implications for seeing a child in this manner are far reaching. For example, education given in groups for children of the same age is very inefficient. Parents and teachers should spend a great deal more time listening and watching than instructing. This would result in a much better use of the child's time and effort. The teachers and the parents must show how and where to look for material, but not dictate what the child needs. In this kind of school, the teacher's main task is to answer the child's questions, not get the child to answer his/hers.

NOTES: 1. A PSYCHOLOGY OF CREATED HUMANITY

'Davis (1928). Cafeteria feeding. Am J Pis Child. 36. 651-679.

[2]Bowlby, J. (1969). Attachment. (Vol. I). New York: Basic Books.

’Luke 23:34.
[4]Psalm 139:19.
’Genesis 3:5.

‘Rayburn, W. et al. (1984). Drug overdose during pregnancy: An overview from a metropolitan poison control centre. Obstetrics and Gynaecology. 64. 611-614.

[7]Gissler, M., Hemminki, E., & Lonnqvist, J. (1996). Suicides after pregnancy in Finland, 1987-94: Register linkage study. British Medical Journal. 313(7070). 1431-4.

"Kid’s First is a child policy advocate group and parent support group. P.O. Box 5256 Airdrie, Alberta. T4B 2B3 Canada.

[9]Gamble, T.J. & Zigler, E. (1986). Effects of infant day care: Another look at the evidence. American Journal of Ortho Psychiatry. 56. 26-42.

[10]Grossman, D. Cl 9951. On Killing: The psychological cost of learning to kill in war and society. New York: Little, Brown.

"Schmitt, B.D. & Kempe, C.H. (1975). Child abuse: Management and prevention of the Battered Child Syndrome. Basle: Ciba-Geigy.
[12]World Bank. (1993). The world food outlook. New York.

"Genesis 1:28.

"Preston, S.H. (1984). Children and the elderly. Scientific American. 251. 36-41.

"Damme, C. (1978). Infanticide: The worth of the infant under law. Med Hist. 22. 1-24.

"Ney, P.G. & Wicket, A.R. (1989). Mental health and abortion: Review and analysis. Psychiatric Journal of the University of Ottawa. 14(41. 506-516.

"World Bank. (1993). The world food outlook. New York.

'"John 12:24.
,[9]Luke 6:9.
[20]Genesis 4:14.

[2]'Ney, P.G. (1974). The law and the essence of love. Victoria: Pioneer Publishing.

[22]Matthew 13:12.

2

PSYCHOPATHOLOGY

1. Measures of Psychopathology

Health is the harmony, joy and efficiency that occur when a person's body, mind and spirit are fulfilling the intentions of the Designer. Illness, then, is the degree to which people are not able or not willing to fulfill those intentions. A dysfunction is a discrepancy between form and function and is measured as griefs and kilogriefs. Pathology is the discrepancy between form and design. There is no discrepancy between design and intent because God "does not make trash. It is easy to understand that, although there are good genes, breaks in chromosomes or difficulties during pregnancy result in the baby being not formed as he or she was designed to be. A tragedy is any lack or attack on the form, function or design that leaves pathology or dysfunction.

We are healthiest and happiest when we are most human. Humans are the apex of God's creation. They were created a little lower than the angels for the present, but will be raised to a higher order so that they will reign forever as kings and priests and judges of angels.' The intent of evil was to frustrate God by dehumanizing this wonderful creature. It was not hard to persuade Adam and Eve that they would be better off by choosing their own intentions and design. If being human is to fulfill God's intended purposes, then to thwart them is dehumanizing.

The tragic cycle began with Adam and Eve. It spirals downward or upward in each family. That tragic spiral can only be stopped by a surrogate scapegoat, that is, someone who is prepared to accept the inevitable pain of changing family patterns. We call him or her the family Pilgrim (see 2.7.d). The downward spiral begins with a selfish choice. Upward spirals are always initiated and maintained by loving choices.

Some people may have many of the characteristics that God intended them to have, but they are missing others. In those areas of their lives they are unwell and need help and healing. It is possible that a person score high on all but enjoying God and His creation. If this lack of joy were added to griefs in other areas, one could say that he/she had between 2.5 and 2.7 'kilogriefs' of unwellness (1000 griefs = 1 kilo grief).

All the attempts to measure the amount of unwellness or pathologies a person has are currently determined with reference to population averages. A patient's hemoglobin is determined by the average most healthy looking men or women would have at that age. Intelligence is determined in relation to an arbitrary norm. Psychoticism or neuroticism is determined by what average people think like. The problem with norms determined by the average is that they fluctuate and may have little to do with reality.

In this psychology, we are attempting to establish norms in terms of an absolute, a real reality. Reality is that which is permanent. Energy and matter are unified in ultimate reality. When a very large particle accelerator was developed with sufficient energy, it was possible to discover the Z-Bozon - which provided evidence that the four unitary forces of the universe could be reduced to three, that is, the weak force and the electromagnetic force could be unified. It took immense energy to discover this unity. It is now more clearly understood that only by approximating the energy of the big bang, i.e. creation, will it be possible to find that law that unifies everything. Since only God has that amount of power, the only route to understanding the unifying forces of the universe is through Him. Since we distort by observing, we can only know real truth by receiving the truth that is declared by itself, i.e. by God Himself.

The deviation from the original plan is much smaller in infants. The amount of distortion gradually grows as people wander away from God. The distortion is progressive to the body. If people accept the Alternative Plan, the distortion can be corrected. With salvation through Christ, spiritual distortion is reversed. The changes in the mind are progressive as people become more mature and loving like God. Although their body progressively decays, they are assured of a new body which will fit their spirit and new mind.

By definition, normal is that which:

- conforms to reality, i.e. will always be.
- is part of God's original plan. Any deviation from the plan produces a distortion, which ultimately results in death.
- has roots that are in God's purposes.

The amount of abnormality can be determined in these ways:

- the discrepancy between design and function.
- the difference between belief and behaviour.
- the distance of alienation between a person and God.
- the degree of dissimilarity between Christ (the perfect man) and any person.

Pathology is the degree of deviation from the Original Plan of each individual. It is the amount of deviation from their Blueprint. The unit of pathology we call griefs. It is the amount of damage to the person as they should have become. Since that damage is a loss, grieving is necessary. A thousand griefs are a kilogrief.

The measure of pathology is individual. Although there is overlap because there are similarities among individuals, the amount of grief for a person is entirely individual. To see the degree of pathology or distortion, one must see the individual's Blueprint clearly. This results in a paradox. For an individual to see his Blueprint clearly, he must be helped to overcome the distortion in his ability to view. It is only after some treatment, when his ability to view his Blueprint, and thus the amount of grief for the person he should have become, is restored.

We use the Hope Alive program to help restore a clear view of the Blueprint. This is done in the first half of the program. After that, it is possible to more clearly see the person he should have become and then engage in the process of grieving. The more whole a person is, the better able to see his blueprint. A well person may see very little need to grieve the person he should have become because he is quite like that person.

Some ways the Hope Alive program uses devices to help a person to more clearly see her Blueprint include:

- helping her recapture the play, visions and dreams of her childhood, both actual and symbolic.
- encouraging her to express her current grief and pain from distortions to her Pilgrim.
- providing a figurative smorgasbord of lessons, careers or families that she can choose from.
- encouraging her to watch children and to pick the ones that she feels are healthy.
- describing activities that are most frustrating or fulfilling.

In God's universe, the person each of us should be is an expression of the person He is. We are made in His image. His intention for creation and His design for humanity is the natural expression of His person. However, because of the temporary disruption caused by evil, human form and human function are, to varying degrees, distorted and to not appear according to the original design.

A person is designed to experience, express and share joy. If she should experience joy continuously and has an experience of joy no more than once a month, she has approximately 1200 griefs or 1.2 kilogriefs of distortion or pathology on this parameter. It may be true that in this world of struggle and pain the average person may experience 4-5 moments of joy per month. According to human average, her pathology on the parameter of joy is 20 griefs. By these standards, she should be content if therapy restores her to 18-20 griefs, but she still feels dissatisfied and may not understand why. Hope Alive counseling, then, measures griefs based on individual norms, and the program helps individuals deal with these griefs and learn how to experience joy.

Other parameters of psychopathology to measure result from a consideration of the other parts of God's intention for humans and encoded in their Blueprints. We are still working on refining and defining these so they are more easy to measure, code and analyze.

Prevention

To help a child become the person he/she should have become, wise parents should provide children with a wide variety of opportunities to express themselves and to pick what healthy activities they are fascinated by. For example, allow a child the opportunity to respond to a whole variety of machines, musical instruments, play opportunities and media in a very large gym. A wise parent would then measure the amount of time the child plays at any particular machine, and the amount of involvement. This, then, becomes a measure of the child's interest, which is an expression of his/her Blueprint.

Education

Education should be designed for individual children after they have been observed under a variety of conditions and their academic needs are understood. In the optimum education environment, children should be asking the questions and teachers providing the answers. Among the first things that children should learn, because they have this tendency in any case, is scientific methodology. They should be aided in their attempts to understand how things work, then to replicate what they believe is happening and then to explain it to others.

Motivation

Since children can read their Blueprint and see the person they should become, thus in descending order of importance, a person's motivation to learning is to:

- share joy.
- express curiosity.
- survive.
- please parents, etc.
- compete with self and others.

COUNSELLING

The Hope Alive program attempts to restore the Blueprint (as much as is possible) to the person. This process requires they regain joy and curiosity and learn to love. The effectiveness of treatment, however, is not determined by how close one can return to the original plan, but what percentage of improvement takes place. In this program we utilize the paradox "unless a grain of wheat falls into the ground and dies it remains alone." Obviously, people are alone and physically separated from their loved ones who died. Their mind is isolated and their spirit alienated from God. Complete treatment requires a new body, a new spirit, and a progressive restoration of the mind.

Effective counseling results in:

- a diminished number of disappointments so that people are not constantly being seduced by those who purport to provide them with what they need.
- a diminished expression of the Dancer and Urchin.
- the ability to mourn the loss of the person they should have become (PISHB).
- people being more thankful, grateful and loving.
- people not wasting their energy, but heading in the direction of the person they should have become.
- using their energy and resources to become progressively more mature and Christ-like.

2. Eight Interlocking Tragic Cycles Leading to the Death of Humanity

It is a principle aim of the "evil one" to destroy humanity. There are reasons to believe he is closer to that goal than ever before. By turning men and women against each other and against themselves, Satan has effectively begun a process that, "unless the days are shortened," could result in the annihilation of humanity.[2]

God created humans with a robust system of self-preserving instincts. However, the fact that these are so strong is partly why, once they are turned about, they can be so self-destructive. Humans are quite capable of destroying themselves individually and collectively. Internal human tendencies and natural laws that govern the universe are there to ensure that humankind survives. I believe that the best ways to understand how and why humans function as they do is to know and appreciate God's intention for His creation, and to know those self and species-preserving mechanisms of body, soul and spirit that He built into humans.

One of the basic paradigms of this creation psychology is humanity's response to their helpless young. At the sound of a helpless cry, everyone becomes caught in a dilemma between wanting to nurture or destroy. Our species-preserving psychobiology is alerted by the attention demanding sound. We cannot relax or rest until the crying stops. It will stop if the child is nurtured, beaten or ignored long enough. The helpless young emits a soul-piercing cry, or, by a look, posture or gesture, appeals for help. That appeal is no less demanding of a response if it originates from the silent, unseen, unborn young.

The unborn child's cry is heard in the biological changes that a woman feels, and in the resulting changes in her behavior. Those behavioral changes are perceived and understood by her mother and her mate. If parents and grandparents respond to the biologically discerned appeal of the silent, urgently demanding unborn young with aggression or neglect rather than with nurture, our species cannot survive.

We love ourselves when we love others as ourselves. That is why it is good to follow Christ's command to love our neighbor and our enemies.[3] The Universal Ethic of Mutual Benefit (UEMB) states that we cannot benefit at the expense of another. Something cannot be good for us alone. If it is "evil" for them, it is "evil" for ourselves. If it is "good" for them, it is "good" for ourselves. It is only and always a choice of good or evil. There is no third option such as silence, inactivity or uninvolved observing. Thus we are always choosing between good and evil, not right or wrong. In situations of need, particularly in matters of life and death, there are no innocent bystanders.

When we injure another, we injure ourselves. When we ignore the appeal for help by anyone, we lose the sensitivity to listen to our own needs. When we kill someone, the dead person cannot be brought back to life, nor can what died inside all those who contributed to the killing grow again, except by the grace of God.

If we kill, the instinctual restraint to our aggression has been broken. From then on, this barrier is weakened with little probability that it will ever be fully restored. From the moment that an individual kills another, they know and we know that their aggressive feelings cannot be trusted. If a woman agrees to the destruction by abortion of her unborn young, she knows that she has allowed, if not encouraged, the expression of a terrible tendency within her. Having killed once, she is cautious about her aggression ever after. If a father severely beats a small, naughty child, he knows that he has "gone too far." After that he must always struggle to control his temper. In war, a relatively small portion of the soldiers fire their rifles to kill, but once they have killed it becomes progressively easier.[4]

Neglect is almost always more damaging then abuse because it kills our ability to develop. Any parent who ignores the pitiful cries of a suffering infant because he/she was too tired to respond and later finds the child to be very sick, feels a justifiable, awful guilt. Having once neglected a child, a person's instinctual drive to nurture and protect is weakened. To make sure it does not happen again, parents often try to compensate by responding too quickly and with great indulgence to any indication of the child's distress.

Killing an unborn infant is qualitatively different. The infant is dead and no perpetrator or observer, even those peripherally involved, can ever be the same. The more helpless the person killed:

- the more damaged the killer and the observer will be.
- the more their instinctual restraint to aggression will be broken.
- the more their natural drive to nurture and protect the innocent and the victim will be weakened.

THE DESTRUCTIVE BOND BETWEEN PERPETRATOR, VICTIM AND OBSERVER: THE TRAGIC TRIANGLE

It is unlikely that any form of neglect or abuse can occur without the participation of the Perpetrator, Victim and Observer (Figure 2.1). This tragic triangle rotates with time and circumstance so that the roles are relatively interchangeable.[5] The Observer has the most critical role in mistreatment or killing. Both the Perpetrator and the Victim are likely to turn to the Observer and ask, "Why didn't you stop us?" They recognize the difficult dyad in which they are trapped and the relative objectivity of the Observer.

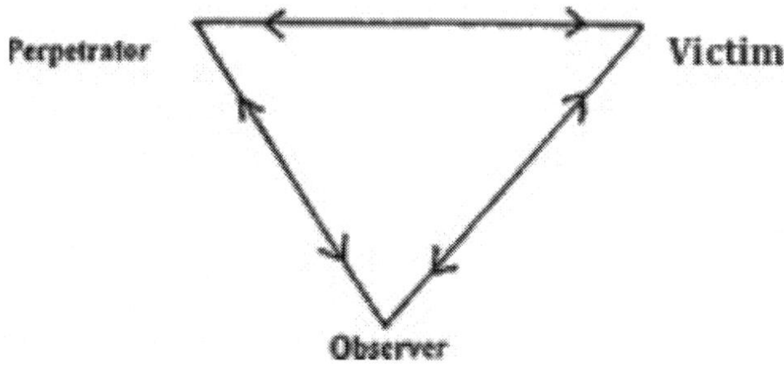

Figure 2.1 The Tragic Triangle of Abuse or Abortion

Some victims, even children, may contribute to their own victimization. This is the most tragic part of any triangle of mistreatment and murder. Once a person has been victimized, a psychological, energy-demanding conflict is formed and the organism must resolve it. The resolution is often sought by contributing to a re-creation of the original trauma, thus appearing to invite re-victimization.

There is a persistent bond between the Perpetrator (P), Victim (V), and Observer (O), which is mutually destructive. Even when there is no apparent action, there is a continuing conflict in the mind among these three that results in fatigue, psychological and/or physical illness, and sometimes suicide or murder. This bond is so strong it can be stated as, "You do not become what you eat, and so much as you become what and whom you hate." This continuing bond among the three parties (PVO) can only be broken, and people released from it, through healing and reconciliation. Although it may be hard to forgive and dangerous to forget, it is the only path to reconciliation. Without reconciliation, tragic history must and will repeat itself. Without peace among them, every P,V and O will have no peace within.

The destructiveness of abortion

In the early years of my practice, I began to recognize that mothers who had pregnancy losses tended to be depressed after the birth of the next child. This interfered with their bonding and it made it more likely for them to abuse and neglect their children. The first paper I wrote on the subject was published in 1979 and created real furor.

It had been argued for years that the major cause for abuse and neglect was unwantedness. If children could be selected, chosen and planned by providing the full range of "reproductive choices," then there would be a major decline in child abuse. This hypothesis had little research and certainly no scientific evidence to support it.

I discovered that the opposite was true. When there was more abortion, there was more child abuse. Later, we did the research to elucidate some of the factors and confirm the positive correlation. To state abortion and abuse are linked is still a very politically incorrect statement. It can get us into trouble almost at any time.

We also discovered that not only did abortion lead to child abuse, but child abuse more frequently leads to abortion. That is, people who are dehumanized by mistreatment in their childhood are more likely to dehumanize and destroy their young. Thus there is a vicious cycle between abortion and abuse that is very difficult to stop. We later discovered that children who grew up in families where there had been abortions, or in countries were abortions were likely, exhibited many of the conflicts and symptoms of survivors of trauma (see Section 2, Cycle 4, PASS). They were abortion survivors. Abortion survivors had little self-respect and gave little to others. Having been dehumanized as a "wanted" object, it was easy to dehumanize others. Thus a vicious cycle of guilt and violence can ensue.

Aborting unborn babies is the most self and species destructive activity known to humanity. An innocent, unique person is killed. Many human qualities in the Perpetrators and Observers also die. Abortion also undermines many species-preserving mechanisms and sets into motion a whole series of tragic cycles. Abortion is the center of seven interlocking tragic cycles (Figure 2.1). Abortion initiates and perpetuates these cycles. They continue from moment to moment and from generation to generation because a number of self and species- preserving instinctual and social mechanisms that become distorted by abortion.

It appears that almost everyone is capable of killing. We all hope that we are never in circumstances where we would be "forced to kill." The circumstances of early childhood abuse and neglect, dehumanization, starvation or chemical dis-inhibition make people more likely to kill. Humans are restrained from killing by three important barriers: the law, morality, and instinct. This is illustrated by the figure on the following page (Figure 2.2).

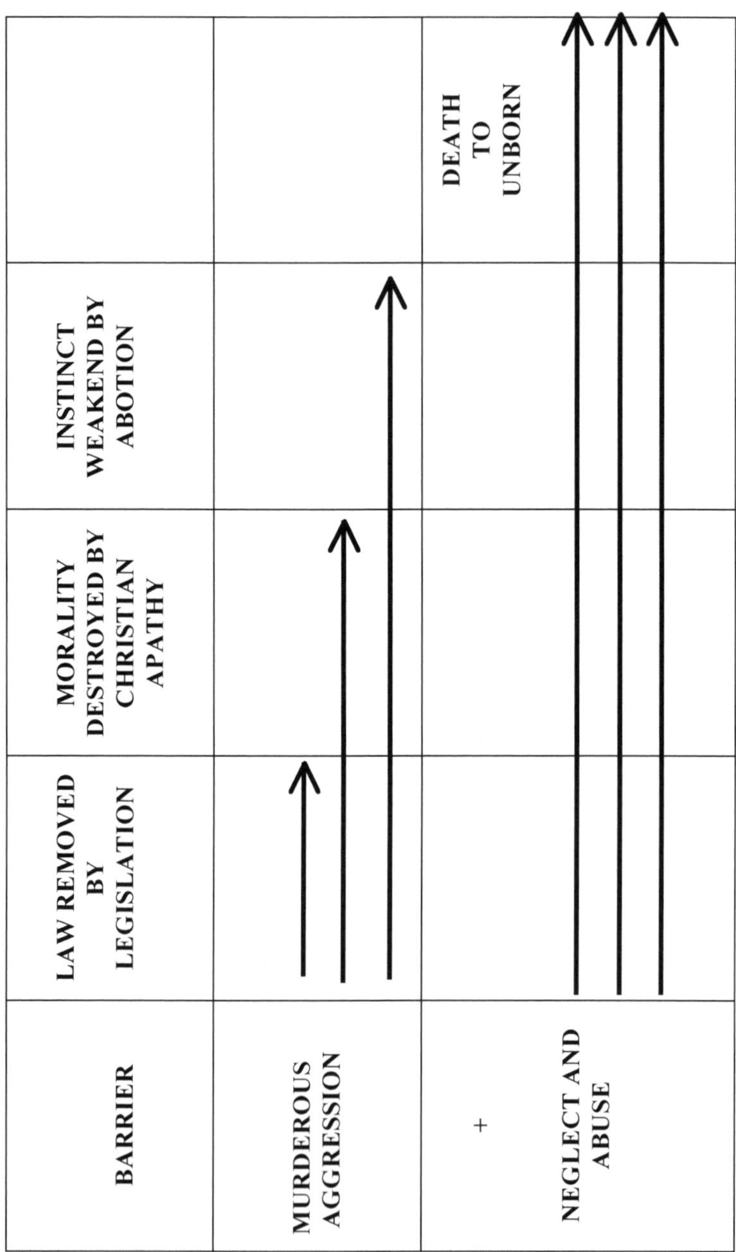

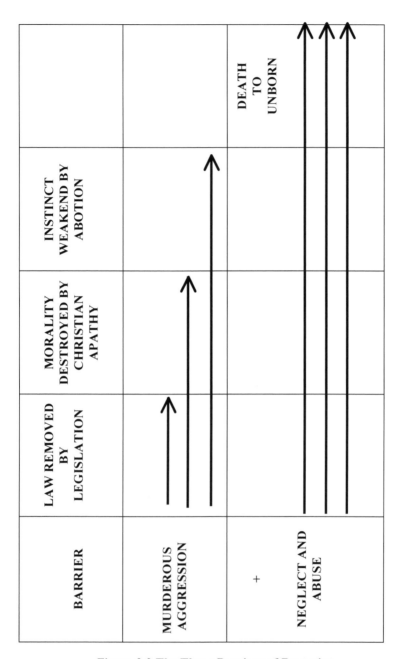

Figure 2.2 The Three Barriers of Restraint

Unhappily, in almost every country, laws no longer restrain, but encourage the killing of unborn young. Established morality is so confused and is so confusing that it no longer keeps many people from their aggression toward helpless babies. Instinct is badly weakened by these seven vicious cycles that are set in motion by abortion. Thus, abortion is cause and effect in a series of events that are increasingly uncontrolled.

The eight interlocking tragic cycles transact with each other, each tending to perpetuate and extend the destructive influence of the other (Figure 2.3). They are all triggered by the "helpless cry" of an unborn child. They all contribute to death by abortion. The whole group of them rotate with time and circumstances. For example, a child who experiences mistreatment during childhood may later become a mother who arranges to have her baby aborted, or a father who does not support his wife, thus making it more likely that she has an abortion. Abortion interferes with bonding to a subsequent child and increases the probability of the child being abused or neglected.[6]

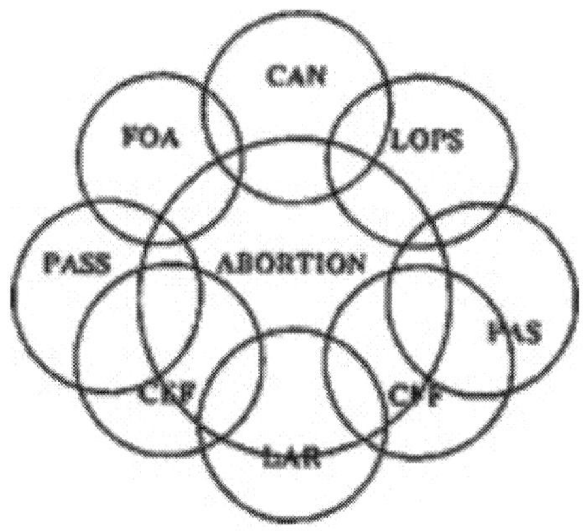

Figure 2.3 The Eight Interlocking Vicious Cycles of Abortion

Cycle 1. Child abuse & neglect (CAN)

Our studies[6] show that women who have an abortion are more likely to abuse and neglect their children. We also found that people who were mistreated as children are more likely to have or contribute to an abortion. The woman who has an abortion is more likely to be anxious during a subsequent pregnancy[7] and depressed and anxious when the child is born.[8] Because of the anxiety regarding her baby (she may be convinced that the baby has some abnormality and/or will die), she is less likely to interact with him *in utero* and is less likely to prepare for his arrival.[9] Because she is depressed, she does not bond as well to her baby. Children who are not as well bonded are more likely to be abused and neglected.[6] Bonding would normally have protected the child from the occasional rage and neglect that can occur in almost every parent. Our evidence also shows that women who have had an abortion react to their infant's helpless cry more often with anxiety, helplessness and/or rage.[6] The normal tension that results in a parent on hearing her/his baby cry in the middle of the night, more frequently results in the parent neglecting or hurting the child rather than picking it up and nurturing him.

The trauma of abuse and neglect creates conflicts that people must resolve.[10] As children, they try to understand what and why during the trauma by helping to re-enact it" (often by subconsciously irritating or provoking their parents). This makes it more likely they will be traumatized again. Parents who find raising children difficult and unrewarding are more inclined to abort the next pregnancy. The surviving child is inundated with the conflicts of abortion survivors. Adults who have been mistreated as children are less inclined to consciously welcome children, and more often abort those whose arrival is considered inconvenient or expensive.

Cycle 2. Post-abortion syndrome (PAS)

Women who have an abortion, and men who contribute to the termination of one of their children, are greatly conflicted by guilt and unresolved grief, fears and anger. These men and women have difficulty resolving the conflicts. Unresolved conflicts result in a constellation of pathological signs and symptoms known as the Post-Abortion Syndrome (PAS). The existence of PAS has been denied by not only the mother but also health care professionals. Our evidence shows abortion results in deeper and more damaging conflicts than almost any other trauma because it cuts at the roots of humanity. It appears there are few people who are not touched. At any time, 35% of aborted women indicate they need professional help.

An abortion is difficult to grieve for many reasons:

- it is not supposed to occur and few feel it must be dealt with.
- the mother does not have the opportunity to hold the infant.
- she has contributed to the loss she must now mourn.
- there are very few professionals who are inclined to listen to the
- affected parents' distress or treat their disorder.

PAS people are more likely to have pathological, incomplete grief, and therefore become depressed and alienated. This depression 1) interferes with the bonding of parents to other children, 2) diminishes their ability to respond to their infant's cry, 3) disrupts their parenting ability and 4) interferes with immune function and thus adversely affects general health.

Women who have been abused or neglected as children have great anxiety about having children for many reasons. One of these anxieties is that they fear they will mistreat their children as they had themselves been mistreated. Left untreated, PAS further undermines self-confidence and confidence in the ability to parent. Thus, abused and neglected people are more likely to abort their infants when they become pregnant. This explains, in part, the high rates of repeat abortions.

Abortion creates deep conflicts that many people attempt to understand by re-enacting the conflict-inducing trauma. Thus abortion leads to repeat abortions.

Cycle 3. **Lack Of Partner Support** (LOPS)

In most countries there are few legal restraints for a woman to have an abortion. Because fathers have no legal right to restrain a partner from killing their child, they are afraid that their partner might have the child killed without their awareness or consent. Fearing that the child may be killed, they do not allow themselves to recognise, love and bond to the unborn infant. Because they cannot attach to and incorporate the child, they are less likely to support their spouses. Our evidence from a large study shows that when the mother is less supported, she is more likely to abort or miscarry.[12] If her spouse leaves her before or after the abortion, she will anticipate rejection from her next partner. Anticipating rejection, she may subconsciously cause to happen the very thing she fears the most. She tends to attract and be attracted to partners who may not support her well. Part of her partner's lack of support comes from his knowledge that she has aborted an infant in the past. In this tragic cycle, fathers do not support their partners, and therefore women are more likely to abort their babies. The reenactment from one generation to the next seems to be due in part to an effort to understand the conflicts initiated by abandonment and neglect in childhood.

Under normal circumstances, males watching their mate grow bigger become very protective of their mate and their territory. This is a result of hormonal changes that take place in them. However, knowing they cannot protect their mate because they are not allowed to legally, they give up and leave or they become angry and coerce a woman to abort, or they become helpless and unsupportive.

Cycle 4. **Post abortion survivor syndrome** (PASS)
When children are raised in families where there has been (or could have been) an abortion, they are "survivors."[1114] We call their resulting conflicts and symptoms the Post-Abortion Survivor Syndrome (PASS). Abortion survivors might have died because:

- other babies in their country are frequently aborted.
- their parents deliberated on whether or not they would abort them.
- their siblings were aborted.
- they were the wrong sex.
- they had a handicap.

There are many types of abortion survivors, but they suffer from similar conflicts. These children grow up with survivor guilt, which makes them doubt the validity of their existence and their future. They do not trust their parents and have difficulty attaching to or trusting them and other authorities. Their anxious attachment to parents tends to make them clinging, demanding, hard-to-raise children who are less likely to explore their environment and develop their own intelligence. Because PASS children are insecure and demanding, their parents find little fulfilment in parenting. They tend to reject their role as a parent, and will then abort a subsequent child.

A child with PASS, when he grows up, is less optimistic about the future in general, and the future his children might have in particular. For those and other reasons, he or she is less likely to welcome children into the world. If a woman does become pregnant, she is more likely to abort the infant. Because PASS people are more likely to have been neglected as children, they will tend to re-enact that mistreatment by picking a less mature, less supportive mate, thus a connection is formed with the cycles of CAN and LOPS.

CYCLE 5. FEAR OF AGEING (FOA)
Not too infrequently, parents coerce their teenager or young adult offspring to abort an embarrassing or inconvenient pregnancy. These parents seem to believe an abortion will save money, save face, and protect their economic future. When an abortion occurs, it sets in motion a vicious cycle. The aborting parents now have PAS. The siblings of that aborted infant have PASS and ambivalent feelings about their parents and grandparents. These grandchildren know that they are alive only because they were "wanted" by their parents, if not by their grandparents. They resent existing because they were "wanted." As wanted children their self worth depends on how much and for what reason they were wanted. They resent their parents' power over life and death. Being wanted is a tenuous thread by which their existence dangles.

As the grandparents grow older they begin to suspect the children (with PAS) and the grandchildren (with PASS) whom they considered so callously may now regard them in their increasing frailty as having an insufficiently high quality of life to deserve living. As they become increasingly infirm, they become increasingly anxious about living because they, too, may become unwanted. An unborn child was killed because he or she was an inconvenience and therefore unwanted. Now, with the increasing prevalence and social acceptability of euthanasia, the sick, elderly and infirm know they may be legally eradicated for convenience. Rather than live with an uncertain future, they may want to determine their own fate and opt for physician assisted suicide or a "Living Will." (See Section 5, Euthanasia and Eugenics)

Cycle 6. **Convenient Eugenic Feticide** (CEF)

With more readily available "diagnostic tests" and technically efficient abortions, people can more easily select their babies according to time, circumstance, or the unborn infant's sex and intelligence, etc.[15] They want a perfect child at a convenient time. Parents and science create a collusion of convenience, each assuring the other that they are killing an inconvenient, handicapped child for the best of intentions, even aborting the baby "so it won't have to suffer." In fact, measures of enjoying life indicate handicapped people are more glad to be alive. Their rate of attempted suicide is lower than that of "normal" people.

With increasing sexual promiscuity and more abortions, there is also an increasing number of pelvic inflammatory diseases, often post-abortion. The consequent infertility results in a greater need for *in vitro* fertilization and fertility enhancement. This often results in multiple fertilization that is then seen to require "fetal reduction." Any extra embryos from *in vitro* fertilization can then be used for experiments, "spare" parts, implanted in sterile women or frozen and stored for some later use.

Amniocentesis or chorionic villa sampling is used to determine which baby should live and which should die. As eugenic abortions increase, more handicapped people know that it "could have been them." Their particular kind of PASS results in untoward behaviors that make them often less appealing, less desirable and less "wanted." "Who would want a handicapped idiot like that? We must make sure we do not have one." Thus more abortions for eugenic reasons are likely. Because women who have had abortions are more anxious during pregnancy subsequent to an abortion, there is a greater demand for amniocentesis and genetic testing to "make sure that the baby is all right." (See Section 5, Euthanasia and Eugenics) A physician can never tell a pregnant woman he is 100% sure the unborn baby is normal, partly because he could be sued for "wrongful life."

Cycle 7. Lessened aggression restraint (LAR)

Abortion can only be achieved by dehumanizing the infant and overcoming the instinctual restraint to aggression against helpless young. Anyone who has abused or neglected a child, or who has contributed to the death of the unborn infant, realizes they have weakened the mechanisms that restrain their aggression and provide an impetus to nurture and protection. Therefore, aborting parents cannot trust themselves as well ever again. They will be constantly cautious about their anger, fearful of their neglectfulness, and guarded in the expression of any strong feeling, lest they get "carried away." Because they fear their own impulses they tend to be very protective toward their children, frequently telling them to "be careful" or "tone it down."

The children who grow up in an overprotective environment learn to suspect their own impulses, partly because they have never had a natural opportunity to fully express them. Constantly guarding themselves against possible expressions of aggression leaves children with little opportunity to encounter and strengthen the normal instinctual restraint against their own aggressive impulses. Thus they are less likely to restrain themselves under circumstances that might incline them to abort their young or assist in the suicide of their aged. Parents who have selfishly neglected a child and ignored his or her cries for love, constantly criticize their children for being selfish. Expecting their children to be like them, they inadvertently make it so. Selfish, unloved children, as adults, have lessened tolerance for an inconvenient or handicapped child.

Cycle 8. Contraception's False Freedom (Cff)

There is a vicious cycle between contraception and abortion. People who use contraception are more likely to seek an abortion because they are angry about "failed contraception." Those who have had an abortion are more likely to seek contraception because they do not want to have to go through that pain again. The mass promotion and hype of contraception, and its gradual acceptance, soon convinced everyone that any kind of sex was fine as long as it did not result in conception.

Summary

These eight tragic cycles usually lie dormant until, in some manner, an individual participates in an abortion. All the tragic cycles initiated by abortion too easily become operative and those caught up in them will find them difficult to retard or stop the cycling. When many people are affected by less-restrained aggression or by neglecting impulses, it is not difficult to predict that the net outcome will be a serious threat to our species.

Abortion not only destroys children but it lessens the desire to have children. Having children requires that people conserve their resources and plan for the future, thereby creating a hopeful expectancy. With fewer children there is less hope. When there is less hope, people are not inclined to have children (Figure 2.4).

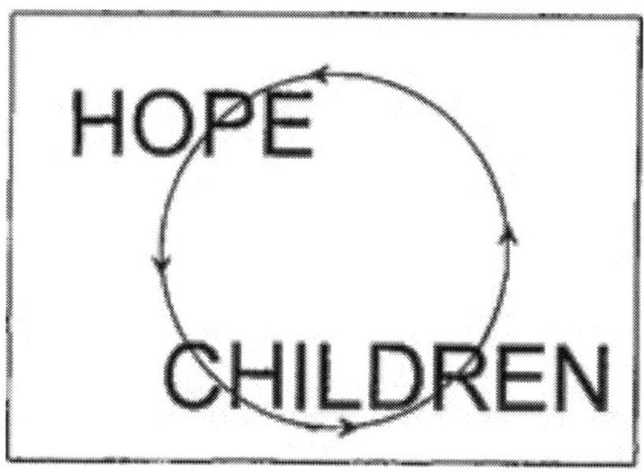

Figure 2.4 The Cycle of Hope and Children

The only way to restrain or reverse these tragic cycles is to allow the Creator of all life to infuse the world with His Hope. People should welcome in the name of Christ all the children He creates, regardless of size, shape, sex, race, intelligence, etc.

3. **The Tragic Triangles** of **Child Abuse & Neglect**

Anyone who cares to look will admit that an infant is the most wonderful creature in all of creation. He or she is the apex of God's mighty creative endeavours. He or she is the closest reflection of God's nature and form that we have on earth. Each baby is an absolutely unique individual, growing into a woman or man who could become God's close friend. To destroy a single infant by abuse or abortion is a terrible insult to God's love and an assault on His person. We believe it is the largest and deepest tragedy there could be, or has been - since that terrible day when angry and ignorant people killed God's Son. It is precisely what His enemy has wanted to achieve.

Infants are destroyed *in utero* by abortion, and after they are born by infanticide. Child abuse and neglect cruelly handicap a child so that he is but a caricature of what he should be. The neglect does not provide a child with what he needs, and therefore he cannot develop into what he was designed to become. The aggression of physical, verbal or sexual abuse aims to destroy the developing child so that he becomes scarred and bitter. A combination of abuse and neglect, especially when the neglect occurs first,[16] so damages children that many would prefer to kill themselves than live so damaged and dehumanized.

Child abuse and neglect are almost always done in ignorance or because of selfishness. Many people might rationalize "I couldn't help myself" or "the child deserved it," or "they got in the way." Whatever the rationalization, everyone knows to neglect or abuse a child is a heinous crime - not only against a child, but against themselves and against all humanity. Yet, children have always been scapegoated for problems adults refuse to tackle.

Parents have the greater contribution for their child's mistreatment, and therefore the greater responsibility for their child's abuse or neglect. However, parents are not the only ones that contribute to harming or ignoring an infant. Sometimes the greatest harm is done by trusted professionals in society who use, or abuse children - physically, verbally or sexually, or misdiagnose their hurts and injuries.

Our data shows that 95% of all children experience a combination of abuses or neglects.[17] We found that verbal abuse has the deepest and longest effect on a child's self esteem and hope for the future.[16] This is partly because it is so subtle and partly because it never stops. The words that are said to and about a child are the words that he/she will use against him/herself, whenever he/she is angry with him/herself, for the rest of his/her life. Sexual abuse creates deep scars by confusing children about who is "adult" and who is "child" and titillating desires that they cannot manage. Physical abuse creates deep conflicts in the child, particularly about aggression and self-worth.

Though abuse is damaging, physical and/or emotional neglects are far more damaging. Our data clearly shows that children who are neglected are both more susceptible and more vulnerable to all kinds of mistreatment.[5] You cannot stop a starving child from eating garbage off the street, literally or figuratively. No matter how you might instruct neglected children or restrain the people who leave garbage, the neglected child will always go for garbage. Why do starving children go to garbage dumps for food rather than to the homes of rich people? It is because they feel that they only deserve garbage. After all, they have always been treated like garbage. In their desperate search for any kind of understanding, nurture and guidance, neglected children expose themselves to all kinds of abuse and misuse. They allow themselves to be repeatedly hurt, almost as if pain was better than the absence of any kind of stimulation. At least it keeps the child in contact with reality.

There is convincing evidence that victims may contribute to their own victimisation in many subtle ways.[5] Even some children may contribute to their own victimisation for the following reasons:

- They are neglected and desperately seek any kind of attention. Even when it hurts, adverse attention is preferable to alienation with its consequent threat of losing contact with reality.
- They are curious and want to see what will happen next, even when intuition warns them of danger.
- They are afraid something worse might befall them. They are easily threatened into not protesting, not running away or not reporting what happened.
- They are protecting the perpetrator from shame and humiliation, partly because they feel sorry for him or her, partly because they know how awful it feels.
- They are trying to maintain stability in their own family. They realize that by their acquiescence they prevent a blow-out that may destroy the structure of the family upon which their survival appears to depend. They feel a bad parent is better than no parent.
- They enjoy a "special" relationship with the perpetrator or get "treats" that their siblings do not receive.
- Their body enjoys the sexual titillation or cuddling, even while their mind is saying it is wrong.
- Like everyone else, they have a tendency to make their worst expectations come true. Being able to anticipate and ready oneself for the future, even if it is bad, is better than a very uncertain future.
- They have a poor self image, and believe that the neglect and abuse are what they deserve, so why should they complain.
- They try to overcome feelings of guilt (by repeatedly doing bad things) or anxiety (by repeatedly re-exposing themselves to their source of fear).
- They hate the anxiety of suspense, and want to get it over with. It is better than waiting to see what happens.
- They enjoy the power they have over the perpetrator and the revenge they will have when he or she is exposed and punished.
- They find unhappy but familiar home life is less frightening than the possibility of a foster home.

- They have a need to understand how and why they are neglected or hurt. They attempt to know the how and why of the original trauma by participating in its repeated re-enactment.

The greatest portion of the contribution for every tragedy is held by those who are supposedly innocent bystanders. Those who observe are better able to react reasonably than the Perpetrator and Victim who are often reacting to each other from deeply buried conflicts. A close examination of every tragic event shows that the key players are those who "could have known" and "should have done something." Unhappily, when bystanders or observers are questioned about a tragedy, they invariably say, "I didn't know what was happening, and besides, I couldn't have done anything about it anyhow." This is why the UN Observers in Bosnia are hated more than the Serbians, Croatians and Moslems hate each other.

History will not judge us by how much we knew but by what we did with what we did know. Did we follow up on our suspicions? Did we try to stop harm and neglect from happening to someone we suspected was suffering? Did we enquire and offer to help both mother and child when we heard screaming from another aisle in the supermarket? Often people are too afraid to intervene, feeling that they would have to become too involved and lose the comfort of their apparent ignorance. More often they would have to admit their complicity and thereby lose their apparent innocence.

When people will not see how they contribute to tragedy they tend to scapegoat the most available vulnerable person. Someone has to be blamed, and it is better to be someone else. The most vulnerable and almost innocent scapegoat is the unborn child.

To protect their sense of social innocence, people will insist that the most obvious perpetrator is imprisoned, hung or exiled. People who are trying to protest their innocence will not acknowledge that victims and observers contribute to the tragedy. To do so would destroy their belief that they were uninvolved or innocent.

The tragic triangle of the Perpetrator, Victim & Observers (PVO) rotates with time and circumstance.[5] The child who was a victim has a high probability of becoming a perpetrator when he or she becomes a parent. Even children who were just observing the fights between parents are likely to become aggressive perpetrators. The person who is a perpetrator (especially anyone who molests children) when thrown into prison becomes a victim at the hands of other prisoners. The victim becomes the perpetrator by insisting the person who harmed them has the maximum sentence or should never be forgiven.

For the purposes of this treatment program, everybody is initially considered to be a victim. Later they must acknowledge and accept their portion of the contribution and responsibility. This is not to say that there are not organisations which cynically use and abuse people for profit, especially the sex, clothing, armament, food, drug, alcohol and entertainment industries. It is to acknowledge that almost every parent at some level of thinking hates to see him/herself doing to their children what was done to him/her. He/she knows that the greatest gift he/she could give his/her children is a better childhood than he/she had. Even while harming their children they are hoping someone will show them a way out of the ever cycling tragic triangles.

The person at each point of the tragic triangle has some characteristics in common with those at the other points. The victim has also some perpetrator and some observer tendencies. If it were possible to know the extent of these characteristics in a person, it would be possible to predict what would happen in the next episode of tragedy. That people have such great difficulty keeping tragedy from repeating seems to indicate that there is evil at work that makes tragedy repetitious. Yet, like many human tendencies, re-enactments may be adaptive, arising from a built-in drive to resolve conflicts and so increase changes of survival (see Section 2.6, Repetitious Re-enactments to Learn).

4. The Damage Caused By Mistreating a Child

Mistreatment of children causes:

- self doubt. Because they could not trust their parents and their parents mistrusted them, they tend to mistrust themselves and others. They may tend to caution their children excessively just as they were cautioned by over-protective, controlling poorly bonded parents.
- a sense of worthlessness. Especially when verbally abused they feel they are not valuable and so subconsciously expose themselves to danger. They feel they do not deserve anything good, so they may spend money they should not or end up as a street kid. This is all in an attempt to validate the feeling that they are rat bags, sluts, idiots, scum because this was what they were called or how they were treated.
- difficulty accepting love. They never were loved so they do not expect it, cannot find the right people to love them and do not believe they deserve it.
- a deep sense of failing even when there is success, because they were never good enough for their parents.
- fear of success and therefore never try their best for fear of outdistancing their parents.

- a tendency to behave like their parents having good and bad features firmly implanted through a process of modeling..
- the need to be people-pleasers. Because they are trying hard to get their parent's approval, they are concerned more about how other people feel they are doing than a self-evaluation of the quality of what they achieve or invent.
- a continuing sense of self-consciousness, wondering what was wrong with them.
- a tendency not to trust their desires, impulses, sensations, thoughts, or emotions, since their parents distrusted their own sensations, they could not trust their children's.
- a persistent sense of guilt that is exacerbated by minor offences which they may provoke by socially offending, because they were blamed for their parent's failures.
- fear of expressing their feelings, thinking they will be scorned, ignored or attacked, because whenever they spoke honestly they were reprimanded (shut down).
- difficulty experiencing joy, there was little reason for and no modeling of joy.
- persistent or frequent sense of hopelessness, and a belief they are likely to die young and violently. They tried hoping as children but they never did get their needs met.
- a tendency to neglect themselves. They were not properly nurtured and guided so how could they know how to care for themselves.
- dissociation. The feeling they are really not in their body during times of stress, because in the past the pain, fear and confusion would have driven them insane.
- a fear of freedom because they were often abandoned.
- many strong emotional triggers and prejudices that they do not like in themselves or others, having learned derogatory discrimination from their parents.
- always trying to resolve the problems created by their mistreatment. They are obsessed with analyzing themselves and tend to become self-centered because there had to be some answers.
- the tendency to recreate in their life the unsolved problems out of their past since internal conflicts drain energy.
- a tendency to punish or flagellate themselves, because maybe if they were good enough, their needs would be met.
- the need to keep pseudo-secrets for fear of disrupting their family or their own life.

- the fear of knowing what really happened in their family and therefore a tendency to avoid investigating anything.
- difficulty adapting, negotiating and compromising.
- difficulty calculating their real advantages in an adult way.
- continually attempting to find the building blocks they missed as a child and being sold a bill of goods for things that are of very little value in their development.
- difficulty enjoying their children's joys.
- jealousy for the things they give their children but which they did not get as children, which they might even give themselves.
- a desire to be perfect and find a perfect partner.
- an overactive sense of responsibility, but will not acknowledge their strengths.
- a tendency to try to re-develop themselves.
- frequent struggles with spouses and often marital breakdown.
- a tendency to be selfish and acquisitive.
- a knowledge of their immaturity that they cannot change makes them feel fragile and/or inferior.
- persistent indecisiveness.
- frequent procrastination.
- often misinterpreting what people say or do.
- difficulty loving and receiving love.
- problem concentrating which interferes with their business and academic success.
- nightmares that diminish their sleep and their ability to learn and which may stunt their growth.
- the lack of modeling from parents on how to conduct interpersonal behavior, especially between the two sexes, with affection and respect. Therefore, it is difficult for them to be easy and spontaneous models to their children.
- developed strong ingrained Dancer and Urchin masks at the expense of their Pilgrim.
- never becoming the PISHB, that person they were designed to be because few of their needs were met.
- as they were treated they tend to treat themselves with abuse or neglect. Similarly, thus they will treat others as they were treated. If they were neglected they will tend to neglect themselves, their children and their neighbors.
- an increase in abortion and in sexual promiscuity. When there has been childhood neglect, the person becomes a nobody, when there has

been abuse, the person considers him or herself as a bad body.

Tragic Triangles of Abortion

Each episode of abortion, as in child abuse, is composed of a triangle. The victim is obviously the helpless, unborn infant. There are many who are perpetrators with a share of the contribution and responsibility, including the mother, the father, the grandparents, the abortionist and staff at the abortion center. These perpetrators can also be seen as victims, for the harm they cause rebounds on themselves. Remember, we are all bound up in the bundle of life and therefore the universal ethic of mutual benefit applies both ways. When an infant is destroyed, innocence, nobility and humanity die within the perpetrators and the observers.

Too often, the Perpetrator alone is condemned. Jesus Christ warns those who provoke or set up the Perpetrator. "How terrible it will be for anyone who causes others to sin."[18] There are no innocent bystanders. Almost everyone in large and small ways contributes to the tragic triangle. "We have all sinned and come short of the glory of God."[19]

There are many observers in the tragic triangles of abortion. These include people in society who know that millions of unborn children are being "terminated" but find it is convenient to designate abortion as a woman's right. Even many God-fearing people tacitly condone abortion because someday they might need to have their daughter's unwanted pregnancy terminated. Many others, while avowedly against abortion, contribute to abortion by not attempting to resolve the underlying problems. It appears that in all tragic situations, especially abuse and abortion, there are no innocent bystanders. If one is not doing something to stop the tragedy, one is contributing to it.

- **The Abuse - Abortion Connection**

Our research has shown that people who have had an abortion are more likely to abuse their children and people who have been abused are more likely to have an abortion.[6] Abortion and abuse and both cause and effect, not necessarily in one person, but certainly within the family. The sins of many generations of a family, selfishness, willful ignorance, pride, etc., find a scape-goat in the child, who is the smallest and the most innocent human. The scapegoating in the family is brought upon a vulnerable child for unresolved conflicts of the parents' families. They attempt to choose their convenience, education or job at the expense of another's life or health, but it is not possible. In the long term, they cannot benefit at the expense of an unborn child.

No one can truly benefit at the expense of another. Therefore, when a child
is aborted, people are abusing themselves. That self-abuse is almost always an echo of mistreatment somewhere in the family. Killing a child produces a partial murder of oneself. It is a kind of self abuse.

That abortion increases the chance of child abuse should be of no surprise. Abortion results in more post-partum depression and therefore less bonding, less touching and less breast feeding. It should be noted that one of the earliest arguments was that aborting unwanted children would diminish the instance of child abuse. Statistics show precisely the opposite, that is, with more frequent abortions all kinds of child abuse have increased.[6]

In summary, our research has shown:

- parents who have had an abortion are more likely to abuse and neglect their children.
- parents who were mistreated are more likely to have an abortion.
- parents who have been mistreated tend to mistreat their children, depending upon the extent and the nature of their mistreatment including; physical abuse, verbal abuse, sexual abuse, physical neglect, emotional neglect and intellectual neglect."
- men and women who were neglected as children tend to neglect their spouses.
- women who are not supported are more likely to have both abortions and miscarriages.
- there is a vicious interlocking cycle between abortion and abuse.

For many years, it was argued by those people who called themselves "pro- choice" that there should be freely available abortion because then there would be fewer unwanted children, and if there were few or no unwanted children there would be less child abuse. Triggered by the reports of some of my patients, I suspected this was incorrect. When I investigated the relationship between child abuse and abortion and reported a direct correlation, people were angry and astonished. It appeared that the rate of child abuse did not decrease with freely available abortions.[20] In fact, the opposite was true. In parts of Canada where there were low rates of abortion there were low rates of child abuse. As the rates of abortion increased, so did child abuse. Lenoski reported that it was not the unwanted children who were abused, it was the wanted children.[21] He used careful measures of wantedness such as when the mother picked a name, when she began to wear maternity clothes, etc. We have now more clearly established that child abuse is positively correlated with abortions. Indeed, it is a vicious cycle. That is, parents who have been involved in abortion are more likely to abuse and neglect their children. Mothers and fathers who were abused as children are more likely to abort their child.

A. Why abortion may lead to more child abuse

There is a significant statistical association between abortion and child abuse. There is also abundant clinical evidence to indicate women who have had abortions (and other pregnancy losses that result in many of the same conflicts) are more likely to abuse and neglect their children. The following conflicts and symptoms help explain why there is this connection. It must be remembered that a statistical association does not mean every woman who has had an abortion is a poor mother.

Choice not to mature

By rejecting the child, parents have rejected the maturing force of a pregnancy and they are more likely to remain less mature parents. Even children can detect immature parents. When asked what was the best explanation for their parents' emotional abuse and neglect, children most frequently chose immaturity.[22] They know that other reasons such as alcoholism, drug abuse, etc. are probably an indication of their parents' immaturity. They tend to be less mature because they:

avoided the crisis of incorporation. Every pregnancy is a crisis. During pregnancy, the body, the mind and the spirit must grow. The body's elastic tissue and pain fibres resist stretching. The mind quails at the task of growing up. The spirit would like not to acknowledge eternal verities. When a person chooses an abortion they have chosen not to face the challenge of growing larger and more flexible to accommodate and incorporate a new baby in and among them. They will persist with their self image of fragility and fun loving young people. Their fear of incorporating the child produces a resentment that too often becomes destructive.

chose to regress. Many parents regress in thought and behaviour in an effort to continue to be considered a child by their parents. They vainly hope that somehow, someday, their parents will give them the things they needed and they will become the person they were designed to be.

chose to remain selfish. Rejecting the child indicates that they have put selfish desires first. Consequently, they have a limited capacity to love and a restricted desire to learn to love a subsequent child.

stopped personal development. By choosing an abortion they have stopped the natural process of their own developing propelled by mating, propagating and nurturing a child.

damaged their self respect. By choosing an abortion they have undermined

their self respect as a human and as a parent. They believe they could not and cannot cope well. Too often their unhappy expectations are fulfilled. For men this often means wanting to stay adolescent. Believing they cannot support their wife, they want to play with their "big toys" and flit from one relationship to another.

ANXIETY DURING PREGNANCY

Women who have had an abortion are often more anxious during the pregnancy of a subsequent child.[7] These are some of the possible reasons:

Anticipate Abnormality. Post-abortion women expect their next child will be handicapped or die as a punishment of God or the natural consequence of having an abortion. Consequently there is a tendency to anxiously look for assurances from parents or friends and physicians. More medical investigations are never able to provide absolute certainty that the baby has no defect or abnormality. Even after an ultrasound or amniocentesis, physicians cannot promise that the child is perfect, increasing the patient's anxiety. The doctor's uncertainty may precipitate a decision to have an abortion. "I cannot stand the thought of having an abnormal child. If the doctor cannot be absolutely sure this infant is okay, I am going to get rid of it."

Patients who do not have good medical insurance realise that they are caught between getting reassurances, which costs money, and not knowing whether their baby may be abnormal. Thus, there is an increased anxiety and an increased ambivalence about the baby.

Women who are very anxious during the subsequent pregnancy tend not to look after their health as well. There is a certain fatalism. "This child is probably abnormal, so it does not matter whether I smoke, drink, do drugs or eat improperly." In their hearts they know they should try very hard to live a balanced life with a good diet but, because they are anxious, they resort to habits that they have used in the past to allay their anxieties. Because in their mind the baby is probably abnormal, they do not prepare for his/her arrival. They do not provide a room, pick a name, buy clothes, attend prenatal classes or develop a network of supporting family and friends.

Conditioned Avoidance. Women who have selected abortion in the past have repeatedly tried to decide whether they would or would not keep the next pregnancy. Their anxieties grew every time they considered the demands of pregnancy and child-rearing. They became relaxed and thus rewarded themselves when they decided not to have a baby. To overcome this conditioned avoidance, they will have had to face a high level of anxiety.

Stress. Because of a previous abortion, women are more anxious and easily stressed during the next pregnancy. Because many have broken relationships, they have to work and look after themselves rather than being looked after by a supportive partner. Animal studies have shown that females stressed during their pregnancy secrete high levels of estrogen. This tends to feminize the offspring. Under extreme conditions the offspring are hermaphrodites. Under less extreme conditions the male offspring are effeminate. More evidence indicates stress during pregnancy results in a lowering of sperm counts and maybe less male libido. We have yet to do the research to determine whether effeminate men are more likely to occur in families where their mothers have had an abortion previously, but there is some supporting clinical evidence. If this is true, it is a vicious cycle. Effeminate men are less likely to commit themselves to a relationship and support their pregnant partners. Because their partners are unsupportive, women have to work and experience an increased level of stress, which increases estrogen during pregnancy, etc.

Parents who anticipate that their child will be abnormal, in spite of knowing all medical evidence indicates everything is fine, have a terror that the baby will not be able to survive or, if he does survive, will be abnormal and ugly to look at. Dr. Agnes Gereb in Budapest runs a beautiful birthing center. She finds that women who have had abortions have great difficulty going through the third stage of labor until she gets them into a hospital environment.[23] There, where they feel more secure and where there are better facilities to deal with a baby who is having difficulty, they are able to accomplish the third stage of labor.

ALIENATED SUPPORT

In most western countries, men have no legal right to protect their unborn babies. They know that their partner, without their awareness or consent, can abort their baby. Not knowing when their baby might die by abortion, they avoid attaching to the baby. Because they are not attached to the baby, they do not support their partner. Our study shows that lack of partner support is the most important factor that determines the number of abortions.[12] Thus, a vicious cycle ensues whereby men, unattached to their babies, do not support their partners who are more likely to have an abortion and, because of that, men are less likely to attach to their babies.

The lack of support by the partner is particularly poignant in situations where an adult, neglected as a child, is terrified about maturing. Thus, the best way to prevent abortion would be to ensure that men are supported so they can mature, support, encourage and love their pregnant wives. Men need to be taught by parents and wise elders. They need a legal right to protect their unborn infants.

The unborn baby should be supported by a series of concentric circles. The baby is supported by the mother, who is supported by the father, who is supported by the grandparents, who are supported by the church and government. It is not possible to short-circuit these supporting circles. A church or agency, attempting to support a single mother, may alienate away the father. This undermines the very thing they are trying to accomplish. Parents and grandparents should be cautious they do not alienate the father in their support of a pregnant mother.

Couples need to be encouraged and challenged to mature before they parent. They should be able to encounter and benefit from other crises in their lives before they encounter the Crisis of Incorporation. The Crisis of Incorporation for the baby involves the body, mind and spirit. If Mary had come from a rigid, religious home, she might have rejected God's surprise loan, i.e. "No way am I am going to have a baby. I am sure God would never make a young, unmarried girl pregnant. Go away, angel - or whoever you are."

Broken Relationships. We found, in a study of those seeking help for an abortion, that 80% of the relationships broke up following an abortion. After an abortion, women are angry for not being supported and not making the right choice. This anger at the departed partner is often displaced, so the infant becomes the target. Men leave women out of feelings of disgust, fear and anger. Women leave men because they can no longer trust and because they are not interested in sex. Women who have been abandoned by their parents or boyfriends are likely to anticipate their present spouse will desert them during their pregnancy. Suspecting he will do it all again, the mother, by her suspicions, can fulfill her own worst expectations. She may suspect that he:

- might have another woman.
- is not really interested in her now that she is out of shape following the baby's birth.
- cannot handle the stress of being a father.
- is drinking when claiming he is putting in extra time at work.

Suspecting that her partner is about to abandon her, she accuses him, which precipitates a vicious cycle in which he eventually leaves.

Lack Of Partner Support. The father, having wondered whether he would lose his baby to abortion at any time during his partner's pregnancy, is not as well bonded to the baby. Fathers who joyfully anticipate the baby's arrival and are confident nothing will happen, often talk to their unborn baby. After birth, the baby often recognizes his or her father's voice. That encourages the father's bonding to the child. Being well bonded, the father is more likely to care for the infant and protect him or her from all kinds of intra-family or extra-family stress or assault. If he is not well bonded to the baby, he is more likely to abandon his family or fight with his wife.

contempt of family or peers. Even though having an abortion appears to be accepted by society, individuals who have an abortion are still looked on with some contempt by family and peers. Having had an abortion, they are more likely to lose the support of their family and peers during the pregnancy, birth and postnatal development of a subsequent child. Being PAS, women may be obnoxious and/or demanding.

POORLY BONDED

It is well recorded in scientific literature that babies who are not well bonded are more likely to be abused and neglected.[10 24] It appears that children born subsequent to an abortion are not as well bonded for the following reasons:

depression. The mother, not having gone through the grief following an abortion, is more likely to have post-partum depression.[8] Women who were depressed post-natally bond less well. Babies that are not well bonded are not protected as a parent would protect a part of themselves, nor looked after as well as a parent would look after themselves. Bonding is not an absolute protection. If the parent disregards him or herself and abuses him or herself, he or she will abuse the child. However, a well-bonded baby is cared for as well as a mother or father would look after their right arm. Well-bonded babies are intuitively understood and nurtured as part of the parent's self.

inability to attach. People, having not detached, i.e. having not grieved a previous loss or person, have a lessened capacity to attach to the next person.[25] If the mother is not detached from the aborted baby, she is less likely to attach to her next baby. She may be afraid to grieve because of the pain involved or because it means acknowledging the death of a precious baby. Often grief is precipitated by the birth of a baby because the mother now realizes what she has done in agreeing to the abortion of a pre-born child. Having her own baby, she realizes the aborted baby was also a child with soft skin, penetrating eyes and a firm grasp.

disappointment. Often the aborted baby is idealized. The subsequent baby may be viewed as comparatively less lovely or intelligent. The mother's disappointment makes it harder for her to see all the lovely characteristics of the baby in her arms. There is less interaction, there is less joyful experience and less of an ability to see the nuances of a growing infant that create pride in the parents. The next child is often seen as a replacement for an intentional or unintentional pregnancy loss, but he/she can never live up to the parents' expectations.

anxious attachment. Without good bonding, babies are anxiously attached. Anxiously attached babies cling and cry more. They do not explore. Babies who do not explore do not develop their intelligence as well. Clinging and crying babies can be very irritating. This may provoke physical or verbal violence or neglect.

DISTORTED RESPONSE TO THE INFANT'S HELPLESS CRY

We found a correlation between how parents respond to the baby's helpless cry and how they abuse or neglect their children. Parents who are irritated or annoyed by a baby's cry are more likely to physically or verbally abuse their child. Parents who feel anxious or helpless in response to a baby's cry are more likely to neglect their baby.

There is also clinical evidence that mothers who have had previous abortions are less likely to respond with nurture to the infant's cry. If parents respond with anger or ignoring more readily than with nurture, the human infant is in danger of abuse, neglect and possibly infanticide. There are increasing rates of "fatal child abuse" and infanticide. It is reported that the most common cause of death to children six years of age and younger in the United States is not infections, cancers or accidents, but being killed by their own parents. The rate of infanticide in Canada is also escalating.[26]

If people do not respond well with care and nurture to the helpless cry of infants, they are less likely to respond with nurture and care to the helpless cry of handicapped, old or infirm people. Since, at some point in their lives, the majority of humans will be helpless and cry out to have their needs met, this means that almost every human is endangered. A sensitive ecological balance has been upset. A distortion in the human response to the helpless cry is a major threat to the survival of the species.

Parents may respond to a child's helpless cry with:

anger. The baby's cry is designed to alert a parent; if necessary, to bring them out of a sound sleep. If the irritation is not controlled and used to drive a nurturing response, it becomes anger. The cry triggers irritation. "Shut up. I need my sleep." This anger arises and is fuelled by unresolved conflicts. There is no question an infant's cry is irritating. It is designed to alert and alarm people, to bring them out of their lethargy or television programs and make them respond as quickly as possible. But if not immediately dampened by an instinctual restraint, the response easily becomes destructive.

helplessness. "Now what am I supposed to do? Why won't someone help me?" A child's piercing cry, indicating distress or needs, may evoke feelings of helplessness similar to those during childhood. If the adult is unable to respond confidently with nurture, they are more likely to call for professional help or leave the child in the care of some other person, usually day care. There is evidence that day-care increases the amount of competitiveness among children, the amount of anxious attachment and the number of intercurrent infections.[27 28]

sorrow. The child's crying may evoke sorrow in the adult. A child's tears may make post-pregnancy loss parents want to shed tears they have held back ever since their unborn baby was killed. They may refuse to grieve, but they cannot control their unhappiness. To grieve would be to acknowledge the unborn was a child, not a piece of tissue. So they desperately try to stop the child's crying, forcibly if necessary. "That kid's whining is driving me to desperation. Dammit, if you can't stop him, I will."

fear. A child's helpless cry evokes the fear of the adult's own aggression. The fear in the child's cry makes them realise they have broken through the instinctual barrier to their own aggression. They will try anything to prevent his/her irritating upset - bribes, threats, force, ignoring for long periods. Post-abortion parents tend to be very cautious with their own anger. They often caution the child not to be angry.

pain from un-expressed hurts and unmet needs. The child's helpless cry can trigger a desire in parents to express their own child-like hurts, confusion, fears and unmet needs. Since it is unlikely these will be met, post-pregnancy loss parents have to suppress their own feelings and consequently need to forcefully suppress the child's cry. As a result of the distorted response to the helpless cry, the parent is likely to:

avoid. They become absorbed in their own disturbing preoccupations and close the door on the baby crying in the crib. They are likely to leave the child to the care of someone else while they go out to have fun and distract themselves from grief and guilt.

attack. The parent may attack the child, slapping it, shaking it or harming it in other ways. Shaking damages the child's brain by resulting in petechia (small bleeds) that later interfere with the child's mental function and contribute to learning disabilities.

control. In an effort to control the child's cry, the parent may be over controlling, constantly telling the child to be quiet, to stop crying, don't get excited, don't be a sissy, etc. Thus they verbally abuse the child if he expresses any feelings that trigger a strong reaction in them.

overprotect. A post-pregnancy loss child may be overprotected, not so much from the environmental threats, but from his parents' own aggression in response to his helpless cry. A post-abortion child is often constantly cautioned to be careful and, consequently, becomes overcautious with his or herself and may be obsessive in his or her thinking.

UNABLE TO TOUCH

There is clinical evidence that babies born after mothers have an unmourned pregnancy loss are not as frequently picked up, cuddled, touched, or caressed. Consequently, they are not as frequently breast-fed. It appears that the flesh of the infant awakens visions of the aborted baby's broken body. Touching the baby somehow taps into painful memories of how the baby's body was tom apart during the abortion. For women who have had RU-486 and prostaglandin abortions on their own and have seen the dead baby, the child in their arms reminds them of the tiny child that died during the abortion.

Because the mother is unable to touch the baby, she is less likely to breast feed the baby. If the baby is not breast fed, he/she does not obtain many vital ingredients, including essential fatty acids. Essential fatty acids are necessary for the formation of the white substance of the brain and the myelin sheath of the peripheral nerves. Thus babies that are not breast-fed are not as smart or as quick as they were genetically designed to be.[29] because the baby also obtains antibodies through breast milk, babies who are not breast-fed are more likely to have infections. Babies who are not breast-fed are not getting the right mix of nutrients and therefore they are hungrier, less content and more demanding. More of the helpless cry initiates more neglecting and aggression by parents.

In one country we studied, the older age group of women breast fed their children at the rate of 87%. Since the introduction of a one-child policy, requiring millions of abortions, the women now breast feed their baby at the rate of 18%.

Babies that are not breast fed are not as well tactually and psychologically stimulated. There is a great deal more eye contact, skin contact and playing with the babies during breast-feeding. Because their bodies are not as well caressed, the babies do not like their bodies as well. People who like their bodies have greater psycho-physiological integration. Babies that are not breast-fed are not held as securely and therefore they are more insecure and cry more often, precipitating more parental feelings of irritation or helplessness.

UNMET NEEDS

Children born to mothers who have unresolved pregnancy losses may not have their needs as well met for the following reasons:

do not know the child. Many post-pregnancy loss parents were abused and neglected as children. They had to dull their sensitivities, or else the pain and grief would be too much to bear. Most post-abortion mothers have blocked out the subtle communication of the baby within them, a still, small voice. They are now less able to detect the subtle needs of the child they have in their arms. They have not listened to their own urges to welcome their previous child and are now less capable of reading their own and the child's blueprints. They do not know precisely what is the difference in their blueprints, between what they need and what the child needs. Thus they tend to deface the child's blueprint and impose their own, feeling that the child needs what they needed as children rather than what the child's own blueprint indicates.

self over-control. Parents who have had abortions realize that they have broken through instinctual barriers to their aggression and try to replace these with rigid self-control and self-criticism. This results in their being more strict and demanding of others. When they are more rigid they are less able to change with the baby's unpredictable schedules and resent demands placed on them by the baby's needs. They are irritated by the child's lack of regular rhythm. They are angry when their own selfish pursuits are interrupted.

dehumanized child. To have an abortion, the parents had to dehumanize the infant. When they did that, they dehumanized themselves. Having dehumanized one child and having dehumanized themselves, it is difficult to see the full humanity of the next baby. This often means they cannot perceive subtle requirements and quiet joys of a fully human infant.

replacement child. Often the baby born after an abortion is a replacement child. The parents tend to confuse the live baby with what they believe the dead baby was like. Then it is hard to understand his needs. They tend to see in the replacement child more demands and less enjoyment than the idealized aborted child would have given them. Because parents cannot read their child's blueprint as well, and because the child's needs are not as well met, the child is more demanding. He may cry excessively, even all night. The parents become more irritable, and the baby more anxious, in a vicious spiral that too often ends in violence. Their inability to satisfy their baby contributes to the parents' perception of themselves as poor parents. This increases the likelihood of them giving up and having somebody else do the parenting for them. With low self esteem as parents, they cannot persist through difficult times, e.g. the child's infections, sleeplessness, bumps and bruises. They are constantly rushing off to find some professional that will resolve their problems.

NOT AS HEALTHY

We have found that all women who have unresolved pregnancy losses are not as healthy as women with full term pregnancies.[12] Many readily acknowledge they need help with their grieving. At any point in time, 30 % or more indicate that they need professional help to deal with their loss. If they had been asked "Have you at any time needed professional help to deal with your loss?" a much higher percentage would indicate so, possibly 100%. Thus the 30% point estimate is a conservative indication of how many want professional help.

There is evidence to show that unresolved grief leads to depression. Although this may be a sub-clinical depression expressed more as backaches, headaches, etc. than as persistent sadness, the depression interferes with the function of the immune system. When the immune system is not working as well, people are more likely to have infections and cancers.

When the mother is not as healthy, she is not as vigorous and responsive to her baby's needs. She is less likely to spend time with the infant. She is more likely to spend time dealing with her own illnesses and conflicts.

In summary, a post-abortion mother may:

have unresolved grief, producing depression or sub-clinical depression with more psychosomatic complaints, resulting in poor immune response and increased infections and cancers.

be more prone to infections, e.g. colds, thus spending less time with her child and more in bed or at doctors' offices.[30] Berkeley, Humphreys and Davidson (1984) found that, following an abortion, women attended a general practice 80% more for physical complaints and 180% more for psychological problems than they did before their abortion.

be less energetic and less responsive to the baby's smiles and needs.

have less sleep, partly because she may be dealing with the nightmares following the abortion. Without sleep she is more irritable and does not respond calmly to the infant's helpless cry.

have breast cancer. Although still debated, there is good evidence post abortion women are more likely to have breast cancer.[31] Having cancer, she is more fearful, more often away having treatments and less likely to be available for the child through his or her full range of development.

PESSIMISTIC EXPECTATIONS

As a result of unresolved guilt and an inability to forgive herself, a post abortion mother is likely to feel God will punish her with a handicapped or unwell child. If she does not believe in God, she may feel a disaster to the child is the natural consequence to having an abortion. Feeling that she is not going to have as happy, healthy, contented, intelligent child, she is more likely to get into drugs and delinquent behavior. She is more doubtful, suspicious and pessimistic. Unfortunately, humans tend to fulfill their own worst expectations. Having had an abortion herself, she may expect her child to get into sex early in life and to have an abortion like herself. This may contribute to the fact that abortions tend to repeat from one generation to the next.[32]

RE-ENACT TRAGEDY

There is considerable evidence to show that when humans are unable to resolve conflicts they recreate them.[1133] They do this in an attempt to understand the salient features of the initial conflict. Because conflict consumes energy without benefit to the organism, humans are programmed to persistently work at conflict resolution. They set up conflict re-enactments by the type of mates they pick, how they interact with their children, places they work and places they live. In an effort to understand why they had an abortion, they may:

- pick the wrong type of mate who is not supportive, which increases their propensity to have an abortion or miscarriage.
- allow or initiate early sexual titillation of their child. This may be through their own provocative behavior, sexual abuse or having freely available pornography.
- push the child to have an abortion. This may be subtle through innuendoes or very overt pressures such as threats that their daughter will have to leave home unless she has an abortion.

Too often, a post-abortion child is involved in early sexual behavior, becomes pregnant and is subtly coerced into having an abortion with threats of abuse or abandonment, thus re-creating for the parent the unresolved problem of their own abortion.

B. A COMBINATION OF POST-PREGNANCY LOSS & POST-PREGNANCY LOSS SURVIVORS

Not infrequently, women who have had abortions are also abortion survivors. The combinations of the effects of the abortion and being an abortion survivor are not merely additive, they are exponential. That is, the conflicts are intensified, one part building on the other. It is our experience that women who have both had an abortion and are abortion survivors are more deeply conflicted and their conflicts are much more difficult to resolve. Although we do not have sufficient data to state it as a significant scientific correlation, there is clinical evidence to show that women who are both post-abortion and post-abortion survivors are more likely not only to hurt their children but hurt their children more intensely for the following reasons:

GUILT ABOUT EXISTING

If a parent feels that because her siblings were arbitrarily killed by her parents because they were inconvenient or unwanted, she feels guilty about her existence. Parents with survivor guilt cannot fully live their lives. If they have difficulty living it is very hard to let their child live fully, joyfully and hopefully.

Although many PAS or PLS or PASS or PLSS women may not want children, their biological drives often override their rational desires and they find themselves inadvertently pregnant. They are then in a deep dilemma, not wanting to kill the child because they know how it would be for the experience of any sibling. At the same time, they cannot welcome their unborn child. Therefore, the child is often allowed to live, but not allowed to fully develop. The child's birth often not only precipitates guilt about having had a previous abortion, but also intensifies their survivor guilt.

HARD TO WELCOME

Because their siblings were not welcomed and because they did not welcome one of their own children, it is very difficult for PAS and PASS parents to truly welcome the next baby as a unique individual. They are more likely to have the child because he/she is "wanted." A wanted child often has often too high expectations placed upon him/her. Compared to what parents' expect, this child is disappointing. The parents react to their disappointment with over control, excessive correction, or frequent verbal expressions of their displeasure. Because this child is not as good as the child they aborted, it is hard for them to enjoy the child's joy. Though there is a wonderful way created human babies might provide much of the encouragement for parenting with their smiling, cooing and penetrating gazes, there can also be bitter disappointment when it feels this never happens.

Re-enact their unresolved PASS conflicts.

Not having been able to resolve their own conflicts about being an abortion survivor (being alive when their siblings died, trusting their parents, etc.), they have a tendency to re-enact these psychological conflicts with the child that was born after an abortion. That child not only has his own PASS conflicts, but now has conflict imposed on him by his PASS parents. These include a tendency to feel guilty about existing, distrusting parents, cynical about love, difficulty making commitments, problems attaching and anger that parents aborted a sibling. They also struggle with narcissism, hedonism and pessimism. In an attempt to resolve their own problems, the parents subtly encourage the child to re-enact their difficulties by having another abortion. Consequently, there are more children whose siblings would be aborted. Thus the cycle of abortion and abuse cycles from one generation to the next.

Distrust

As PASS parents, they have difficulty trusting their own aborting parents. Therefore it is harder for them to turn to their parents to ask for help. Trying to deal with all the problems themselves, they may exceed their ability to withstand the demands of the child, child-rearing difficulties and insecurities of job, housing, etc. In their frustration, they attack and possibly kill the child. All these factors contribute to the increasing rates of infanticide (now often known as "fatal child abuse").

Guilt

Because of their guilt about existing, PASS parents may expect an early death. They may also expect their children to be injured or die. They may engage in risk taking for themselves and their child, e.g. smoking, driving too fast, taking drugs. If they become suicidal, they tend to want to kill their child with them. Whole families have been killed by PASS mothers and fathers who later kill themselves.

Difficulty mourning the person I should have become

PASS parents have difficulty accepting life. It is much more difficult to relinquish and mourn the person they were designed to become. This makes it more difficult to accept the person they are and any child as he or she really is.

C. HOW CHILD MISTREATMENT CAN INCREASE THE PROPENSITY TOWARDS ABORTION

The connection between child abuse and infant abortion is reciprocal. One leads to the other in a cycle that seems to spiral downward from one generation to the next. These are some of the reasons found in the conflicts of approximately 5, 500 men and women we have interviewed over the years and about 4, 800 additional subjects from whom we have collected research data. To some extent, these conflicts effect both men and women - sometimes more deeply affecting a woman and sometimes more the male partner. These twenty-one factors arising from child abuse and neglect are not the only factors, but can often be observed in women who propose to have or have had an abortion.

Increased crisis of incorporation (ICI)

Every pregnancy is a crisis. The baby demands that the parent's body, mind and spirit expand. This is always resisted, e.g. the body's collagen and elastic fibers work to retain the body's pre-pregnant shape. If the ICI is accepted, the person incorporates the child and consequently grows in all three dimensions.

People who have been abused have a greater crisis during pregnancy for the following reasons:

fragile body. Those whose body has been securely held, warmly washed, soothingly dried and gently brushed as children like their bodies. They live comfortably in their bodies. There is greater physiological harmony. They trust their body to deal with stress. If, as a child, her body has not been gently caressed, a mother feels her body is less elastic. She fears her belly might burst during pregnancy or her vagina tear during labor. This may be expressed with "I cannot take the pain. I cannot go through with this."

Immaturity of mind. When emotions are heard and intelligences guided and challenged, the personality matures. Children who have been abused or neglected do not have as mature and as flexible thinking. The demands of the pregnancy and child are considered too great. "I'll go crazy." Therefore they abort the child.

Undeveloped spirit. Those who have a personal relationship to God through Christ at an early age can trust Him in crises. People who have been abused or neglected as children have a misperception of the nature of God. They tend to see God as over-controlling, angry, authoritative, punitive or neglecting and abandoning, much as their parents were. Because they avoid dealing with God and cannot comprehend Him as He is, their spirits do not develop. They think that God "will disown me because I am pregnant out of wedlock." Therefore they abort the baby.

Pregnancy out of wedlock and (in ancient times) pregnancy during a betrothal before the marriage was to be consummated, were always looked upon with great skepticism and disapproval. It is a wonder that Mary did not seek to have her baby aborted or run away and hide herself. It is of great credit to both Mary and Joseph that they saw the hand of the Lord in the whole matter and obeyed His instruction. They decided not only to keep the baby but to marry and bring up the child in a family with love and nurture.

FEAR OF ABANDONMENT

Children who have been neglected or abandoned are terrified that it will happen again. Every child knows that if they are abandoned they cannot survive. Abandonment is the worst experience of a child, much worse than any other kind of abuse or neglect. Unfortunately, too many parents use threats of abandonment as a type of punishment. Often children are abandoned by a mother pursuing a lover or a father pursuing a job or new relationship.

The parent who has experienced abandonment may react to a pregnancy with:

Suspicion. She suspects her partner is going to desert her, and therefore tends to fulfill her own worst expectation. She thinks, "You are just like my father." She can make her own worst fears come true by amplifying small neglects and suspecting other women. She may believe the time that her husband is working extra hours is time that he is spending at the pub with a girlfriend.

Amplification. A woman may acutely feel small neglects which may arise from the fact her partner feels inadequate or afraid. She amplifies these; "I knew you would. I know you were going to ignore me. I can tell you are losing interest."

Despair. Many women neglected or abandoned as children are confronted by an impossible choice posed by their partner, i.e. "You have to make up your mind and choose it or me. You can't have both. " She may react with, "1 cannot stand this. To avoid being rejected by my partner, I have to abandon my baby and arrange to have him killed by an abortionist. What a terrible choice. I guess 1 have to look after myself first. I know nobody else will."

A feeling of being threatened. Many young women are directly threatened with abandonment and some with assault if they do not have an abortion. In some circumstances, even well reared women feel coerced into aborting their baby because of difficult circumstances of poverty (hunger, lack of housing) or friendship. Too often, a young couple use threats of abandonment on each other. Yet, even the most destitute who choose to welcome their baby find a way, "God provides."

Because pregnant women so badly need a supportive partner, if a man threatens to leave or just is not definite enough in his commitment to a woman, it is unlikely she will ever trust him.

Distrust of parents

Knowing that her parents have abused and neglected her, a woman feels quite convinced that they will not help her during her pregnancy. They did not care during other periods in her life when she desperately needed help. She is sure they will not now. So without even appealing for their help, she aborts the child.

Vulnerability

Because the young father or the mother has been neglected or abandoned, they are very vulnerable to small amounts of rejection. Even suggestions of rejection during the pregnancy hurt disproportionately and evoke unresolved conflicts arising from previous neglect. "Crisis pregnancy counseling" seldom recognizes how much hurt a previously neglected young parent feels by a small amount of rejection. Literally two words can precipitate a man or woman into deciding to terminate their baby. Simply being ignored or told "Not now!" may be enough to trigger the rejection and death of the pre-born child.

ANTICIPATE ABANDONMENT BY CHILD

The mother or father who was abandoned as a child anticipates that no sooner will they attach themselves to the child, than he will abandon them by either running away as a child, or leaving home when he is older. Being so sensitive to abandonment, they would prefer to abort the child than feel abandoned later. If they have abandoned previous mates or friends, they find it easier to do the same with the baby.

ANTICIPATE HATE

They fear that their child will grow up disliking or hating them just like their parents did. Rather than re-experience the hate, they would rather abort the baby.

RETAIN CHILDHOOD

If a child was neglected or abused, he did not get many important ingredients that would make him into the person he was designed to become. To have a baby catapults young people into adulthood. They are quite sure they will lose their last chance of being nurtured by a parent. They falsely assume that if they could stay single or childless, there is still the chance a parent would provide them with the things they needed but never received as children. They not only want to retain their status as a child, they also tend to regress and hope that as a poor, sick urchin having had an abortion, their parents will take pity on them. After all, they had the abortion partly to please their parents.

During early pregnancy, a young father and mother tend to regress. They watch to see if anyone will pick up on these indications of dependency and give them the nurture and support they need. When nobody responds, some feel abandoned all over again and scramble to get rid of the unborn baby.

Young parents are very susceptible to the media that constantly tells them they can only have a good time as a single adult. To have a child means giving up smoking, cars, travelling, partying, etc.. According to the media, it is apparent you can only have fun drinking Pepsi when you are young, active, single and childless. Forgoing fun is particularly difficult for those who were not allowed to play as children or were given the responsibility of looking after younger siblings.

SCAPEGOATING

Adults who have been abused or neglected as children are often painfully aware of the fact that they were scapegoated for family problems - unresolved conflicts that may have been handed down for many generations. If they cannot deal with that scapegoating, they will hand the scapegoating down one more generation. Since they were selected as scapegoat, it is easy for them to select their unwelcome, innocent, defenseless child as the next scapegoat. They realize that, once their baby is aborted, their family will at least temporarily stop blaming them for the problems nobody has the courage to deal with. This happens with a combination of the following mechanisms:

Projection. They project into the infant bad family characteristics or undesirable characteristics of the deserting or unsupportive father, or unwanted aspects of their own self, failure, selfishness, etc. To get rid of those unwanted characteristics, the parents subconsciously believe the child must be destroyed.

Innocence transfer. By scapegoating and destroying the child there is a symbolic transfer of the evil from themselves to the child and the innocence of the child to themselves. The scapegoating may temporarily stop the problems of the family from being expressed, but it will soon accentuate and intensify those problems and require further scapegoating. Thus, a sibling may become pregnant and have an abortion, or else they may have a second abortion.

SAVED FROM THE SAME FATE

Parents who have been abused and neglected as children sometimes want to save an infant from the same awful experience they had. Intuitively, they perceive that they would not be a good parent because they were not well parented themselves. They assume that the child will receive as bad or worse parenting than they did. Therefore they think to abort the child is to save the child from the same suffering that they experienced.

Some parents believe the world is too cruel or uncertain. Rather than expose the child to the experience of uncertainty, cruelty and discrimination that they experienced, they will abort the infant. When people feel hopeless, they do not welcome children. Then, when there are fewer children, people feel hopeless. There is little reason to plan and save for the future.

LACK OF AWARENESS

Women who have been abused or neglected as children have poor self-awareness. In order to survive, they learned to dehumanize themselves to feelings of pain, fear, despair, confusion and joy. They are not as sensitive to their inner strivings and urges. They will not admit the cry of their own pain. Not hearing themselves, they cannot hear the still, quiet voice of the infant inside them. Children who have been sexually abused or verbally attacked because they were fat or misshapen are ashamed of their bodies. Girls reject the idea of their breasts or their tummy enlarging. They want to keep their good figure.

If this means aborting the baby they will do it. If they were neglected during childhood, their blueprint was misread or defaced and therefore they may not see that being a parent is part of the person they were designed to become. They would rather believe their lifestyle does not include being responsible for the life and future of a child.

CONTROL

Too often, aborting the baby is an expression of a desire for control. This can arise from a number of mechanisms:

Control over their destiny. If they were over-controlled as children they want to be able to make up their own mind, even going against what is expected of them. This particularly occurs in children who come from childhoods with authoritarian parents.

Control over their body. If they were sexually abused and had no chance to protect themselves, to abort the baby is an expression of regaining control over their body. This is re-enforced by feminist rhetoric that tells a woman the baby is part of her body and her body is only her business.

Control of their partner. Some women who, having had a traumatic experience with their father, brothers or partners, want to exert control over a man. Threatening to abort the baby can make him sweat. Leaving him in a situation where he does not know what is going to happen makes him very worried. To abort the baby is to express hate to their partner.

Revenge on parents. Kent, Greenwood and Loeken-Nicholls[34] have shown that women may have abortions as an expression of their anger at parents, who may have had abortions or may have misused them. It may also be an attempt to keep their parents from experiencing the joys of being a grandparent.

Vulnerable women. Some men may try to find and manipulate a vulnerable woman - someone who had a poor or non-existent father and is trying somehow to find a man who will father her. This man may hold considerable control over her with threats of abandonment. She may respond by aborting their baby to show him he has no power. She may feel a certain sense of satisfaction in rejecting his baby because he rejected her.

IMMATURE

Men and women who have been neglected have not completed their development. Their needs have not been met or, when they were partly developed, somebody attacked and destroyed part of who they were. It is hard for a child to have a child. Even though there are strong biological drives to propagate, immature people are more likely to abort their babies for a number of reasons:

Women and men may feel they are too young. did not have a reasonable childhood or adolescence, and still have much exciting travelling to do or education to complete.

They anticipate the child as competition for their needs. They expect their child is very demanding and therefore they would have no time for their own needs.

Conflict with the desires for vicarious gratifications. Often a young woman gets pregnant hoping that if she had a child, he would gurgle and goo, smile and delight her with such enjoyment that she would gain pleasure from providing what he needs. Therefore, she would vicariously have her own needs met. Then she begins to realize that babies can be demanding and less enjoyable. Rather than face that disappointment, she aborts the baby.

Men realize that they would have to sacrifice much of their sports, fun, big toys, etc.. Rather than forgo these, they coerce a woman to have an abortion.

DEROGATORY DISCRIMINATION

If, as a child, she was brought up to believe that some minority or different group is inferior to her, she may then re-enact the conflicts of her parents by mating with someone of a different race. When she realizes they have a child of "mixed blood," the derogatory side of the conflict comes out and she aborts the baby.

DISPLACED AGGRESSION

Often the aborted baby is being attacked as a displaced object of the parent's aggression. This occurs when:

- the parents feel abandoned or are threatened with abandonment.
- in the parent's own aggression there may be fantasizes of revenge against his/her own parents. The parent could act out his/her revenge on his/her child if the child was born, therefore it would be better to abort the child.
- children who have been neglected or abused have greater anger. It does not take much to precipitate this anger. Since they are unable to express the anger directly at the parent, they direct it at their unborn

sibling.

- men, knowing they have no opportunity to protect their babies, often expect their children to be aborted without their awareness or consent. They feel enormous rage at women for being deprived of their paternal rights. Feeling that rage, they direct it at the infant, especially if they anticipate she is a girl, and insist that "it" be aborted.

REJECT PATERNITY

Men, rejecting the idea of being a father, coerce their partners into aborting their babies. They may pressure women with threats of exposure or abandonment. They tend to reject paternity if:

they were rejected by their father.

having seen their fathers abuse their mothers, they are disgusted at what men do to women. They would not want to be men like that.

they feel impotent. Their normal nurturing and protective instincts are frustrated. They may protest on behalf of their babies, but soon sense the futility. Legally, men are unable to protect their children. They feel helpless, and question how they could be a father.

legal threats. In some parts of the United States, men cannot renew their driver's license until they pay for child support. On one hand, this might increase the amount of support women get from men who impregnate them, but on the other hand, it strongly increases a man's desire to force a woman to have an abortion.

impact of the media. The advertising media more frequently depicts men as having fun when they are single. In movies, books and other situations, it is the single man who appears to have all the adventures and all the women. It seems it is better not to have a wife or family.

conditioned passivity. By the age of seventeen, it appears that the average

American has seen sixteen thousand murders and other desperate situations that would normally call them to react with protection. They cannot rescue or protect the endangered person. They can only sit and watch because the emergency is happening on television. This tendency to passivity while people (women, in particular) are in desperate circumstances, becomes the conditioned response in real situations that appeal for their protection.

Interrupt pursuit of pleasure

Many adults abused as children are fighting against depression and despair by keeping themselves busy, high on drugs or drunk. To have a child would mean having to give up that pursuit of pleasure and face the depression.

Many children grew up in families where both parents were working. The parents often provide toys to their children as the substitute for their presence. The toys may make the child temporarily happy. This encourages the child to expect the best way to deal with unhappiness is to buy things for themselves. To have a child means that they would have to buy things for the child and deprive themselves.

Dehumanization

Child abuse and neglect dehumanize a child. Dehumanized parents find it easier to dehumanize their unborn infant. Because they feel worthless and because the best effort they could bring to the world is a child, they see the child as worthless also. It is less difficult to destroy a dehumanized, pre-born child. They expect the child to be just like them and since they are less than human, the child must be less than human also. Having been abused, they have little self respect. Therefore they feel they are not increasing the damage to their self respect by having an abortion.

Disrupt false ambition

Abused and neglected children are often struggling to obtain their parent's affirmation and affection. They think somehow they could still please their parent by making a lot of money or getting more education. A pregnancy is a disruption of their aspirations. In the sense that they are ambitious only to please somebody else, these ambitions are false. Because they cannot disrupt their strivings, they must abort the baby.

Not welcomed

When young parents were abused and neglected as children, they had a distinct feeling that they were not welcome. Therefore it is harder to welcome their baby just as he/she is, when he/she is, and where he/she is. They sense that because they were rejected, they will automatically reject their baby. They think it would be better to abort him/her than not be able to welcome him/her.

Fear of pain

Having been beaten or burned as children, parents anticipate childbirth and parenting as a painful experience. They believe it would be better to abort the baby than re-experience the fear and pain of their own childhood. They are given false information that it is safer to have an abortion than have a baby. It is obvious to anybody who understands statistics that you cannot compare a phenomenon that lasts for twelve weeks (average pregnancy duration to abortion) with one that lasts for forty weeks. On a totally random basis, a person is 3.3 times more likely to get sick or die during a full-term pregnancy. In fact, the odds of maternal mortality are equal at 15 weeks. Thus, pregnancy protects, not harms, health. If people are trying to protect themselves and their health, they will accept the lie that it is safer for them to abort the baby. If they were sexually abused and associate pain with their vagina or other sexual organs, and they do not want to experience that pain again, they will prefer to abort the baby. Unfortunately, they underestimate the amount of pain that occurs with the regular abortions.

NOT HOPEFUL

Abused and neglected children had their hopes and dreams dashed. Because they have little hope for their own future, they see there is little hope for the child's future. Because they believe there is little hope for the child to have a good, secure life, they will abort the child. Unfortunately, without children, parents do not conserve, plan or look to the future. With fewer children there is less hope. With less hope there are fewer children.

GIVING THE BABY A CHANCE LATER

New Age religions have re-developed the idea of reincarnation and state the aborted baby's soul will come back at a more convenient time. This false idea is falsely comforting to those who want to avoid the guilt and grief after abortions.

D. A COMBINATION OF CAN AND PLS

If an adult has been abused or neglected as a child and he/she is also an abortion survivor, all the conflicts previously written are intensified.

SURVIVOR GUILT

For people who do not allow themselves to fully live their lives and feel guilty about their existence, it is hard to allow a pre-born baby to exist. People may feel the Cain complex - feeling guilty for killing their brother. This happens

if they were born before a subsequent sibling was aborted. People may have been told that they were difficult pregnancies or deliveries or that they were difficult children. Because they were so difficult, their mothers decided to abort subsequent siblings. They feel it was their fault younger siblings died. Now they cannot allow their children to live.

They may experience the Jacob complex if they were born after a sibling was aborted. They feel they have been a supplanter, a person that took the previous baby's life and place.

Because of their survival guilt, they have been living a half-life seeking fun, fun, fun, work, work, work, sex, sex, sex, etc.,...to avoid their inner turmoil. To have a baby would disrupt this defense, and therefore they select abortion.

NO FUTURE

As an abortion survivor, they have a sense that the same force that arbitrarily destroyed their sibling could still take their life. Because they cannot be sure when they might die, they do not plan for their future. Having a baby means planning for the future and this is something they dare not do; they do not buy insurance, they do not visit the doctor and they do not save money for the baby's future. In their thinking, it would be better to abort the baby.

IMMATURITY

Because they do not fully live their life or plan for their future, they do not develop all their abilities nor utilize their opportunities. Thus, they tend to be more immature. Being immature means it is very hard for them to accept the responsibilities of parenthood. They are afraid they cannot cope, so they choose to terminate the baby's life.

DISTRUST

Abortion survivors were distrusted as a child by their parents, who could not trust themselves, and therefore they do not trust themselves as a parent. They feel they might be overprotective or unable to contain their rage, therefore they abort the baby.

Their parents may have told them they aborted their sibling out of love for them. Therefore they tend to become cynical about love. If they are told they are loved even though they have an unexpected pregnancy, they doubt it and reject both offers of love and the baby.

RAGE

Being a wanted child, a child who was selected to live when a sibling was terminated, he has to go on being wantable. This means he cannot be himself. He constantly has to wonder if he is pleasing others. This keeps him from developing into the person he should be. He develops more into the person others expect him to be. He pleases his parents for much of his childhood, but during his adolescence he rebels with rage. That rage may be expressed as a rejection of a pregnancy, even when his parents insist he and his girlfriend should have and keep the child.

WANTEDNESS

Being wanted children, abortion survivors learn to suspect their parents' motives and therefore their own motives for wanting a child. They may be persuaded by Planned Parenthood or the United Nations rhetoric that the first right of every child is to be wanted. They know within their own heart and experience that if the first right of every child is to be wanted, then if the child is not wanted he or she has no right to be. Since every parent is ambivalent about every child, part of them, at least at some time, does not want a child. The parents who were abortion survivors or wanted children use this concept of unwanted children to justify aborting their baby. They have been persuaded to think that if their baby were unwanted they would probably abuse him or her. There is no evidence to support this notion. In fact, the best evidence shows that wanted children are more likely to be abused.

If she is trying to stay wantable as a wanted child, then a young mother knows that she has to please her parents. If parents express displeasure, disgust or threats about her teenage pregnancy, she is likely to quickly acquiesce and have her baby aborted.

NOT HOPEFUL

Many abortion survivors dare not be hopeful about their future. Intuitively they realize the child will make them think about and plan for their future. To reject hope they have to reject the baby.

CANNOT COMMIT

Abortion survivors are often unable to commit themselves to relationships. They cannot commit themselves to each other in a marriage nor can they commit themselves to the child. Therefore, they reject each other and abort the baby.

SELF DOUBT

Pregnancy loss survivors doubt their ability to handle a baby lovingly or handle the stress that is imposed by a baby's demands. Because they doubt their abilities, they reject and abort the baby.

DISLIKE CHILDREN

PASS adults who were also abused and neglected as children tend to envy children's pleasure. They dislike children for the joy they express. Rather than enjoying the child's joy, they feel jealous. It reminds them of what they did not have as children.

SIBLINGS UNPROTECTED BY FATHER

Abortion survivors know that their father was unable or uninterested in protecting them. The father, in particular, not feeling the protection of his own father, feels unable to protect his children. Being angry at being rejected or not protected by his own father, he displaces his anger at his father onto the preborn child.

RE-ENACTMENT

In an attempt to resolve the conflicts arising from childhood neglect and abuse and being abortion survivors, many subconsciously attempt to re-enact the problems of abortion by having the baby aborted. Unfortunately, if there is no one there to help them understand the essential conflicts of the re-enactment, the reenactment only intensifies the conflict and thus the propensity to have another abortion. Our results show that the first pregnancy is the best predictor of subsequent pregnancies.[12] A full term pregnancy the first time is more likely to result in a full term pregnancy the second time. A woman who has an abortion in the first pregnancy has a much higher propensity to have an abortion in the second pregnancy.

7. REPETITIOUS RE-ENACTMENTS TO LEARN

Humans have known for a long time that unless and until they learn from their mistakes, they will tend to repeat them. They may have tried hard to learn from the past through history lessons, moral instruction, and legislative prohibitions. But still tragedy is repeated, especially when that tragedy happens to small or dependent people. The greater the crime to humanity, the greater the internal conflict and thus the greater the tendency to repetitious re-enactment. From our studies, it appears repetitions of tragic history are attempts to understand what happened the first time a person was neglected, used or abused."

When a traumatic event (neglect, accidents, deaths, repeated moves, etc.) happens to a child, it creates a conflict. Until the conflict is fully understood and adaptably externalized, it destabilizes a child's mind, which then must work on the problem in order to regain stability. Instability in the human microcosm produces inefficiency in the efforts to fulfill its purpose to develop as designed.

Children would normally deal with every conflict immediately, but their first priority is to survive and develop. Because children have no one to help understand and resolve their conflicts, and because too often one trauma is piled on another, most abused children do not have time to contemplate what has happened to them nor understand the reasons why. There is nobody available who seems willing or able to help them work through the complicated dilemmas caused by abuse and neglect. Those who might help the child understand are seldom able to rescue the child from the recurring tragic circumstances that create the abuse and neglect.

Even one trauma can create a major conflict in a child's mind. Mental conflicts deprive children of the peace and security they need in order to explore and thus develop their intelligence. Mental conflicts rob children of joy and frequently of innocence. They make children introverted and less capable of loving. They diminish a child's capacity to procreate beauty and life. They impede a child's quest for truth and limit his/her chance of becoming God's friend. In short, they dehumanize the child.

At a biological level, these imbedded conflicts create an inefficient use of energy. Thus, children are frequently unable to make efficient decisions and are often embroiled in unnecessary interpersonal conflicts because of psychological conflicts. To avoid entropy (loss of energy and order), children must resolve each conflict. Children could possibly do this by understanding the essential components through quiet contemplation or by discussing complicated issues with somebody who could give them insight. Since the roots are deeply dug, gaining understanding is difficult and confounded by the many mixed feelings and motives. Neither contemplation or discussion work very well. When they do not, a child must help make the event re-occur, a not-so-instant replay the child can watch to try and detect who did what and why.

Surely the most tragic part of child abuse and neglect is that mistreated children have the propensity to contribute to the re-enactment of their early tragedies. The child who has been physically abused becomes aggressive, often provoking fights (not only with his peers but with adults who could really hurt him). The verbally abused child cannot control his/her tongue and so elicits a constant stream of verbal put-downs. The child who has been sexually abused, in an effort to understand why it happened, may become seductive (not infrequently becoming a prostitute in his/her adolescence). Children who were physically neglected often seem unable to find or hold jobs, so they end up on welfare with barely enough to eat. Children who lacked touch and affection seem to select emotionally cold partners. All of this looks like the pointless repetition of tragedy, yet it can be viewed in a different way. Tragedy is repeated not because we do not understand, but because we are trying to understand.

If a child could re-create, re-experience and (hopefully) review his early tragedy, there is a better chance that he will understand how it happened than if he just mulls it over in his mind. With increased understanding of how it happened, he will have a greater chance of avoiding similar conflicts in the future. Having a replay can help resolve the conflicts in his mind that have been tying up so much energy or obstructing curiosity and the development of intelligence. Sadly, understanding happens only when a wise person can instruct a child about the critical components while the tragedy is recurring. This seldom occurs. That is why much of Hope Alive group counseling is interpreting the dynamics as the conflicts are re-enacted in the group setting.

People re-create or re-enact early tragedies by first locating and then engaging people who will help them perform the replay. There is a subtle interchange of signals that alert them to potential tragedy partners. Not infrequently, they will find precisely the person who begins to mistreat them as they were abused and neglected as children. People who were mistreated both discover and construct the tragic triangles that reoccur in their lives. They find fertile soil in some of the people they meet. They plant the right signals, and soon the tragedy grows without much effort on their part. On the surface this appears to be such a waste of time, yet it is done precisely so that the person can understand and resolve their earliest tragedies.

More frequently, people with unresolved conflicts that grew out of their experience of abuse, neglect and/or abortion uncannily locate and often mate or transact with a person who has the potential to become their tragedy partner. In short order, they bring out or amplify characteristics in each other that result in a painful re-enactment of earlier tragedy. For example, she marries a nice, social-climbing lawyer. After one cocktail party she says, "I think you had one too many." He replies, "I don't like you trying to control me." In all too short a time, she has an alcoholic husband "just like my father" and he has a nagging, bitter wife "just like my mother." Should they part, the chances are they will do it all again.

The tragedy partner becomes a kind of magical mirror. When one looks in this mirror one does not see the reflection that one expects. One frequently sees the other half of oneself. Having seen that reflection, a person starts a tense and sometimes angry transaction that tends to accommodate this hidden, and often disliked, aspect of oneself.

Often the tragedy partner, at least in the early stages of the relationship, is idolized. Like idols, they are not allowed to talk or to see the other's needs. That would entail recognizing that they are both wounded and needy. The partner usually falls off her/his pedestal with a bang of disappointment. This is often followed by brief mourning, then a determined effort by the other to place the partner back on the pedestal or find a more attractive idol.

I was once asked to see a woman who was quite depressed, partly because she was going through her fourth divorce. This woman had been mistreated by her father, who was occasionally violently drunk. When drunk, he would curse his wife and beat the children. When sober he tried to compensate for his misdeeds with extra kindness and gifts. She could not understand how such different behavior could come from the same person. She determined not to marry any such man and indeed selected a kind, caring person. After five years of marriage she decided that he was a "wimp" and divorced him. She then had three successive marriages to violent, drinking men. I was able to help her understand the nature and origin of the conflict in her childhood. She divorced her fourth husband and remarried the first one who had become available again. I do not know if they lived happily ever after, but she had learned that until people learn from their history, they must repeat it. When they have useful insight into the truth of themselves and their tragic relationships, they are free to choose to be different people.

When a child is traumatized, the abuse or neglect invariably creates a conflict in his or her mind. The mind is programmed to retain the essence of the conflict so an individual can survive and adapt, learning how to avoid or overcome that kind of situation should it re-occur. The conflict occurs because the traumatic event sets in motion many mixed feelings and opposing desires, e.g. to love or hate, to fight or to run away. If the debate in the child's mind is not resolved, it results in a psychobiological disequilibrium. The human must maintain a careful homeostasis in order to use time and energy efficiently. Conflict results in inefficient imbalances and thus must be resolved.

Because of unresolved conflicts, the child also has a tendency to re-enact tragedy. Any repetition of the traumatic event increases the internal debate, further fixing the conflict. It is not just the traumatic event, but the enormous energy that is put into attempting to resolve conflicting thoughts and behaviors that creates a neurotic, subconscious conflict. This is illustrated by the following diagram, which shows increasing conflict-fixing, neuro-psychological oscillations that might take place in the child's mind.

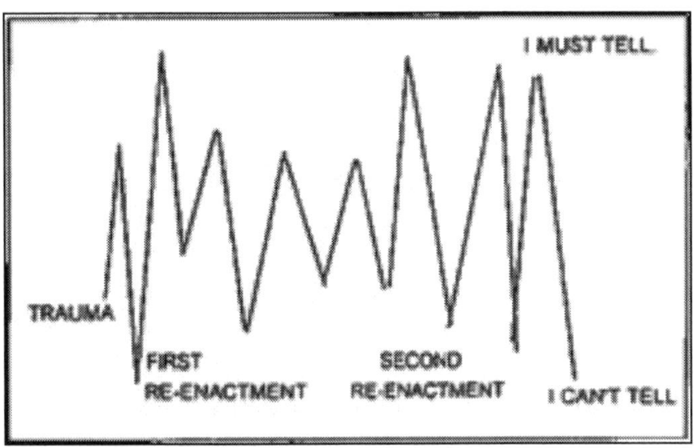

Figure 2.5 Repetitious Re-enactment of Trauma

Traumatic events in a child's life usually engender deep conflicts that she cannot readily untangle and which result in conflicting desire and confused emotions. She may want to run away, but she is frightened to do so for fear of being left totally alone or eaten by some monster. She may want to fight, but the person who is attacking her is much bigger and would attack back. That conflict between fight and flight, between keeping quiet or telling someone, and its associated emotion becomes a fixed, subconscious conflict, especially if the trauma recurs. Even if the traumatic experience does not recur, the debate in the child's mind develops into a major conflict.

For example, having been sexually fondled by a respected uncle, the child may lie in bed at night debating with herself about how she should react, e.g. "Should I, or should I not tell my mother what happened? If I do tell, what will happen to me or the family?" The debate in her head goes back and forth, "Yes. No. Maybe later?" The longer and harder she tries to make the right decision, the more intense the emotions become. These strong, oscillating emotions help imbed the conflict. In an effort to understand the how?, why? and why me? questions arising from the traumatic experience, she may help recreate it. The second traumatic event sets off even more reverberations of indecision and mixed emotions. Again she is alone and must decide whether to act one way or another, but by now the decision is much harder. Conflicts engendered by neglect and abuse in children consume an enormous amount of energy, attention, and mental capacity, thus interfering with their ability to learn and truncating their emotional development.

Many people find ways to avoid making the decision to tell someone about neglect and/or abuse, or to protest directly. They procrastinate, hoping some event will decide for them. This is especially true for abortion survivors. What is initially a small yes-no dilemma in her mind becomes "I cannot possibly decide, but I cannot just ignore it either." More and more energy is expended trying to control the ambivalent oscillations of intense feelings and a desperation from trying to resolve the underlying conflict. This going to and fro in her mind will continue until at some point she attempts to resolve the underlying issues by helping re-enact them. In adult life this becomes "I agreed to marry him only because he was so persistent, not because I decided to. Now I am stuck with a situation which is worse than the one with my ex."

CASE EXAMPLE: THE BLACK STRAP AND JOHNNY

Until recently, some school principals used a thick leather strap to punish children by repeatedly assaulting their most sensitive tactile organ (i.e. the hand). One particular principal in Northern Canada was very irritated by a particularly hyperactive and mischievous child. Johnny never forgot the principal, and the principal never forgot the child because he had strapped him so often. Shortly after Johnny left school, the principal retired. He went to his neighbor, Johnny's father, and said, "Undoubtedly you are having trouble with Johnny. He certainly was a troublemaker at school. Now I have retired, I would like to give you the black strap that I used on him." The father readily accepted it and used it on his son. When the young man grew up and had his own children, his father presented him with the black strap. Although he had vivid memories of the pain it had caused him, he now used the strap to inflict pain on his own son.

I was asked to examine Johnny Jr. and found this bright-eyed, tousled haired youngster to be just as constitutionally hyperactive as his father. No amount of strapping would restrain his impatience or make him concentrate. The father, once the Victim and now the Perpetrator, could well remember the pain, but still he felt that it was the only thing he could do to correct his son. It was not until I suggested that he did not really want "the black strap" to be passed on from one generation to the next that he stopped to reconsider. He recognized that each time he hit his son he also felt the blow. He vicariously relived the pain of his childhood, each time feeling the burning anger at his father, the humiliation and the thoughts of revenge. With growing insight, he could put the strap in the garbage. Thus, this tragedy did not have to be re-enacted by successive generations.

8. PERSONALITY SPLITS

A. THE CAUSE OF SPLITS

Every child is created in the image of God. He enters life with great hope for a fulfilling life and with the in-built expectation that his needs will be met. Even if he is badly neglected or repeatedly traumatized, he will still struggle to develop, but the frustration is so great that he begins to develop false faces. This tendency to try and obtain the necessary ingredients to build the Person I Was Designed to Become happens in anyone who does not readily obtain an optimum childhood, i.e. nearly everyone at least to some extent.

The core conflicts that result in the initial tendency to develop and use false faces by using masks may begin during earliest infancy. The cold, wet and hungry child lies in the crib feeling, "Why are they not responding to my cry of distress?" or "Why do they respond with aggression and not nurture?" or "Why did they use me for their gratification instead of giving me what I need? I must know, do they ignore me because they are incapable of parenting or because I am not worthy of their love? Maybe if I'm a pleasing child they will love me, or maybe if they see how hurt and sad I am they will take pity on me."

Even a badly wounded child cannot ignore her Blueprint. Though she cannot find the family or situation that will provide the necessary developmental building blocks, it is hard to stop searching. Seeing both what she is and what she could be and trying to keep trying or giving up is the central conflict engendered by mistreatment. "Why don't they love me and give me what I need? Is it because they can't or they won't?"

I cannot survive if my parents are incapable of meeting my needs for touch, food, affection, affirmation, guidance, protection, etc. Therefore I prefer to believe I'm not worthy of my parents' love. Maybe if I punish myself or change I will be good enough. But I've tried that so often that I'm bruised and broken. Since I can't resolve this dilemma, I could go crazy." She recognizes this deep tension might result in losing touch with reality. That tendency to go crazy (become psychotic) results in a terrifying anxiety. She is faced with almost impossible choices; 1) find defenses that will keep her together; 2) kill her family and hope to find a better one; 3) kill herself or; 4) become psychotic.

When an infant lies in her cot, cold, alone, hungry and wet, she cries for attention. Almost any attention would be better than nothing. What she desires is someone, preferably parents to whom she is bonded, to pick her up, see her distress, understand her need and meet them all with grace and enthusiasm. "Oh, my poor little darling! I can see you are in a bad way! Let me hold you. Your mummy will look after you. I know exactly what you need ... Now, you are all dry and well fed, come lie in my arms while I sing you a soft lullaby. It is such a joy to have you. I thank the Lord everyday."

Many children are ignored or aggressed when they most urgently need loving care. "Just ignore her, she is being naughty and just wants attention. If we ignore her long enough she will go back to sleep." or "Stupid little brat, she keeps me awake! I better go and give her a good spanking." If there is no response, her cry goes into the void and she begins to wonder if she exists. From that neglect, there is the beginning of a tendency to try to defend the small, fragile sense of self by elaborating two false faces.

Every small creature, at the sound of the approaching footsteps of the one that cares for them, "smiles" in anticipation. If she was a puppy, she would wag her tail. If that sound of approaching footsteps is also accompanied by sounds of aggression, an infant might still "wag her tail" by smiling, hoping desperately that the caring adult will see how appealing she is, suppress any anger and, in love, pick up and nurture her. If those footsteps appear to approach part way and then fade into the distance, the happy expression on the child's face quickly disappears. It is replaced with the enormous distress that comes from being neglected when she is desperately needy and dependent.

Neglected and abused children have repeatedly experienced the need to wear a happy-looking face at the approach of possible nurture. They automatically feel and express their sadness when the sound of the nurturing adult fades. Alternating between smiles and sadness soon becomes mostly automatic. This is the beginning of the two false faces. The "approach smile" becomes the Dancer. The "disappearing sorrow" becomes the Urchin. The child reasons, "If I was good enough, they would love me. Yet, if I were loved, then I would be good enough." The neglected child cannot resolve this dilemma and thus must defend herself from psychosis or annihilation with false faces.

The neglected and abused child is in an impossible situation. She is caught up in the vicious cycle of hurt and hope. Because it is too difficult to believe that parents are not capable of nurturing her, she must believe that she is incapable of being loved. But that thought creates an impossible dilemma that can only result in self-annihilation. It is no wonder that the child elaborates these defenses, which become increasingly set and difficult to discard.

B. TWO FALSE FACES

The human is designed to survive through adaptation, therefore the tendency to elaborate masks is almost universal. He/she defends against annihilation or psychosis by wearing two false faces, the Dancer and the Urchin.

THE DANCER

Wearing the Dancer mask, the individual tries to please by always being optimistic, compliant, ready to help, eager to learn, affectionate and amiable. She creates the illusion both for herself and others that she is full of potential, and given a little encouragement she could do much for others. She offers to others more than she is able to give. She is terrified that someday someone will detect how needy and/or ungiving she really is. She believes that if uncovered she will be rejected. She dresses well, is full of energy, smiles a lot and in an outgoing way, attracts others who might provide her with what she lacked as a child.

This image can only be maintained for a limited period before she runs out of energy or positive feedback, at which point it collapses and she quickly reverts to being an urchin. She wants to attract someone who can give her much of what she lacked as a child, thereby giving her a chance that she will continue to grow and develop according to her Blueprint.

Unfortunately, there are few friends or partners who are also willing to be a partner's parent. She normally attracts somebody much like herself who is looking for a parent rather than a mate. They may both want a child to be the source of vicarious gratification. The impossible expectations of her man as husband and parent, father and lover, are seldom met. They usually become mutually disappointed in each other. This results in increased efforts to make the other person into someone who is really as good as they appeared to be at first meeting. When these efforts to change his/her friend or partner fail, they attack each other and/or split up only to seek another opportunity for conflict re-enactment in another potential mate. If she is pregnant, it is hard to dance. Therefore, it is easy to persuade her that the unborn child must be terminated.

On the surface, Dancers seem to be vivacious and loving, but beneath the mask they can be cynical and manipulative. By their effort and talents they can also make other people feel inadequate. They can be seductive, or self-righteous, or selfish behind the facade of selflessness. The Dancer has a self-destructive tendency. She may deliberately do something self-injurious to evoke her Urchin. She does so because she has a sense that the Urchin following along behind is going to replace her at any moment anyhow, especially because she is tired of dancing. She painfully realizes people use her as a Dancer and becomes increasingly cynical.

Some of the many types of Dancers are described in the following paragraphs. Some people have more than one Dancer or Urchin mask.

A Ballet Dancer is always on her toes, bending over backwards to please people and always presenting a stiff and stilted smile. She pushes herself to the limit, and generally wants a perfect body full of grace. She may become anorexic. She is not really aware of her audience but exalts in any applause, although it is never enough. She continually looks for an ideal partner who will dance the perfect *pas de deux* forever. She is usually attractive and seductive, but prefers an impotent partner because she cannot give herself.

A Tap Dancer is generally stronger and tougher than a ballet Dancer. She has a busy, sometimes funny routine, clowning, and hoping for laughter, if not appreciation. She makes a big noise for attention. She was often hyperactive as a child.

Jazz Dancers are accepted in a small group of like-minded people. They state that they don't care what happens to the rest of the world as long as they can "do their thing", but underneath they are desperate for acceptance. They become vitriolic when they are not accepted by the "square" world. They engage in outrageous behavior and often wear outlandish dress, which effectively gets them the attention, which they assert they do not want.

Ballroom Dancers want to be part of a large and snobbish crowd, but also to be so attractive that they stand out. They hope that the charming prince/ princess will spy them and carry them off to the castle where they will be cared for, just out of his/her sheer admiration for their loveliness. In a lovely gown with a perfect partner, they yearn to waltz gracefully through life.

Disco Dancers are desperately neglected and often sexually abused children grown older. They engage in angry seductiveness, less for money than for power. This sordid re-enactment of the sexual abuse that they experienced as children seldom ends in anything but disease or death.

The Pied Piper is a solo Dancer who, because of her charm, can seduce children. She may even believe that she is doing children a favor by leading them away from their parents to unsavory pleasures under her mountain. They select social work or childcare as professions.

The Liturgical Dancer is ostensibly performing for the glory of God. She is really showing off her body and her talent for her own glorification. She wears a pious face and has exaggerated gestures of praise but, for both herself and the audience. She is more the focus of attention than is God. This solemn person wears black most of the time, not to be plain, but to dramatize how sincere and holy they are attempting to be.

Tragic Dancer. These people are forever showing off their wounds or their abuse, seeking commiseration and approval. "Oh how brave you are." They are a little bit like the tragic figure in the grand opera. They can only see themselves as Victims, but get pleasure out of seeing "that dirty 'bugger' put away in prison."

The Dance Teacher is a person who is conducting courses to help people look prettier and be more pleasing, either to make their marriage work or sell more. She appears to be very successful at what she is teaching. Beneath the facade she knows she is false and constantly worries that someone will discover how little she really knows.

The Heroine Hero loudly commiserates with "you poor women" or "you down-trodden peons." "Join me and we will assert our rights, overthrow the (male) oppressor and create a state of bliss and harmony for all. Both the empathy and rage are sham. What is real is their desire for power. They go into politics or, with bluff and bravado, work themselves into powerful bureaucratic positions.

The Copy Cat Dancer imitates all those who dance well enough to get lots of attention they too would like. They are continually dancing to a different tune, trying to be somebody else, and have very little idea of who they are even as a Dancer.

The Mime or Chameleon Dancer. The mime or chameleon dances to imitate anyone so they too can be enjoyed and accepted by everyone else. This dancer is the life of every kind of party.

It seems that in human relationships every audience needs a dancer and every dancer needs an audience. They need each other. Whenever either the audience stops applauding or the dancer stops dancing, the whole charade collapses and people go their separate ways, grumbling in their disappointment. When alone, discouraged or so frustrated that they begin to become destructive, the Dancer's "smile" is replaced with the Urchin's "scowl."

THE URCHIN

This false face is depressing, despairing and self-pitying. The Urchin often has psychiatric and physical complaints. The Urchin metaphorically huddles on the sidewalk against a cold, stark building, hoping that somebody will notice and give her a pittance to keep her alive. She searches every face hoping to find somebody that recognizes her deep desires. In her heart she knows it is unlikely to happen. She struggles home at the end of the day with just enough on which to survive, crawls into her hovel, and cries herself to sleep. Occasionally, someone gives her a few extra dollars.

Sometimes the Urchin attracts a Dancer who sees in her some potential to become a loving parent to him. The Urchin resists the push to change and, with ugly determination, keeps making the Dancer fail until she reverts to being an Urchin, e.g. those who try to rescue alcoholics. The Urchin is often tagging along immediately behind the Dancer, ready to quickly take the Dancer's place when she becomes exhausted.

The Urchin often hates her mother or her father, especially for the damage that follows being neglected. She knows in her heart that those early injuries will not heal very readily, if ever, and she will drag herself through life with at least a permanent psychological limp. But the Urchin cannot hate her mother without at least momentarily hating herself. Hating of oneself must eventually be self-destructive. Eventually the Urchin gives up hating a parent and ends up either hating anyone that makes her feel uncomfortable or engaging in self-destructive behavior.

Usually the Dancer is seen in public - at parties, work, entertainment, etc. while the Urchin is seen only by family or close friends. This is partly because most people are ashamed of their Urchin.

Some of the various types of Urchins are:

The Beggar is slumped into the comer of a damp, dark subway or propped against a grey concrete building. Her hand is outstretched until it is stiff and cold, waiting for a meager handout. When she gets a little more than she expected, she gloats, dresses up and suddenly becomes a Dancer. When she gets very little, she becomes bitter and shrunken. In her hunger, she eats a crust, falls asleep, only to wake up with a desperate and dying hope that people will be kinder the next time. She becomes increasingly angry with the government, the church or the rich people who ignore her plight.

The Troll is an angry, destructive Urchin who defends her "bridge" from other people who keep trying to cross to wonderful opportunities. If she can catch one of these opportunists she hauls them into her domain under her bridge so they can witness the miserable conditions in which she lives. Hopefully that person will rectify them. But even when she captures someone, she usually lets them escape, or drives them away, not without some "marks" from their experience. They hurry away wondering what they ever saw in her that attracted them in the first place.

The Hobo is always moving on, never satisfied with where she is; hoping against hope that some other place or some other partner will be better. She hitchhikes or rides the rods on the railway. She is miserably alone but she is unencumbered. She laughs sardonically at constrained society, but cannot help longing for a home of her own. Covered partially by a leaking tarpaulin, she sits beside a sputtering fire and watches the evening lights come on in the homes in the valley below.

The Derelict has an almost absolute disregard for her health and safety. She is frequently drunk, asleep on the streets and expects to wake up dead after being stabbed. Often she ends up in jail, complaining, but glad of the security and routine. She wishes her misery would end but is too afraid to kill herself. There is just a faint possibility that at the next rehabilitation centre someone will see her inherent value and rescue her.

The Miser hoards both her wealth and misery, which she carefully counts each morning. Her only pleasure is vicariously feeding on the misfortunes of other people seen in television news. She makes frequent comparisons and considers that her misery is greater. She waits for death, anticipating the obituary that will disclose how much she really was worth. Everyone will react in surprise. "We should have been more friendly."

The Prospector lives alone in the mountains or delves in a mine. There is always just enough showing of gold to keep her struggling by herself. She is secretive and afraid to share. She hopes that someday she can be so rich that she can buy any amount of time and attention from people. It won't matter if they are really friends or not.

The Penitent is repeatedly confessing and asking for forgiveness. The pardon has already been given but not accepted. She frequently flagellates herself in hopes it will forestall or prevent real discipline. The Penitent gladly accepts or seeks adversity as being good for her soul. Underneath she is proud, rigid, self-righteous and judgmental. Often she is found in legalistic Christian congregations.

The Drug Addict and Alcoholic are stating to the world, "Can't you see I'm killing myself? When I succeed you will be really sorry." Her fix is less to make them temporarily numb than it is to heighten the subsequent misery. She attracts rescuing Dancers then sets out to make them as miserable as themselves

C. FUNCTIONS OF THE FALSE FACES

The two false faces have two functions:

- they are a lure, attracting possible affirmation to keep the blueprint clear and to provide the material for the building blocks that would buil the Person 1 Should Become.
- they are a decoy, diverting aggression or the arrows of adversity fro hitting the Pilgrim.

The false faces may insist theirs is the only way of existing. They sometimes reflect components of a person that could not develop because she did not receive a reasonable childhood. These undeveloped, and now undevelopable, components are split off to preserve the life and sanity of the core person. They become false faces of the real person, but though very demanding, they cannot develop and cannot be reintegrated into the core person.

Each image has an aggressive, as well as a fearful and wounded side to it. The Dancer can also be willful and manipulative like a spoiled prince or jealous fairy. The Urchin can rage, even murder, wanting to destroy himself and others. Like a troll, or a mean leprechaun, he lays traps for the unwary and laughs sardonically when someone falls into them.

Letting go of the Urchin and Dancer results in high levels of anxiety, an awful struggle in removing them, and mourning when they are gone. Some patients and counselees argue, "If I let go of these [false faces] then there will be nothing left of me. I risk losing friends and family because they expect me to be this way. I risk losing my sanity or of being annihilated." This is a similar anxiety to that which initiated the whole destructive, defensive process.

More than one counselee has said they couldn't let go of the false faces because they had no knowledge who their Pilgrim was. They had lost touch with their core person and felt now there was no way to recover a sense of who they really are.

People use false faces to defend themselves and to gain some form of attention, hopefully to get the building material that they need to develop. Many family, friends and foes help them develop and maintain those masks in order to be entertained, looked after and to have someone carry or express their anger and grief.

Anyone who detects and understands the Dancer and the Urchin in a person can easily manipulate them, e.g. "You are so good at..., e.g. organizing a party. We know you can do it better than anyone else. We can always count on you, can't we?" (Dancer) or "You poor little thing, no one understands you like I do. Join my army and fight for your rights. When I'm president I will make sure that no one mistreats you ever again."

The Dancer and the Urchin, in full regalia, are very convincing. Many people know the person as nothing but one or the other false face. The Pilgrim feels desperately tired from maintaining the false faces of the Dancer and Urchin. She would like to give them up but cannot for fear of:

- defence. "Nobody would like the real me."
- alienation. "If I don't keep dancing for them, they'll just ignore me."
- deprivation. "I get so little now. If I stop trying to please them, I'll get nothing."
- losing touch. "I only know me as a Dancer or Urchin. Without my masks, I'll go crazy."

She earnestly wishes that people could get to know and accept her as she really is. Because she is so afraid that she will not be accepted (as she was not as an infant), she will not let people really get to know her, even though she protests all the while that she wants them to "just accept me as I am."

The Dancer may become weary but her act is so well practised that it becomes a familiar and an acceptable public image of her. Dancers too often respond to the call for an encore, "One more dance, please." They keep performing even though inside they are crying out, "I can't dance anymore." There is a hidden wish sometimes expressed as a fantasy to stand centre stage, drop both images and say, "This is me! I want you to believe that this is me and accept me as I am." Yet, they are terrified. They cannot believe that anyone would want them without dancing so pleasingly.

The false faces of Urchin and Dancer have some utility, but wearing these masks is maladaptive because it is automatic and compulsive. They cannot put them aside, even when the occasion allows it. One beautiful young woman, adopted and then extensively abused from an early age, had severe Crohn's Disease - literally and figuratively turning herself inside out trying to please her parents. As a child she worked hard around the home, got good marks in school, went to Girl Guides and took ballet six days a week. Her mother would only criticize and beat her. Her father was away or ignoring the strife between mother and daughter. After fights with her mother, she would disappear to her room, put on some ballet music and dance in a frenzy until she fell from exhaustion into a sad heap and wept. Then curled up into a ball on the floor, she would not let anybody touch her. Though driven to despair by her demanding abusive mother, she could not feel or express her real feelings until she was utterly exhausted and then she became the Urchin. Very few people ever saw that sad and angry Urchin.

Parents who were mistreated as children have an enormous difficulty intuitively and joyfully responding to the needs of their children. Many who were mistreated as children can be good parents, but only at great cost to themselves and only with single-minded determination. When their children act like Dancers, they tend also to become Dancers - more like friends instead of parents. When their children act like Urchins, it brings out the Urchin in the parents. You find parent and child vying for attention and, like children, fighting with each other when they do not get it.

A. THE WOUNDED PILGRIM

Masks have holes for eyes. If anyone closely looks into the eyes behind the masks of Dancer and Urchin they will see the real person, the Pilgrim. Most people avoid looking into the eyes behind the mask because they might see a real person who might communicate with them on a real basis. They prefer to see the mask of either the Dancer or the Urchin. Masks are much more in tune with how they see the world themselves.

The central and integrating authentic person is the Pilgrim. She is often travelling through a wasteland of small hopes and big disappointments, but she clings tenaciously to her Blueprint. She must decide under what circumstances she will use the false faces of Dancer and Urchin as a shield or a trap. However, the more often she decides to use them, the more she depletes the knowledge of herself and the more her blueprint fades. As Pilgrim, she is usually rational and reasonable, and is able to communicate, negotiate, and compromise. The Pilgrim is struggling to develop into the person the child initially should have become. Unfortunately, the Pilgrim gets very little recognition, partly because she is not often visible and thus is not well known by others, partly because she is too honest.

Without the proper nurture or affirmation she needs, the Pilgrim begins to shrink and to submerge. Eventually, she lives as just a shadow of what she could have become while the Dancer and the Urchin become more firmly fixed. These are two alternatives and often quickly alternating ways of living.

The Pilgrim is on a journey through life, seeking to find a permanent home where she can be her real self. She carries a burden of pain, fear and anger. Carefully folded in a secret pocket is the Blueprint of what she should become. Walking silently beside her is "My Name", her indestructible self that she wants to know but cannot without God's help. Often the Pilgrim sits down in despair but something stirs her to try again. It is probably the quiet prompting of My Name and/or God's Holy Spirit.

When a person has been damaged by neglect, abuse or abortion, her Pilgrim is wounded and walks with a limp. It is hard to believe anyone would love her, but she knows she needs love. If she has not had a decent home, it is hard to think there is one anywhere. If her parents have used or misused her, it is hard to imagine a loving father. Yet, the wonder of the world and the picture from her Blueprint (which she occasionally examines) tells her there must be something better somewhere, sometime, somehow. Even when her mind tells her it is all useless, her biology prompts her to walk a little further, for in her biology is much of the Blueprint of what God intended her to be. In addition to her biological drive, somewhere ahead "someone" is faintly calling her name.

The Pilgrim hides for fear of being exposed to annihilation from attack or being rejected because of being too needy or unworthy. The false faces, to be convincing, have to be invested with some portion of the Pilgrim.

The Pilgrim is longing for an opportunity to be recognized and to develop. The Pilgrim knows that she must get rid of the Dancer and the Urchin because these impede her progress. Her Pilgrim is unable to develop because the necessary childhood experience never happened. Now that she is chronologically an adult, those building blocks never can be found. Yet the Dancer and the Urchin cling to a type of existence, whispering lies. "We can still do it. Just try harder. Get some more counseling. Nurture your inner child."

The Pilgrim is often badly wounded and very fragile. The Pilgrim is usually weary, trying to find growth, joy and peace The Pilgrim has warts or imperfections. The Pilgrim is not fully integrated. It is this wounded, weary and warty Pilgrim who maintains both the Dancer and the Urchin in an effort to protect the true Pilgrim, "My Name." Too often, the Pilgrim, in utter frustration, will despair and either commit suicide in an attempt to retain some integrity, or will become psychotic.

There are many representations of these three images in Art, Drama and History. The two faces of the earliest theatre (Tragedy and Comedy) are the Dancer and the Urchin, while the chorus of the Greek theatre represents the Pilgrim. The chorus told the story and was endowed with reason and memory. The Two-bit players Comedy (Dancer) and Tragedy (Urchin) would drop their masks at the end of the play. Similarly, counselees are enabled to discard their masks and assert their Pilgrim in the Hope Alive Program.

Cinderella sat in the ashes until magically transformed into a Princess (Dancer). But, at the stroke of midnight she would become Cinderella (Urchin) again. Both Princess and Cinderella knew this was not their true self. The Pilgrim is obviously the story teller.

Experience has shown us that the more severely a child is neglected and abused, the more clearly they can identify the Urchin and the Dancer and the less clearly they can see the Pilgrim. Abortion survivors also have great difficulty describing their Pilgrim. They have felt too guilty about existing to let their Pilgrim grow and assert herself.

Table 2.1 shows a list of the characteristics written by a young woman who was extensively damaged by neglect, abuse and abortion. The two false faces were very clear to her. It took her only three minutes to completely describe them, but it took a long time for her to discover that there was a Pilgrim, let alone describe who the Pilgrim was.

DANCER	URCHIN	PILGRIM
* Optimist • manipulative • lying * dramatizing * expectant lively • challenging • angry * smokes for effect tries to please to the point of changing self to suit others ♦ bright and clean clothes with well cut collars, high heels, and makeup adolescent • put down ♦ chocolate biscuits	• pessimistic • seductive • closed * sad and shy • expect and want rejection in order to confirm complaining ♦ trying to get without giving self • deliberate sickness for attention • playing of less attractive characteristics • childish • chocolate biscuits	• open * giving freely * joyful • confident • courageous * truthful with self and others as appropriate * accepting of self and others the appropriate clothes for the occasion, enjoys wearing but ready to improvise if need be • being realistic in expectations of health and disciplining self to come to good health and optimize chances of well being of self and others. * chocolate biscuits

Figure 2.1. Characteristics of Three Images

A. "MY NAME": THE INDESTRUCTIBLE YOU

Behind the false faces and beside the Pilgrim, there is the indestructible self for which we have given the term "My Name." The unique person who was created by God as essentially spirit is also given a unique, individual name that encompasses who he/she is.[35] That person and that name are eternal. One's real person is given a first name, usually by parents, in some type of ceremony that has great significance. It is amazing how people stick with their first names, even long after they may change their last name.

The eternal name and the core person are, for the purposes of this treatise, one and the same. Your name is who you really are, with all the faults and foibles that God uses in a transcendent manner to create the eternal characteristics of a person. This is why there will be no difficulty recognizing the person in heaven. All that has affected people in their earthly life is re-worked together with the essential spirit to form an absolutely unique and very interesting person.

When persons come to know Christ as Saviour, their names are recorded in the Book of Life from which they can never be blotted out. They are adopted into the Family of God. They are continually challenged to trust, love and obey. Even their own rebellion cannot separate them from the love of Christ[36] or change them from being a daughter or son of God and a sister or brother to Christ. A person will never know her eternal surname if she never knows Christ, for He is the only one who can absolutely protect her integrity.

The eternal name of the person embodies his eternal spirit and his human characteristics. It has profound meaning and deep significance that only a person can discover as he walks and talks with Christ. In treatment, the false faces (Urchin and Dancer) must be set aside. The PISHB must also be buried and mourned. God uses His Alternative Plan to recreate a new creature: a spiritual person who, with human characteristics, will someday get such a wonderfully new covering (body) that it will fit exactly right. Then there will be no pain or grief. What could have been, will be.

Figure 2.6 is a copy of an advertisement for a theatre presentation in Paris. The Dancer, who is faceless, can quickly take on the Urchin, whose mask she is holding. Figures 2.7 and 2.8 are a counsellee's rendition of the Dancer and Urchin.

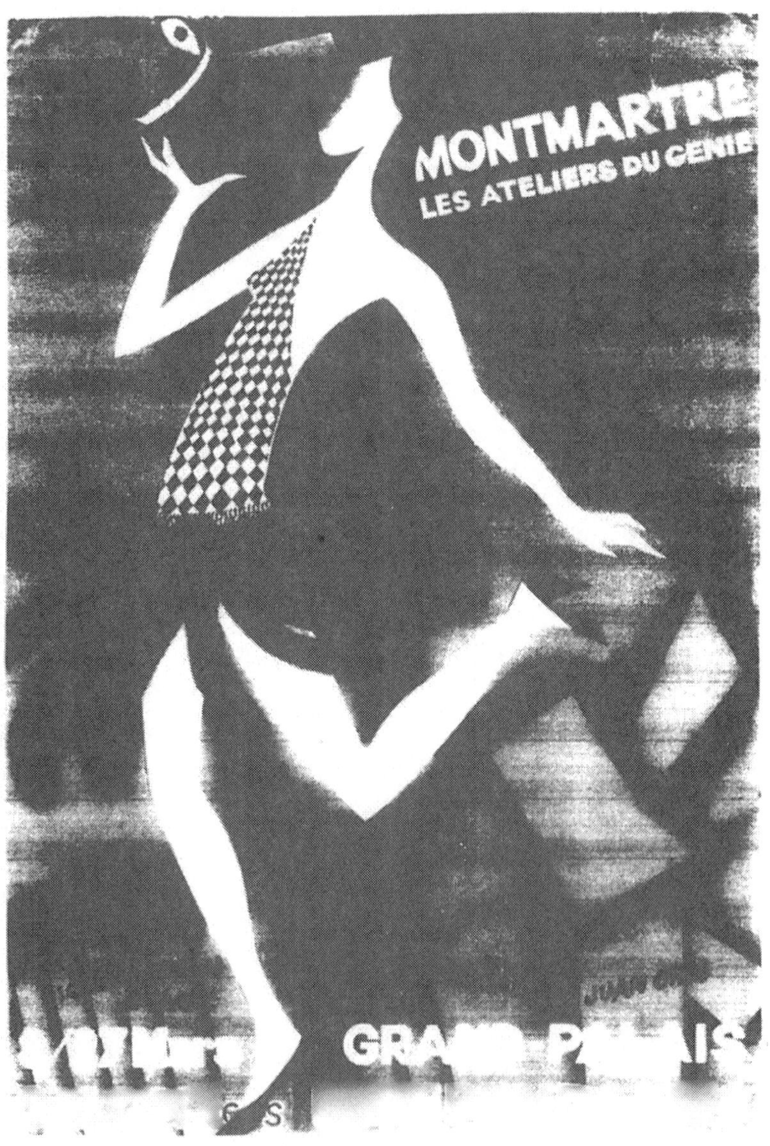

Figure 2.6 The Dancer and Urchin as portrayed in theatre

Figure 2.7 The Dancer

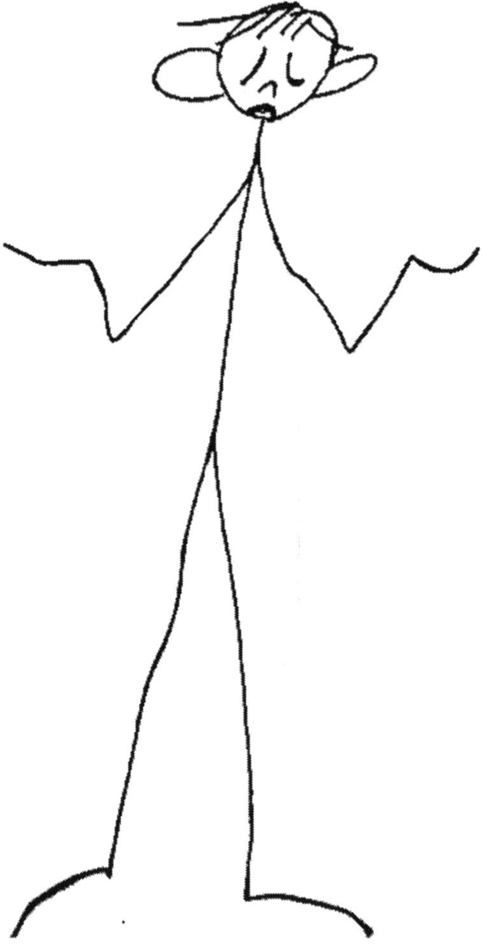

Figure 2.8 The Urchin

NOTES: 2 PSYCHOPATHOLOGY

'I Corinthians 6:3.

[2]Matthew 24:22.

'Matthew 19:19.

[J]Grossman, D. (1995). On Killing: The psychological cost of learning to kill in war and society. Little. Brown.

•'Ney, P.G. (1988). Triangles of abuse: A model of maltreatment.Child Abuse & Neglect. 12.363-373.

[6]Ney, P.G., Fung, T. & Wickett, A.R. (1993). The relationship between induced abortion and child abuse and neglect: Four studies. Pre & Peri-Natal Psychology Journal. 8(11.43-63.

'Bradley, C.F. (1984). Abortion and subsequent pregnancy. Canadian Journal of Psychiatry. 29.494- 498.

"Kumar, R. & Robinson, K. (1978). Previous induced abortion and ante-natal depression in primiparae: a preliminary report of a survey of mental health in pregnancy. Psvchol Med. 8. 711-715.

"Coleman, A.D. & Coleman, LL. (19711.Pregnancy: the psychological experience. New York: Herder and Herder.

'"Martin, H.P. (Ed.) (1976). The Abused Child. Cambridge: Ballinger Publishing.

"Ney, P.G. (1989). Child mistreatment: Possible reasons for its transgenerational transmission. Canadian Journal of Psychiatry. 34. 594-601.

[12]Ney, P.G., Fung, T. & Wickett, A.R. (1994). The effects of pregnancy loss on women's health. Journal of Social Science and Medicine. 38(91. 1193-1200.

[13]Ney, P.G. (1983). A Consideration of Abortion Survivors. Child Psychiatry and Human Development. 13(31. 168-179.

[14]Ney, P.G. & Peelers, M.A. (1995^ Abortion Survivors. Pioneer Publishing, Victoria, Canada.

[15]Peeters, M.A. (1995). Human and ethical aspects of genetic engineering. Hearth. (WinterV 8-12.

[16]Ney, P.G., Fung, T. & Wickett, A.R. (1993). Child neglect: The precursor to child abuse. Pre- and Perinatal Psychology Journal. 8(2). 95-112.

[17]Ney, P.G., Fung, T. & Wickett, A.R. (1994). The worst combinations of child abuse and neglect.Child Abuse and Neglect. 18(9). 705-714.

'"Matthew 18:7.

'"Romans 3:23.

[20]Ney, P.G. (1979). The relationship between child abortion and child abuse. Canadian Journal of Psychiatry. 24. 610-620.
[2l]Lenoski, E.F. (1976). Translating injury data into preventative health care services: Physical child abuse. Dept, of Paediatrics, University of Southern California, unpublished.
[22]Ney, P.G., Fung, T. & Wickett, A.R. (1992). Causes of child abuse and neglect. Canadian Journal of Psychiatry. 37. 401 -405.
[23]Gereb, A. Birthing Centre, Budapest Hungary. Personal communication.
“Klaus, M.H. & Kennell, J.H. (1976). Maternal-infant bonding. C.V. Mosby: St. Louis.
[25]Lindemann, E. (1944). Symptomatology and management of acute grief. American Journal of Psychiatry. 101. 141-148.
[26]Statistics Canada (1996).
[27]Ragozim, A.S. (1980). Attachment behaviour of day care children: naturalistic and laboratory observations. Child Development. 5.409-415.
“Goodman, R.A., Lie, L.A., Deitch, S.R. & Hedberg, C.M. (1986). Relationship between day care and health providers. Rev Infect Pis. 8. 669-71.
“Hardy, S.C. & Kleinman, R.E. (1994). Fat and cholesterol in the diets of infants and young children; Implications for growth, development and long-term health. Journal of Pediatrics. 125(S). 69-77.
“Berkeley, D., Humphreys, P.L. & Davidson, D. (1984). Demands made on general practice by women before and after an abortion. J R Coll Gen Pract. 34.310-315.
“Melbye, M., Wohlfart, J., Olsen, J.H. et al. (1997). Induced abortion and the risk of breast cancer. New England Journal of Medicine. 336. 127-8.
,[2]Ney, P.G. Ongoing study. Pregnancy Loss Survivors. Unpublished.
“Ney, P.G. (1988). Transgenerational Child Abuse. Child Psychiatry and Human Development, 13(3), 151-167.
“Kent, I., Greenwood, R.C. & Loeken Nicholls, W. (1978). Emotional sequelae of elective abortion.
C. Medical Journal. 20. 118-119.
“Revelations 2:17; 3:5.
“Romans 8:35.

3
A DIFFERENT APPROACH TO POST-ABORTION SYNDROME

1. THE CONTINUUM OF GRIEF

Although in this book we have used the term Post-Abortion Syndrome (PAS) as the best example of the problems we describe, it is obvious that other kinds of pregnancy losses can result in many of the same conflicts. The reason for this is that rejecting the child and consequent grief are on a continuum.

Table 3.1 shows the intersection of the welcome curve and the grief curve.

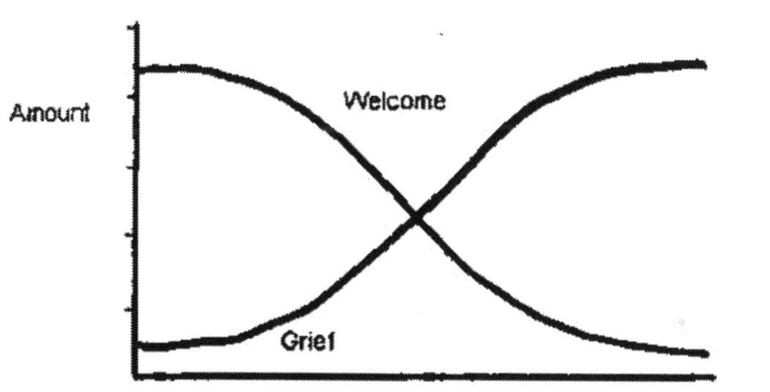

Table 3.1 The Welcome Curve / Grief Curve Intersection

Table 3.2 on the following page shows an inverse relationship between how well a child is welcomed and how much grief occurs if the unborn baby dies or is killed. Because there is a continuum of conflict and grief, we prefer to use the term Post-Pregnancy Loss Syndrome.

Welcome	Grief
As is, where is, a delight and joy.	Good parents soon realize they cannot provide everything for the child's amazing potential, so some sadness.
As is, even though handicapped, bad timing, miscarriage.	Brief, uncomplicated grieving, then growing effort to learn and
As is, but reluctantly, because of disappointment, i.e. boy, not a	Transient grief and uncomplicated adjustment
As should be, because misread the Blueprint.	More difficult adjustment and grief. Periods of post-partum blues.
As might have been, e.g. replacement child. Now disappointing.	Must mourn the loss of a previous child and learn to properly read the Blueprint of the existing child.
As want to be, i.e. a wanted child for many mixed motives.	Difficult adjustment. Often grief plus unrealistic expectations leading to
Miscarriage or stillborn. Not welcomed, but would not kill.	Major grieving and re-assessment of priorities.
Welcomed, but forced to abort because of governmental regulations, e.g. one child policy.	Major grief complicated with anger at authorities because of their power and at self because of powerlessness.
Not welcomed during pregnancy, miscarriage, SIDS, stillborn or handicapped child.	Major grief complicated by guilt and mixed motives that may take a long time to understand and may re-occur
Not welcomed, coerced to kill by threats of abandonment by partner, parents, etc.	Pathological grief complicated by fears and anger associated with those who did the coercing. Disgust with self for being so weak.
Not welcomed. Chose to kill.	Major pathological grief that recurs and often results in clinical or sub-clinical depression that may produce symptoms of nightmares, depression, etc.

Table 3.2 The Continuum of Grief

The amount of grief is equal to:

- how unwelcome the child is +
- the number of conflicts associated with the child +
- how well the child is known, i.e. the duration of the pregnancy, +
- the way in which the child died, i.e. abortion versus miscarriage.

At one end of the continuum is a child who is absolutely not welcome. The parents, without any qualms, choose to kill the child. That is not to say that a biologically based desire for that child does not exist, but it is true that some people (partly because of the current situation and attitude about abortion and unborn children and partly because of their experience of abuse and neglect) have an apparent, almost unequivocal desire to get rid of the child. They will do it in any way that is most convenient. We say "almost" unequivocal because as long as there is a biologically based attachment there is also a psychological desire for the child.

At the other end of the continuum, a child is welcomed just as he/she is, when he/she arrives and however he/she may be. The child brings delight and joy. But still, good parents realise that they are inadequate to bring up a child and allow the child to use all the potential, so he/she becomes the person God designed him/her to be. There is a certain amount of grief associated with every child. Every parent realises they are not adequate for the task. That is part of the sad, sorrowful sickness the evil one has visited on the world.

Between the two ends of the continuum there is a wide range of responses to the child. Couples who have a pregnancy when it is most inconvenient and they are struggling with other issues may wish that the child was not there. If the woman miscarries her un welcomed child, she feels a large amount of guilt. There have been instances where women have not wished the unborn child was dead. Although this child was carried to term, he died shortly thereafter due to Sudden Infant Death Syndrome or the consequences of some abnormality. Then there is much grief.

The continuum can be represented as above (Table 3.2). There is plenty of room for other possibilities not mentioned here. This is briefly described to convey the idea that there is a continuum of welcome and, consequently, a continuum of grief. Women who welcome their babies but who, under pressure of losing their home, job and the opportunity to educate their children, are forced to abort them, obviously feel a great deal of grief. Yet they are not nearly as conflicted in their grief as women who reject a child. The ability to grieve is proportional to how uncomplicated the grieving is. We believe that the most difficult grief, i.e. the most complicated grief, is the grief following the rejection of the child and a willful, callous determination to kill him or her as quickly as possible in the least expensive, most convenient way possible.

There are many other factors that make grieving difficult, one being the duration of the pregnancy. Men and women who abort a child because he/she is handicapped have difficult grief and high rates of depression.[1] Guilt and grief is also reported among couples who, having "pregnancy reduction following multiple fertilized ova implantation."[2] Obviously, the longer the pregnancy, the more the child becomes a reality in the minds of the parents. Thus, a death produces a greater sense of loss. However, we found that grief following the miscarriage of a baby was less difficult and less prolonged than grief following an abortion, even though, on average, the pregnancy of the miscarried baby was longer.

2. Unavoidable Attachment

All parents attach to all children. Everyone who loses someone he/she is attached to must grieve. Every unborn child is a person whose identity is known to the family. Therefore, any loss of an unborn child is inevitably going to result in grief. This is because the way humans were designed makes attachment necessary for the survival of the child.

Very shortly after conception, the fertilized ovum burrows into the folds of the lining of the uterus. Very quickly thereafter a placenta develops. In this way, the mother enfolds the baby and the baby attaches in a very intimate way to the mother. Between the mother's bloodstream and infant's blood stream there are only two cells. Every second, mother and child are monitoring each other's blood chemistry and emotions. There is no greater human intimacy.

What is happening biologically in the body is recorded and reinforced in the mind. Hormones produced by the placenta and the mother's hypothalamus effect the thinking of both mother and child. If she allows herself to sense these hormonal changes, her mind very quickly begins to know and welcome the baby.

In many species, the changes in the behavior and/or appearance of the pregnant female produce territorial, and sometimes aggressive, behaviors in the male. Very shortly after the goose starts laying eggs, the gander takes a protective stance not far from his mate. Woe betides any creature that intrudes on their territory. In a similar manner, the changes in a pregnant wife produce in most men a very protective attitude, i.e. "Don't you dare lay a hand on my wife, just stay clear. If you are not good to her, you get out of this house."

As the biological attachment grows and becomes more intimate, so does the psychological attachment. The idea that there is a child in the mother's mind quickly changes to "This is a specific child."

Any ambivalence about being pregnant is greatest during the first trimester. During that time the mother is just getting to know her baby. There are uncomfortable psychological, hormonal and physical changes that are not easy to adapt to. In a similar manner, the young husband has to grapple with the idea that he is becoming a father, that he must change his lifestyle, possibly get a second job and give up many of the exciting pursuits of a young man. In time, however, the attachment becomes stronger and the baby becomes more definitely an individual in the minds of both parents. It is tragic that people who support, promote and perform abortions persuade people of the "benefits" of abortion, are taking advantage of a young couple at their most vulnerable, ambivalent stage of the pregnancy, i.e. the first trimester.

Not welcoming a child does not stop the attachment from occurring. However, it does intensify the conflict. At a sub-conscious level the mother is becoming increasingly attached, both biologically and psychologically, to her child. Another part of her mind may reject the baby or she may be under considerable coercion to reject the baby. This conflict may intensify as the pregnancy continues. The conflict is best resolved by welcoming the baby.

It is important to emphasize that there is no scientific evidence to show that abortion solves any major conflict. Abortions are contraindicated in psychiatric illness. If a woman is suicidal, the best treatment is a pregnancy. She is thirty- five times less likely to commit suicide when she is pregnant then when she is not pregnant.[1] Obviously, children create and demand a future orientation. Children create hope and hope prevents people from killing themselves.

Because the attachment to an unborn baby is unavoidable, grief is inevitable when that baby dies. To become available for a subsequent baby attaching, the mother must let go of the previous infant.[4] This is something like the bonds of a carbon atom. If those bonds are all taken up it is impossible for another element to attach.

Grieving also involves recovering part of the mother and father's self that they have invested in the baby. It also means that they are not preoccupied with that child, so that they can get to know a subsequent child and read his or her blueprint clearly.

When grieving, it is vitally important that they do not communicate with the spirit of the dead baby. Scripture makes it quite clear this is forbidden partly because it is very dangerous.[5] Humans cannot discern very readily between spirits. Too often evil spirits have masqueraded as dead people even when they seem to be saying benign things. Communicating with a dead spirit also interferes with the grieving process.

To grieve the baby, the baby must first be re-humanized. It is vitally important that the baby be seen as an individual with characteristics of personality and body. However, it is very hard to re-humanize a baby if the mother and the father have themselves been dehumanized by previous child abuse, neglect or surviving their parent's pregnancy loss. Once they are able to re-humanize their baby, he or she can be welcomed into their heart, home and family. They have to be able to bond to their baby before they can let he or she go. We help people recapture their impressions of the baby and to use their imagination to touch, hold and welcome the baby before they see him or her die. Then they can more readily grieve his or her loss.

3. The Indelible Imprint

From the time of conception, the body increasingly becomes highly organized. In the early stages of a child's life, his/her brain is being wired by experiences and perceptions. By the age of one year, 75% of the wiring has been completed. During that time, the connections made between axons and cells are partly determined by the baby's emotionally charged experience. This new discovery gives greater importance to the quality of early experiences. It has become increasingly apparent that if there are traumatic experiences to a baby, these are recorded, not only in the biochemically-based memory, but also in the hard wiring of the brain. Thus, some of these early damages are untreatable. They become a defect, a disability for the rest of the person's life. That is why it is so vitally important to welcome the baby, to recognize the baby's blueprint, then hold and nurture the baby very carefully.

Babies can be taught before they are born in California, there is even a university for the pre-born. Babies can be taught music. A well-known conductor in Canada, when following the cello line of a composition he did not know, began to feel that he remembered the score for cello, even though he was quite sure he had never seen the composition before. To test himself, he said "I will write down what occurs on the next page before turning it." What he wrote was correct. Later, he checked with his mother and she confirmed that during his pre-born life she was practicing this piece for a concert. The baby was very close to the cello, heard the music and remembered, even forty-five years later.

There is no greater intimacy than between a mother and an infant. They have a moment-by-moment monitoring of each other's blood chemistry and thus the changes and emotions of each other. This intimacy creates an indelible imprint in the mind of the mother. In her memory is stored the individual characteristics of this child, even when she denies that she knew or wanted the baby.

In Hope Alive therapy, people are asked to visualize their miscarried or aborted child or sibling. It is fascinating how accurately people seem to be able to describe the sex, physical characteristics and personality - and provide a name. When this is done by couples in separate groups and they compare notes later, there is often 100% agreement. It seems that God makes families aware of a child's Blueprint. This would be in order that they can be in a better position to meet the child's needs. Unfortunately, in the hurly-burly of family life, parents and siblings are caught up in their own problems. They seldom pause long enough to examine the child's Blueprint. It is only when they pause during Hope Alive counseling and they are given an opportunity to listen carefully to their own inner thoughts and feelings that they are able to discern the child's Blueprint. Sadly for abortion children, this is always too late.

We have many stories of how accurately mothers and fathers can remember the details of their pre-born babies. Paul and Laura, from Washington, D.C., were remembering their first miscarriage. Quite independently, they wrote down the sex, personality and physical characteristics, and the name they would give to this child. Later, they found that they were in agreement on every point. How the information is conveyed to the father we cannot tell.

A woman in a group I was conducting was asked to imagine her pre-born, aborted baby. She responded with dismay and disgust, stating this was a terribly stupid exercise. She would have no part of it because there was no way she could know that child. However, once persuaded that she should try, she took two seconds and said, "He was a boy and his name was Paul."

As much as there is a memory of the baby, there is a memory of the event in which the baby died. It is not hard to understand how there is a sudden expression of extreme hormonal changes in the baby's blood as he or she anticipates being aborted. It is possible to sense and remember the baby's fear, cry, despair, pain and anguish as he or she dies. If mothers can listen to that cry they can recover their ability to sense the subtle cries within themselves. It is important that they imagine the death of the baby, partly because it is necessary to externalize the experience and to remember in order to resolve all the conflicts surrounding the baby's death.

The baby has definite memories of her experience within the mother. Since these occur before the baby has speech, they cannot be expressed in words. However, they are sensed as vague biological sensations. When the appropriate word is put to that sensation, there is a sudden recognition that, "Yes, that is what I felt." The baby's mind, like all of our minds, is an incredibly accurate black box, far more accurate and sensitive than the black box of a 747. She sensed all the experiences and, by laying down neuronal connections within the brain, has indelibly recorded that experience. The early recording may influence the way people behave for the rest of their life.

4. Why the Post-Abortion Syndrome is Real

A syndrome is usually defined as a constellation of symptoms (complaints) and signs (evidence from medical examination) that occur in patients because of some pathological process. PAS is not well recognized by physicians or counselors, partly because they have difficulty believing that an abortion is a significant event in any person's life. They can only recognize its significance only if they realize that the death of an unborn infant is important. Many people want to believe the infant is only a "fetus" or "blob of tissue" and not a person. Thus an abortion, or "termination of pregnancy" (TOP), is not supposed to affect anyone. Yet, casual or clinical observations convince many in the healing professions that the frequently damaging and often debilitating post-abortion syndrome in women is very real. There is a similar corresponding affect in men who are or were the partners, termed Post-Abortion Husband Syndrome (PAHS).

The loss of an unborn child by abortion appears to have significant impact on the parents of the mother and father (Post-Abortion Grandparent Syndrome (PAGS)). Aborting unborn children also affects the physicians who refer the parents, the abortionists, the counselors and any who assist or promote abortions (Post-Abortion Providers Syndrome (PAPS)). There is real damage done to children who were considered for a terminating of their lives and to the siblings of those who were aborted (Post-Abortion Survivor Syndrome (PASS)).

Human attachment and psychodynamics provide *a priori* argument for Post-Abortion Syndrome because there is:

A SIGNIFICANT LOSS

There is a real attachment to a real person who consciously or subconsciously exists in the minds of parents and relatives. The live biological entity in the uterus is recognizably human. Although he or she is chemically different, thus foreign or antigenic to the mother, the baby would normally be rejected immediately. But this baby must hang in there. He uses his placenta to both attach himself to the mother and protect himself from antigen antibody reactions that could destroy him.

Because the unborn baby looks and reacts as a human, we react to it as human and under normal circumstances call it a baby human, him or her, our baby. His determination to attain and maintain attachments create reciprocal hormonal and psychological desires to attach in the minds of his parents. What happens in the body is recognized and recorded in the mind. The mother's body is attaching to the baby, and the baby to her. That physical event creates a psychological attachment in the parents, whether the baby is wanted or not.

How much a woman or a man is aware of her/his attachment to the unborn child depends on many factors, particularly how well he or she was welcomed as an infant. It is easy and natural to sense and visualize their unborn child because there is a receptive mindset formed by physiological changes in both parents. From conception, there are hormonal changes that influence the mother. Changes in her stimulate subtle but important changes in her spouse if he is at all concerned and observant. Although almost every parent has strong mixed feelings about a new baby, particularly at the beginning of the pregnancy, their attachment will grow as the baby grows.

Parental ambivalence

There is considerable parental ambivalence about terminating their unborn child. There is an internal debate, if not interpersonal discussion, about the method by which his or her life is terminated. All the anxiety that surrounds being pregnant, all the turmoil that affects the decision about what to do with the baby, all the aggression that goes into destroying the developing infant, and all the pain arising from the loss, creates difficult, deep psychological conflicts that are not easily resolved.

Mourning and grief

Since they were attached to the unborn baby, eventually the parents will have to mourn the loss the abortion produced. Every human detachment requires grieving. If they do not mourn, they will begin to develop symptoms from the conflicts of partial or pathological grief. Every loss must eventually be mourned, the more ambivalent the attachment, the more difficult the mourning. Denial is not effective for very long. The usual defenses of isolation and distraction cannot last indefinitely.

Unresolved conflicts

Unresolved conflicts are debilitating. Although individuals may have a plethora of defense mechanisms to avoid feeling the distress and deal with the conflicts surrounding an abortion, these will collapse as soon as she or he becomes weak, experiences another loss, or is involved in interpersonal conflict. The intensity of the symptoms depends upon the number of previous losses, the strength of the parent's ego, the ability to rationalize or deny her or his feelings and the determination to suppress any attempts by people to bring the conflicts to light. The symptoms may appear only after a relatively minor trauma that triggers a resurgence of the conflicts engendered by abortion.

DEPRESSION

Denied grief, plus fear and angers, tends to result in an agitated depression. The type of clinical symptoms that develop will depend upon the reasons for the abortion, the duration of the pregnancy, the sensitivity of the parents to their inner workings, their defenses and what help they may receive.

AN UNRESOLVED CRISIS OF INCORPORATION

Every pregnancy results in a crisis of incorporation. To welcome and accommodate a new baby, the mother's body, mind and heart must expand. The father's image and pocketbook (and often the house) must grow. The extended family must enlarge. The church and community must be prepared to grow. If the process of incorporation is truncated by an abortion, everyone involved is left feeling empty and often with a sense of withering up.

BROKEN HORMONAL CYCLES

Much of human thought and behaviour is governed by regular cycling hormones that create a sense of beginning and ending. When cycles are completed there is a sense of well being and satisfaction. If the cycle from intercourse to pregnancy to full term delivery is truncated by an abortion, the body and the mind are harmed (e.g. breast cancer, agitation).

5. DRIVES AND EMOTIONS; TWENTY-TWO STAGES OF PROCREATION

Though instinctual drives and most emotions are organically predetermined, external pressures, and therefore some emotions that surround pregnancies, are very mixed. They fluctuate quickly and widely. The whole process of procreation is filled with ambivalence. At any time it is virtually impossible for anyone to say they are absolutely sure they want only one outcome to a pregnancy, either a dead fetus or beautiful baby. The direction taken by any individual depends on many factors: maturational changes, hormones, childhood experiences, social mores, personality attributes, personal ethics and the law of the land.

Under natural conditions the process unfolds in an orderly sequence.

Spirit, mind and body in harmony anticipate a happy, full term delivery. Yet, even under the most ideal conditions, there are many mixed feelings, motives, and conflicts that create a crisis that demands the mother and father must change. When a person has been mistreated as a child or if as children they grow up in a world where enduring life-oriented values are destroyed, this progression can be badly distorted.

The usual sequence of events that may culminate in a live baby, or a dead fetus, is described in twenty-two stages of procreation. We recognize that many women appear to make any decision about their pregnancy alone, but most women have some dialogue with their partner and their family, even if it is only in their mind. These stages are the ones that a relatively intact couple goes through. It is often quite different for a woman who is on her own. The stages are as follows:

1. Anticipation

With puberty, in each youngster there are hormonal changes that stimulate an interest in the opposite sex. "Puppy love" is deeply rooted in the desire to propagate and procreate and thereby contribute to the survival of their species. It also stems from the growing awareness of the joys of knowing and being known, friendship, intimacy and loving.

2. Yearning

As they mature, anticipation within adolescents gradually becomes a strong yearning for a mate. It is coupled with some thoughts of caution about the anticipated responsibility of a baby, and/or fear of what might take place if they did become pregnant. The yearning grows with increasing contact with the opposite sex, titillation by the media, and so-called 'sex education.' The anxieties about changing as a person and fears of being abandoned grow also.

3. Bonding

The increased yearning for a mate results in various kinds of flirtation and often a struggle arising from an almost equal desire to withstand the seduction by the opposite sex. Usually, as one person advances, the other resists. Then they exchange the initiative. Sometimes it is a bitter fight. Then there is a sudden yielding and the pair fall in love. In the proper order of mating, before becoming too enthralled, they should discuss terms of their marriage, then have a formal betrothal in front of family and witnesses, then a private marriage.[6]

Intercourse results in pair bonding. This is a strong persistent attachment that, to some extent, always takes place between sexual partners. Regardless of what the situation or who the partner, a mysterious union occurs. It takes place partly as a result of stage-specific imprinting, partly from the powerful reinforcement of endorphins and partly from the vaginal absorption of male generated hormones. To this organic union, "the two shall become one flesh," there may be added personal commitment and parental, social or religious approval, according to custom or belief.

Whether there is a ceremony or blessing, pair bonding is the basic marriage in every part of the world. The two become "one flesh" partly because the rich abundance of hormones in his seminal plasma is quickly and efficiently absorbed by her vagina during intercourse. Pair bonding may create ties that can be resented and lead to bitterness. Multiple pair bonds result in people who are tom and scattered in different directions.

4. Reconsideration

After the couple has bonded (married), there are usually thoughts of reconsideration. This often happens after the honeymoon, or when the period of sexually driven euphoria wears off. "What have I done? Am I stuck with this man or woman for life? Can this whole thing be undone?" But the bonding, plus the social pressure and personal commitment, keeps the couple together through most of life's vicissitudes. If the formal aspects of marriage are nullified, the bond still lasts - ask any divorced couple. Only in the worst marriages does intercourse, or making love, stop altogether.

5. Conception

With normal conception (fertilization of the egg then implantation), hormonal development results in profound psychological changes. The first result is usually a growing awareness. "I'm feeling quite different. I wonder if I'm pregnant?" Some people seem to be much more aware than others, "I know the day I conceived." Some have a spiritual awareness of the baby's arrival upon fertilization. Yet this awareness can be suppressed so well that some can state, "I did not realize I was pregnant until I went into labor." The vast majority of women are somewhere between, sensing to some degree that they are pregnant even before signs such as the cessation of menstruation has occurred. A woman's awareness seems to depend on her sensitivity to her body, mind and spirit. This sensitivity may be lost as a result of child abuse and neglect. (The male will notice the changes in his wife and tend to become protective.)

Intercourse results in pair bonding. This is a strong persistent attachment that, to some extent, always takes place between sexual partners. Regardless of what the situation or who the partner, a mysterious union occurs. It takes place partly as a result of stage-specific imprinting, partly from the powerful reinforce

6. Realization

With that inner realization of a pregnancy, there comes joy, doubt and fear. No one is content with only a suspicion there is a pregnancy. Yet the awesome implication of knowing there is a baby on the way makes people hesitate. "I must know, but I'm afraid to know the results of the pregnancy test." Once a pregnancy is confirmed, the couple's mixed feelings are greatly intensified. Some jump for joy. Some cringe in terror or beat themselves down with guilt. Realization always results in intense mixed feelings that fluctuate rapidly. The outcomes of the following phases are critical in determining whether the baby will be joyfully welcomed or bitterly rejected.

7. Confirmation

Once the pregnancy is confirmed, the young couple engages in an almost desperate search for approval, nurture, and support. They are afraid of being rejected for what they have done. Yet they know they cannot have and raise a child on their own. They begin by trying to guess how people who are important to them will react. They hope someone, if not everyone, will be glad and rejoice that their baby will be born.

8. Announcement

After they divulge the information they are going to have a baby, there is a predictably mixed response from their peers, parents, and the public. These responses can be categorized into three groups, but obviously there is a continuum that blurs the boundaries:

Wonderful. The most hoped for response is, "What wonderful news. When is the baby going to be born? What can I do to help?" The couple will tend to hear positive responses if they are glad of the pregnancy, and negative reactions if they think the baby is an inconvenience.

Terrible. "You had better get rid of it. Don't burden me with any of the responsibility." "If you don't get rid of it, I don't want to see you." These could be said by partners, family or friends. The closer the relationship, the more a couple will be affected.

Uncertain. "Well, I don't know. Do you think you can afford it? Maybe you should see a genetic counselor before you get too excited?" Depending on the type of response, the couple's joy, fear, or doubt is reinforced.

9. Crisis of growth and incorporation

Every pregnancy stirs deep-seated ambivalence in men and women about becoming an adult and a parent. Every young person senses he/she is now being propelled into the future faster than he/she may want. Suddenly, being carefree without a financial burden looks very good. Now they realize they must continue a career or finish their education.

Every pregnancy is a crisis. If the pregnancy is not a crisis, then the couple do not go through the necessary changes to become a parent. Becoming a parent always creates "kiros," or a series of crisis. It initiates profound changes in the young couple if each partner is prepared to deal with them. These series of crisis are:

- self perception: The crisis results in a major reorientation toward oneself and life. "I am now a mother and we are a family."
- enlargement: The two must enlarge physically and emotionally to incorporate a new little life that will live in and among them for many years to come. "My body is getting bigger" or "We need a bigger house." Just as the skin of a woman's enlarging belly resists stretching, so does the mind.
- child bonding: This requires a loosening up of parents' personal perceptions and boundaries - allowing themselves to become attached to the baby.
- maturing: They must mature, otherwise they have a limited capacity to nurture, guide, and protect the infant. "I hate to do this, but I've got to sell my motorcycle, settle down and grow up."
- hope: The infant demands the couple make provision for the future. "I just realized our city needs more parks for kids."

Thus, every pregnancy must be a crisis, otherwise the infant will be born to adults who are still children resenting his/her intrusion.

A favorable outcome to this crisis of growth and incorporation for the infant. This is determined by:

- nurturing support from friends and family.
- social and moral approval.
- a determination by all who are involved to be single-minded in supporting the couple through that pregnancy till birth and beyond, i.e. not consider having the pregnancy terminated.
- legal restraint.
- resolution of conflicts arising from childhood mistreatment.
- quality of partner support.
- outcome of previous pregnancies.

The crisis of pregnancy can produce both negative and positive changes in the parents. They are more likely to be negative if there is:

- denigration by society of the parents. "You're only a teenager" or "Anyone with your background could never be a good parent."
- diminishing the value of the child and, consequently, the value of

raising children. "Who needs another mouth to feed? The world is already overpopulated."

- unresolved personal or interpersonal conflicts. "My mother never really loved me, how can I love a baby?" or "We've already got a very strained relationship, this will make it much worse."
- unmet developmental and emotional hungers that are intensified by pregnancy, "I can't feed and look after a baby, I was never properly fed myself," or unrealistic expectations, "Maybe when I feed the baby, he'll be so happy, I will feel less alone and abandoned. When he is full and smiles with gratification, I will feel so good inside that it will be like being fed myself."
- the threat of loss of love from a partner, "Get rid of that fetus, or you'll never see me again."
- anti-life rhetoric. "It's a woman's right to choose, it's her body. Don't let men use you. It isn't a baby anyway; it's just a blob."
- materialism. "I've got to refinish this house, and then I must buy a new car. I'll have a baby after that."
- selfishness. "I need to complete my career first, then get a good job. I can't let a little brat interfere with my plans."
- lack of identity. "I don't know who I am, so how can I have baby?"
- legal approval for the termination of the pregnancy. "I guess abortions are okay because there isn't a law against them."

10. UNWELCOME ATTACHMENT AND CONFUSION

In the crisis, the couple may grow to accommodate the infant person, or stay as they are and reject him, or keep struggling. Then there is a period of considerable confusion of acceptance and attachment. It is in the crisis that the real decision to welcome or reject the baby is made. If confused, the pregnant couple tries to find information that would resolve their conflicts and help them decide what to do. In this state, they are very impressionable. The information provided by society, government pamphlets, and by the physician in particular, makes a great impact. The more comforting, the more reasonable, and the more authoritative it sounds, the more readily they will accept the information, whether it is right or wrong.

11. A FORK IN THE PATHWAY

Most of the crisis ends when the mother or couple decides to welcome the baby into their hearts and minds, body, family and home. If she/they do, the following events (11A-F) result in growth and joy. If the baby is not welcomed, she/they still must decide between the remaining options (see Nine Alternatives, section 2.9). They can make decisions at any time, but the usual events are 12-22.

A. Welcome Attachment

If the baby is welcomed, so is the increasing attachment. A mother even welcomes the growth of her breasts and belly. A mother buys maternity clothes and almost struts, protruding her belly so that others may see her and congratulate her. The father feels a growing sense of territoriality and pride in his family. He is very quick to accept accolades and good-natured jibes from his work mates, but is ferocious with intruders. Together they begin planning for the baby's arrival and think of names.

If the mother and father can accept the crisis of incorporation and if they can allow themselves to change, they can more readily welcome their baby. The better they can welcome the baby, the more secure their attachment to him. They need to welcome the baby into their heart, mind, family, home and soul as well as into their body. They give him a name and a family home. They welcome him in whatever size, shape, sex and I.Q. he might be. When they welcome the baby in Jesus name, they welcome Jesus. If they welcome Jesus, they welcome Jesus' father. If they welcome God, they welcome the resources of the universe. There is no lack of resources in God's creation.

If they welcome the baby they welcome themselves because the baby is an expression of themselves. If they reject the baby they are rejecting unwanted aspects that they projected into the baby, aspects of themselves that they hoped somehow would disappear if they abort the baby.

B. Growth and joy

There is a powerful push from biology and from the psyche and the soul to have and nurture children, yet there is a great deal of uncertainty. The uncertainty results in a variable resistance. People have to recognize that there is a resistance, learn how to overcome the resistance and mature as the baby impels them. Their growing maturity produces an increasing sense of responsibility. As parents become more aware of their responsibility they become more awe-struck by the wonder of a new life in their midst. With that awe, praise and thanksgiving will bubble forth. Even when they have grown with the impetus of the newly arrived child and every subsequent child, they will still have more opportunity and room to grow with every grandchild. As they grow, they will become more aware of the world and their place in it. This brings both joy and sorrow.

The placenta produces hormones which stimulate changes in the mother that are usually felt as good health, a sense of aliveness, and growing awareness. The mother becomes increasingly grateful for what her baby is doing to her. This is partly because as she becomes increasingly aware of the baby she becomes less preoccupied with herself. Loving others is always good for one's health. Normally the husband and wife will take prenatal classes and exercise together in anticipation of a joint experience of labor and delivery.

C. Crisis of delivery

The baby within the mother is being formed in the dark. It is a little bit like sculpting with your eyes closed or developing a film. There is always the eager, yet somewhat anxious, anticipation "what is he/she going to look like?" The prenatal bonding increases as the baby becomes more definite in its responses to the mother's emotions as it skips and kicks and somersaults. If the parents have an opportunity to see the baby on ultrasound there is a very quick bonding. No longer is the sensation from "it." There is a definite baby that they want to know the sex of and give him/her a name to.

If there has been a previous abortion, there are acute anxieties:

- fear that the baby will be abnormal.
- fear that they will not be able to handle the children.
- fear of how his/her personality will develop.
- fear he will be angry with them for aborting a sibling.
- fear the baby will not survive.

No matter how well couples are prepared, a delivery creates an additional crisis. What they have internalized now must become external. Their highest hopes and deepest fears are about to become apparent. No longer can they fantasize. They have to face a stark reality.

It is amazing that in God's alternative plan some of the best events happen with the most acute pain, i.e. the death and resurrection of Jesus, salvation for an individual, the birth of a baby, the death and home-going of family and friends.

Women who have had an abortion tend to imagine that they are being punished by having an abnormal baby. Dr. Agnes Gereb in Budapest, Hungary runs a beautiful birthing center but found that women who have had previous abortions have difficulty going through the third stage of delivery. They usually have to be immediately transported to a hospital before they will expel the baby. Part of this appears to be their fear of an abnormal baby who might need the technical care of a hospital.

Men and women who have had good nurturing as children have strong egos and flexible bodies. It is not hard for them to stretch, both psychologically and physically. There are individual anatomical and physiological differences, yet there is a remarkable connection between how lax a pelvis is and how relaxed and mature a woman is. Old obstetrical nurses used to tell me that you could tell how well the cervix will dilate by looking at the lips of a woman. If they were full and expressive it usually meant the woman could easily expel the baby through the uterine canal. As anyone knows, there is immense tension in the delivery room as the baby comes forth. That tension is broken by the cry of a healthy infant. At that point mothers laugh and fathers cry and medical staffs heave a collective sigh of relief. At this point begins a unique period of bonding to the infant. Our research has shown that mothers who have had previous abortions tend to be depressed and cannot bond as well. Women who aborted a previous baby have a diminished ability to touch, examine and breast-feed the baby.

1. Depletion

Shortly after birth, mothers feel physically and emotionally drained. Hormones that promoted their health and vigor suddenly subside. Because they are not engaging in sex, they are no longer having the estrogen, estradiol, prostaglandins and other hormones that are normally supplied by their husbands in seminal plasma.[7] Thus, it becomes vitally important that mothers in this period are well supported. For many generations mothers were allowed to stay in hospital. As this is being curtailed by demands to cut health care costs, there is an added need for home care by the family. The mother should have F.R.A.P instead of flap. The four F's - food, flowers, fanfare and family. The three R's - rest, reassurance and routine. The two A's - acceptance and affirmation. One P - prayer.

At this point, grandparents and family need to rally around, support, and nurture the mother. From ancient times, this is a time when the mother needs to be kept in bed, brought flowers, candies, well-wishes and tucked in by a nurse. The growing emphasis on short postpartum hospitalizations plummets the mother into another round of looking after that she is ill able to afford. Jews, Chinese, and many other cultures know this is a time for the mother to be given chicken soup. Nobody knows exactly why it should be chicken soup, but it may be related to nutritional needs for calcium and protein. It is amazingly cross-cultured and seems to be well appreciated, if not for its nutritional content, then for its emotional meaning.

c. Renewal

If the mother is well nurtured, supported, congratulated and blessed, she is gradually able to turn out from herself toward the baby. She sees the baby smile. That smile evokes in her a warm response as she becomes increasingly interested in and bonded to her baby. This turning from herself to the baby and its intricate needs is very good for the health of the mother. She is better able to do that if she is well supported by the husband. The husband, in turn, can better look after the needs of his wife and not feel jealous and rejected if he was well supported by family and friends.

The child soon becomes the focus of the parents' life. This means many changes in their other interests and ways of relating to each other. This calls for great patience, and the child is the parents' best coach. If they watch him carefully he will draw them out of their regrets and self-centeredness. Children produce hope. As hope grows, the family becomes increasingly interested in the world around them.

D. Nurturing and being nurtured

There is a beautiful symmetry to the family in which the mother cares for the baby and the mother is cared for by her husband and the husband by extended family and friends. This cycle is quite robust but also fragile insofar as the exigencies of employment or political necessity can too easily interrupt or distort this process. I have always felt that the way to resolve the tensions between family and state, men and women, grandparents and children, and law was to make sure everybody's focus was on the well being of the baby.

Children give as much as they get from their parents. As parents watch their children they become much more aware of the beauty of human development. Too much time is spent in attempting to train children and not nearly enough time is spent in getting to know them and their individual Blueprint. Parents soon realize that as they love children they are being loved.

Every child has some challenging characteristic that calls for great patience. Children who are handicapped can turn parents into bitter recluses or into joyful, patient, wise people - depending upon whether they will accept the joy and challenge of their particular child.

12. Conflicts when the child is not welcomed.

Now parents have the information and must make a difficult choice. They want guidance, preferably from someone they know well and can trust, but often they do not know how to ask. Those they turn to can make a very big difference. Too often they are told by friends, counselors and society that abortion is legal, without hazards and quite okay. A quiet conversation with a positive pro-lifer who points out benefits of babies, hazard of abortion and routes to ongoing support and affirmation makes all the difference. Most importantly, the baby must be welcomed and the couple supported. This is a good opportunity to ask them about their own childhood, their earlier pains, fears and confusion. If they are able to express their emotions and conflicts, feel understood and nurtured, there is a much higher probability they will change their minds and have their baby. If they see their baby healthy and active on an ultrasound scan, almost 100% will welcome their baby.

13. Decision

At some point they make a decision, sometimes too late in the pregnancy, to abort the infant. There are at least fifty-three separate factors to consider in order to make a truly rational decision about abortion. Deciding should take six months or more, but most mothers make snap, emotionally driven decisions in less than one week. There is a sense of relief at having made any kind of a decision. After the anxiety of trying to decide, the relaxation is often seen as confirmation they made the right decision. With a decision to "terminate," there comes a grim determination to "go through with it," indicated by the way they disregard any further advice. Yet, sidewalk counseling is demonstrably effective in conveying factual information so women and men change their minds. Once a decision is made, the couple hates anyone to confuse them with facts. It usually means they must again go through the agonizing process of deciding will they or will they not terminate the pregnancy with an abortion. Intuitively realizing what impact it will have, most avoid seeing their infant on ultrasound even though it is offered free of charge. If they do, 80-100% of people change their minds about having an abortion.

14. Submission

Having made a decision to seek an abortion, parents seem to readily submit to the humiliating and frequently painful process of the abortion procedure. Once they have been referred, there is sad resignation, "Now it's out of my hands. I'm beginning to hate this whole thing, but I can't upset everyone by changing my mind. Besides, they are professionals and should know what they are doing. Just hurry up and get it over with." But in most, if not all, women's minds there is a persistent hope that someone will rescue them.

15. Passivity

Having submitted themselves the couple move in dazed detachment. They arrive at the abortion clinic with a remarkably passive attitude. They often feel as if they were observing the whole process happening to someone else. Having dehumanized their baby they now allow themselves to be further dehumanized. If they submit to hate and accept the experience as hateful, they will become increasingly angry. If they accept it as punishment, they will accentuate the pain, and even hope to be injured. If they submit to it as an authority, they will weakly protest so they can blame someone else. Yet, loving sidewalk counselors with prayer and genuine concern for a woman are able to break through this barrier of detachment and help a woman see the impending tragedy. We are studying the impact of sidewalk counselors and have not yet found any deleterious consequence. Hope dies with difficulty. Even while they walk into the clinic or prostrate themselves on the operating room table, women often protest. One of the greater tragedies of the abortion procedure is telling women to "stop making such a fuss" or forcefully restraining them if they attempt to leave.

16. SHOCK

To abort a child, a person must first be dehumanized (usually through child abuse and neglect). Then she must desensitize her own feelings and natural instincts. Then she has to dehumanize the infant she is about to destroy. Once she and her partner have done this, they accept any rationalization against an inner warning or cherished morality. They block out their awareness that this is a unique individual, with a God-given right to life. The mother is purposefully unaware of many inner voices, so it is not surprising she notices little of what happens to her. The pain of the abortion shocks her into reality. It is hard to hide from what is happening when it hurts so much.

As the abortion routine begins, questions arise, "Is this really happening? Can't somebody please stop it? I can't believe what I'm doing." Similarly, women and men do not speak out or seek help in the early stages after an abortion, even though they yearn to be understood and comforted. During the abortion there is often a hyper-awareness so that many details are later remembered. Women remember the tone of voices, the colors of the room, the coldness of the furniture, etc. Coming out of an anaesthetic, the sight of blood or the crying of other women suddenly makes many women conscious of what has happened. Then they want to scream or sob with grief.

17. NUMBNESS

Following that hyper-awareness during the later stages of the abortion, there is a period when everyone who is party to the abortion feels very little of anything. They want to be left alone, but not too alone. They have a sense of being overwhelmed. As in war, having killed, it is hard for a person to believe that he/ she actually did participate in killing a baby. They certainly do not want to keep feeling all the aggression, despair, and horror that went along with the deed. To stay sane and functioning, they block out all feelings. Both men and women feel a need to talk to someone, but they know if they did, they would feel awful all over again.

18. Desperate reconstruction or distraction

After the numbness, the abortion participants make strenuous attempts to reconstruct their lives. During this time, denial, detachment, distraction, rationalization and repression are the main defense mechanisms. They often try to keep the guilt, shame, anger and fear out of their minds with "fun, fun, fun" or "work, work, work" or "sex, sex, sex."

19. Defenses crumble

The attempts to reconstruct their life fail when:

- they have too much time alone.
- some trigger in their environment sparks the memory of the abortion or its anniversary.
- they become tired and ill.
- there is a quiet conversation with a friend or relative that makes them face the reality of what they have done.
- they see a baby the same age as their own would have been.
- they again become pregnant.

Their defenses are supported by both the denial and rationalizations provided by abortion advocates. There is an understandable reaction in many women to defend themselves against the accusations of others of having killed their baby. On analyzing the data of the Abortion Recovery Canada Helpline, we discovered the calls for help most frequently occurred at 5-6 months, when the baby would have been born, and at 12 months, on the first anniversary of the abortion.

20. Clinical symptoms

When defenses crumble, people may become depressed, weary, morbid and sleepless. They experience nightmares, loss or gain of appetite, disruption of biorhythms, uncontrollable weeping, mood swings, flashes of anger, etc. Often they have psychosomatic illnesses with headaches, abdominal pain, backaches, diarrhea, etc.. They can also have psychological turmoil which is expressed in poor relationships, disinterest in sex, social withdrawal and/or excessive use of drugs and alcohol.[8] Some people become very suspicious, and some paranoid, to the point of a psychotic breakdown.

Nightmares are often the first sign that defenses are breaking down. These uncontrollable, frightening dreams often indicate the beginning of the collapse of conscious defenses. The dreams are often of blood, darkness and despair. Many hear a baby calling out in fear or pain. The contents of their dreams seem to indicate that although they may have been unconscious or unaware of what was happening to the baby while he or she was being painfully killed, their body and mind recorded her/his struggle to live.

7. Treatment and Resolution

If treatment is available, both women and men can relive the experience, understand the conflicts and reconstruct their lives after having properly mourned the loss of their child. Most frequently, people struggle without good professional help, often becoming increasingly angry and bitter. Many are drawn into quack or ineffective therapies - especially those which assure them they have no need to feel guilty or claim painless, mystical or religious quick-fixes. They often try to forget the experience and ignore their distress in excesses of work or pleasure, but every now and then the painful memories and conflicts resurface. Often they complain to physicians of head or stomach pains, indirectly seeking inner relief, only to be given another pill. Most physicians are unconcerned or ill informed. Others cannot face their culpability.

8. Reconciliation and Rehabilitation

It is impossible to properly recover from having an abortion without also reorientating one's life. One must affect reconciliation with oneself, baby, partner, family, society and God. Rehabilitation must include a repudiation of the motives that killed the baby and a determination to try one's best to prevent a similar occurrence to other unborn babies. Most of all, the underlying conflicts from childhood mistreatment must be resolved, and new ways of thinking and acting must be taught.

Although this sequence of events is described for an abortion, many of these mechanisms apply to other types of pregnancy loss. There are important reasons why abortions are more difficult to mourn.

Many women who have had miscarriages may have thought or done something they believe contributed to the loss. They might have simply wished that they were not pregnant. They may have prayed God would take the baby. When the baby dies, they feel considerable guilt. Yet, their conflicts are qualitatively different from those of a person that has deliberately considered the options, decided that the baby must die, and participated in his or her painful destruction.

Parents of stillborn infants, or those whose babies died of crib death, are also racked with guilt. But it is nothing like those parents who, after having an amniocentesis, decided that their baby was the wrong sex or had some imperfection that they did not want, and therefore he or she must be terminated. They suffer not only from having killed their helpless, possibly handicapped child, but also from the fantasies associated with having conceived what others regarded as a child not worth living. They realize they have acted out the worst kind of derogatory discrimination.

6. The Development of Conflicts Surrounding Abortion

The conflicts that develop before, during, and after an abortion can best be understood by considering the dynamic process that leads to a pregnancy or a pregnancy termination. All individuals, female and male, contemplate their life with a mixture of motives and feelings: hope and despair, love and cynicism, gratitude and bitterness, procreation or destruction. They approach the procreation of other human life with the same mixture of feelings. They all have some biologically driven hope that human life will continue with their own genetic contribution to the survival of their species.

The cycle of life begins with the mutual interest between a man and a woman that develops into intense pleasure and joy as they turn away from themselves and toward each other. There is love in the giving of themselves and the powerful drive to meet the needs of the other person as best they can.

Pregnancies may result from many reasons and usually there is a combination of reasons. Some of these reasons may be: an attempt to dispel loneliness, a sexual drive, a desire for excitement, a fear that they cannot resist advances, the insistence by one of the couple, or brute force. Sometimes pregnancy results from desperation when an individual tries hard to save a relationship. Some pregnancies result from intercourse that is mostly power and anger. Sometimes pregnancy stems from a desire to share the joy of life and wisdom hard-gained. Too often children are wanted, not welcomed. But once the ovum is fertilized and once the hormones, produced by the mother, placenta and fetus, start circulating, there is a miraculous change in attitude and behavior, especially when people do not resist these changes.

The miraculous changes in perception, outlook, emotions and consequent interpersonal relationships that accompany pregnancy mostly result from profound chemical changes in the mother's body. These changes must and always occur. Without the hormonal changes the woman would not change, and without profound changes in her, the child could not survive. The mother must be changed so that she is able to accept and bond to the child. The mother-infant bond protects the child from any episode of rage or abandonment that may occur in any parent (more frequently in some than in others). She must change because she also must spend time and energy preparing for the arrival of the child. She must be able to meet its nutritional needs, and so her own nutritional needs, and therefore tastes, change. She must be enabled to accept change to her physical shape and psychological state, figuratively and literally, to accommodate the growing child.

As there is a dependent child within the mother, so she also becomes demanding and dependent. Her somewhat helpless behavior evokes corresponding changes in the mature, concerned male who fertilized that ovum. He responds to his mate's physical and psychological changes with a greater effort to provide a home, income, and security for his family. With his mate's dependency and his outlook on himself, his mate and the world will change. Thus children are the most maturing and civilizing forces to men and women anywhere in the world and anytime in history.

The survival of the human species depends on both the healthy procreation and the optimum nurture of children. It cannot be left to chance or to human morality, desire, intelligence, culture, education, philosophy or religion. Because the underlying mechanisms that ensure survival must always work in every male-female couple, they were encoded in the genes and expressed in hormonal changes. The drives to have, hold, and then let go of the human child are best protected from environmental changes, human folly, self destructiveness, flattering philosophies and any force that seeks to destroy our species, through genetic codes. This means that, for the young, there are essentially no exceptions to the order of mating, propagating, educating, and separating. Whether the conditions are right, whether the child is welcomed, whether the parents are intelligent or irresponsible, these events and changes will always happen to some extent. To deny this to oneself or to others will only result in confusion and conflict.

7. CORE CONFLICTS AND SYMPTOMS OF POST-PREGNANCY LOSS SYNDROME (PLS)

There are always at least two sides to conflicts, whether they are interpersonal or intra psychic. There is as much time and energy put into attempting to resolve inner dilemmas as there is in settling international disputes.

These symptoms arise from various deep psychological conflicts. Serious physical or mental difficulties often begin developing during the whole chain of events leading to the abortion and intensify years after. Rather than describing the symptoms, we concentrate on the underlying conflicts because treating symptoms, whether with pills or with prayer, does little to resolve the basic problems. A symptom-treated person may feel better for a while, but they almost always relapse and then usually feel worse.

1. GRIEF

"I know I must let go and mourn my dead child, but it is so painful I don't want to start."

Because every mother and (to a lesser extent) every father is biologically attached to the infant, they are also psychologically attached. Whenever humans lose the person they are psychologically attached to, they must go through the experience of grief, but grieving is hard work. Grieving the loss of an aborted child is probably the most difficult kind of grief known to humans for the following reasons:

Not Held. To initiate grieving, an individual must see and preferably touch the body of the person they have lost. In times of war, governments tend to ship dead soldiers back to their families. Modem obstetrics has shown that mothers must be given stillborn babies. The parents examine the dead baby carefully, hold the baby to them, own the baby, caress the baby and name the baby. Then, when they bury the baby, they can properly grieve. Unfortunately it is not possible for parents to look at the tom apart body of an aborted baby. Even so, many parents have expressed a wish to see what was their baby, or at least know the baby's sex.

Contributed to death. Psychiatry has known for a long time that if an individual contributes to the death in fact or in fantasy, the grief is more difficult. If you were driving through the streets of your city late at night with your best friend at your side and suddenly, out of nowhere, came a car that crashed into you and killed your best friend, it makes a lot of difference to the grieving process if you were driving through a green light or a red light. Many people have had the experience of wishing a beloved mate suffering from cancer would hurry up and die. They cannot continue witnessing the pain and the ravage of the disease. Even if in their subconscious mind they wished for the death of that person, it is more difficult to initiate and complete the grieving.

Socially prohibited. People who have lost their pregnancy, particularly by abortion, are prohibited from expressing their grief. Much popular opinion says that abortion is a non-event, therefore one should not have to experience any grief. Although it is natural to grieve, people who were informed the abortion was a non-event begin to question their sanity when they experience a very normal phenomenon. Too often, post-abortion parents are ignored, shamed or gossiped about if they try to express grief or remorse.

Baby dehumanized. The baby has to be remembered as a baby before it can be grieved. It was dehumanized in order to abort it, now it must be dehumanized. This is difficult for people who have been dehumanized by their experience of child abuse and neglect.

Ambivalence. Abortion represents the extreme ambivalence people have toward themselves, significant others, life in general and their baby's life in particular, their baby. On the one hand, almost everyone yearns to have a child, but on the other hand many feel intense anger and fear of the responsibility. The baby is the focus of this ambivalence. It is very difficult to grieve the loss of that child without first resolving the intense ambivalence.

No social support. For all other kinds of grief, family members tend to be supportive and lenient. People are given time off work and allowed to regress. Not so with an abortion. People are supposed to carry on. No time or attention is given to them in order to talk about their grieving.

No professional help. Most physicians, specialists, social workers, clergy and counselors of all kinds are totally uninterested in helping people grieve the loss of a pregnancy, particularly an abortion. One wonders why this is. It is possible that this occurs because they are implicated in contributing to the abortion by overt or covert consent or coercion.

No explanation. Most people feel much better in struggling with deep conflicts when they understand the process - where to begin and how to end. Because people grieving a pregnancy loss are not given an explanation of what is involved, they often find it a strange experience and feel very alone.

Tight defenses. There are many readily available supports for defense mechanisms, e.g. pills for distressing feelings, inexpensive fun and games, pre-recorded rationalizations and causes of all kinds that are empowered by anger. As long as their defenses hold up, post-pregnancy loss parents seldom acknowledge the need to grieve.

No time. Grieving takes time and energy that many people who were part of the abortion never take, or think they need to take. Grief is always more difficult when there is ambivalence directed at the lost object, and when one has in any way contributed to the loss. This is partly why women who have aborted feel a greater sense of loss than those who have miscarried an infant of approximately the same maturity.

If the loss is not sufficiently mourned, the ensuing pathological grief makes people apathetic, fearful, tense, irritable or tired. Unresolved grief often leads to depression, often sub clinical. Depression can interfere with the immune system. Poorly functioning immune systems increase the chance of infections and cancer.[9] The Post-Pregnancy Loss Syndrome may have all the features of a major depression. Some severely depressed individuals become psychotic.

2. GUILT

"Deep in my heart I know I've done something very destructive, but, if I acknowledge the extent of my aggression or ignorance, / won 7 be able to live with myself"

We define guilt as the intuitive awareness that one 1) has made a mistake, 2) cannot easily, if ever, reverse the situation and 3) will soon experience uncomfortable consequences. Guilt is the awareness that we have broken a universal law or ethic, e.g. the Universal Ethic of Mutual Benefit (UEMB). If we transgress the UEMB we know we have attempted to benefit at our neighbor's expense and survive when another dies. Guilt is innate. It always occurs whenever we damage ourselves or a member of our species, alienate ourselves, or rebel against God.

Guilt can be either an emotional or legal state. Many people feel emotionally guilty when they are not guilty. Some feel they are not guilty when they are. There are many types of guilt. Some guilts associated with abortion are:

Biological. No species can survive if it destroys its own young. There is not only a restraining mechanism that prevents them aggressing or neglecting their helpless young, but every member of every species feels very bad if they destroy a youngster. This feeling is a biologically based guilt. Any individual who has injured or killed a member of their species, especially helpless young, will feel at least a biologically based guilt because they instinctively realize they have done something that undermines the survival of their species. When the unborn are destroyed, everyone, regardless of race or religion, feels a sense of having broken the instinct to propagate and preserve. "I know I am designed to pro-create and enhance my species. I feel bad when I am preventing or distorting that deep drive." This also might help explain guilt about masturbation, seductive teasing, using condoms, abortion, etc.

Existential. "I don't deserve to be alive, especially when an innocent brother or sister of mine was arbitrarily aborted." "I haven't suffered enough to be in a position to help others."

Ontological. "I haven't developed all my talents with all the opportunities I have been given. I didn't because I suspected someone would kill me just like they killed my sibling."

Spiritual. "I know I shouldn't ignore God. I must not damage anything He has created, including myself."

Familial. "I feel awful for hurting all of those who depend upon me, especially my trusting child."

Guilt. "I feel guilty for feeling guilty. I know I am forgiven, but I can't accept it. I can't forgive myself for the abortion. I know I need to."

Lack of Appreciation. "I should try to show my appreciation better and more often, especially to my parents, but it is hard when I know how they treated me in the past and pushed me into having an abortion."

Not Good Enough. "Somehow I feel the reason my parents abused me was because I was bad, and they neglected me because I wasn't good enough for their love. Maybe if I could make myself better I would be worthy of their attention, but I suspect I can never be as good in their minds as the aborted baby I am replacing."

Unacceptable Feelings/Impulses/Fantasies. "I can't control what I think and often feel. I feel guilty when I do, partly because I don't shut it off when I should. Since the abortion, I feel I can't restrain all these aggressive thoughts."

Inadequate Parent. Every parent realizes he/she is not adequate to properly raise his/her children. There is so much potential in a child that will never be realized because parents are human. They cannot avoid realizing what a child needs if they ever look into their eyes. That is why parents often avoid looking into children's eyes. Children know that we are not giving them the materials they need to build according to their blueprint.

Partner pain. Men feel terribly guilty watching their wives during or after childbirth or abortion. "Oh God. For a few moments of pleasure, I caused her all that pain. I'm ashamed of myself. I don't blame her for wanting to abort a fetus."

Lack of Loyalty. "I know I am supposed to keep the secrets in the family, especially about abortions, but I am never too sure when I am letting something slip."

Family Disharmony. "I feel guilty when my parents fight or when they threaten divorce. Maybe if I hadn't been born they wouldn't fight."

Traditional. "I can't see why we keep having to do it this way, but I feel awful when I step out of line. Our family has never talked about anything personally. They'd be shocked if I brought up my abortion."

Authoritative. "They tell me to do it one way, but I don't believe that it is the only way it can be done. I like doing it my way, but boy I sure feel awful when I do."

Jealous. Parents who were deprived themselves try so hard to give their children what they did not have. But when doing so, they feel jealous. Then they feel guilty about feeling jealous.

Social. One sex tends to make the other sex feel guilty for having characteristics of that sex, men for being assertive, women for being dependent.

Trespass. "I feel guilty if I think I am on somebody else's property, or if I flirt with another woman's husband." There is a certain biological basis for this exclusivity of partners and children, 'my husband,' 'my dad,' 'my son,' etc. Some think a baby is trespassing in their body, yet they feel few qualms about killing the trespasser.

Ignorance. "There is so much I don't know. But I know that I am not even trying to find out. I should have looked into other options before having the abortion."

Privacy. "I know that it is none of my business. I shouldn't have listened in on that conversation about her abortion."

Lack of Love. - to God, family, neighbors, and self. "I should have loved, not killed my unborn baby." "I should have supported my friend when she was pregnant."

Guardian Guilt. We feel guilty when we realize that we have not carefully kept the world God made, and cared for all the fauna and flora therein. We especially feel guardian guilt for not trying to save unborn babies from abortion.

Non-Reciprocal. "I feel I am supposed to love people as much as those who love me, but I don't."

Dishonest. "I know it is wrong to lie to myself or mislead others. I lied when I said I would commit suicide if I didn't have an abortion."

Vicarious. "When I see other people being punished, I feel I deserve to be punished for agreeing to an abortion."

If guilt is not acknowledged and properly dealt with, people tend to use a variety of maladaptive coping mechanisms. These include:

Distraction. Attempting to distract oneself from inner turmoil by excitement, work, travel, sex, impulsive buying, horror movies, novels, danger, alcohol, drugs and ultimately war. "I cannot let myself think about it, so I will continue this until I am exhausted or run out of money." When the excitement of the usual distraction wanes, people look for or demand something more thrilling. Eventually, violent movies or violent sport does not distract enough, so people get their distraction from war.

Rationalization. Employing a number of ready-made rationalizations that are often more persuading to others than to the person who is using them. "It was not a baby, besides the baby would have been unwanted. Unwanted babies are abused, everyone says so."

Self-Injury. Engaging in self-destructive or self-injurious behaviors, e.g. promiscuity. "I am worthless, so who cares if I die."

Recrimination. Incessant recriminations and self-abnegation. "I'm just no good for nobody, no how, no more."

Denial. Oft repeated denial of responsibility, e.g. "I didn't do anything wrong. Besides which, I was forced into it."

Projection. Believing others are the source of some undesirable thought or feeling, e.g. "I'm not guilty. It's you pro-lifers who try to make me feel guilty."

Reaction Formation. Trying to make themselves look and feel good by helping others, e.g. caring for old people, even attempting to save babies. Unfortunately, trying to solve the problems for others without resolving them in oneself result in contributing to or compounding the very problems these problem-solvers are ostensibly trying to resolve.

Self-Denial. Recognizing that a baby has been denied life, women and men who have been part of an abortion try hard to deny life to themselves. They make sure they do not enjoy anything, e.g. failing at exams or jobs, and keeping themselves poor.

Scapegoating. Many women who are feeling both guilty about an abortion and angry for not being supported, are looking for some male to blame. Men blame women for seducing them. Not being able to accept their contribution to the tragedy, parents must blame some innocent, powerless person, too often their own small child.

Incessant Therapy. Often, people who are trying to resolve underlying conflicts that are the result of an abortion, seek out therapists who are not interested in the effects of abortion, or who try to make post-abortion people feel not guilty.

Numbing. To keep themselves from the fears, pains and guilts following an abortion, many pressure physicians to prescribe anti-depressants or hypnotics. Others use alcohol and street drugs.

Hypochondriasis. Some post-abortion people develop an unending string of physical complaints that demand much investigation but can seldom be diagnosed or treated.

Getting tough. "I felt guilty right after the abortion, but nothing bothers me know. What is the matter with those wimps, anyhow?"

Incessant confession. "Maybe if I keep going to confession God will eventually forgive me for my abortion."

Railing at God. "Religion is stupid. Besides, if God really loved me He would have stopped me from doing it."

Opposite Sex Hating. "The bugger/bitch forced me. I am going to get even someday."

Re-enactments. Too often people recreate their unresolved tragedies to learn from them. Thus abortions are repeated.

If guilt is repressed, most people try one defense mechanism after another. If the guilt is accepted, there results a depressive effect with sadness, weeping, negative outlook and pessimistic feelings about oneself. If the guilt is seen as important, it can result in self-destructive or self-injurious behavior. Helping people deny their guilt is a disservice and will eventually be resented. Helping people express, examine and deal with their guilt through full acknowledgement and reconciliation is always eventually appreciated.

3. FEAR

"I am afraid that what I've done to my baby will be done to me. I avoid thinking about it by staying busy, drunk or angry with everyone."

It is not easy for people to kill other people. There is an instinctual restraint to aggression that keeps humans from wantonly killing each other. That is why in war, in genocide and in executions, often people are first dehumanized by mistreatment before they are killed. People are given a blindfold to help the executioner, not the victim. Without seeing the person's eyes, it is easier to believe that they are not really human and so it is easier to shoot them. It has been shown that once a person has killed another human, it is much easier for them to do so again. Civilizations have reinforced the instinctual restraint to aggression with moral and legal prohibitions.

Every species has an instinctual restraint to aggression, especially towards members of one's family. In humans, this restraint explains the low occurrences of matricide and patricide. Even though children are very provoked by cruel abuse, they seldom seek revenge and attack or kill their parents.

People who have killed a helpless, unborn child have gone against and broken through the strongest instinctual restraint to aggression known to humans. Humans have always protected their unborn, knowing that the species could not survive without doing so. When a man and a woman have consciously killed a baby, they know they can never be the same. If a person overcomes the instinctual restraint to their aggression against their young, they fear their aggression from that point on.

People who have had abortions tend to be very cautious with their emotions, particularly their anger. They also tend to project their aggression into others. For example, "I didn't do it. He made me do it." "The Doctor wanted me to agree so he could kill the baby like my parents wanted." Because they see aggression in others, they become more fearful and withdrawn. In addition, they tend to be controlling of children, frequently badgering them to "stop fighting." If they were honest, they could see that their aggression of others stimulates their aggression and they are already struggling to control their anger.

Part of the psychological conflict from abortion is a result of recognizing the extent of one's own aggressiveness. It is as if a primitive death drive to destroy the innocent little scapegoat was activated when the abortion occurred. Realizing one is capable of killing one's own innocent child is to realize the existence of one's vulnerability to coercion and a destructive force within. It is small wonder people try to deny the impact of abortion. The deep fear of one's aggression may result in a general inhibition of all assertiveness.

The fear of aggression within is often greater than the fear of aggression without. Everyone feels that they might hurt or kill under certain circumstances, and therefore try very hard to avoid those situations. Many mothers have told me, "I get so frustrated I could murder my child." Knowing the mother and her track record, I do not usually take that threat seriously. If she has lost control and injured her child, then we all take it seriously. She knows she has broken an instinctual barrier to her aggression. From that point on, the mother can no longer trust herself, and the child must struggle between trusting her and being on guard. If this is true with child abuse, it is even more true with abortion.

A woman, having broken the instinctual restraint to her aggression, will tend to avoid situations that make her angry. She tries to suppress the expression of her anger at her children, but is often telling them to be careful. The father and the mother may, from the time of the abortion onwards, generally inhibit all their assertiveness and turn into outwardly meek people, but underneath their passivity there is a high level of aggression. Fearing their own aggression and not being able to acknowledge the hateful thing that they have done, they may project their aggression into others, e.g. "Abortion is a woman's right and I'll kill anybody that tries to stop it."

4. WANTEDNESS

" *I couldn't welcome my baby because I was afraid and/or selfish, so I told myself that if I didn't want him, it was all right to get rid of him.* "

Since much of the abortion decision depends upon whether the unborn is "wanted," it brings into sharp focus the parents' own wantedness. If adults involved in abortion think about being wanted or not wanted, they soon become aware of a sense of alienation from others. This produces a sudden desire to cling, resulting in desperate dependencies that are hard to tolerate. For example, "You still like me, don't you? Please tell me you still love me." These statements are expressed many times in many ways.

If a mother and father reject their child because he or she is "unwanted," they then begin to worry about their own wantedness. If the first right of every child is to be wanted, then if this child is not wanted, he or she has no right to be. If that applies to unborn children, logically it will apply to everyone else, particularly all those who are voteless, voiceless and/or helpless. The parents,

having aborted a baby, worry about whether they are liked or wanted by others and govern their lives according to what is popular or socially correct.

Anticipating they might be rejected, they pick up on small cues of disapproval, amplify these, and may recreate for their own lives the rejection that their baby experienced.

Adults, seniors in particular, worry about what might happen when they become dependent and/or senile. This tends to make them very conservative, holding on tightly to their belongings and money. Being tight-fisted may make their children more inclined to wish euthanasia on them. The ageing parents, fearing their abortion surviving, wanted children, will be more inclined to try to maintain control over their lives. This may mean deciding when they die. Thus they seek a doctor assisted suicide.

Knowing their right to life was decided by whether they were wanted or not, children worry about whether people want or like them. They become increasingly dependant on each other for peer approval. It makes them very vulnerable to popular opinion. This dependency focused on their parents keeps them from maturing. It makes it very difficult for them to express independent actions or ideas.

5. ANGER

'I *don't know why I'm so angry, but everything irritates me. I fly into a rage for no apparent reason. I must learn to control myself, but I would like to let people know why I am so mad.* "

Anger is a common affect of post-abortion and results from a number of conflicts. Often the women, and sometimes the men, feel they have been abandoned just at that moment when they most needed support. From that point on they are angry with those who abandoned them and less trusting of everybody.

They feel cheated of being a parent, of having a beautiful child that really appreciates them, of having real meaning in life, of propagating oneself in one's progeny. The anger can be directed at governments and the medical profession which, instead of supporting an individual in their time of need, made it all too easy to kill the dependent unborn infant. The anger can be directed at oneself in verbal and physical expressions. It could be directed at physicians, especially those who did the abortion or made the referral and many others who are lacking the courage to stop the abortion.

The anger is particularly intense for those who come from deprived homes because once again they have been deprived. It is even more intense when someone has persuaded, coerced or threatened them into having an abortion when their mind and body told them they should keep the baby. Abortion highlights a person's early deprivation and can increase the desire for a baby. Having been deprived of the chance to have vicarious gratification, i.e. to enjoy the baby's enjoyment of being looked after, they hope once again to have a baby that will fulfill their needs for recognition and nurture.

A woman is most vulnerable to abandonment when she most needs the support of her partner, which is during a pregnancy. The partner himself needs to be supported. Men and women who have been neglected or abandoned during their childhood fear that this could happen again during the pregnancy. If the woman has been abandoned, she easily submits to an abortion when she is threatened by the abandonment of her partner or family. Unfortunately, if she has not resolved the abandonment issues of her childhood, she tends to pick a partner that will help her recreate the unresolved problems of her earlier tragedy. If she is abandoned during her pregnancy, she feels very angry and easily becomes bitter. She usually dumps her unsupportive boyfriend. All too often, she finds a new one much likes the old one.

The symptoms of these conflicts regarding anger are often: anger, uncontrollable episodes of rage, growing bitterness and icy isolation. Bitter women may become extreme feminists who enjoy putting down men. Men embittered by an experience of helpless anger - when his partner aborted his baby against his wishes, begin to seduce and use women with little care about the destructive consequences. Many others fear their own bitterness, knowing that it can lead to illness and even cancer, yet do not know how to resolve it. They search and often are attracted to superficial therapies or New Age religions.

The anger in PLS results from:

- being neglected or abandoned as a child.
- being deprived of the vicarious pleasure of parenting given by an appreciative infant.
- knowing they were robbed of real meaning in life.
- the loss of reflection of self in one's progeny.
- being abandoned again by parents and/or partner during pregnancy.

Teenage PLS parents realize they were rejected (by the mother, father, grandparents or society) and to be re-admitted back into the "community," they had to sacrifice their babies. Their anger is expressed toward themselves, partners and families - but also toward the physicians who referred or did the abortion. Curiously, they do not often admit to anger toward the abortionists.

"He was just doing what I asked."

The argument that a physician is only authorized to do what is good for the patient and is no longer a professional if he accedes to her choice, is usually lost on PLS parents. This anger is particularly intense in adolescent girls who come from deprived homes and encountered someone who persuaded them to have an abortion. Many of these adolescents were looking for the vicarious gratification from an appreciative infant for unmet childhood needs. The abortion highlights their sense of deprivation and increases the desire for a baby.

6. TRUNCATION OF THE HORMONAL CYCLE

"I can't really describe it, but I feel off balance, something like jet lag only much worse. Maybe I need more sleep."

Humans are biologically rhythmic. They have short and long biorhythms that sustain and change them according to the light and darkness, summer and winter and environmental exigencies. One long biorhythm is a pregnancy. When abortion artificially and abnormally truncates this biorhythm, women are left in a state of psychological and neuro-hormonal suspension. It is like being wakened from a deep sleep. It throws one's mood and one's neuro-hormones off balance.

During early pregnancy, breast cells proliferate wildly. When examined under a microscope, these cells could almost be mistaken for cancer cells due to the frequency of cell divisions. During later stages of pregnancy, these cells mature because of the influence of other hormones. If the pregnancy is truncated by an abortion, these unstable cells can more easily become cancers.[10] Although it has been claimed this study disproves an abortion cancer link, closer reading demonstrates there is a correlation and the authors agree with this reasoning.

The sudden disruption of a complicated hormonal cycle by abortion also leaves the mother feeling deflated, empty and aimless. Often women desire to return to and finish the cycle of a pregnancy and thus become promiscuous.

7. SELF WORTH

"I never did feel very good about myself. Now I feel I'm absolutely no good for anything."

At a biological level, the most valuable activity of any human is to recreate one of his/her own kind. Since it is the most driven biological activity, it is an activity that can strongly enhance the person's sense of worth. If a person was hurt during childhood, he/she has a diminished self worth that, following abortion, is damaged even further. When one has low self-esteem, he/she treats him/herself with disrespect. During a pregnancy, women with low self worth do not look after their health.

The symptoms of the above conflict expressed, as "I am no good, especially now that I have destroyed the most valuable thing I could ever create," may result in self-destructiveness. This may be overtly suicidal and risk-taking or self- injurious behavior, e.g. getting drunk or neglect.

8. RETALIATION

"Why is it only me that has to suffer? My boyfriend got off scott free and now he is dating someone else."

Sometimes PLS women have a sense of being the only victim of the abortion. Some angry PLS mothers want revenge on those who did the abortion, those who persuaded them to terminate the pregnancy or at the men who impregnated them. But, fearful of abandonment, they express their hatred indirectly.

9. ANNIVERSARY REACTIONS

"It has been six months since my abortion and I feel worse than ever." or "Suddenly I can remember every detail of my abortion one year ago."

One year after an abortion there is an intensification of many kinds of symptoms, particularly abdominal pain. Grief and anger also surface at the time the child would have been born. We analyzed data collected by Abortion Recovery Canada's Helpline, which showed the highest frequency of calls was at the time the aborted baby would have been delivered. This is strong evidence for the biorhythms of pregnancy seeking completion. Strong reactions occurring on the anniversary of the abortion may continue for many years.

10. SENSE OF INCOMPLETENESS

"I feel something is missing even though I am sure I did the right thing."

There is often a strong desire to replace the aborted child. This desire for a replacement child is mixed with an intuitive awareness that problems might arise with the next child because of difficulty attaching. The next pregnancy may be delayed but the desire to have a replacement child gnaws away in the hearts of the parents. Being a replacement child is difficult. This child must try and fulfill impossible expectations. Using a Survivor Analysis, we found that previous abortion lengthens the average interval between pregnancies and a miscarriage shortens it. It seems people are aware they must grieve before again becoming pregnant, and that grieving an abortion takes longer.

11. FEAR OF BEING A PARENT

" *I will probably never have another child. Now I realize what I have done to my baby; how could I every be a decent parent*?"

Having lost control of the destructive tendency toward a child, which resulted in abortion, both men and women fear they will abuse children and so may decide not to have any. Somehow they know the abortion has damaged their ability to understand a child's deepest yearnings (see section 2.5.c).

12. DISTRUST

"I want to be loved and supported more than ever. I do not like being alone, but who can I trust?"

Having given way to one's own destructiveness, the destructiveness that resulted in the painful death of a helpless and innocent child, people begin to distrust anyone who might be aggressive. They think they perceive aggression in others. They will try to correct in others what they will not acknowledge in themselves. "We must stop war or jail those aggressive men." Having been manipulated by someone they trusted into having an abortion, they fear that they can be manipulated again. They then fear the intentions of anyone close to them. They need someone to lean on but, having experienced lack or withdrawal of support when they needed it most, they wonder whom they can rely on.

13. LOSS OF PERSON I WAS AND THE PERSON I SHOULD HAVE BECOME (PISHB)

"How I wish I could go back to the way I was before the abortion. Now me and my life can never be the way they might have been. "

There is no possibility of regaining the innocence a man and a woman had before they procured an abortion. If they cannot mourn the loss of the PISHB, they will tend to take a cynical view of themselves and others. It is difficult to grieve the loss of a baby before they grieve the PISHB.

13. MEMORIES

"I *have forgotten so many things about my life. I don't want to remember because I am afraid something terrible may have happened to me.* "

Humans are equipped with very accurate sensors that record in the brain every aspect of their function. This is why parents' minds become increasingly aware of the baby's presence during pregnancy. The mind has also recorded the death of the baby. The mind has recorded the baby's intense fear, their unspoken cry for help, their agony and death throes. It is possible for the mind to recall that baby and visualize his/her painful death. That memory is much too disturbing and is deeply repressed. Unfortunately, the mind is not precisely selective and this tends to mean other related kinds of memories are also repressed. There is also a tendency to become more forgetful when they are repressing painful memories.

14. Disrupted sleep

"I cannot sleep because I am afraid to dream."

Many PLS parents have great trouble sleeping or are plagued by terrifying nightmares, especially when the mind's capacity to repress memory is lessened by lack of sleep, alcohol and some medications. The nightmares are often filled with blood, pain and darkness. Some believe they hear the voice of the spirit of the aborted baby. All too often their physician will prescribe a REM (dreaming sleep) suppressing hypnotic. The improved sleep is only temporary because REM dreams will start breaking through again, requiring even more hypnotics. It is not surprising so many Doctors who referred their patients for abortions seem to select REM suppressing hypnotics. Pharmaceutical manufacturers may subtly encourage freely available abortions because millions of people now require their hypnotics.

15. Unresolved crisis of enfolding and incorporation

"This is stretching me beyond my limits. It is too much. I can't change for this."

To enter the ovum, the sperm must "toughen up'' while the ovum has to "loosen up." To allow the fertilized ovum to implant in its wall, the uterus has to soften up, and then grow many times its original size. For the baby to grow, the woman's body has to expand and change shape. Her mind must also become more flexible to accept and accommodate the existence of the infant. The father must grow in strength and character to accommodate the added responsibility. If one or both of their egos are rigid and/or fragile, they feel they cannot expand without falling apart or losing themselves.

The natural crisis of pregnancy is something like the challenge of climbing an unfamiliar mountain. If they accept and overcome the challenge, they mature rapidly. If they abort the climb from fear, it is much harder to accept the same challenge in the future.

Rather than accept the crisis and grow, some couples abort their baby to protect their psychological immaturity. If they are post-abortion survivors, their core being is even more fragile. Thus they are more likely to seek an abortion and experience both PAS and PASS.

16. FRACTURED FEMININE OR MASCULINE IDENTITY

"I just don't feel very feminine anymore."

Having a child is the most feminine or masculine thing a person can do. When they reject the baby, they reject that part of their identity. As a result, men rejecting their masculine identity may tend to identify with women. They become more passive and dependent in their attitudes and behavior. Women, having rejected their feminine identity, may identify with men and become masculine in dress, attitudes and behavior. They enjoy competing with men, especially when encouraged by "affirmative action" (they can have a legitimate, unfair advantage).

A woman whose biological make-up is to love, mate, procreate and nurture has now destroyed a new life within her. After an abortion, she has difficulty believing that she is a gentle, loving and nurturing woman. She may struggle to re-establish her femininity and may become a professional caregiver. On the other hand, she may decide it is impossible to be soft and feminine ever again and so she allows herself to become hard and bitter.

The father is biologically equipped and psychologically driven to protect his pregnant mate. When he does not have the legal right or when he will not, being too afraid or selfish to protect his young and support his mate, he loses much of his masculinity. He knows she will have difficulty trusting him and he will have difficulty trusting himself.

17. PARENTING PROBLEMS

'I sense the abortion did something damaging to my ability to relate to children. My nieces don 7 seem to trust me like they used to."

Our evidence shows that women who have had abortions are more likely to have difficulty touching babies and therefore are less inclined to breast feed. They are more likely to respond to the infant's helpless cry with helplessness, anxiety and/or aggression. Post-abortion children are less well bonded and therefore more exposed to the parents' anger and neglect. Because of the resulting anxious attachment, children born after an abortion cling, and thereby cause more irritation and anxiety in the mother. She may abuse and neglect the infant, or try to avoid harming the child by placing him in a day care. Clinging children do not explore or relate as well. Their parents may have difficulty dealing with their delayed development.

18. Re-enactment of tragedy

"I still can't figure why I did it. Sure there were lots of reasons why abortion seemed best, but they don't seem very important now. Maybe the only way to really understand what was going on in my head is to get pregnant again."

Having had one abortion that resulted in conflicts that they could not resolve, a woman and her partner are now likely to re-enact the tragedy by having another abortion. They are also more likely to re-enact the tragic abuse and neglect of childhood by having an abortion. They may re-enact their mothers' abortions, trying to resolve their own abortion survivor conflicts. In revenge, they may destroy infants that their mothers would have claimed as grandchildren.

19. Psychosomatic illness

"I should know by now it is no use trying to keep quiet about deep problems. My body always lets me know something needs expressing, but I can't talk about the abortion."

The unresolved conflicts surrounding abortion may contribute to or activate anorexia and bulimia. With these, a woman may attempt to fill her empty feeling by compulsive eating or punish herself and avoid men by denying her sexual attractiveness. She allows herself to put on weight, but that worsens her damaged self-esteem. Many unresolved conflicts in men and women create muscle tensions, physiological instability and hormonal imbalances that result in aches, pain and dysfunction of all kinds. Pre-menstrual symptoms are often exaggerated by abortion.

20. Depression

"My life is going well – good job, nice apartment, new boyfriend, but I find myself feeling gloomy and suddenly crying."

Depression is defined as such extensive sorrow and anger that the person's physiology is changed. Often people are depressed, but are so well defended that they do not feel sad. There are signs and symptoms of physiological disharmony and biorhythm disruption. In its adaptive form there is, a) a slow metabolism to conserve energy and avoid entropy, b) regression in a search for caring, and c) an inward turning, in an effort to resolve psychological conflicts. The sorrow and intense conflicts from an abortion are major contributors to depression.

Depression is maladaptive because family or friends do not deal with, or care to respond to, the demands of the depressed person. The person becomes increasingly desperate and anxious, resulting in agitation. Though most depressed people withdraw, very few gain either insight or resolve their psychological conflicts by turning inward. The associated biological slowing may progressively get worse until people become vegetative. Depression can continue toward death. Although depressions are on a continuum, they should be treated with antidepressants when physiology is disrupted and people have vegetative signs. Unfortunately, treating depression with anti-depressants because there is a "chemical imbalance," without addressing the underlying conflicts, may perpetuate and exacerbate the symptoms. It is not surprising so many anti-depressants are being prescribed since the advent of freely available abortions. Many people use distraction and denial to suppress their post-abortion emotions and conflicts. It may work well enough until some other relatively minor trauma precipitates a major reaction, stemming mostly from an unresolved pregnancy loss.

21. **POOR PHYSICAL HEALTH**

'I am eating the right foods, exercising regularly and making sure I get enough recreation, but I keep getting sick."

Often depression is sub-clinical (not severe enough to impel the person to see a physician). Even mild depressions tend to suppress the immune system. A poorly functioning immune system allows a person to become sick from infections or cancers more frequently. Our research has shown significant correlation between pregnancy losses, particularly abortion, and poor physical health.[9]

22. PUNISHMENT

' I did what I though was best for everyone, but now I see nobody really benefited. I was really being selfish. I won't be surprised if I can never get pregnant again or if the baby is abnormal."

People are aware of the fact that we are tightly bound in the bundle of life and that what we do to others, we do to ourselves. They anticipate what could happen to them as a result of their destroying an unborn child. They know the consequences are inevitable and will be difficult to deal with. They try to avoid this with self-imposed punishment.

As a result of the above conflict, people are very frightened that during the next pregnancy they will be punished with an abnormal baby. They seek many reassurances and frequent tests, including ultrasound. They tend to insist that the baby be perfect. They have a greater propensity to sue obstetricians if there is anything wrong with the baby. As a consequence, there is a higher incidence of caesarean section. Since no physician will promise the baby is normal, PLS parents become even more anxious, and consequently more demanding of examinations and tests.

As a consequence of the desire to punish themselves in order to avoid the natural consequences of the abortion, PLS people tend to hurt themselves. There is an increasing rate of self-injurious behavior with PLS such as; cigarette smoking, cutting, exposing themselves to dangerous situations, or soul-destroying violent or pornographic media.

23. MATURITY

' I *know I have to grow up, but I feel so cheated of what I needed as a child. I keep hoping that if I stay as a child, somehow, someday, someone will give me what I need. If I accept this baby, / will have to become an adult. "*

Children are the most civilizing and maturing influence in the world of humanity. To reject children tends to leave couples immature, narcissistic and usually materialistic. To reject a whole generation of children leaves a nation barbaric.

It is amazing that it takes human young so long to mature. You would think that the Great Designer would have created children with intelligible language at birth. Then they could easily and accurately tell their parents what they need. Instead, they can only emit a piercing, non-descript cry that rapidly alerts parents to the fact something is wrong, but without much indication of what precisely is needed. Is it food, warmth, diaper changing or cuddling the baby needs and needs right away? The only way a parent could know, is to recognize their own "gut reaction." To be able to read a child's individual blueprint, each parent must regress and ask "what would I be trying to communicate if I screamed like that?" Thus, parents are forced to re-live aspects of their childhood and grow up with the development of each child. By re-developing in synchrony with their children, adults can mature and, to some degree, correct developmental aberrations of their first growing up. To reject an unborn baby is to reject opportunity to change and mature.

Why would God not give an infant the ability to communicate his/her needs with clear language? After all, it happens in every other species. A kitten's mew is not qualitatively different from the mother cat's meow. We expect the reason is that the infant's immaturity and lack of ability to communicate makes us go through our developmental stages again. It is an efficient way to make us mature. To understand an infant's howl, we have to remember how we felt and what we trying to communicate when we howled in the same way as infants. We have to remember and maybe express our own deepest feelings, which are without words, in order to empathize with a child's. In addition to understanding the child's needs expressed in his/her flushed face and piercing cry, we must become more sensitive to our own biology. This is more evidence that children are the most civilizing, maturing force in the world. To re-grow up as our children mature and as our children's children develop, gives us the necessity and the opportunity to become wise and mature. God earnestly wants interesting, mature friends, so I suspect that is why he designed children this way.

These twenty-four major conflicts must all be addressed and at least partially resolved. It is small wonder that weekend retreats and other quick fixes do so little to properly treat a PLS person. In an effort to provide more complete and lasting relief, we designed the Hope Alive group counseling program. Hope Alive is no panacea, but it does take these issues seriously.

8. DESPAIR FOLLOWING ABORTION

When an abortion takes place, a woman is abruptly brought face-to-face with the death of two people: the person she "should have become" and the child in her womb. In most instances she wouldn't have killed her child if she had a supportive, protective mate. This accentuates the despair that she has already been feeling. Because a mature mate could have prevented the tragedy of abortion, much of the grief-driven anger is directed at men. As much, maybe more, is directed at the parents who mistreated her as a child. The despair and anger are expressed usually in one of four forms:

1. CYNICISM

'The world is a terrible place and men are the worst part of it", or "Get what you can, but don't trust yourself to anybody", or "My parents were no good, why should I try to be a good parent?"

2. UNREALISTIC HOPE

'There is just the right person for me out there somewhere, sometime. I'll just keep searching." or "I can do it entirely on my own. I'll show the world I don't need anybody."

3. **DEPRESSION**

"I'm no good and shouldn't expect anything better than the garbage I keep getting. *If I had the guts, I would end it all right now." or "The only thing that keeps me going is my job, but I'm beginning to hate it."*

4. **ALTERNATING STATES ARE MOST COMMON**

"I gave up trying. But since he said something nice, I'll put on a happy face and try once more." Then, "Well, that was a blow out. Now I'm back to square one with my miserable self plus some more self-recriminations."

There are only two ways to deal with this deep kind of hurt—either healing or continued cynicism and wounding others. Either the woman is healed so that she does not need to go on suffering or killing, or else she will continue to harm herself and others, in particular her children.

The process outlined in this manual is not perfect or complete and for this reason we continue revising it. We are trying to get at the core conflicts. So many people who have tried some or all of the following, end up saying, "There's got to be something more, because I still hurt like heck." This is a partial list:

"Forget it." She is told by some counselor or magazine article that abortion was not important, so she should not worry about it. She tries to forget the abortion with a continual round of distractions such as trying new jobs, new clothes, and new relationships. It does not work so she seeks out more of the same advice, trying hard to be convinced she has nothing to feel guilty about.

Sublimate. "Put your anguish and anger into having another child or into a worthy cause." Eventually the woman gets tired and the whole effort seems futile.

"Get angry." Encouraging anger results in militant feminism and often serves to increase the chances of encouraging others to have an abortion. She is told to look after herself and not let anybody invade her space. The resulting loneliness only accentuates her grief and despair. Without forgiveness and reconciliation, the effects of anger soon wear off and the vicious cycle closes.

Self-punishment. By repeated confessions or self abnegation the woman is supposed to be able to forget her abortion.

Ritual cleansing. Continuously cleaning the house or washing one's hands could remove the guilt of blood. No amount of washing removes the guilt and shame but she will often keep trying because, for a moment, it decreases her anxiety

Healing the "inner child." There are modern therapies that make the woman think she can overcome her grief by healing the wounded child inside her. She soon realises that her "inner child" missed critical ingredients at critical times and now cannot develop any more than a child starved of protein can be healed of the brain damage with a protein rich diet in adulthood. Too often she will keep trying with modifications of the same hypothesis.

Grieving the loss of the aborted child. This is valuable but does not deal with the loss of the child who was herself. Without a deeper healing she senses she might abort another baby.

Psychotherapies of all sorts that give her insight but no hope. With good treatment she may gain insight into all the reasons for her destructiveness, but without a more definite purpose to life this insight only increases her sense of responsibility and therefore her guilt.

"Do it again and you'll get over it." Women try to overcome their hurt and anger by having repeated abortions. Scientific studies show that the second or third abortion is no easier for women. Generally they feel as much pain and now twice as much guilt.

Suicide. Sometimes suicide is committed slowly through a self-destructive lifestyle, and sometimes it is a quick, final act. It is the final statement of anger at life and loved ones who now must carry her unresolved conflicts and guilt.

Religious 'Band-Aids' or Rituals. "Just let go and let God heal you." "Have faith and all will be well."

New Age Beliefs. Not uncommonly, people accept the bizarre idea that babies choose their earthly life. Therefore, no one else is responsible for what happens to them.

9. NINE ALTERNATIVES

It is vitally important that pregnant women understand they are not trapped into making an impossibly difficult choice between the three limited alternatives that are usually presented; abortion, adoption or keeping the baby. The more alternatives a woman has, the better able she is to choose, and the more sound will be her decisions. There are at least nine alternatives available to pregnant women with the choice to give birth to the baby.

A. Give birth to the baby

TO HAVE AND TO KEEP

1. Single mother with help from the baby's:

a. Grandparents who care for the child as foster parents.

b. Grandparents who care for the child as theirs until it is well grown and then return him or her to the mother.

2. Single mother with help from a Christian Parenting Centre.

3. Single mother with help from the State (Welfare).

TO HAVE AND TO SHARE

4. Marry the father and develop a home.

5. Fostered with the child in a family home, i.e. both the mother and child are taken in and cared for.

6. Fostered with the child in a group home run by caring Christians. In this group home the mother may leave her child with loving staff, e.g. nuns, while she goes off to complete her education, work at a job, or find a mate. When she has settled, she can take the child and go on with her life. She has the opportunity of seeing her child every moment of the day she is not working or studying.

TO HAVE AND TO LET GO

7. Open Adoption. Choose parents before birth, have yearly reports, etc.

8. Closed Adoption. Not know the adopting parents, no ongoing contact.

B. TO KILL

9. A woman must know that there are no scientifically established benefits to abortion. She should also know that the Universal Ethic of Mutual Benefit will always apply. She cannot benefit at the expense of another human, especially her own baby.

NOTES: 3 A DIFFERENT APPROACH TO POST-ABORTION SYNDROME

[1]Dallaire, L,, Lortie, G., Des Rochers, M. et al. (1995). Parental reaction and adaptability to the prenatal diagnosis of fetal defect or genetic disease leading to pregnancy interruption. Prenatal Diagnosis. 15. 249-59.

[2]Kanhai, H.H., deHaan; M., VanZanten et al. (1994). Follow up of pregnancies, infants and families after multifetal pregnancy reduction. Fertil Steril. 62. 955-59.

[3]Rayburn, W. et. al. (1984). Drug overdose during pregnancy: An overview from a metropolitan poison control centre. Obstetrics and Gynaecology. 64. 611-614.

[4]Lewis, E. (1979). Mourning by the family after a stillbirth or neonatal death. Arch Dis Child. 54.303- 306.

[5]I Chronicles 10:13.

[6]Ney, P.G. (1974). The Law and the Essence of Love. Victoria, Canada: Pioneer Publishing.

[7]Ney, P.G. (1986). The intravaginal absorption of male generated hormones. Med Hypothesis. 20. 221-231.

[8]Drower, S.A. & Nash, E.S. (1978). Therapeutic abortion on psychiatric grounds. S Afr Med J. 54.604- 608; 51 643-647.

[9]Ney, P.G., Fung, T. & Wickett, A.R. (1994). The effects of pregnancy loss on women's health.Joumal of Social Science and Medicine. 38(9). 1193-1200.

[10]Melbye, M., Wohlfart, J., Olsen, J.H. et al. (1997). Induced abortion and the risk of breast cancer New England Journal of Medicine. 336. 127-8.

4
POST-ABORTION SURVIVOR SYNDROME

1. THE HELPLESS CRY: THE ESSENTIAL CRISIS FOR EVERYONE

Human response to the helpless cry of their young will determine if the human species survives. The helpless cry is any sound or signal that alerts a person that some creature is in distress and cannot help him/herself. The signal may be very subtle, e.g. a small hormonal change in the pregnant mother telling her she has conceived, or the quick tearful glance of her child. It can be as loud as a lion in pain. Every species has its own signals, but there is also cross species sensitivity, especially to the helpless cry of the young. Humans react to the helpless cry of puppies, kittens and lambs. Dogs, particularly bitches, respond with distress at the sound of a human infant's whimpering. The full range of subtle signals is known only to the receivers. They may be particular to a couple, family, tribe or nation. They are emitted whenever a creature, in pain, fear or need, perceives there may be someone who is better able to help them than they are themselves. The helpless cry is piercing. The physical and emotional response it elicits is anxiety or irritation.

The helpless cry creates a crisis in everyone who directly or indirectly hears it. People are unable to not respond to a baby's helpless distress. Anyone with any humanity in him or herself must react in one way or another. The helpless cry is an essential crisis. It forces a decision and consequently a change in anybody who is involved. The helpless cry insists that we exercise whatever limited freedom of choice we have. It is an accurate gauge of how human we are as individuals and how civilized we are collectively. It will determine whether we become more free, more mature and more loving or whether we become insensitive, dehumanized and hateful. The response to that cry determines the fate of the individual who cares, but also the person who receives the cry, groups and nations. It forces us to acknowledge and deal with our own helplessness. The helpless cry creates a critical balance on which the survival of the species is delicately poised and on which it depends.

The essential message of the cry is "Please help me. I cannot help myself, but I believe you can. Please hear, understand, and aid me." The type of cry is determined by who emits the cry, the quality of the signal and the situation in which it is emitted. There is the soundless cry of the unborn infant, "Please welcome, nurture and protect me." There is the exhausted cry of a starving child, with a message conveyed more eloquently by eyes than lips, "Can't you see I do not want to die? Please give me food and drink."

There is the angry cry of the abortion survivor, "I want to believe I have a right to exist that is not determined by whether I am wanted or not." There is the terrified cry of the tortured prisoner, "No more pain, please. I must keep some dignity." There is the sorrowful cry of the aged and infirm, "I don't really want to die, but I see no reason to live any longer, especially now I have been asked by my children to sign a living will."

A. WHY THE HELPLESS CRY IS CRITICAL

The most critical cry is that of the most helpless and the most innocent human, the unborn child. The moans and mute appeal of those who are dying are often more palpable and are almost as critical. Our responses to the helpless cries at the beginning and the ending of life are important for the survival of our species.

We have all been endowed with a sensitive and receptive body, mind and spirit so that we will hear a helpless cry, no matter how faint, if only we will listen. The cry of the helpless is designed to be piercing, to gain our attention whatever we are doing. That cry disturbs our equilibrium and irritates us until we respond. There are cries that are almost impossible to ignore. When a sick child cries, the mother becomes increasingly tense until she reacts one way or another. If the crying is made to stop, her tension diminishes. That state of relative relaxation strongly reinforces (i.e. strengthens) the mother's tendency to respond in the same way next time, whichever way she responded, punishing or nurturing. If she does not respond, she will feel increasingly angry, helpless or desperate to help. If the mother responds with nurture, she is not only motivated by the child's quick relaxation, but also by her pleased expression and her soft murmur, which reinforces the same action again. If she responds with avoidance, going to another room and ignoring the child's cry, the very fact that she cannot hear the pitiful sound reinforces what she has done. Ignoring the child and walking away also allows her to relax. If she responds with aggression by hitting the child and making it stop crying even momentarily, the lull in the crying allows her to relax a little. The relaxation she experienced will reinforce her aggression. It is small wonder that some parents say "Of course I hit her when she cries. It's the only thing that works." The release of her angry tension also increases the probability she will hit the child when she cries. The mother's rationalizations, e.g. "spare the rod and spoil the child," have little to do with the real reason, which is that she has been conditioned to hit.

We must hear the helpless cry. Our biology, if nothing else, knows that if we hear and respond appropriately, our species will survive. We cannot ignore the helpless cry in part because it is persistent and insistent. The young have been given enormous determination to make themselves heard. They will alter the pitch and the duration of the cry, the words or the behavior, until we respond. Yet we can rationalize our self and our species' destructive tendency to ignore an infant by saying, "She just wants attention and I already gave her what she wants." Usually, the more desperate the child the higher the pitch, and thus the more irritating the cry. Too often parents put their crying, neglected children in front of the television, hoping something will distract them. The net effect is to neglect their children even further and to expose them to violence.

If, for no other reason, we cannot ignore helpless cries because eventually they will be heard. Even if many are allowed to die or are killed, there are nearly always some survivors. They will continue the cry. The survivors of the Nazi Holocaust are determined to make sure it never happens again by reminding people of that awful tragedy. There are survivors of abortion who, more eloquently than anyone, tell humanity what a tragedy it is to kill unborn infants.

B. FACTORS DETERMINING THE NATURE OF RESPONSE

The way people choose to respond to the helpless cry is determined partly by how well their own cries of helplessness were responded to, especially when they were young and helpless. If they were well heard, understood, and nurtured it will be much easier for them to respond to others with nurturing. If they were neglected or aggressed when they cried, they will tend to neglect or assault other helpless life. In doing so, they will relive their early traumatic experience without learning. This is partly why the tragedy of mistreatment or abortion is perpetuated from one generation to another. To understand and resolve the underlying reasons for the hurt of not being heard when in distress as a child, people tend to help recreate the tragedy in adult life. They sometimes recreate abortion tragedy by finding an insensitive mate and sometimes by helping to foster demandedness in their children.

The unborn infant's soundless cry can be responded to with protection and nurture more readily if the mother is also nurtured by her mate and family. Not only must she have been nurtured as a child, but also she must be nurtured especially during a pregnancy when she could become relatively deaf to the demands of her totally helpless infant. Those who nurture her, particularly her partner, must also be supported, and he must be supported by others in widening circles. Even governments have an important supporting role to play. Fears fostered by the United Nation's frequently quoted, false statement that "the world is overpopulated," set the stage for many to conveniently ignore the helpless cries of the poor and unborn.

The individual type of response to the helpless cry is also determined by previous choices to nurture, neglect or aggress. Although we always retain some freedom to choose, the amount of freedom to choose is partly determined by how often we have consciously chosen in the past rather than let others or circumstances decide for us. Because of the powerfully reinforcing properties resulting from diminishing tension when the child stops crying, similar choices we make tend to be repeated with each crisis.

We cannot easily make a decision to assist or hinder helpless people without help. Many factors influence us. Our biology impels us to respond. It also generally guides each person to respond with nurture, because otherwise the species could not survive. Often people feel helpless when an irritable infant whines or a dying person groans. Because they feel they are not equipped to deal with the cry for help, they get angry or avoid those situations. Their tendency to ignore or become enraged is often an appeal for assistance from those who could respond with nurture, "Please, will somebody help me help this person." Hopefully they may turn to a friend or a professional, or to God. "Please, God, help me nurture this desperate and demanding person, rather than wound him or her. Help me enliven, not kill."

Since God designed our biology to sustain the species, it is very natural to respond with nurture and protection and guidance for the young, especially those most vulnerable. In some instances, the helpless state of those who are crying is sufficiently demanding or complex that people who might respond may feel inadequate and therefore angry. Mothers and fathers usually need someone to support and encourage them to respond appropriately to their young one's helpless cry with nurture and understanding. The pregnant woman's partner must be supportive. Husbands need to be supported, understood, and helped by their families, and the family by society, church and government.

The opposite could be just as true. When people have selfish motives they seek encouragement to overcome their biologically determined desire to respond with nurture. They may appeal to others for help to ignore or rationalizations; receive justification from those who are also bent on ignoring or killing, even asking Satan in rituals to assist them in their determination to be destructive.

There are no innocent bystanders in matters of life and death. We all either help or hinder, kill or cure. The crisis of a pregnancy is a crisis for everyone within hearing or seeing distance.

The choice of response to a helpless cry is critical for the person who is emitting the cry, and critical for the person who should respond, and critical for everybody who could be affected by the choice of response and for all who may be observing the event. The choice is influenced by many factors over which some people may have little control. The amount of freedom to choose may be small, but it is still there. When people are properly informed, their choice is clearly for life.

It is as if a pregnant woman is pushed by a crowd of aggressive or uncaring people to the edge of a swimming pool. Although heavily influenced, she usually makes the final choice to dive in, or push her way back through the crowd to safety. She may decide to abort the unborn child because she sees little option. Yet whatever she decides, she is exercising choice. Everyone must exercise their ability to choose no matter how small; otherwise they are not free even with wide-open choices all around them. Sadly, the so-called pro-choice people are anti-choice. Just like the serpent in the Garden of Eden, they talked of all the supposed benefits without mentioning the deep and extensive damages.

c. ESTABLISHING PATTERNS OF GROWTH OR DECAY

As individuals walk through life, they are suddenly confronted by a helpless cry. Each cry causes an unavoidable personal crisis in their lives. Now they must choose how to respond. There is now no possibility of living life as a straight, uninterrupted line. They may want to comfortably continue along the path that they were walking, but the helpless cry will invariably result in a change in their direction. The cry insists on a choice. Even those who think they can ignore they cry and pretend they never heard it, have made a choice. The cry creates a bifurcation in life's path.

On the path of life of a person who becomes pregnant, the direction of the infant and the parent intersect as soon as she is aware she is pregnant. Those paths cross each time the infant emits any helpless cry, even the silent cry heard through the hormonal changes of pregnancy. Now the mother has three choices; to nurture, neglect or to assault.

This situation is a crisis for both child and parents. The child must also make a critical decision, to cry or not to cry. What if he cries and no one responds? Intuitively he knows that if that happened his world would fall apart. What if he cries and he is attacked with a slap like the last time? Would he dare to cry again even if very lonely, cold or hungry?

If the child is nurtured, he or she grows and matures and so does his or her parent. If the child is attacked or neglected, both the parent and the infant tend

to diminish. Whichever the choice, that downward trend becomes a progressive course because each instance of their infant's cry tends to be met with a response which is similar to the last one that allowed the parents to relax. It takes enormous effort to change the direction of the path from destruction to health. The parent and infant have a parallel trajectory that must intersect each time the infant cries for help. Each intersection is a new opportunity to change the course of events. The ultimate trajectory is the sum of the direction of those intersections.

Any individual who hears the cry must respond with love or hate. As Christ pointed out, you either do good or evil - there is no intermediate response. To love is to nurture the individual according to her/his particular needs and according to the person he or she could become which are determined by their design as seen in their Blueprint. To respond with aggression or neglect or by confusing the cry or misreading it so that the response is inappropriate, is always harmful to both child and parent. If a person loves her/his child, he/she too is being loved and the parent will grow and mature. If a parent mistreats the child, the child's life is being destroyed progressively, but so is the parent's.

D. SUMMARY

The response to a helpless cry will determine what becomes of the person who is crying and the person who receives the cry. Since everyone encounters these cries, the general response of people will determine what we become collectively. As in the individual, so in society. There is a sensitive balance. The balance can be upset by a host of factors; biological, psychological, social and spiritual. The most critical cry for individual and society is that of the most helpless and the most innocent, the soundless cry of all the unborn infants in our world.

How societies respond to these cries will determine the nature of how they respond to all other helpless cries in their tribe or nation. If they become insensitive to the cry of the unborn infant, they become less sensitive to all cries of help from the poor, sick, disabled and dying, including those cries within themselves. If they respond with neglect, they neglect their own person. If they respond with aggression, particularly killing the unborn infant, they kill an important aspect of themselves. How people respond to a helpless cry will determine the nature of society. It will determine how human we are individually and how civilized we are collectively.

2. WHY CHILDREN ARE SCAPEGOATED

Wherever there are abortions and child abuse, children are both scapegoats and survivors of the ultimate discrimination. The scapegoat is any convenient person upon whom difficulties, errors and omissions of others can be displaced. Scapegoating gives guilt-ridden people a temporary sense of righteousness and justification for their indignation. Though scapegoating may temporarily suspend a sense of guilt and the subsequent need for reconciliation and forgiveness, it usually only perpetuates the underlying problems.

Scapegoating has existed through all history in all cultures. The usual scapegoats are those who are small, voiceless and voteless. The disabled, the mentally handicapped, the poor, the imprisoned and those with any kind of observable difference that makes others feel uncomfortable, have been frequently scapegoated. Unborn children are the ideal scapegoats. They are small, voiceless, innocent, and unprotected. In our generation, the unborn are the most frequent, but the least obvious, scapegoats. Each year, approximately sixty million die for the sins and omissions of their parents, grandparents and governments. The unborn are scapegoated for overpopulation, the distress of pregnancy, economic difficulties, the invasion of privacy, the time and energy required of parenting, broken relationships, hedonism, and their tendency to evoke painful, repressed memories and emotions. They have no inherent right to life and must die by abortion if they are "unwanted."

Children, particularly the unborn, are scapegoated for the adults' unresolved problems. When adults have unresolved conflicts arising from their childhood, they project them into their children, born and unborn, who then becomes the apparent cause of those problems. When adults are unable to mature, they blame children for holding them back.

Children are scapegoated for adult narcissism and frustrations. "It's your fault I cannot become the person I should be or obtain the goals that I want for myself." Children are scapegoated for the incompetence of the adult population in their efforts to solve world problems, e.g. the arms race, ozone layer depletion, etc. They are scapegoated for excessive demands on natural resources by the adult population, who will not admit to their insatiable desires and self-exploitations.

Children are scapegoated when governments divert health and educational funds to the ageing population. Evidence clearly shows there is a decreasing amount of the gross national product of western countries spent on the health and welfare of children. There are more of them living in poverty each year. Children are scapegoated by adults insisting they attend schools that gradually kill the child's curiosity and hamper his unique development. The adult population refuses to learn from children or accept their joy and spontaneity.

Children are scapegoated in custody battles and marital disputes. They are scapegoated for adult anger with physical, verbal and sexual abuse. They are scapegoated for adult self-indulgence with physical, emotional and intellectual neglect.

Our evidence indicates there is a correlation between child mistreatment and the abortion of unborn babies. One affects the other in circular causality. Women who have been mistreated as children are more likely to have an abortion. Those who have an abortion are more likely to abuse or neglect a subsequent child. The rate of child abuse and infanticide, now called "fatal child abuse", is increasing, even though it was argued that freely available abortion would get rid of unwanted babies and thus diminish abuse. Developmentally delayed and handicapped children more often have their medical treatment terminated at the expressed wishes of their guardians who say their "quality of life" does not warrant the expense. Adolescents are designated as the source of societal delinquency and are imprisoned, although anybody who studies them knows they represent the repository of many kinds of adult mistreatment and misunderstanding. The only time delinquent adolescents are treated as adult is in the court, which does not recognize their immense immaturity and confusion.

3. THE SCAPEGOAT'S RESPONSE

The general public, in its enthusiasm to punish delinquent young people, tends to forget that the vast majority of them are children who are being scapegoated. Most young offenders come from terrible backgrounds of abuse and neglect. Consequently they are easily persuaded by peers and titillated by the excitement of crime. They are also easily preyed upon by cons and pimps. More often than not, some of the worst crimes are the first crimes for these young people. Delinquents may serve lengthy prison sentences. While out of sight and sound they are out of the public mind. They are truly driven into the wilderness of a prison system, bearing the sins of a large group of people. The case described below, as others in this book, is based on real patients that I have examined and/ or treated. The identifying data has been sufficiently changed so that they cannot possibly be identified. George and Joelle illustrate how some of these young people who are charged with major offences are victims more than perpetrators.

CASE EXAMPLE: GEORGE AND JOELLE

George, 16, and his sister, Joelle, 15, were born into an alcoholic family on the south end of the southern island of New Zealand. At an early age they were apprehended by Social Welfare and placed in a series of foster homes, but finally were adopted. Although they were wanted by their adopting family, they were frequently told that they would have to leave if they did not behave themselves. George and Joelle did not feel very welcome at home but, having experienced early neglect, they tenaciously clung to their adopting parents. They tried to behave well and work hard in school. There was no major delinquent behaviour until they were both charged with first degree murder.

George awoke late one night to hear sounds he thought were that of an animal whimpering in his sister's bedroom next door. Thinking that it must be a puppy (and being very fond of animals) he went happily to investigate. He found his sister lying in her bed crooning softly to a new-born infant lying on her tummy.

Because she was rather chubby, Joelle had managed to hide the pregnancy throughout the full term. Alone, she gave birth to her firstborn in her own bedroom. She tied the cord, bathed the baby, and now lay on her back with the contented babe on her tummy. She softly sang "My little one, I'll never leave you, baby. I'll never let you go."

George's first reaction was disappointment, then fear, and then rage. "Joelle, you know we can't keep the baby. They will throw us out of the house." Though George had always protected his beloved little sister, he was so afraid of losing his home that he insisted that they get rid of the infant.

George and Joelle had a literal "tug of war" with the baby. George, being older and stronger, overcame his sister. The baby was placed in a cardboard box. As gently as possible, George wrapped the infant in some spare bedding. He then rushed out of the house, down a back alley and placed the baby on the back steps of a home several blocks away. He rang the doorbell, covered the baby as best he could and ran back home.

One month later, the police found the baby frozen stiff. Nobody had been home and the weather had turned very cold. The police had little difficulty in finding the perpetrators. They rounded them up and placed them in the youth detention, where I was asked to examine them. There were no major psychiatric problems, but they were full of guilt and fear. Curiously enough, at least while in prison they knew they had a secure home. They were both charged with murder.

A child knows she cannot survive without a caregiver and guardian; therefore she will protect her parent and scapegoat herself. She knows that her security and development depend on the guidance of a pair of parents of opposite sex. Intuitively knowing she needs two parents, she will intervene in their quarrels, directing their anger at herself and thus lessening the anger between them. Children scapegoat themselves because they know that eventually they must be heard and attended to or they will die of neglect. Even into their teens, they feel that it is better to receive parental anger than alienation.

Neglected and "wanted" children attempt to acquiesce but often fail to meet the demands of the adults. This results in increased adult anger and more scapegoating. Scapegoated children have poor self-images and easily become depressed. Parents become angry and demanding as they try to propel the child to greater efforts. When they fail, many parents become guilt-ridden for mistreating their children, so they start looking for some other scapegoat for the child's problems, often their child's peers, "Those terrible children in that awful school."

Children tend to accept the scapegoating more readily than adults. People reject scapegoating when it becomes too threatening. They blame their siblings, their friends or their teacher. Some eventually blame society and become anti-social. Some children accept the scapegoating and invite more by their irritating behavior. This may result in the eventual alienation, imprisonment or self-destruction of the adolescent, scapegoated for continuing family conflict.

The most frequent causes of scapegoating are denied, false and unresolved guilt. Terminating one's dependent offspring will result in the greatest sense of biological and psychological guilt. Attempts to avoid this guilt are made by dehumanizing the unborn. There is also an increasingly elaborate rationalization that produces a distortion in the language and logic of adults, for example, "the only reason people become guilty is because they are religious" or "because prolifers insist that blob of tissue is a child."

When rationalizing guilt is no longer effective in forestalling its impact, adults attempt to relieve their discomfort with increasingly bizarre and violent betrayal of human relationships shown in the drama that the media readily offers. With more abortions, the need for these distractions increases and so does the need for the money to pay for them, but as the birth rate declines, there will be fewer taxpayers in future. Thus, people become increasingly materialistic and narcissistic at the expense of children, and so this becomes another vicious cycle.

4. Welcomed; The Real Choice That Decides Which Child Survives

Margaret Sanger, the mother of International Planned Parenthood Federation (I.P.P.F.), proclaimed, "the first right of every child is to be wanted." Jesus Christ, God's son, stated, "Whoever welcomes a child in my name welcomes me, whoever welcomes me, welcomes my father."

Wanted or Welcomed? Is there a difference? And, if so, is it important? We believe there is a vital difference between being wanted or welcomed, a difference sufficiently important that the life or death of our species depends upon it.

A friend, Dr. Rose Shvela, survived five selections in the Nazi death camps. She lived because she was chosen to live. Another friend, Dr. Wanda Paltawska, survived Ravensbriik because she was wanted for "medical" experimentation. There are approximately sixty million unborn babies who die each year because they are unwanted and about two hundred and ten million each year whose neighbors or siblings are terminated but who are allowed to live because they are wanted. But is it a joy to be wanted and wonderful to be alive because somebody wants you? The follow up studies of the death camps found survivors had high rates of depression and suicide. Many of their psychological conflicts about being alive were also found in their children.[1 2]

It appears that many survivors do not find great pleasure and peace in life. Somehow they feel guilty that they are alive when others, just as good as they, died because of circumstances over which none of them had any control. One of their greatest difficulties is guilt, survivor guilt. Those who are alive because they were wanted also seem to have an impending sense of doom or existential anxiety. They fear that someday their lives will be snuffed out by circumstances similar to those which killed their siblings; inconvenience, imperfections, wrong sex, too many, etc. For children who are alive when their parents killed their little siblings, or chose them to live, there is a deep distrust of all parental figures. They have an anxious attachment that interferes with their ability to question their family and explore the world. This interferes with their intellectual development. It limits their freedom to know and express their thoughts or feelings more effectively than any totalitarian regime.

That simple sentence of I.P.P.F., "the first right of every child is to be wanted," is the death sentence for millions of children and threatens many millions more who become abortion survivors. Thus Planned Parenthood is creating a culture of death and disharmony. Is it any wonder we see so many young people that are apathetic, antisocial, distrustful, pessimistic about their future, and with little natural affection? The wanted survivors of abortion are deeply unhappy people who disturb those around them. They have a deleterious impact on the culture and economy of our current civilization.

It is always better to prevent then to treat. Therefore it is vitally important that all children be welcomed to the world whether they are wanted or not. Blessed are all those children who grow up in families where abortions have never been done or even considered.

We believe that it is important to discuss the abortion of siblings with a child. This makes it possible for parents to talk about anything without having to maintain pseudo secrets. This allows children to investigate everything they want to in the family and learn from the families past mistakes. This diminishes the restriction of expressing feelings and the need to maintain pseudo secrets. Disclosing and discussing with abortion survivors makes it possible for parents not to worry about an unwelcome surprise when their children find out from someone else. Parents might know something is wrong only because there is a sudden alienation in their relationship for reasons the children are afraid to talk about. From the data we have gathered, it appears that children are less affected about being abortion survivors when they are told by their parents. It is better that the children find out gradually rather than being told everything suddenly. The parents should explain more in keeping with the child's curiosity and according to their ability to understand.

The Universal Ethic of Mutual Benefit states you cannot benefit at the expense of another. If it's not also good for your neighbor, no action or acquisition is really good for you. There are no proven psychiatric, medical, or social reasons to do an abortion. The unborn child cannot benefit and the mother does not. If the mother cares for her baby, she is caring for herself.

When a child is welcomed in Christ's name he is welcomed to be (to exist), to be here (anywhere), and to become (what God intended him to be).

Wanted children are more fearful, distrustful and prone to hedonism. The wanted abortion survivor is also guilt ridden, anxious, and angry. The advantage of being an unwanted child is that he is free to be himself instead of always worrying about being good enough to stay wanted. The child who is welcomed regardless of whom he/she is or where he/she is can have a greater sense of purpose and joy in being alive.

5. PASS CONFLICTS AND SYMPTOMS

For the purposes of this book, a survivor is anyone who did not die when the chances of being killed were much higher than usual. A person is a survivor when: somebody attempts to kill them, or when the chances of them surviving are statistically low, or when they were sentenced to death and are reprieved, or when those near and dear to them were killed. There are many situations in which people become survivors, but abortion survivors are unique. The very parents who conceived them and who would normally love them, have plotted to take their life or the life of their sibling. There can be no deeper enigma or more difficult psychological conflict. "My parents considered killing me" or "My parents killed my innocent little brother" or "My parents hired someone to kill me" or "How could they? What does it all mean? Why am I alive?"

People also become survivors when:

- some evil power tries to destroy their family tribe, race or religious group, e.g. Jews, Caribs, Newfoundland natives, etc.
- there is a local or area wide disaster that wipes out large numbers of people nearby, e.g. volcanic eruption, famine, disease, plane crash, etc.

- they are assaulted with an attempt to kill them.
- they survive some other type of possible pregnancy loss or their mother died in childbirth.

All of these groups have aspects of survivor guilt but they experience much less existential anxiety, anxious attachment, self-doubt, ontological guilt and secrecy than abortion survivors. In all of these other situations their parents almost invariably attempted to protect them against the force that threatened them all. PASS (like all syndromes) is a constellation of signs and symptoms, most of which appear in the majority of the people affected by a damaging agent.

Since there are approximately 60,000,000 abortions each year, there are 150,000,000 to 200,000,000 new abortion survivors each year. These people have deep psychological and social difficulties that express themselves in pervasive inter-psychic conflicts and persistent personal problems.

It is generally accepted in medicine that the majority of distress and illness comes from conflict engendered disharmony of mind and body. Conflicts arise when humans cannot resolve competing or opposing tendencies within themselves or when they cannot accept and deal with difficult realities or when there are major discrepancies between belief and behaviour. The following is a brief summary of the conflicts and symptoms that arise as a consequence of being an abortion survivor.

SURVIVOR GUILT

"I should be grateful to be alive, but I should not have lived when others died. I experience guilt because I feel I contributed in some way to the decision to terminate them." People who feel this existential or survival guilt, because they were not aborted, believe that it is not fair that they are alive. They often feel they are not as worthy of life as those who died. People with these conflicts are always apologizing for who they are or trying to justify themselves and their existence. They feel guilty about their needs and their dependency. When they become depressed, they usually become suicidal. If they are anxious they tend to be almost hypomanic, desperately trying to please other people. Some feel haunted by the revengeful ghost of the aborted sibling.

Abortion survivors are desperately afraid of death, yet they court it all the time. They are afraid to die because they have never really lived. They are afraid to live because they feel that those who did not survive would be angry with them for enjoying life. One woman, who had survived the stillborn deaths of three male siblings, had early in her life bought herself a grave plot that she frequently visited. She expected to inhabit that plot at any moment, yet she was terrified of dying.

"Why am I alive? It may be some outside circumstances, something I did or did not do. I do not deserve to be alive. I feel guilty. I am taking up somebody else's space, time. I wish I could regress to the moment it happened and analyze what happened. I want to fuse with my mother again. "[3]

EXISTENTIAL ANXIETY

"I want to live, but I fear I am doomed." People whose mothers have considered killing them or whose parents arranged for an abortion that failed, feel that they have escaped a death sentence. They believe that the death sentence is still in effect and may be carried out at any moment. They believe that because only "chance" kept them alive, "chance" will probably kill them. If they are alive because they were "wanted," they feel that they must stay wanted or they will no longer have the right to live. It is easy to make them feel ashamed. They are continually pleasing, fawning, "dancing," and hoping for applause. Eventually this becomes so tiring or time consuming that they become rebellious. The mindless vandalism of many adolescents seems to be an expression of their anger at being dangled by the tenuous thread of "wantedness." They quickly destroy or discard gifts given to them in an effort to remove any evidence of their parents' trying to buy their love. They tend to be fearful people who expect the worst. When they are no longer able to cope with normal defense mechanisms they engage in a variety of types of self-injury. The pain or the blood is a reassurance that they are alive and not going crazy. It also seems to be a message, "Look, ye gods, I am trying to kill myself so you do not have to do it."

Because they are so uncertain about the future, abortion survivors have problems making real commitments although they readily make promises they know they will not be able to keep.

" I do not want others to change their minds about me. It is important to be well perceived by others. Therefore, I will make a commitment even if I know that I will not be able to keep it. A commitment is a real burden. "

They tend to procrastinate. *" I cannot solve anything, so I procrastinate until eventually the other person breaks the commitment. I feel guilty about procrastinating, but I cannot stop myself. "*

"I want to do what others want, so I wait and see what they decide."

"I prefer that somebody else decides for me. I had no right to exist. I am still a child trying to find a place in this world, like a little lamb, walking along side my mother trying to find a tit, a child

wandering around, carrying the weigh of something on my shoulders. I had so many unanswered questions which I could not ask because nobody would answer and besides which I could not even formulate them. All my life I have been running, running away from death, no from something worse than death."

" *I suffered from a sense of impending doom which made me decide not to have children. Not having children made me suffer from biological guilt, because I knew I should have had children. I procrastinate then I feel guilty. I feel spiritual guilt. I am just caught up in a web of guilt. Everything in my life is guilt."*

ANXIOUS ATTACHMENT

"I want to be close to my parents, but it does not feel right. The closer I get the worse I feel." A mother who has had abortions refused to hear the helpless cry of her unborn child. Subsequently, she has difficulty hearing her own helpless cry and those of others. She often responds with feelings of helplessness, anxiety or rage to the other children's cries. Clinical observations show those children born after an abortion often cry without any obvious cause for several months after their birth. Mothers testify that they have great difficulty in responding to their child's helpless cry.

"My son was born two years after my abortion. He screamed day and night for two years. He needed constant body contact. No doctor knew what was wrong with him."

The anxious, ambivalent and tenuous attachment between parent and surviving child arises from three sources:

- Women who have had an abortion have difficulty in bonding to, touching and breast-feeding subsequent children. The mothers and fathers realize these basic difficulties and attempt to compensate with extra effort, doing it "by the book" and buying their child's love with gifts.
- The abortion surviving child is suspicious of parents and their expression of love. They think, "How could you, my father or mother, be a loving parent and ...kill one of my siblings ...consider killing me ...have tried to kill me." "I do not trust you and I do not trust the anger that I feel toward you as a consequence. I must hide my anger or it will destroy us both."
- Abortion surviving infants often emit abnormal, anxious cries when their mother is out of sight. The toddlers cling persistently to the skirts of

> their mothers. One mother attested to the fact that her new-born child had screamed for two years without interruption and had needed continuous body contact during that period. This evokes in the mother very ambivalent feelings. She will try to push the child away, increasing his anxiety and his tendency to cling. Thus, a vicious cycle is initiated. Older children either are never at home or they hang around the house. Either way, this is detrimental to their development. Children need to feel confident to explore their environment and test their observations in order to develop their intellect.

As adults, abortion survivors with anxious attachment are continually asking each other, "Do you still love me?" They often say:

"I needed other people around me otherwise I felt that I did not exist. I was afraid in any silence there was nobody around me."

"How could you, my parents, be loving to me and yet have killed one of my siblings or considered killing me or have tried to kill me? I must be on my guard. They might do something with me. I do not trust you and I do not trust the anger I feel towards you. I want to kill you. Yet I need you. It is safer if I can see and observe you all the time. I will do that until I am old enough to run away."

'I l*iked to be alone, my mother was dangerous. I had to be good. I could not upset my mother.* "

Because they have no stable attachments, abortion survivors experience multiple fears: fears of death, of darkness, of a "boogie man" that will take them away, sometimes of fire or of knives. They think that the arbitrary event that took their sibling's life will eventually get to them too. As they live in fear of being terminated, they do not make plans for their future. Anticipating the worst, they try desperately to remain in control of things.

"I often had terrible dreams, of great loaves of bread falling on me and engulfing me. When I told my mother she did not reassure me, she was even more frightened than I was. 1 did not understand why. My mother always told me that I was her favored child, and I always thought to myself, "Why does she always have to insist that she loves me?"

"My life stopped when I was ten. My mother came and woke me up one morning at six. She said, "Do you want a little sister? We would not have time for you anymore and we would not be able to go on holidays with you." 1

answered what she wanted to hear. I was half asleep, she was in a hurry, my father was in the car waiting to drive her to the hospital for her abortion. She left and my life stopped."

"My mother was always distant, busy with a hundred things. She never hugged me. On the other hand, she was so anxious that I should not get hurt. I never understood this distant but excessive control over me."

PSEUDO-SECRET COLLUSION

"I desperately need to know what you did to my unborn brother or sister, but I am afraid to ask." This conflict arises from two major sources:

- A child is afraid that what he or she will find out is too awful. In knowing the truth about his/her parents having killed his/her sibling or wanting to kill him/her, the child would despair. The child may refuse to eat, wondering whether he/she could ever know for sure that when they feed him/her they are not trying to poison him/her.

  " I *was afraid of what I might discover. The worst thing would have been to discover that I was not loved even though they told me I was.* "
- The abortion survivor knows that were he/she to bring up the forbidden subject, it might destroy his/her parents or their relationship, and therefore the family upon which the child depends.

Children caught up in conflicts about secrets tend to be very careful about what they hear. They avoid the normal child's curious "eavesdropping." They are careful about what they see and avoid poking into family correspondence or archives. They are careful about what they say and will not ask things that normally tweak a child's interest. Their own anxiety and anger arising from a subconscious awareness of the pseudo-secret must be hidden. Therefore, they lend to repress all of their feelings. Children cut off the questioning of normal intellectual development. They must limit the expression of their speech and the expression of their emotions because they could be too dangerous. They become fearful children who do not express spontaneous joy and enthusiasm. As growing adolescents and adults, they tend to trust the media because they are confident it will lie to them and help support their and their parents' pseudo-secrets, e.g. "abortion does not kill a real child.'' They are very curious in spite of their determination not to know what really went on in their family. They have a voracious appetite for newspapers, magazines, novels, television, and almost any media that will provide them a certain amount of excitement but never reveal the real truth. The news creates a modicum of tense anticipation from expecting a disaster. They do not like to worry, but they feel worse when the tension stops. This vicious cycle is a major contribution to media addiction.

DISTRUST

"I want a committed relationship with people but I do not know who I can trust." Abortion survivors do not trust men because men, particularly their fathers, could have made a much greater effort to protect them from their mother's compelling interest in abortion. They may not trust men because many men have pressured women into abortions. Survivors later tend to look upon their fathers, as "wimps" who were cowardly and could not provide a model for courage and tenacity in the face of destructive forces. It is obvious to the abortion survivors that males have a seldom mentioned self-interest in having ready access to abortion. Survivors do not trust women because of their murderous or fearful selfishness. They cannot believe their expressions of affection are genuine. After all, they have killed a helpless sibling, often declaring, "It is best for everyone." Survivors do not trust authority and cannot recognize leadership. Politicians and judges appear to cave into popular demands for abortion.

Abortion survivors become skeptical children who do not appreciate efforts made on their behalf and will not help around the house. As adults, they have great difficulty with committed relationships, but keep searching for someone that they can really trust. They experience a string of broken relationships, which only further convinces them they may as well be hedonistic. They tend to be narcissistic and cynical. Instead of seeing sex as sacred, they use it for self-gratification.

Abortion survivors have a strong but repressed fear of their parents. They realize their parents not only had the power of life and death in their hands, but their parents were not inhibited or hindered in exercising that power over them and their siblings. Besides the fear of being abandoned, children most fear being killed and eaten by their parents. An abortion is basically that primitive. These are some statements from a number of abortion survivors.

'I *felt my mother was dangerous. I had to be good and not upset her. She had so many phobias, especially with knives. She was afraid of being left alone with old people or with babies. When I was nine years old she became pregnant and I was ill for nine months. I was so anxious I thought I was going mad. I could not eat anymore and was in a state of constant anxiety. I felt I was floating, I withdrew into an imaginary world of books. I felt like a dummy, not alive. I showed no interest in anything. "*

"After her abortion, my mother slept with a butcher knife under her pillow. She scared me but I did not want to hurt her."

"I always feared my grandmother and did not like to be around her. She seemed strange. It was only much later that I found out that she had had an abortion."

"I had an acute panic attack in hospital one day when I was twelve. I had relapsed leukemia and had had a bone marrow transplant. My mother told me she was going for prenatal diagnosis to make sure the baby was all right. I knew what would happen if the baby wasn't. One night I thought perhaps if I did not get better the doctors would get rid of me too. I never trusted my mother after that. In actual fact I never trusted anybody after that."

"I never knew where I could turn for help, to whom could I talk? I didn't trust my parents, they aborted two of my siblings. Luckily I had a good girlfriend with whom I was able to talk."

"During my psychoanalysis, I underwent a regression to the womb experience. I found myself on the floor, in fetal position, begging my mother to let me live. I promised her that I would be a good girl. I spent my entire life trying to justify my existence and being good to my mother. I still fear her, although she is 86.1 never had any interest in anything except in books, because they allowed me to escape to an imaginary world."

In summary, abortion survivors distrust:

- God because He did not intervene to protect their siblings. Now they are angry at Him and do not want to get to know Him.

- Parents, because selfishly they aborted one of his/her siblings (even while saying they were doing it out of love).
- Government. The government supposedly is there to protect those who are most vulnerable, but, in most Western countries, it actually pays for the death of unborn babies.
- Self. In their fantasies, many children feel they have contributed in some way, even by being bad or demanding children. They do not trust themselves and they do not want to become parents. If they do become parents, they distrust their parenting ability and intend to quickly put their children in the care of somebody else, e.g. day-care.
- Important concepts. (Love, Parent, etc.) Knowing that their siblings were not protected but aborted, often out of "love," children do not trust the idea of love, parent, etc.

APATHY

"Abortion is terrible. Somebody should do something to stop it, but what can an individual do? Everybody seems to think it is a good thing. Maybe they are right." Abortion survivors, finding that there was nothing they could have done to protect their unborn siblings or neighbors, feel very passive. They have attempted to help others in their community, only to no avail. Finding the forces of abortion just too powerful, they become increasingly apathetic about the destructive force of abortion, and may even begin to rationalize to themselves or to the rest of the world that it is a good thing, if not a thing that is too powerful to stop because this is what people want.

VICARIOUS GUILT

Many abortion survivors, intuitively realizing their mothers are suffering the guilt of an abortion, and, wanting to protect their parents because they know they need them, will take the parents' guilt upon themselves. They then begin punishing themselves or flirting with death.

One woman remembers how, at the age of four, she began having no interest in her dolls and wanted a real baby. She painted male genitalia on one of her dolls, took it down to the end of the garden, and buried it. Many years later, she realized that was about the time when her mother had an abortion. She also realized how desperately guilty she felt for her mother's abortion and how for a great deal of her life she has tried to understand and deal with that guilt.

POOR RELATIONSHIPS

"My parents did not care for me. Why should I care about them? My friends understand me. They know how angry I am. Maybe the only thing that makes sense anymore is being violent." Abortion survivors have difficulty trusting and attaching to their parents. Their parents have difficulty bonding to them. Because of this combined effect, there is an anxious attachment that shows in the child's desperate clinging at some times, and at other times wanting to avoid the parent altogether. Because of the poor attachment, children do not feel safe to explore their environment. Children learn so much by exploring their environment. The lack of interacting with their environment limits the development of their intelligence.

The development of intelligence is also interfered with by:

- Having to be careful about asking questions.
- difficulty expressing thoughts and feelings for fear of upsetting guilt-ridden parents.
- not wanting to use such concepts as love, family, fatherhood in their communication or exploration.

Because of the poor relationships with their parents, they have difficulty relating to others, except in a few superficial ways. They are attracted to peers who are also as angry as they are, and are careless with their safety. They have difficulty falling in love, making commitments or having intimate sexual relationships.

A combination of their deep anger, plus their distrust, plus their guilt, often results them in being careless with their own lives and randomly violent. Because of their interest in peer approval, they often become involved in gang violence.

POOR HEALTH

"I have never liked my body. There has always been a struggle with my weight and I really don't trust any of my appetites." Because of their poor bonding and the diminished chance of being touched by their mother, they often do not feel good about their own body. When people feel awkward in their own body, there is not as good psycho-physiological integration. They tend not to have easy control of their body functions and often struggle for respiratory, bowel, menstrual and weight control.

People with PASS frequently feel imprisoned in their body. Their body was possibly considered for an abortion, and therefore they feel vulnerable in that body. Many of them would not be alive if their body did not persist in sustaining them.

Abortion survivors who have not been well held and caressed by their mother feel an ongoing need for touch. Because of their loneliness, there is an increased propensity towards promiscuity.

WORTH

"I never did like... They are not very intelligent. I don't really care if they kill themselves off. There isn't enough room for all of us anyhow." When children are wanted, their worth is determined by the degree to which they are wanted. There is no sense of intrinsic value. Because they have relative worth, they believe others have relative worth also. They begin believing they must compete with others to ensure that their relative value is greater, thus ensuring their survival. This increases the tendency toward derogatory discrimination against minorities and a tendency to scapegoat.

SELF DOUBT

"I want to live a spontaneous, natural, free and easy life, but whenever I try to, my impulses lead me into all sorts of trouble. I cannot trust myself and

I cannot trust my parents. They obviously do not trust me because, having killed a helpless child, they do not trust themselves. They are continually hassling me about being careful and looking after myself, so how can I trust my emotions, desires or biological functions to guide me?" Abortion survivors tend to overeat, oversleep or drink in binges. In their most extreme form, they are anorexic and bulimic. They like to be "greenies" and/or hippies that turn into "yuppies" who compulsively watch their weight, diet and exercise. They aggressively defend their possessions and pleasures.

"I had so many fears during my childhood; fear of darkness, fear that something would destroy me, that somebody would take me away. I slept all covered up so that "thing " would not find me and destroy me. I think it is because my mother aborted my brother. I have so many aggressive feelings towards women. I long for fusion with my mother or with somebody, but I feared women. I want to hurt my girlfriends. I have difficulties making decisions. I am afraid of my past, afraid of what I might discover."

ONTOLOGICAL GUILT

"I know I am talented and have lots of opportunities. I could have a good future, but I can't seem to get my act into gear." Survivors with the conflicts described here find it difficult to finish work projects, their education, or raising their family. They often feel that the future is too uncertain and they should not be alive anyhow. They continually quit and start again. Eventually they develop many rationalizations for their failures and become fully occupied with just living and entertaining themselves. They seem to be waiting for a major catastrophe that will propel them into doing something meaningful. They might subtly contribute to the promotion of a catastrophe, even those they ostensibly are trying to prevent. Unfulfilled, ontologically guilt-ridden parents often push their children into filling their own dreams that are usually inappropriate for the child's personality or intelligence. They are often good at rationalizing their lack of effort. When asked to contribute in some way to a worthwhile endeavor, they are full of excuses.

"My existence depended on being wanted, but there is a lot of effort that I must put in to remaining wanted. I cannot be myself, I am vulnerable to all sorts of manipulations."

" What do I do with my anger? What do I do with my fear? There is no reality, only my reality. "

"You cannot live, you cannot die. You cannot pass on that kind of life to others."

"I had to look at other children to see how they behaved and I copied them. "

If a child cannot trust his/her parents, if he/she must always be on the lookout, then he/she does not feel free to explore the world. In addition, mothers who suffer from post-abortion syndrome are so afraid of losing their child, they constantly tell the child to be careful. The anxiety is therefore reciprocal. Because these children are not free to explore and ask questions, the development of their intelligence is hampered. They become passive absorbers of information. Creativity, one of the greatest human gifts, is stifled.

"When I was four years old I suddenly decided that I did not want to play with dolls anymore. I wanted a real baby. One day I took my doll, painted male genitalia on it and then strangely enough I buried it at the end of the garden. It was only years later that I realized that my mother had had an abortion when I was four years old. Only now I see that to protect the image I had of my mother as being innocent I tried to make myself responsible for my mother's abortion. I have been carrying her guilt all my life and have suffered terribly from it."

BELIEVING THE LIE

Children feel it is too awful to acknowledge, "my parents killed my sibling." They do feel, "Who can I trust?" So they join with their parents in awful rationalization/denial. "It wasn't a baby." But if it was not a baby, PAS Survivors must conclude, "I wasn't a baby or human until my parents said I was." This makes them dependent on parents for life and truth. What a terrible, frightening enigma. The most frequent conclusion is "Now I will strive to gain that same power over life and truth - But it is too awesome, therefore I will never have children."

ESCAPE FROM INNER TURMOIL

"Hey, man. That was some fight. Next time I hope he kills him. Maybe I should join an army and get involved in the real stuff." The guilt, anxiety, distrust, rage and sense of apathy create such enormous tensions and turmoil within the young abortion survivor that he feels he can survive only if he is distracting himself. Some examples of distractions can be; fun, sex, murder mysteries, violent sports, or the vicarious enjoyment of watching increasingly violent sport on television.

Abortion survivors, in an effort not to feel, are also more likely to become involved in the use of drugs, alcohol or prescription drugs.

DISLIKE OF CHILDREN

Abortion survivors tend to be unsure of their identity and existence. Therefore they are threatened by children. They avoid having children or committing themselves to family life. They will engage in any kind of sex that has little chance of propagating, e.g. "outercourse." If they have children, they tend to put them in day-care at a very early age. Many abortion survivors have a death wish which they know is incompatible with having their own children.

DISTORTED IDENTITY

PASS attempting to live a life for their dead sibling may deny their own identity. If he was a boy sibling, a girl may feel she has to deny her feminine identity.

Men with PASS often have specific variations of these major conflicts. They may experience:

- shame of their masculine sexuality from the fact that sex resulted in the death of a baby, and they are shamed by their female partners
- rage at not being allowed to protect their baby and not being allowed to produce a child in their image.
- distrust, which results in inability or disinclination to commit to their partner, which increases promiscuity.

The net effect of the above may be a sham gentleness, or rape, or homosexuality.

In addition to these major conflicts, most abortion survivors tend to have an undeveloped or poor self image. It is hard to have hope or experience joy. They may have perceptual abnormalities and be suspicious of being followed or spied upon. They try to avoid any real pursuit of truth and are easily swayed by the politically correct opinions. They inadvertently trouble women who are suffering from Post-Abortion Syndrome by contributing to the woman's painful awareness that she has destroyed something very precious, the survivor's equally loving sibling.

CASE EXAMPLES

Isabella, 37, was an obstetrician/gynecologist in Europe. Her mother had four abortions after she was born. She had three abortions before and one abortion after her only child. She had been an abortionist for a number of years, but was becoming increasingly selective about whom she terminated. She seemed to be a pleasant, energetic person but felt she did not know who she was. She was not happy to be alive, had insecure human relationships, and often thought of injuring herself. She was frequently sad about life and angry at her husband or little boy. She often thought that she was losing her mind, and was bothered by ideas she could not control. She had many broken relationships, poor physical health, difficulty being a good parent, suicidal thoughts, repeated depressions, sleeplessness and difficulty trusting people. As she became increasingly aware of the roots to her problem, she became better able to express her tears and sorrow. She began looking for ways to give up her lucrative practice of abortion.

Alexandra, a 26 year old psychology student in Europe, had one older sibling who had been aborted. She had aborted her only pregnancy. Although she was bright and energetic, she was not happy to be alive. She didn't have a good idea of who she was, thought she was not using her abilities, had many insecure relationships, had often injured herself, and had a persistent feeling that something terrible was going to happen to her. She had many broken relationships, repeated depressions, persistent grieving, low self esteem, and troubling, frightening dreams. As she discovered the roots of her conflicts in being an abortion survivor, she began expressing more feelings. As she grew in awareness, she lost her suspicious defensiveness.

During the many encounters with children and adults born into families where there have been abortions, we realized that children intuitively "knew" that there was somebody else in the family, somebody that was missing. This is often expressed in dreams, imaginary siblings who have names and with whom they play, and/ or in feeling the presence of somebody who is constantly with

them (a weight on their shoulders, somebody following them). One young woman stated that she could not look in a mirror because she was afraid that she would see some other person. She could sense an "evil" presence and felt there was somebody missing. *"I* felt *it was somebody very close to me, almost a twin brother or sister. "* Many children will spontaneously draw these missing children when they draw pictures of their families.

A woman told telling her nine year old son about her abortion, which had taken place years before he was born. He said, " I *knew, Mom, that there was something wrong. I always have nightmares about knives and my mother killing me. I have an imaginary brother who wants to kill me. If you had not aborted the other, would you have aborted me?"* Later in life he said once in anger, "*You should have aborted me.* "

When she looked at the picture she had drawn of her childhood and "saw" the little brother she had always imagined she had, a thirty-five year old women suddenly understood that all the tragic history in her family was due to an abortion. She said, *"As a child, I was too shut up in my own problems to even think I was an abortion survivor. I was just trying to survive and clean up the mess in my home. "*

There are many far reaching consequences to being chosen to live because you were wanted. These children are angry because their siblings were killed, thus preventing the subsidiary attachments to brother and sister that might be necessary when they lose their parents. They feel a deep and sometimes overwhelming guilt for surviving. "It was my fault my siblings died." or "There were too many of us." or "I was such a burden to my parents they didn't want any more children."

There is a strong resistance to the idea that people suffer when they know they could have been terminated. Yet, abortion survivors do exist. They will not go away just because it is difficult to think about them. Their distress and clinical illnesses should be recognized and treated. If this requires changing one's view about the world, maybe it is about time. After all, if these observations and deductions are correct, millions of people are badly conflicted and, often as a result, seriously ill.

When one infant is aborted the parents may seek to absolve their guilt by pouring their love into the replacement. This displaced compensation only makes the survivor's life more difficult. Being a replacement child is its own hell.

CHILDREN KNOW

Do the children know they are abortion survivors? As a rule, child psychiatrists understand that there are few real family secrets. Children have a way of perceiving what is going on in the family but often do not talk about it, for fear of upsetting the family. These become very damaging pseudo-secrets. It can also be assumed that it is impossible to avoid communication following an important event in one's life. The trauma changes behaviour, perceptions, and personality which let others know that something critical has taken place. Thus it is essentially impossible to keep the secret of abortion from children. It may be possible to collude with them to maintain pseudo-secrets.

Children learn about abortion in a number of ways:

- They have intuition. Through their dreams and their drawings they often convey the fact that they know that their mother was pregnant and lost that pregnancy. In one instance a little girl told me about a terrifying dream in which three of her siblings had become buried in a tunnel they made in the sand. The mother insisted there was only one child. She later admitted she had three early miscarriages, but insisted her daughter could not have known about them. Often children show their awareness of other family members by drawing extra children when asked to provide a picture of their whole family.
- Children overhear conversations between neighbors, or through the bedroom walls, or hear their parents talking on the telephone.
- Some children are told directly by parents; sometimes in sorrow, sometimes out of guilt.
- Recently, it has become popular to involve the children in decisions about whether the next pregnancy should be aborted.
- Some children are threatened, "I could have aborted you."
- Children are very curious about events that affect their survival and may ask directly.
- Some people believe the spirits of aborted children who are not committed to God linger and have ways of indicating their existence, especially to children.

Children are heard to comment to each other about whether or not they were wanted. It has become a major preoccupation. Many suspect their mothers have had abortions. Many learn from overheard conversations, or make deductions from circumstances. Because children's fantasies are worse than the facts, some experts advocate letting children know where their mother was (having an abortion) or why she is so upset.

Because marriages are less likely to be stable nowadays, and because children need to be cared for by someone, they tend to form increasingly strong attachments to their siblings. This means that, although there is sibling rivalry, there is a greater desire to have a brother or sister than there has been in the past. Thus when a brother or sister is killed through abortion, they feel loss, anger, and a whole constellation of symptoms known to survivors.

Surviving children often live with a fear of non-being, feeling they are alive only because they were wanted. They wonder what would happen if they were no longer wanted. Knowing that they are alive because they are wanted, they must go on pleasing their parents. Being always compliant and agreeable is an awful obligation against which the adolescent will rebel. His/her rejection of the burden results in a rejection of his/her parents, particularly of mother, who placed it upon him/her. For adolescent boys, this may result in a diminished regard for women and an increase in the amount of parental abuse.

The child may subconsciously know he has an aborted sibling but is afraid to face the facts. So he will not ask questions about himself or his family. Limiting his curiosity in one area will make it more difficult for him to learn in others. He will collude with his parents in maintaining pseudo-secrets about abortions in the family, but this makes him generally less communicative.

Some abortion survivors feel overwhelmed by the forces that so capriciously determine their existence. They feel afraid to do anything brave with their lives lest they upset some balance and destroy their family. Other abortion survivors know that they are the substitute child. There are expectations placed upon them in place of their aborted sibling. These often well exceed the child's capabilities and his parents try to make him more successful by telling him how badly he fails. As a disappointment to his parents he becomes a disappointment to himself and his self-esteem develops poorly. He is often corrected with violence which begets violent feelings within him. These may be expressed toward his siblings, himself or his parents.

Since the state could not or would not protect his intrauterine life, this child has a diminished regard for the laws of the nation, "If my country won't protect me when I am most vulnerable, why should I respect its laws?"

Evidence has shown that those who survived abortions have a tendency to abort their own children. It is a type of revenge upon the grandmother. "You almost killed me so I will punish you by not having grandchildren for you." It is also an expression of how little they value their own lives and the lives of others.

The father was powerless to protect his children's lives when they most needed the protection, so children will grow up regarding their father as powerless and not an authority to be respected. A man cannot be a good model for a boy who knows his father could not keep his wife from killing the infant for which he is half responsible. Because many women so capriciously kill their offspring, girls will tend to reject their femininity. Boys who reject their manhood and girls who don't want to be feminine tend to increase the number of adults who are almost neutral in their sexual orientation.

Many survivors feel they do not deserve to live. More frequently they feel they deserve to die. When troubles accumulate, they feel suicide is the most logical option.

CASE EXAMPLE: JANICE AND HER UNWELCOME BABY

I saw Janice in New Zealand when she was going through her second divorce. She was struggling with depression, anger and difficulty in raising her two sons. Her husband, an ex-biker, had little time for her or the children. Though he struggled, he could not stop drinking. When he was drunk he would beat the children and curse his wife. She had been adopted as an infant. Though she was very wanted she did not feel welcome. For reasons that she could never understand, her adopted brother was treated so much better than she was. He was a good boy, who in manhood was a well respected but "stuffy" professional. She was always "the black sheep" and drove her parents to distraction with her delinquent behaviors.

Although she is a tall, graceful, good-looking woman she frequently found herself with men who didn't treat her with respect. Janice admitted that there had been many men in her life and she always managed to choose the wrong one.

While still a teenager, after one of these liaisons, she found herself pregnant. Still wanting to "enjoy life", she chose to abort the child. For many years she denied any negative impact of that abortion. As she became increasingly depressed, she began to examine the roots of her depression. She had to admit that she had always struggled with knowing that she had aborted a baby because, much like herself, he was not welcome. By rejecting him, she had done the very thing that she so resented having been done to her. There had been no place for her and there was no room for her unborn baby. It was not until she humanized, welcomed, then mourned the baby that she was able to experience any joy.

6. TEN TYPES OF POST-ABORTION SURVIVOR SYNDROME (PASS)

Abortion survivors have similar conflicts to those people whose family members died in accidents, illnesses[4], or by genocide. There are at least ten types of abortion survivors.[5] Their situations and conflicts are different, but they have in common deep questions about whether they should be alive, whether they are worth anything to anybody, and whether they should develop their abilities. These people are not easily treated, but insight is valuable. It seems that when they sublimate their deepest anxieties into helping to prevent people from becoming abortion survivors, they are functioning best.

The ten types of Post-Abortion Survivor Syndrome (PASS) are:

STATISTICAL SURVIVORS (PASS TYPE 1)

These are people who survived in countries or cities where there is a statistically high probability that he/she would have been aborted. In most of North America, there is at least a 25% chance of being killed *in utero.* In some parts of eastern Europe there is a 80% chance that a survivor would have been terminated before he/she was born. If a person has a statistically slim chance of living through an event that kills many like him/her, he/she is truly a survivor and should be considered as such. Though many of these people were told they were definitely wanted, they know the odds were stacked against them. They wonder why they were allowed to live while others died. To be alive because you were wanted is not necessarily a pleasant experience or reassuring knowledge. It becomes quickly apparent, even to children, that if you live because you were wanted, then when you become unwanted you may not be allowed to live. Agnes stated:

"Our country (Ukraine) is committing collective suicide. When I look at my family tree, I realize the number of people who are missing, missing in wars, sent to camps and who never came back, but most of all, all the children my own family killed. I would have had five brothers and sisters. My childhood would have been different. I would not have been so lonely. The state became my family, a big anonymous, protective family. It was a good system for me because I always needed to have people around me; otherwise I felt that I did not exist. However my

peers never replaced my brothers and sisters. I always had to compete with other children trying to be first and be well recognized by others. I guess that it just the way it was."

WANTED SURVIVORS (PASS TYPE 2)

There are millions of children who have survived a serious deliberation by their parents or physicians about whether they were "wanted" and therefore should live, or "unwanted" and be aborted. Their parents may have calculated whether there was enough money, the grandparents wondered if they could endure the embarrassment, and society may have questioned whether there were too many people in the world. The parents may have consulted a geneticist to determine whether the child was handicapped or the wrong sex, and if so, made decisions whether the child should or should not be allowed to live. Unborn children are affected by hormonal changes that result from major conflicts in the mind of the mother. There is also growing evidence that unborn infants not only hear, but also remember conversations about them.[6] the implications are subtly conveyed to the child after he/she is born about whether he/she should have been allowed to live.[7]

"My parents always said they had wanted me. I often wonder what would have happened if they had not wanted me? I feel I must stay wanted. Being wanted means existing."

"I had fourteen years of psychotherapy because every year, as a child, I tried to commit suicide. I did not want to live. After many years of therapy, I found the cause of my distress. My mother had wanted to abort me but when she arrived at the abortion clinic, when she was on the table, she changed her mind. I do not know how I knew, but I knew there was something very wrong between my mother and I. Now I understand why I never wanted to live."

SIBLING SURVIVORS (PASS TYPE 3)

Many children are born into families where one or more of their siblings were aborted. Although parents believe it would be impossible for children to know about them, there are many clinical examples where children know that a brother or sister did not survive intrauterine life. One mother asked me to interpret the dream of a very distraught girl, age 7. Her dream so disturbed her, she was afraid to go to sleep. In the dream she had gone to a riverside to play with three young siblings. Together they had tunneled into a sand bank, which had then collapsed, burying the three siblings. She alone escaped. She could not tell me the age, name or sex of these children. It turned out the mother had had three more pregnancies than she had live children, but insisted her daughter could never have known about these very early pregnancy losses. In one study of the impact on families of pregnancy termination for genetic reasons, it appears that, "Even very young children, and those sheltered from knowledge of the events, showed reaction to their parents' distress and maternal absence."[8]

"I had no right to exist. I never grew up. I am still a child trying to find my place in this world. I have no goals. I am not attached to anything and never had a secure relationship. I was never a part of anything. I felt alone and threatened. My life, my existence were in question. I had insane explosions of anger and an uncontrollable rage. I was enraged at some vague thing that appeared life-threatening. It had to be life-threatening for me to feel such rage. I wanted babies, but when I had them I abandoned them. I went into drugs to escape this reality. It is only now, at the age of 55, that I am beginning to understand. A few years ago, just before dying, my mother told me that she had an abortion before I was born. Knowing about the conflicts of being an abortion survivor helps me understand, and it reassures me because now I know that I was not crazy."

THREATENED SURVIVORS (PASS TYPE 4)

I have heard parents shout to their frustrating teenager, "You'll never know what I had to put up with having you, and you do not appreciate all my effort. I could have aborted you." Even if that parent never seriously considered aborting the child, that kind of outburst has a major effect on children, making them hateful toward their parents and destructive toward themselves. These children feel an awful obligation to their parents which they accept as a terrible burden or angrily reject. They do not appear to enjoy life because they feel that they should not be alive. They do not develop their talents well, and are often seen as lazy, sometimes aggressive, and not infrequently antisocial children.

> *"I was fifteen when my mother, in a rage, told me she wished she would have aborted me. I was too much trouble. I left home shortly after that and lived with a man. We drank a lot and got into drugs. My life did not mean anything to me anymore. Two years later I had my first abortion."*

HANDICAPPED SURVIVORS (PASS TYPE 5)

Modem diagnostic techniques make it possible for parents to choose unborn infants who do not appear to have recognisable defects, or are the preferred sex. The knowledge that they might have been terminated fills the hearts of many developmentally delayed and handicapped children with dread. They know that many like them are being terminated, and that makes them feel vulnerable and ashamed. Even when a great deal of effort goes into giving these wounded people a sense of self worth, the efforts are undermined by the many implied messages in the media, that in the best interest of their parents or society they should not have been allowed to live.

Karen, an intelligent woman in a wheelchair because of *spina bifida* stated:

> *"It is really hard having a handicap in today's world. Life is a struggle, every day is a struggle. Now when I hear that they abort people who have the same handicap as I do, I feel fear, real deep fear. With euthanasia and all, I feel that my life is threatened. Now it is not only a struggle, I feel I am being persecuted. I have to be careful. I feel that people are starting to look at me differently.*
> *Almost as if they were asking: "Why is she alive? Did they not do prenatal testing in those days? I guess she was born before that."*
> *I am ashamed to be alive yet I love life. I wish I didn't have this feeling of overwhelming rejection."*

CHANCE SURVIVORS (PASS TYPE 6)

There are children who would have been aborted if the mother had been able to obtain an abortion. These survivors are explicitly or implicitly told they were lucky to be alive because "if I had discovered I was pregnant earlier" or "if my parents had given permission" or "if someone had been willing or allowed to do it, I would have aborted you."

Sometimes circumstances arise that prevent a woman from having an abortion. Evidence shows that the largest numbers of women who are prevented from having an abortion are grateful once they see their beautiful child. There was no significant rise in the rate of maternal deaths due to "illegal" or "back street" abortions when funding for abortions was curtailed in the U.S.A. There are a few mothers who are resentful and convey this resentment to the child, "You are lucky to be alive." Unquestionably, children who are caught in this situation feel a great deal of ambivalence toward their parents. They may feel sympathy for parents about their dilemma and anger at themselves for being alive. Sometimes they reject and leave their parents. If they can find some other kind of parent, they may eventually gain a good impression of themselves. If there is no one to parent them, they quickly form an attachment to some type of leader or gang and thereby become delinquent.

> *"I heard my mother telling her friend that if abortion had been legal, she would have aborted me. It was a real shock to me. Now I do not believe her*

when she tells me she loves me. "

"I am alive by the skin of my teeth, or perhaps by the grace of God. '

AMBIVALENT SURVIVORS (PASS TYPE 7)

Children whose parents contemplated aborting them, but could not make up their minds until it was too late to do an abortion, are also a type of survivor. Later in the child's life, the mother is likely to indicate that, "It would have been a lot easier and simpler if I had not had you." A child in these circumstances can easily conclude that his parents are still looking for an opportunity to terminate him. The delay in making the decision is an expression of the universal ambivalence of people about new babies as they go through a crisis of incorporation.

There is no doubt that almost every pregnancy creates a personal crisis. In the early stages most women are at least, for a period, unsure whether they want a child at this time. Often they debate whether they will or will not have the child, adopt out the child, or abort the infant. There are approximately fifty-five factors that a woman needs to consider carefully before she can make a rational decision. It is likely that most women eventually do not make a rational choice at all but are swayed by circumstances or emotions. Some women later convey to the child, "I could not make up my mind, but now I wish I had aborted you. Life would have been a lot easier and simpler." Some children who grow up under those circumstances are caught up in their parents' continuing ambivalence. Sometimes they are loved and other times they are hated. That ambivalence becomes part of the child's attitude toward him/herself and others.

TWIN SURVIVORS (PASS TYPE 8)

Even when the most modem methods of locating and aborting a child are available, twins are sometimes missed by the abortionist. Those who have survived the abortion of their twin feel a great deal of anger and grief. One man, whose twin was aborted, becomes dangerously suicidal on the anniversary of that event. It is now known that twins communicate, touch, and even caress each other *in utero.* They have a very close intrauterine relationship,[9] and when parted grieve deeply. When one is killed, the other's grief is long and difficult. But when the grieving is for a twin they knew but never saw, it is almost impossible.

"My mother aborted my twin and then four months later she aborted me. I lived, but there is no sense in my living. I got into alcohol, drugs and child prostitution. I am not worth anything.

Every year I try to commit suicide on the anniversary of my twin's death. I know that a death sentence was passed on me by my mother and that it still has to be carried out. That is why I always live on the edge. I cannot live and I cannot die. There is so much anger in me. I hate my father and I long for my mother. "

ATTEMPTED MURDER SURVIVORS (PASS TYPE 9)

Gradually coming to light are a number of people who have survived attempted murder *in utero.* Giana Jensen survived a saline abortion. She has some handicaps, but lives a full life. She overcomes much of her fear and resentment by speaking out for unborn children. At one point she had nightmares of abortionists trying to kill her. Ana-Rosa Rodriguez survived an attempted abortion. She lost one arm in that attempt. One man, during his primal therapy, recovered a very early memory in which he felt extremely nauseated, suffocated and near death. He concluded it could only mean one thing. When he checked it out with his mother, she had indeed attempted to abort him. These survivors struggle with deep and difficult conflicts, "Why would my mother or father want to kill me?" "Am I supposed to be dead?" "Does she still want me to be dead?" "How can I trust myself?" "How can I trust her?"

Helen survived an abortion many years ago with few physical effects, but has been plagued by psychiatric problems that require both medication and psychotherapy. She states,

"The knowledge I was a failed abortion makes me feel I have disobeyed and should not really be here; that I have no right to be a real person, and have no proper place in the world. I feel I was judged and sentenced, but his punishment was not carried out and is still in abeyance. The hardest thing to accept is that someone who professes to love me did try to kill me. For this same reason of broken trust, I have been unable to discuss this with my general practitioner. I have to overcome feelings of dread and panic when I visit him."

BRIEF SURVIVORS (PASS TYPE 10)

Not infrequently, an infant that is aborted in the later months of pregnancy is born alive. Almost always, regardless of their viability, they are left to struggle alone and die on a counter or in a garbage can. Sometimes nurses are ordered to smother them with the placenta. It is the worst experience for any human to have to deliberately stifle the pitiable cries of a naked and helpless infant. Though these tiny survivors' lives are so short, they leave an indelible imprint on the minds of those who kill them. Neither time nor alcohol can erase the memory of having destroyed an innocent fellow human.

The child who is born after an abortion is, from a psychological point of view and for the parents, a replacement child. He/she carries the weight of parental expectations both for him/herself and the aborted child. He/she is often haunted by the presence of this "other" person. The "other" child, the aborted one, might have been better, even a perfect child. A child born after an abortion usually arrives into the family while the mother is still grieving the loss of that "other" child. These children usually know that there is somebody "missing". Being alive because they were wanted, they believe they must always please others and therefore have difficulties being themselves.

Today more and more children are being brought into the abortion decision especially in the case of a eugenic abortion. They cannot remain neutral. The decision to abort a child because he/she is handicapped has terrible consequences on the surviving child. They are led to believe one is allowed to kill a person because he/she is not perfect. Their perception of any suffering persons will never be the same again, but they will experience relentless guilt that will plague them throughout their lives. They feel guilty because they feel they participated in the abortion decision, in fact or fantasy.

Children feel they have magical powers and can make things happen. In the abortion situation, their very existence precludes the existence of anybody else. "Because I am alive, my sibling would not be allowed to live. I have decided that it would be better that my brother die because he would have been a burden." Or they feel: "Had I been a better child, less demanding, would my parents have aborted? Perhaps they dislike me so much, they do not want to have other children like me. I was a difficult birth and a difficult child." This results in what we call the Cain Syndrome.

A sibling who believes he partook in killing an innocent human being, i.e. an aborted brother or sister, feels a double guilt. He was not punished. He suspects someone will discover what really happened, then everyone will know he is a murderer and want to kill him in revenge. He may now feel that he has an evil power within him. He may feel it is better to kill again rather then await a more terrible fate. Besides, the uncertainty is killing him. If he kills again at least the secret will be out that he is a killer and deserves to be punished.

Today there are children who kill in vicious murders, choosing victims who are readily accessible. How many of them partook at an early age in the decision to terminate a sibling? By murdering, they try and resolve the deep conflict they felt by having been brought into the abortion decision. "I stood by helpless, ambivalent, unable to defend my brother." "I wanted to be the only child. I was glad they aborted it." "I thought it would be the best thing for my mother so I agreed. It was really bad for her and now I am guilty of two horrible harms." "I helped kill a baby and I agreed to something that harmed my mother. I am the one who should not be alive."

The psychological consequences of some abortion survivors are like those Cain suffered; being a wandering soul who must try and work hard (become an achiever) even though he knows that his efforts are not going to amount to much. He has a deep fear that somebody is "out to get him" and that he will be killed sooner or later. In our generation, it is becoming safer either to kill yourself before somebody else does (a quick death by suicide or a slow death involving drugs, casual sex or smoking), or to be so strong that nobody will dare touch you. This tendency profoundly alters normal human relationships.

Parents who have survived Nazi Death Camps have difficulty talking to their children. Often it seems easier to suppress the communication, but then the child's curiosity, fear and fantasies intensify. Professionals conclude it is better to deal directly with the subject of surviving. Parents who have dealt with their abortions find it is most useful to speak frankly with their children.[10] Initially there is an outpouring of grief, many fears, some nightmares and psychosomatic complaints. However, children deal with the reality better than with innuendo and pseudo-secrets.

We hope that it is not trivializing to make such a comparison with death camp survivors, but there are many basic similarities." Helen states that

"Most disaster survivors are threatened by impersonal accidents of nature or, in the case of concentration camp survivors, by a hating adult enemy. Survivors of abortion attempts are threatened by those who profess to love them and it is this dichotomy of love and killing that causes the unresolved problem. I was told by my psychotherapist that terminating a pregnancy is not the same as trying to kill someone, but speaking as and for the fetus, it does feel like it. I have the feeling that I disobeyed in not dying when it was required of me. The medical profession has been very kind although what I really want is for a doctor to put his arms around me and say that he is sorry and that I am worth something after all."

CASE EXAMPLE: JEAN-PAUL

Jean-Paul[12] discovered that he was an abortion survivor in two ways. His mother had aborted his twin, and he himself was aborted later in the same pregnancy. Jean-Paul's parents conceived him under bad wartime conditions. His mother attempted to terminate her pregnancy when her husband was at sea.

She succeeded in aborting Jean-Paul's twin. She later discovered that she was still pregnant. She aborted Jean-Paul at seven months gestation in the brothel that her husband frequented when he was in port. The Madame noticed that the infant was still struggling and so she kept him warm and someone rushed him to a hospital where he was successfully treated. Jean-Paul had a tumultuous childhood and an even worse teenage period, but he turned out to have a loving concern for suffering people and a wonderful artistic talent. He cannot enjoy any of his talents and opportunities because of his survivor guilt, his fears for the future, and his difficult interpersonal relationships. Even though others tell him how loving and talented he is, he can see very little value in anything he does. On each anniversary of the abortion of his twin, he seriously tries to kill himself.

Abortion survivors realize that they are alive only because they were wanted. They fear that if they do something wrong they will no longer be wanted, and have no right to exist. Thus they have an existential anxiety that exhibits itself in repeated attempts to exclude the painful reality of their parents' fluctuating love for them.

7. HOW PASS INTERFERES WITH KNOWING GOD

Most abortion survivors are skeptical about love and fatherhood. Because their parents aborted a sibling out of "love for them," they feel that love does not exist. They have difficulty reaching out to God in a trusting way. Because they have not experienced truly solid and trusting relationships within their family, they avoid acknowledging people as parents and have difficulty seeing God as a loving Father. Abortion survivors may experience a deep sense of hopelessness, and cannot relate to a helpless Christ on the cross. Knowing a sibling died instead of them, abortion survivors are often repelled by the idea of the Son of God dying for them.

8. CONCLUSION

Since everyone is ambivalent about everything almost all of the time, there are few, if any, children who are completely "unwanted." Besides that, even if their parents don't want them, there are many others who want them as adopted children. In addition, the human organism is primed to maintain every healthy pregnancy. What the body does to hold onto and nurture the unborn infant is echoed in the mind. Thus every child is wanted by someone in some way. The real choice is whether to welcome a child.

If a child is unwelcome, the door to life or real living is slammed in his face. Whether he is allowed to live as an abortion survivor or not, if he is not welcome to be who he is, where he is, his life is alien to him. A child can be unwanted, a great inconvenience, but still welcomed. That child has life and liberty to become what God intended him to be.

It is vitally important to illuminate the muddle-headed idea of wantedness because it determines whether people live or die. Wantedness is very destructive philosophy and applies not only to unborn children (abortion) but handicapped people (eugenics) and the aged (euthanasia). The philosophy of wantedness is destroying the life and light God put into our planet earth.

It is time that all God-fearing people welcome every baby in Christ's name. For when we welcome babies we are welcomed by them and thus welcome ourselves. When we welcome a baby in Christ's name we welcome the light and love of Christ. We also welcome God the Father. When we welcome Him we also get all the resources of the universe. How then could there be any child who is unwanted because there is over population?

Having children makes us plan and conserve for the future. Thus the children make us hope. Without children there is no hope. Without hope we do not want to have children. This vicious cycle of diminishing hope and fewer children being allowed to exist is creating social despair and economic chaos in many parts of the world. For our own benefit, and that of our children and the world, we must welcome every child of every size, shape, race, or wantedness in the name of Jesus Christ. Try it. It will change your life. Welcoming every child will go a long way to making the world into a better place in which to be, to be here and to become.

NOTES: 4 POST-ABORTION SURVIVOR SYNDROME

[1]Krell, R. (1979). Holocaust families: The survivors and their children. Compr Psychiatry. 20.560- 568.

[2]Krell, R. & Rabkin, L. (1979). The effects of sibling death on surviving child: a family perspective. Fam Process. 18. 471 -477.

[3]Italicised quotations indicate actual comments made by counsellees in Hope Alive groups. They have only been edited for some grammatical correction.

[4]Ney, P. G. & Barry, J. E. (1983). Children who survive. New Zealand Medical Journal. 96. 127-129.

[5]Ney, P. G. (1983). A consideration of abortion survivors.Child Psychiatry and Human Development. ii 168-179.

[6]Chamberlain, D. B. (1992). Is there intelligence before birth? Pre- and Perinatal Psychology Journal. f>(3), 217-237.

[7]Cavenar, J. O., Spaulding, J. G. & Sullivan, J. L. (1979). Child's reaction to

mother's abortion, case report. Military Medicine. 144. 412-413.

"Furlong, R. M. & Black, R. B. (1984). Pregnancy termination for genetic indications: The impact on families. Social Work and Health Care. 10. 17-34.

*[J]Piontelli, A. (1989). A study on twins before and after birth. Lt Rev Psvcho-Anal. 16.413-417.

[10]Ney, P. G. & Peeters, M. A. (1995). How to talk with vour children about vour abortion. Victoria, Canada: Pioneer Publishing.

"Kestenberg, J. (1985). Child survivors of the holocaust forty years later: Reflections and commentary. Journal of the American Academy of Child Psvchiatrv,.24,804-812.

[u]Real name used by permission.

5
EUTHANASIA AND EUGENICS
(Authors P.G. Ney & M.A. Peeters-Ney)

1. THE RIGHT TIME TO DIE: WHO DECIDES?

There are few questions in life as important as what is the right way and the right time to die. Death is one of life's greatest challenges. Until the Lord returns, it is something that every man and woman must face. Everyone is ambivalent about life and death; their own and that of others. From ancient times there had to be social mores and legislative restraint to protect humans from their own worst tendencies, i.e. to kill themselves or each other.

Death has always been a fearful enemy. Humans intuitively understood that even if death could not be overcome, it could be fought to a standstill. Whenever humanity has embraced death vast numbers of people have died. No one will forget Jonestown; how the desire of some people to kill themselves became enforced death by cyanide for men, women, and unsuspecting children.

Everyone has an ambivalent regard for life and death. There is hardly anyone who, at some time, has not thought about wanting to escape the pain and confusion of living. Virtually everybody who apparently wants to die also wants to live, given a change in their painful condition or confusing circumstance. Although no one really wants to die, there are large numbers of people who are quite prepared to kill themselves and to kill others. It is not hard to persuade people to do one or both. Life and death are in a balance, a finely tuned ecological equilibrium. With very little influence it can be tilted in the direction of death. It behoves humans to understand the balance and consider all those factors that may contribute to a fascination with death and a tendency to kill or to succumb to dying.[1]

This is not a question of a "right to die." Everyone has that "right." Saving the Lord's return, that "right to die" will be granted. This issue is how, when, and in what manner people wish to die. Those who desire Doctor Assisted Suicide (DAS), for example, want to die in the time, place, and manner that they choose, regardless of how it affects others. This is a selfish luxury. The right to DAS may become an enforceable obligation imposed on some medical practitioner whose refusal may not be protected by his ethics.

If we have an inherent ambivalence about life and an occasional desire to kill, what must be done to restrain us from expressing our own fatal aggression?

Will anything but an absolute prohibition work? Humans are exceptionally good at rationalizing. They can make all sorts of foul deeds look fine.

Humans have a tendency to dichotomize phenomena on a smooth continuum such as the desire to live and let live. The advent of the computer has made it easier to digitalize and categorize and thus discriminate in a derogatory fashion. It becomes increasingly easy to decide which group is "worthy of life." The capacity to measure, coupled with humanity's tendency to discriminate, can easily make one group appear to be worth all the efforts and the resources of concern compared to others. This is not because of what has been arbitrarily judged to be inferior or unequal.

All of life is on a continuum. The qualities of each person and each group are on a continuum. There is no real difference or distinction between all shapes or sizes or colors. The criteria by which people live and die can be easily shifted. History records that once society starts shifting toward death, it is not easy to restrain the trend to killing.

Only the self-righteous and arrogant believe they can choose between right and wrong, who is worthy of life and who deserves to die. In reality, in this world we can only choose between good and evil, killing and curing. There is nothing in between, no comfortable, "I am not involved in this." We are known by the intentions of what we do, not by our political correctness. Each choice we make influences the next. The precedents we set result in both individual and legal trends.

It appears that the waxing and waning of civilizations have less to do with a nation's gross national product, than with how well they care for those who are poorer, weaker and more dependent. If a nation is to stay civilized, it must promote care for those apparently less deserving. How then must it encourage its citizens to participate individually and collectively?

Courage and wisdom have always been the keys, not time, money or technology. Resources seem to expand according to how concerned people are for their neighbors. No one has yet demonstrated the world lacks the necessary resources to provide food, water and adequate medical care for every citizen of the earth. The problem has always been distribution, which relates to people's selfishness. Although there are elaborate, and sometimes forceful, justifications of those who have against those who have not, even a cursory scrutiny can detect the real issues are not adequate resources.

If we do not learn from history it must repeat. For the individual, family, or nation, unresolved conflicts generate chaos and result in entropy. Unless we learn from the first tragic experience, we will continue re-enacting tragedy precisely because we must learn. We must learn or we will die. This is true for individuals and nations. Unfortunately, it usually takes many repetitions of history before anybody is wise enough to detect the essential conflict. Could DAS be one of those?

The different approaches to addressing this question can agree on an answer because there is only one truth. There is pragmatic alternative to DAS, one that will show the agreement of good morality, good law, good science, and good economic efficiency.

If everyone is not welcome in this world, no one is safe. Jesus Christ stated that if we welcome the smallest and most helpless person, a child, in His name we welcome Him. When we welcome Him we have His Father and thus all the resources of the universe. It is not a question of having to throw somebody out of the lifeboat because there is no room or insufficient resources. As far as we know, the universe and its resources are limitless.

Distrust is bound to increase when the very pillars of society, namely religion, law, and medicine, are shaken. It is the obligation of both the professional associations and the public, to maintain the immutable ethics and integrity of these three professions. Why would anyone want to make the pillars he leans on crumble when he needs them most? From ancient times, medicine, law, and religion have been the pillars of society. When these become shaky, people are more likely to respond with "who can you trust nowadays?" The law is now often arriving at a decision that it is permissible to kill helpless people. Some religions may support various methods of killing for those who wish or "need" to die. Medicine obviously now has mixed tendencies derived from mixed motives. Some of these are to avoid inconvenience, the desire to gain public approval, and the desire for money.

Without trustworthy pillars of society:

- society becomes increasingly distrustful.
- patient confidence declines.
- legal matters become more complicated.
- the desire to know and worship God declines.
- people become increasingly hedonistic and materialistic.

Eventually, living becomes so confusing and conflicted that people tend to embrace death as a friend.

As the distrust of physicians increases, so the patient's willingness to co-operate diminishes. This increases the demand on the physician to persuade them to co-operate with examinations or procedures and increases the need for more records, expensive investigations, detailed lab tests, etc., all of which increase medical care. The lack of trust results in considerable conflict among physicians. It increases the proliferation of false remedies.

When children fail to care for their parents, especially when they are aged, disabled or infirm, they begin to lose trust and love of their children. Thus, when they are old they will likely be treated in a similar manner. When they disregard their aged parents, the aged are more likely to accept doctor-assisted suicide. As a consequence, they become partly responsible for murder. As such they have many of the conflicts of those who are partly responsible for abortion and/or child abuse. In addition, they become increasingly fearful and consequently conservative as they begin to grow old. We have termed this the Fears of Ageing Syndrome (FOAS).

The survivors of a death always have difficult issues to deal with. When children in the family realize that a loved one was accorded DAS, their normal conflicts following the death of a parent have added to them those of being a DAS survivor. "Was it something I said or did or did not do that made them want suicide? If it was my fault, maybe I am the one who should die next." Survivor guilt, shame, and fear increase the likelihood of anger or withdrawal in children especially and these difficult conflicts interfere with their schoolwork and personal development.

2. ARGUMENTS FOR EUGENICS: A RESPONSE

As society in general, and medicine in particular, lose the direction once provided by ancient morality in determining medical ethics, the void is being filled with a variety of arguments all of which are mostly sophistry in the interest of self. People must be careful to avoid rationalizing thoughts that are basically hedonistic. Arguments between the "haves" against the "have-nots" constitute much of what currently passes for ethics.

Humans need to be able to face the crisis created by a helpless cry and come away more mature and wise, not better able to argue against the desperate, poor and needy of society. If the human body neglects an infected toe, the gangrene can quickly spread and the whole body dies. History teaches us any civilization that neglects its more dependent citizens will eventually collapse. We have a skeptical attitude toward arguments that favor eugenics and the selective destruction of Down's syndrome and other handicapped children. There is a reasonable alternative.

Many arguments have been made to try and justify the eugenicisation of Down's syndrome and other handicapped children. Some of these arguments, and our response to them, are:

POOR QUALITY OF LIFE

It is frequently argued that because handicapped children are not fully capable of knowing and understanding they cannot possibly have a high quality of life. Therefore, they should not have any life at all. The facts are that Down's syndrome children do enjoy life. They smile with small pleasures and bring joy to others. There are fewer suicides among handicapped people than there are among those without handicaps.

BURDEN TO THE STATE

It is argued that the money that is spent on the continuing care for people with Down's Syndrome and other handicaps could be better spent on research and the provision of care for "more important problems." Most of society deems the problems of the rich and powerful more important. Thus middle-aged people get expensive medical treatment, e.g. heart transplants.[2]

It is argued that Down's syndrome children also interfere with their parents' pursuit of pleasure and fulfilment. However, Down's syndrome children have a lower per capita cost than most chronic disabilities. If a family is provided with occasional relief and a small maintenance, most families are quite content to have the Down's syndrome child live with them. They realize the child's special contribution. People with Down's syndrome can also be taught to do piece work. Although not able to earn standard union wages, they can work in well-organized workshops and make enough money for their own keep. As will be pointed out, with modem educational, psychological and biochemical treatment, they can have near normal intelligence.

THEY CANNOT CONTRIBUTE TO SOCIETY

It is argued that people with Down's syndrome cannot make a meaningful contribution to society. This generally means that they do not have a well paying job that allows them to become good consuming citizens and thus support a materialistic society. In fact, they make a whole variety of contributions of a nonmaterial nature.

IMPROVE THE GENE POOL

It is argued that eugenics is necessary to improve the gene pool. Careful analysis shows that selective diagnosis and destruction of Down's syndrome children do not improve the gene pool. It may, in fact, worsen it. At the age of forty, a woman has only a one percent chance of carrying a Down's syndrome child. The insistence that pregnant women over age 40 have amniocentesis raises considerable stress. That stress can increase a woman's level of estrogens and may feminize both male and female offspring. There are many clinical examples of women who, with an uncertain diagnosis of Down's syndrome, have aborted a totally healthy child and spent much of their lives in self-recrimination.

3. THE VALUE OF DOWN'S SYNDROME AND HANDICAPPED CHILDREN

Down's Syndrome and handicapped children enrich society in many ways without any of the following justifications:

UTILITARIAN ARGUMENTS

People with Down's syndrome teach people to be patient and loving by stopping and waiting while they finish an activity and observing small things more closely. They teach people gratitude for all the gifts that they receive. Responding to their dependency with compassion, people learn to be sensitive to the needs of the handicapped and caring in their behavior. Without the dependency of needy people, our world would become cold and dehumanized.

People with Down's syndrome have a different view of life. They seem to be able to detect the essential elements of life. By their frankness and lack of social constraints, they can cut through many formalities, disarm our aggression, soften our prejudice and get to the heart of relationships. Jean Vanier, taking a person with Down's syndrome to a wide beach in France, asked him to draw a picture of joy in the sand. After some thought, this person replied, 'The beach is not big enough."

People with Down's syndrome and other relatively helpless people force people to deal with their own helplessness. Sooner or later humans must recognize that we all have handicaps and that we are all dying. The sooner we learn to deal with our helplessness, the better we are able to maximize our opportunities and utilize all our God-given abilities and opportunities. Down's Syndrome children create a helpless cry. When faced with a Down's syndrome person's inability to deal with many of the complexities of life, we are forced to decide whether we want to grow with them by nurturing them, or we die from within when we are not able to hear their cry and respond to it. Their helpless cry is the cry of our own helplessness.

MORAL ARGUMENTS

Down's Syndrome children force us to question many of our cherished moral tenets, such as the equality of all humankind. They force us to re-evaluate, rethink and restate assumptions that must guide us in critical situations. People with Down's Syndrome force us to question the ethic of "wantedness."

SPIRITUAL ARGUMENTS

People with Down's Syndrome point us to God. They help us to see ourselves as we really are. They help us to know God's mercy and love, for if God loves the weakest and poorest among us, then surely He will love us in our weakness and poverty. We need never be ashamed or afraid of it.

4. PROGRESS IN THE MEDICAL MANAGEMENT OF DOWN'S SYNDROME

Aborting children with Down's Syndrome will put a halt to research into therapeutic possibilities, not only for patients with Down's Syndrome, but for a great number of mental disorders. It has become medical practice to kill a patient one cannot cure. A small number of researchers are continuing to investigate biochemical defects and treatment possibilities for Down's Syndrome and other genetic defects.*

5. PROBLEMS UNDERLYING EUTHANASIA AND EUGENICS

The ethical questions surrounding euthanasia and eugenics are really a response to some deep underlying problems that humans have always had difficulty in grappling with.[4] These are:

DENIAL

We would like to forget or ignore the fact that everyone is ignorant (lacking knowledge and insight), disabled (many mathematicians cannot carry a tune), dying (it is only a matter of time before ageing overcomes regeneration) and mentally ill (we all do self-destructive things for subconscious reasons).

THE DICHOTOMOUS DIVISION OF CONTINUOUS REALITY

The digital computer has helped us ignore the fact that almost every aspect of reality is on a continuum, e.g. weight, distance and radiation. By imposing arbitrary dichotomous distinctions on continuous variables, we can characterize others as essentially different. Then the human propensity to derogatory discrimination takes over, and it is not hard to convince ourselves that those in the other group are less human and do not have a sufficiently high quality of life to warrant existing. We would like to convince ourselves that we are not one of the dying, because we do not belong to the group in which we have placed them. We are not one of the disabled, because they exist in a class we have created for them.

SUPPOSED LIMITED RESOURCES

The life boat mentality is maintained for those arguing that handicapped and Down's Syndrome people use up precious resources, that their existence will mean either the whole boat sinks, or somebody else has to be thrown out.

"WANTED" CHILDREN

It has been widely taught, and frequently believed, that the first right of every child is to be "wanted." This sentence is a death sentence for millions of handicapped and normal pre-born people. To be alive because you are wanted is to be sentenced to a life of existential anxiety, survivor guilt, anxious attachments, ontological guilt, self doubt, distrust and the inhibition of expression to maintain pseudo-secrets. We do this in an effort to provide ourselves with a sense of security and immortality. The net effect is that it alienates and destroys many people upon whom we depend.

We must face these false securities and deal with the underlying dilemmas. We must measure things on an analogue scale. We must remember that there are no essential differences apart from being or not being a child of God. We are different only to some degree on a few variables. We must recognize that there is no limit to certain resources. We should recognize that everyone must be welcomed. Because one is welcomed, one is worthy, and not vice-versa. When one is worthy, one has a self-worth that one can pass on to others and to the world. Thus, we look after each other and the world in which we live.

We believe that Truth is unitary. There cannot be a division between science and ethics, otherwise there will be continuing conflict and no guidance provided for those who must make decisions daily about the existence of other people. We must learn from history. If we do not, we will repeat it. We must recognize that as we treat the smallest infected part of the body for the benefit of the whole body, so, for the benefit of us all, we must care for those whom some in society designate as the lowest and the poorest.

6. A SOLUTION: THE UNIVERSAL ETHIC OF MUTUAL BENEFIT

We are all part of the bundle of life. What happens to others happens to us because we are intrinsically united. The Universal Ethic of Mutual Benefit[5] reminds us that we cannot benefit at the expense of our neighbor. If it is not good for him/her, it is certainly not good for us. If it is not good for a woman it is not good for a man. If it is not good for a person with Down's syndrome, it is not good for anyone else. Science supports this proposition.

We propose the Universal Ethic of Mutual Benefit as a practical alternative to euthanasia, eugenics and DAS. We want to make every living person feel welcome. Being welcomed into existence in this world will increase everyone's self-esteem and self-worth. As people value themselves, they will value others,

care for their neighbors, and protect their environment. Devaluing any person diminishes the value of all people. When society considers some people are unworthy of life, so everyone begins to devalue themselves, each other, and the world in which they live. This results in increasing competition, discrimination, and selfishness.

We are all bound together in the bundle of life. We now live in a "global village." It is not possible to benefit at the expense of one's neighbor. The Universal Ethic of Mutual Benefit that we hold states that only what is good for one's neighbor is good for oneself. This restatement of The Law of Love has good moral and scientific support, so why is it not more widely accepted?

The Universal Ethic of Mutual Benefit always applies in every situation of life and death. What is good for one's neighbor is good for oneself. As we treat others, we treat ourselves. When we kill others we die inside. When we disregard their helpless cry we become deaf to our own helplessness. When we love our neighbor as ourselves, we are loving ourselves. Insofar as we meet their needs, ours are also filled. The hallmark of civilization is respect for the apparently undeserving. If our country is to have a place of honor among the nations and in history, it cannot allow doctor-assisted suicide. There must be an absolute prohibition because no other type of restraint works.

We are commanded to love our neighbor as well as we love ourselves. To love yourself you must know yourself. Insight is vital to loving yourself and your neighbor. You are not able to know your neighbor better than you know yourself for what you cannot see in yourself you will not see in your neighbor. Loving means meeting real needs. Therefore people must know the needs for both themselves and their neighbors. Needs are scientifically definable. Thus it is possible to know when and how to love.

When we are loving our neighbor, we are also benefiting ourselves. We benefit partly by being focused on another's welfare. When our attention is on the ones we love, our mind is in less conflict and our body in greater harmony. Consequently, by obeying Christ's commandment of love we are more likely to live long and stay healthy. After intensive, insight oriented psychotherapy; people naturally tend to become self-centered and introspective. It is an essential that part of any treatment program is to redirect the patients' focus outside themselves. This is best accomplished by teaching them to be loving toward others. In Hope Alive this is done as part of the Rehabilitation phase by making sure patients use their bad experience to prevent happening to others the tragedies that dehumanized them.

The Universal Ethic of Mutual Benefit is that we must love our neighbor as ourselves. We must not try to benefit ourselves at our neighbor's expense. It is good for us only if it is good for our neighbor. It is good for whites only if is equally good for blacks. It is good for a man only if it is also good for a woman. It is good for a woman only if it is also good for her children, born and preborn.

Because of good and evil in the world, we must make very hard choices. Rarely can we choose between right and wrong. We can only choose between good or evil. Often we have to choose between two evil (harming) options. Every time we choose we can love or hate. There is no third alternative. When we choose selfishly, it ends up evil anyway. In the Nazi death camps the guards would sometimes tell a mother she could choose to die with her child or choose life without him. Most mothers chose to die with their children, but many of those who did not were gassed anyway. A few were allowed to live, but that life was a life of constant recrimination and guilt.

Rarely must a physician choose between the life of the mother and the life of the unborn child. It is now generally understood that this never, or almost never, has to happen where there are good medical facilities. Certainly there are no scientifically established psychiatric, psychological or social indications for abortion. Eminent gynecologists state there are no known medical or surgical illnesses that cannot be treated just as well while the mother is pregnant. Ectopic pregnancies must be removed, but if there were techniques available, that baby would be replanted in the uterus by an ethical physician.

If a physician has to choose between life for one and not the other, he does so on the basis of an ancient principle known as "triage." The doctor will choose to treat the person, regardless of their age, sex, size, race, and quality of life, who is most likely to benefit from treatment. If that principle was properly applied, that may be a choice for the infant's life.

Child abuse and infant abortion are selfish choices and they are always destructive for everyone involved. It is rarely a conscious, willful choice by an individual. Frequently it is self-imposed or other imposed because there appear to be no options. In most instances, abortion is a combination of willful choice, lack of option, unconscious conflicts over which mother and father have very little control, and coercion or lack of support from many self-proclaimed innocent bystanders. For these reasons, unless the basic issues are treated there is a high probability that abuse and abortion will be repeated. To treat the underlying problems is what we are attempting to achieve with the Hope Alive treatment process.

We must welcome everybody and love them as much as we love ourselves. If we do so we mature, become freer, learn more about ourselves and become loving and joyful. When we do not welcome and love, we begin to encounter rejection and hate. For what we do to others we expect from them. What we expect we soon begin to get. Even from a small insult we soon realize our worst expectations were justified, and so we become even more pessimistic and isolated until people want either to ignore us or treat us with contempt. What we do to others, we do to ourselves in ever rising or falling spirals.

NOTES: 5 EUTHANASIA AND EUGENICS

'Peeters, M.A. & Ney, P.G. (1994) The abortion-eugenics-ethics connection. UN Conference. NGO Forum. Cairo, Egypt.

[2]Peeters, M.A. (1993). Religion, family planning and abortion (letter) Lancet. 342.808.

'Peeters, M.A. (1995). Therapeutic approaches to Down's Syndrome. Proceedings of thelnternalional Down's Svndrome Meeting. Antalya, Turkey. [4]Peeters, M.A. (1995). Human and ethical aspects of genetic engineering. Hearth. (Winter). 8-12. 'Ney, P. G. (1994). The universal ethic of mutual benefit. T Klin Tibbi Etik (Turkey). 2.53-56.

6

THE HEALING PROCESS

1. The Underlying Philosophy

God has built into every human being the ability to initiate and maintain her/his own inner recovery process. If it were not so, humanity would have died from disease or despair long ago. The therapist's job is to create conditions that are conducive to setting the natural healing process in motion. The surgeon, by careful suturing, brings together the edges of the wound, but he does not make the skin grow. Healing is always a mystery. We acknowledge that at best we are partners in what God is doing. All life is created, sustained and healed by God. Therefore, He should receive all the credit.

In addition to the natural healing and growing process evident in all of life, God (upon request) can, and will, intervene in the lives of individuals. In our experience, those who are seeking God's guidance and help, and those who are supported in prayer, heal more quickly and more completely.

The techniques used in the Hope Alive program, like those of a surgeon, are designed to be as accurate and scientific as possible. They are based on the model of human thought, behavior and relationships that God has helped me develop. These techniques do not require a high degree of psychological sophistication. However, those who use the program should be mature, intelligent, reasonably healthy people who can tolerate their own anxiety without acting out and can deal with high levels of patient stress. They must be eager to learn and have a professional attitude toward patient or client treatment. They must be able to empathize, observe and comment accurately. They must be reasonably firm to insist on completion of treatment. They should have good backup for situations when there are untoward effects of treatment or emergencies.

Although the Hope Alive group therapy process has some elements of transactional therapy, behavior modification, group analytic process and existentialism, it also emphasizes the need to deal with spiritual difficulties and become reconciled to the Maker of humankind. The theoretical foundation is not found in other professional literature. Almost all the techniques are unique to this program. We are happy to share them, but we hope people who use them will understand them properly and cite their source. The material is under international copyright.

The healing process includes:

1. Re-experiencing and re-enacting the original conflict-inducing trauma, this time with a purpose and an alternative outcome. This includes remembering painful events, dealing with denial, and accurately identifying a full range of feelings.
2. Learning new behaviors and ways of thinking. These include learning to assert oneself appropriately, put words to feelings, overcome internal and external resistance, negotiate expectations and roles, modify one's own behavior, acquire parenting skills, and develop better ways of communicating.
3. Gaining new insights. Learning why and how the psychological conflicts arose, what defenses are used, and learning to trace and unravel the intricate puzzle of conflicted thoughts and feelings.
4. Grieving "what should have become" so that "what can be" is allowed to grow. This includes; 1) the death, burial, and mourning of false faces and 2) grieving one's lost childhood, the PISHB, unborn children, and the "what should have become" for one's own children.
5. Renewal and the establishment of realistic relationships. This includes redefining oneself and the expectations of others, and the painful process of reconciliation (including compensation and forgiveness).
6. Forgiving, forgetting and reconciling. Forgetting cannot happen without forgiving. Reconciliation means being able to conduct necessary personal business in an adult fashion, but not necessarily being friendly.
7. Establishing and carrying out the Alternative Plan. This means identifying, in the Blueprint, what has already unfolded, utilizing discarded parts and pieces and then working with God to rework the original design from the inside.

Various parts of the treatment process are more difficult than others. For many, the idea of shared responsibility is particularly difficult. Some patients may have already encountered therapists who tried to convince them that they do not need to feel guilty, "You were just a victim." "You were innocent and helpless." As patients become more aware of how they contribute to their own victimization, it becomes increasingly difficult to retain defenses of denial and projection. It usually means a large shift in their view of what happened and who they are.

CLINICAL EXAMPLE: PAUL STABBED A TAXI DRIVER TO DEATH

Criminal law assumes that everybody has the opportunity to make a free choice. If a person commits a crime, they are culpable, and usually the only ones charged. From a scientific point of view, very few people can make a choice unencumbered by physical or social circumstances. Their crime is also partly determined by their intelligence, education and personality, factors over which they had little, if any, control. Thus there are two paradigms; the law, which holds that people can make choices to do right or wrong and must therefore be held responsible for what they do, and science, which shows that there are a multitude of factors, all of which impinge on a person's ability to make a choice and therefore diminish his/her individual responsibility. It is sometimes difficult to realize how many people contribute to any one episode of tragedy. This case illustrates how, though many people contribute to a tragic death, only one person is held responsible. This perpetrator is then treated as though he/she alone is responsible and had a free choice in the matter.

Paul, 16, grew up on the Canadian prairies in a home racked by alcohol and violence. He was badly neglected, even to the extent of going without food and clothing. His mother drank and took drugs while she was pregnant with him. He suffered some of the effects of Fetal Alcohol Syndrome. After he was born, he was physically and emotionally neglected. His mother kept on "partying" and his father seldom saw the children, except to berate and beat them. Paul was small for his age and often teased by his peers. The teasing became even worse when he went to school because he could not learn some of the simplest things. Yet he was good in sports and could pick off gophers with his "22" better than anybody in the area. Because of his continued failure in school he became depressed and had frequent headaches. The physician who saw him didn't have time to listen to his deep complaints but tried to ease his sadness with an antidepressant. That only made him drowsy and less able to concentrate in school. Eventually he dropped out of school and tried to find a job. Possibly because of racial discrimination, and possibly because of his bad work ethic (he had had no model), he was soon fired.

One day, Paul and his friends were given some LSD and robbed the local hardware store of a collection of knives. That night they went out looking for "trouble" and it was not hard to find. A local bootlegger supplied them well with alcohol. They caught a taxi and ordered the man to drive down a lonely road, pretending that was where they lived. At the end of the road they threatened to kill him if he did not give them all of his money. The taxi driver attempted to resist and called for help on his radio. Paul, frightened, angry, hallucinating, and quite paranoid, stabbed the driver fourteen times. He was soon arrested and brought to trial. I tried to point out to the judge that all the factors that made his parents incapable of properly providing him nurture and guidance, his severe learning disabilities which were not properly diagnosed or remediated in school, his inadequate treatment by the over-stressed family physician, the persistent teasing by his peers, the store-owner who enticingly displayed the knives, the person who gave them LSD, the bootlegger who provided them with alcohol, and even the taxi driver who should have known better than to drive down a lonely road with a group of drunken young people, had all contributed to the tragedy. Why were they not also on trial? How much free choice did Paul really have?

2. THE OPEN-ENDED, FOUR LEVEL MODEL

In most treatment, the doctor is the doctor and the patient the patient for always. Ours is an open-ended model whereby the counselee may become a counselor and even trainer of others. Someone who begins as a counselee and does well is asked to become a sponsor of someone in the subsequent group. If they do well and enjoy sponsoring, after one or two experiences of this they are invited to sit in on a group as a facilitator. A facilitator has a major role in encouraging people as they speak from their own experience. A few who have enjoyed and done well at facilitating are invited to apply for the training course.

The large majority of trainees are professionals from a wide variety of disciplines; physicians, nurses, teachers, psychologists, clergy, religious, etc. and experienced lay counselors. Those who are accepted after application and interview take an intensive 60-hour residential, experiential course. Upon completion of the course, they are evaluated by the trainer and facilitator to determine whether they should be invited to 1) obtain treatment for deeply rooted problems, 2) take the training again and 3) write the examination.

Those who pass the examination are required to commit themselves to the *Commitment to Professional Conduct.* On doing so, they are given a certificate that allows them to work as a co-counselor. Having done a number of groups as a co-counselor, they are invited to take more intensive training to become an independent therapist and supervisor of co-counselors. If they do well at this, they are invited to take a subsequent level of training and become a trainer. Because of the increasing need and demand, we are very keen at this point to train independent counselors and trainers.

The basic training is usually done in a rural setting that provides for good support and nurturing in a quiet environment. The reasons the training is experiential are:

- The best training for clinical work is practice. People learn by doing. In this instance, they learn by counseling and experiencing counseling in a group.
- They understand how it feels to become anxious, unhappy, resistant, etc.

as they learn about themselves.

- They become personally convinced of the efficacy of the program.
- They will not be asking others to do difficult tasks that they cannot or will not do themselves.
- They gain insight and become more mature.
- They discover that personal prejudice and ignorance prohibit them from seeing and hearing in others the truth that is being communicated.

People formally associated with IIPLCARR are members or associate members in one of four categories:

1. Supporters. Those who have taken the training course but have yet to pass their examination and those who are friends and interested parties who support the aims and objectives of IIPLCARR.

2. Co-Counselors. People who have passed their Level I examination and are working with a Hope Alive colleague or some qualified person who agrees to help and will adhere to the procedures of the Hope Alive program.

3. Counselors/Supervisors. Experienced people who have passed the Level II examination and now can function independently. They can invite trainees to join them and can supervise co-counselors.

4. Trainers. Those who have passed the Level III examination and are actively training others in the Hope Alive method. They must have acquired a high level of skill, read widely and engaged in at least one research project.

3. THE ALTERNATIVE PLAN

For one to be able to know and become known, barriers of the impermanent, unreal human must be allowed to die. Unless an individual, in dealing with the conflicts engendered by trauma, can significantly change, his/her personal and interpersonal history of tragedy must repeat. If all tragedy repeats, then there is no hope for humanity. Everyone would soon die in spite of a securely protected blueprint. The process of death and rebirth is an integral part of this treatment program. It is an essential component of the way God uses the original Blueprint to re-create the person from the inside.

The Original Plan for all infants coming into our world is that they are welcome into a family with two happy, healthy parents. All the child's needs will be met, and he/she will grow into full maturity and have an adult relationship with his/her parents. The Alternative Plan is that persons who have been mistreated by abuse or abortion will have their wounds healed and be able to transcend their handicaps, use even their misfortunes to their advantage and become as mature as possible, so that they can have an adult relationship with someone, if not their parents. Included with this is the hope that their spirit be made alive, so that one day they will have a new body and a new start to developing the person they should have become under the original plan.

Though the abused, aborting or surviving person will always have scars and/or the handicaps of personality defects that may never quite disappear, God can start the rebuilding from the inside. He takes the discarded bits and pieces of one's past and reorders them so that, although the outside of the house may still look very dilapidated for some time, the interior becomes beautiful. One day the inner changes will also show on the outside. Metaphorically speaking, the building is not what it should have become. It is battered and distorted on the outside, but inside it is remarkably true to the original Blueprint.

When people are able to mourn the loss of the PISHB, they can accept the person they are. People who accept themselves are much better able to accept others just as they are. When they are not as ashamed of whom they are - figuratively speaking their incomplete and battered house - they are better able to invite people in. Intimacy improves.

After treatment, patients must continue letting go of the false faces (or fake front) because their facade is rigid and prevents the Master Builder from completing the renovations. For God first renews our spirit (salvation), then gradually our psychology (counseling), and finally our body. In the process of renewing all three, it is important to lie to rest "what was" or "should have become" in order that something new may grow. When an individual gives his/her life to Christ, God makes his/her spirit alive by infusing His spirit into him/her. Before resurrection and re-creation of the body can take place, one must recognize the pain, evil and disobedience in one's life and identify with Christ in His death and burial.

The Alternative Plan is therefore not the "second best" but a different, more painful route. With God, nothing is lost or destroyed, unless He destroys it Himself. When people get to heaven, they will see both the inside and the outside as God had originally designed it. The design was kept safe as it was encoded in the genes, and the Blueprint was kept intact by the Pilgrim for "Your Name." God will then take our Blueprints and show that what was tragic can be triumphant.

The worst event in human history (when we killed God's only Son) was both the greatest tragedy and the greatest triumph. The man Jesus Christ, as

Pilgrim, was killed, buried and mourned. He came to life again with a new body that is not confined by time and space and was given a name above every name. Interestingly, even that new body has the scars indicating the trauma Christ went through. These scars will always remain part of His risen body, but they do not hurt or hinder Him.

One of the most basic tenets of Christian theology, and also basic biology, is that "unless a grain of wheat falls into the ground and dies, it remains alone." The patients in our therapy groups are surrogate scapegoats. In a very real sense, they take upon themselves the sins and grief of their family of past and present generations. When their false faces, their childhood, and the person they "should have become" die, family members realize the change and often follow them, for they come to the understanding that they, too, need help in healing.

4. ENDURING DISABILITIES

Healing begins when individuals wounded by mistreatment or abortion, begin to recognize how:

- the neglect and abuse experienced in their childhood, or arising from traumatizing situations in their adulthood, have deprived them of essential nurture and guidance.
- tarnished is the Blueprint of whom they should have become.
- repeatedly damaged the wonderful personality structure they were building is.
- drained they are of the energy needed to keep working on their development.

They must recognize not only what damage was done to them, but also see the harm that they have done to others, particularly by aborting children. Only then will they be in a position to let the Dancer and the Urchin go. Then the person they "should have become" must be properly buried and adequately mourned. Out of that deep sorrow and despair, the Pilgrim will emerge, i.e. the authentic person.

The Pilgrim knows that, even though she cannot become all that she was intended to be by God's design, she can be a lot more than she has been. She will always have scars and disabilities, but she can learn to accept love, love herself, and love others. Once that takes place, the Pilgrim is able to objectively appraise all her relationships and establish expectations that do not continually result in attracting other wounded people. She more easily finds people who are mutually building toward maturity.

Once realistic expectations and mutually encouraging relationships are established, she is able to engage in reconciliation, not only with herself, but also with those around her and with God. When reconciliation has been accomplished, the Pilgrim can reach out in a meaningful and trusting way to help and heal others. Only after she is actively involved in helping others, or preventing a tragedy similar to hers, can she become whole. Now she can rejoice knowing that God has healed her. Now she can love life and make it loving and useful for others.

5. MODEL FOR HEALING

The model for this healing program comes from basic Christian tenets, but has universal application. Life comes from death. Healing comes from burying false hopes and false faces. First, parents who have aborted must recognize and discard the two false faces and assert their Pilgrim. They must mourn the loss of the PISHB before they can mature and enjoy nurturing their children. They must be re-humanized. Only then can they humanize and mourn their aborted babies. Once the mourning process is completed, they can mature and enjoy nurturing their children.

Humans have always wanted quick and painless treatment for what ails them. God could easily provide any number of instantaneous miracles, but He does not. He is more interested that we participate in the painful process, thereby becoming more mature and wise and thus we are better friends for Him. Although God is always doing the healing, most miracles are slow miracles.

You might look at a huge tree and say "What a miracle of design and construction." In fact, it may be a four hundred year old miracle. God acts in time and through pain. It always requires thought and energy. When we participate in His healing process and facilitate the knowing and growing of others, we will understand a little of what God experiences. For the man who was born blind, Jesus made mud from spit then rubbed it on his eyes (not his eyelids).[1] This poor man with the pain from mud in his eyes was then required to find his way to a pool and wash the mud out before he could see. You might ask, why would God, who can make things better so quickly and painlessly, use such a painful procedure. Only God really knows, but I believe it is because He wants us to join Him in a process that is not without effort on His part.

We are involved in physician-assisted miracles, or counselor-assisted miracles. We have an integral part, but still they are initiated and completed by God. The process involves an equal amount of knowing and growing. Gaining insight and gaining new skills.

For the counselors, it is important to know that because they are constantly the recipient of a stream of the most awful stories, they eventually have a mind clouded with empathetical pain and grief and filled with sordid memories and sullied perceptions. This will affect their behavior. Thus they must understand that they are a conduit for all of that suffering. They must pass it on to Christ, who has amply demonstrated that He can deal with all the grief humanity has ever concocted.

6. MOST DIFFICULT GRIEFS

The grieving of an abortion is particularly difficult for both mothers and fathers for the following reasons:

- They contributed to, or caused the death of, the very person for whom they are now trying to grieve.
- Abortion is a concrete expression of the hate dimension of ambivalence toward the lost child. They have to face the aggression in themselves that would otherwise be denied.
- They cannot see or hold the body, for it was tom into pieces (this is critical to all grieving).
- According to many of society's standards, it is not a grief they are supposed to have to talk about - after all it was, "just a piece of tissue." This is unlike other types of mourning, such as the loss of a spouse, where social structures encourage people to talk about their loss.
- There are few people who are sufficiently skilled to deal with the post abortion grief. The vast majority of professionals want to ignore it, and most pastors and priests can only deal with it by listening to a confession.
- To abort the baby, the mother and father had to first dehumanize the child. Mourning requires that the infant be re-humanized. One cannot mourn a "blob of tissue."

It is difficult to initiate a conversation about the grief and conflict of abortion, but it is well worth it. Like many taboo subjects, the abortion is always referred to as "it." The abortion should be called an abortion and talked about in a calm and non-judgmental fashion. Knowing what types of mechanisms are used to deny abortion, and what kinds of symptoms can arise from abortion and its related conflicts, makes it possible to suggest to neighbors, friends or patients that they need to talk about all their pregnancy losses. Quietly suggest that the pregnancy losses include miscarriages, abortions, etc. and must be mourned. Very frequently, there is a flood of tears as the person realizes that someone is prepared to talk about the taboo subjects of abortion and their grief.

If bringing up the subject of abortion does not provide an avenue for discussing abortion, you can mention that since abortion is such a difficult subject, many people tend to deny their abortions, but that abortions cannot be denied indefinitely. Experience shows that abortion needs to be identified and talked about. Unresolved grief does affect both physical and emotional health. Unresolved grief results in pathological mourning. Pathological mourning is a significant cause of depression, self-injury, suicide and psychosomatic problems.

The loss of the Person I Should Have Become is also something that needs to be grieved. People keep clinging to an unrealistic hope that someday they will become the person that God intended. It is difficult to mourn the loss of the childhood that they should have had and the person that they should have become. Going through this mourning is a prelude to mourning unborn infants. Both are essential if one is to continue growing and maturing.

When people hint that they want to talk about their abortion(s), it is vital that friends, neighbors, and particularly professionals, respond. If they try to talk about an abortion and they encounter an unsympathetic ear, then it will be a long time until they try it again. In the meantime, there is persistent suffering. "I tried to talk about this terrible secret. Nobody was interested. Why should I bother trying again? It hurts too much. It would be better just to forget the whole thing."

When talking to people, it is important that the hearer convey:

- a willingness and ability to understand.
- competency to help them (if in no other way than to refer them to a competent therapist).
- a commitment to hear them out and stick with them until there is some kind of resolution.

7. THE TREATMENT PROCESS

Because of the link between child abuse, neglect and abortion, and because abortion is the most deeply dehumanizing experience there is, therapy must be aimed at the deep damages to the human person. The treatment process is very painful and very demanding. It entails deep mourning. One cannot avoid despair. Deep sorrow always occurs when the individual must let go and bury:

- the opportunity to build according to the Original Plan for his/her life.

- the childhood that they should have had.
- the parents and family I needed.
- the Person I Should Have Become.
- the false faces of Dancer and Urchin.
- the loss of the children through abortion, miscarriage, stillbirth, etc.

The Hope Alive process is very difficult and many people are reluctant to participate. In many instances, it is as if the person is using one hand to hold onto "what should have become" and the other to grasp "what could be." Until they have completely let go of "what should have become," they will not see themselves clearly. They will not see their Pilgrim, or if they do, they will see their Pilgrim as faceless. But when they completely let go of the PISHB, the Pilgrim takes on definite dimensions and characteristics.

During this process, they must be allowed to be as sad and mad as they need to be. Unfortunately, in usual social situations, most people are not allowed to be sad, although they are allowed to be as angry, frustrated, or excited as they want to be. Usually, if there was no deep sorrowing there was no real letting go. It is important to realize during this process that if this sorrow is mixed with anger, the person may become suicidal.

Many years of clinical experience have shown that the anticipation of the grieving process creates high levels of anxiety. They desperately hope that there is another way. A careful look at the dead end options forces them to recognize that they cannot go around; they must go through this experience.

Guilt is a difficult feeling and an even more difficult concept to deal with. For the purposes of this manual, guilt is defined as the awareness of having broken some universal law. Guilt could be likened to that hypothetical situation where somebody has, in desperation, jumped from the top of a tall building. Between jumping and hitting the ground they may be thinking, "I have just made an awful mistake... I wish I could undo it and go back to where I was... Very soon I'm going to have to pay dearly for my wrong choice."

The more one is aware of the natural order in the world of people, objects, and forces, the more guilty one feels, regardless of whether he/she knows God or not. The guilt results from recognizing we have transgressed a law of God's universe. There are "unreal" guilts, i.e. uncomfortable sensations from breaking an ancient tradition or social more, but not a "real" natural law. Guilt may be something one is made to feel for hurting one's parents. Much of the treatment process at this stage is not only to grapple with guilt, but also to differentiate between real and unreal guilt.

Once they begin working through all the losses, patients recognize that there are spontaneously occurring changes within. These are like the renovations on the inside of a dilapidated house. They know that the outside structure may not be improved upon. It may always look worn, dilapidated and sometimes half built, but there is a beautiful warmth emanating from the newly renovated kitchen and living room. They are now experiencing God's alternative plan for them. When this happens, they begin to see the abuse, the neglect and survival in a different light. They begin to recognize that even the worst tragedies can be used to advantage in that they promote maturity and a better understanding for the sufferings of others.

A frequent question is, "Will treatment outcome result in something as good as the original plan?" This is like questioning "What would humanity have been like if Adam and Eve had not succumbed to the temptation to be like God?" In this life, people can never answer certain questions. Disease, despair and death are still tragedies brought about by evil. But, the glorious fact is that God transcends those tragedies and makes something beautiful out of something ugly and discarded.

8. TECHNIQUE AND PERSON

There is no excuse for ignorance or sloppy technique or incoherent theory. At the same time, just because one is technically excellent does not mean one should not also pray for patience and give God the credit when one gets good results. Sadly, those who are good technically soon begin to rely upon their technique and give themselves the credit for any success.

For a critical operation on your heart, would you choose a technically expert Buddhist surgeon or a sloppy Christian surgeon who believes that because he prays over his patients he does not need to update his knowledge or improve his technique? Christians need to be both technically proficient and relying on God; always praying for their patients to get well, acknowledging God's guidance as they work, and giving Him the credit when people become well. Not everyone is cured, but everyone can mature. Not every counselee works through the process or faces the hard tasks, yet he/she learns something useful.

In counseling, the counselor is both the technician and the tool. You will not hear from others what you do not wish to hear in yourself. You will not understand in others what you are blind to in yourself. All other factors being equal, the most important determinant of good counseling is a wise, mature counselor who has dealt with his/her own grief, despair, etc.

9. THE END RESULT

Our experience shows that the newly emergent person, even though scarred and handicapped, has realistic expectations of him/herself and others. He/she has the ability to see and utilize all the pieces that he/she was given. Nothing is wasted from the experience. He/she will be able to:

- convert the anger arising from his/her wounds and wants to indignation and, in this way, protect his/her children against exploiting industries, e.g. distilleries, tobacco, clothing, pornography.
- transform his/her sorrow into sympathy for wounded parents and children.
- change his/her guilt to prayer for the sins of commission and omission of him/herself.
- transcend continuing pain and become sensitive to the subtle expressions of trouble in the lives of other people.
- develop an overriding love that "fulfills all the demands of the laws and the prophets," and "covers a multitude of sins."

People who are healed through this process experience great peace due to acceptance by others and themselves. They are better able to use all their strengths and abilities to start developing and maturing more rapidly. There is a spontaneous resurgence of hope with all the strength and joy that accompanies it. They are more spiritually aware, stronger and more resistant. The childlike qualities of exploring, inventing and playing will gradually surface in them. Consequently their children can more easily identify with them. They are now able to accept the offerings of love from their children, and thus their children's ability to love develops and grows.

When this process has been initiated, the integrated Pilgrim begins to emerge - the one who guarded the Blueprint so tenaciously. Once the Pilgrim is recognized, i.e. the authentic core personality, the patients are no longer forlornly expecting someone else to create a proper childhood and provide them with the necessary building blocks for their personal development. They are now able to provide for themselves and accept the love and help offered by others. They are not repeatedly disappointed in relationships. They can now see more of what they receive, rather than what they are not getting. They are no longer continually burdening their children with expectations of their own that were never fulfilled.

Successfully completing this treatment program helps the person to let go of resentment, bitterness and hate and become forgiving. When one forgives, there is a great release of energy that was bound up in anger. This energy is now directed to releasing others from the hate and guilt that had made one cling to being a victim. The new energy and joy begin to show on the outside. The body straightens up, and the eyes are alight. There is a greater internal physiological harmony that improves health and creates optimism. With diminished bitterness, there is decreased damage to the immune system so that there is less likelihood of cancer and infection.

6. WHAT IS TRUTH? - AND A DISCUSSION OF THE FALSE MEMORY SYNDROME

The dehumanizing damage of childhood that most frequently leads to later abortion is neglect. Because the most damaging neglect occurs before language development, and because non-events are hard to remember, the damage of neglect is frequently attributed to sexual abuse. Many poorly trained therapists, who are looking for a cause to a counselee's distress, readily imply sexual abuse, partly because it is politically correct to do so. If the counselee does not remember any sexual abuse, it is suggested it probably did happen, but because it was so traumatic the memory was repressed. A false memory is inculcated by small increments. Once the false memory is fixed, the counselee feels justified in making sure the supposed perpetrator, usually a father, is prosecuted. This has tom apart thousands of families. The fact that the real cause, neglect, is not dealt with, is equally tragic.

Pilate asked Jesus, "What is Truth?" Jesus said, "I Am the Truth." Jesus is the embodiment, the epitome of Truth, the object and the culmination of all research.

We are more curious about ourselves than anything else. Modem science is discovering the amazing complexity of the person. A person is always learning, and with learning one establishes neuronal outgrowths, making axonal connections that were not there before. Like every science, the study of humans has a curious result. The more that is learned, the more questions are raised.

I AM A TRUTH

Every individual is a truth. Every individual's existence is a fact. Each component of their existence is also a fact. Even the errors, the lies built into them, are facts. People, and their experiences, are somewhat measurable and, to some extent, predictable bits of data.

There are many errors built into a person, especially memories of false perceptions... theirs and others. When their perceptions are false, their memories are false. More often their memories are false because of the misunderstandings that are built into the misperceptions of others.

Since no one is capable of fully, accurately and objectively recording any event, every memory is partly inaccurate. Yet, everything a person says is a useful statement about themselves. No one can create a completely false fabrication. Indirectly, they are always commenting on their characteristic way of viewing things, whatever they describe. Therefore, I will accept everything a person says, but I do not believe any of it is a factual or complete account.

People first lie to themselves and then to others. They lie because:

- they choose to. There is a benefit of power or pleasure.
- they are forced to. What is said about them is an error, but they must accept this to gain the approval or the treatment of those who purport to understand or heal them. Often the patient or client has accepted a diagnosis when he/she knows it does not fit him/her nor explains what he/ she knows about him/herself.
- they are conditioned into lying by a series of subtle mechanisms about which they may or may not have any conscious recognition. "Nobody knows me like I do. I know my painful experience. These are recorded in my whole being, body, mind and spirit. I cannot forget them, even when I try to. If anyone cares to examine me closely they will see them."
- they do not know the truth so they do not know they are lying.

Painful experiences are more easily forgotten when:

- a person understands where they came from, what happened, and how painful experiences continue to operate in their lives.
- people forgive and are forgiven.
- they have matured beyond a desperate desire to find the building blocks of their early development.
- they use the lesson to help prevent the same sort of pain happening to others.
- they can use the critical elements of the traumatic experience to avoid or solve similar situations in the future.

People will lie to a professional because they are so intent on knowing, growing and forgiving. They need to understand themselves. Part of this is being understood and that is why psychotherapy or counseling is in high demand. During psychotherapy they are very vulnerable to giving up the truth about themselves.

The mechanisms of learning to fabricate about themselves in treatment arise from:

- operant conditioning. There are subtle reinforcements that occur during the relative social deprivation of psychotherapy or counseling. These are powerful in shaping the patient to eventually adopt the assumptive form world of the therapist. The therapist's "uh, huh" occurs selectively, i.e. when the patient says something that is of interest to the therapist. The therapist's interest is in those matters she/he thinks important.[2]
- direction. The person in the powerful position of therapist can insist that their perception is correct. "You must believe me, you are depressed, and this is the correct treatment for you."
- suggestion during visual imagery or hypnosis or other interchanges. Suggestions can be planted in the patient's or client's mind that the therapist's perception, and only the therapist's perception, of reality is correct.
- mutual distortion. There is a transaction in which the patient and therapist subconsciously collude with one another to believe something for their mutual convenience.

OH, TO BE KNOWN

Everybody needs to be heard and to be known. There is, of course, major ambivalence about this because there is an underlying fear of rejection. With the breakdown of families and social structures, more and more people feel alone and fear rejection. Once a therapeutic relationship is well established and the patient is relatively confident that they will not be rejected, then they are more prepared to disclose who they are. Those who are alone and those who are in pain are particularly eager to be heard and known. If a counselor adheres to a particular diagnosis or treatment prescription of therapy that is wrong, i.e. it does not fit the patient, the patient is gradually impelled to accept the therapist's perception of what is wrong. This is often seen with the post-abortion situation. Then the patient must either:

- blame themselves and flagellate themselves. "I guess I'm stupid, I can't express myself properly ... that is why I'm not understood."
- withdraw into themselves and regress. "I don't believe that what he says is true about me, but I can't make him understand. Therefore I will

gradually stop trying to explain myself in an attempt to protect that kernel of truth that I have." As a person retreats, it becomes more difficult to reach him/her in subsequent therapy.

- become cynical. "No one really knows anybody, why should anybody know me?"
- become hopeless and self-destructive. "What's the use? No one will ever understand me. There is no point in living."
- keep searching for a suitable therapist. "There has got to be somebody out there who can understand me."
- accept palliative treatment, e.g. aspirin, religious Band-Aids, magical cures. "I know this isn't treating the underlying problem but at least I feel better."
- distort the truth of themselves to accommodate the assumptive form world of the therapist. "I know I am lying to myself but maybe I am wrong and she/he (the therapist) is right."
- fight with the therapist. This usually results in the patient being discharged in a rush. "Man, he's stupid! Why can't I convince him that he has me all wrong?"
- Find some other avenue of expression. "Well, I'll lie to my therapist about myself, but I will talk about what I really know about myself to my friends or I'll write it on a piece of paper."

10. THE PURSUIT OF TRUTH

Everyone, in reading any particular theory or treatment technique, must wonder "Is this true? Is this the most beneficial way of doing things? How can I know?" Everybody should be skeptical about whatever they are taught, but not so much that they blind themselves. They should have reasonably objective tests for truth. I suggest the following Fifteen point test:

1. Resonance. Does it evoke internal resonance? "It sounds right to me." This is because:
    - the Spirit of truth in you helps you understand what is true.
    - it fits with God's design for your person.
    - it helps you understand more about yourself.
    - it agrees with what you have already got to know about yourself.

2. Scripture. Does it agree with Scripture as a whole? It is important not to take Scripture, or this theory, out of context. It must not be seen or reacted to from any particular passage (or section), but as we understand Scripture and as we understand God.

3. Person of God. Does it fit with God' personality as I know Him and know that He would do that?

4. Motivation. Is it written or spoken by a man of truth? "The man that seeks to glorify the person that sent him is sent by God. He is a man of truth."[1] Avoid gurus, for they seek only their glory.

5. Wisdom. Is it understood and accepted by wise elders and peers?

6. Science. Does it agree with and align with good science?

7. Utility. Does it work and produce long-term benefits?

8. Popularity. Is it particularly popular? Very few truths were widely accepted by the generations in which they came to light. It is possible that the more unpopular a theory, the more likely it is to be correct.

9. Change. Does it make me uncomfortable. "If it demands a change in my thinking and behaviour, it could be right even through I don't like it."

10. Mutual Benefit. Does it benefit both the doer and the receiver? It should agree with and support the Universal Ethic of Mutual Benefit.

11. Healing. Does it diminish the number of kilogriefs of a suffering person?

12. Time. Does it stand the tests of time, being reasonably consistent or modified in a consistent way?

13. Peace. Is it blessed by the sense of God's Spirit, and not necessarily success? Does it bring more peace within and between people?

14. Glorifying. Does it show more of who God is and how He functions?

15. God's will. Does it fit in with what God is doing generally through all eternity, and what He is doing specifically at this point in history?

It is important to recognize that not one of the above criteria are enough to determine truth, but seldom will you find agreement on all fifteen. Hopefully the Psychology of Created Humanity theory satisfies most of these tests.

Truth is a description of reality. What is real is what is permanent. Scripture teaches that what we see is impermanent. Only what is unseen is permanent.[4] This seems to indicate that matter, as we know it, will disappear and some other form of matter, e.g. anti-matter, will endure. We see the body, and it will disappear, but the spirit, which we do not see and made of anti-matter, will be permanent.

Ever since Heisenberg introduced the principle of uncertainty in 1927, there has been some concern about whether it is possible to know truth. Quantum mechanics implies there are parallel truths. If you are on one track you will never know the other track, although it is just as real. If these are parallel realities there are parallel moralities. This position creates a number of problems for people who believe there is one real and knowable reality.

The problem of the pursuit of reality is that when you try to measure it, it escapes you. If you measure an electron as a particle, it behaves as a particle. If you measure it as a wave, it is a wave. Thus, the process of measuring distorts the phenomena that you are trying to observe and describe.

I believe there is a solution to that dilemma. Namely, that instead of attempting to find reality, you let reality find you. Instead of futile attempts to measure and describe things that are real, you allow the reality that is out there to impress itself upon you. Reality is centered in God and God is always declaring Himself. He wants us to know him. Thus, we can, in the reception of truth, be childlike, yet scientifically so.

Truth is unitary. Scripture and science must and do agree. When physicists discovered the Z Bozon and thus unified the electromagnetic and the weak force, it increased the possibility of finding one force, one reality that would describe all of nature. The difficulty has always been that to find that unitary force would require an immense amount of energy that humans at this time cannot create or harness. This seems to be additional evidence that order and power go together, thus pointing to one source of knowledge, power and truth centered in God. In my experience, scripture and science do agree. There may be times when there seems to be a discrepancy, but later discoveries support the truth in Scripture.

Truth is self-declaring. Since truth is centered in God, He finds us before we search for Him. We must search accurately and with determination and always be ready to receive and observe the unexpected.

Truth is powerful. Truth must and will prevail. It may appear that people can benefit at the expense of their neighbors and that when they bend or break the rules they get ahead and become famous and rich. But rule-breakers end their lives or their family's in ruin. The reason it is better to keep the rules of the game is that it eventually pays off. To be loving will always result in being loved. To show mercy always results in being shown mercy. Those who are peaceful will always find peace. Those are the rules that order our universe. Like gravity, they always apply. You might defy them briefly, but too soon you will feel the painful consequences.

Truth is correcting. With an honest pursuit of truth it is possible to find reality because every time we distort reality, it lets us know. God also lets us know when we are seeking off target. Our task is to be clearly receptive and curious, like a little child. How to be a child-like scientist is an interesting situation. This is not to say one should be unsophisticated in one's scientific pursuits, but it does say that one must always be open to surprises.

Although much is made of statistics, it should be remembered that the key to science is observation. When one observes a very important phenomenon, there are major associations that do not need the fine-tuning of statistics. If one discovers a new treatment modality and the patients become well twice as quickly or live twice as long, one does not need statistics. Statistics, after all, are significant or could happen by chance.

Gravity always applies; so does the Universal Ethic of Mutual Benefit. Reality is not tolerant. People complain about God's intolerance, but they should remember that God is no less tolerant than gravity. Reality is not tolerant of ignorance. Thus, it becomes vitally important for people to know the truth about God and the truth about themselves.

Truth is eventually seen because truth always prevails. Eventually families can only suppress their conflicts, shame and guilt to the third and fourth generation. At that point, the truth comes bubbling to the surface in the form of pain and confusion in the most sensitive people of that family. Although other family members would continue to hide things, the sensitive and vulnerable eventually draw attention to their plight with loud complaints so that those who honestly wish to understand can uncover the roots of that family's dysfunction.

To have family conflicts concentrated on one person is scapegoating. That individual who comes for counseling must realize that he/she is a scapegoat and agree to be a surrogate scapegoat, standing in for other small scapegoats in their family. This is the way to help heal an individual and stop tragedy from cycling from one generation to the next.

The most tragic aspects of individual or national history are:

- when people do not learn from their mistakes they will be repeated by the most unsuspecting, vulnerable people in the next generation.
- those who create problems scapegoat the most helpless and innocent for those problems.
- most people are afraid to unearth and examine painful history, usually because they are implicated in contributing to the tragedy.

To avoid False Memory Syndrome, counselors need to have a good grasp of reality, listen objectively, know themselves, recognize their tendency to react to their counselees projections and remember the damaging impact of neglect. This requires good training, accurate supervision, corrective feedback, analyzing their counseling results and keeping up to date on good research.

There is a dogma of victimization. False Memory Syndrome and false religion become increasingly entrenched by a combination of support and opposition. People, particularly women, are encouraged to feel sorry for themselves. This appears to be part of an old technique now used by militant feminists to recruit support so they can gain power.

PARABLE: TWO SPACE SHIP PILOTS

Bravo Zulu One. You are off course. You are heading straight for the big black hole in Sector nine, Galaxy Charlie two four.

Bravo Lima Two. This course seems fine to me. Who do you think you are to say I am off course?

Bravo Zulu One. I just checked with Starbase Eternity and I know where I am heading. Your course compared to the Eternity Nav Chart Romeo eight-three-two looks wrong, but don't take my word for it. Check it out with Starbase Eternity Nav Centre.

Bravo Lima Two. Yeah, I read Romeo eight a while back. That is a very old chart. It doesn't apply anymore. I am a pretty good pilot. I have made a few mistakes, but I get through okay and I try to be helpful to other pilots. Maybe if I get desperate I will radio for help.

Bravo Zulu One. You are further along that course than you realise. I suspect you must feel the acceleration of the black hole's gravity by now. You must change course 180 degrees and accelerate with all you've got and ask the Nav Centre for the best route out.

Bravo Lima Two. You're crazy. I'm having a great time. If I feel I am off course, I will pull up before it is too far. Besides which, I am sure Starbase Eternity knows that I am a good pilot and they will rescue me.

Bravo Zulu One. Man, don't be so crazy. That thing will crush you. If you get ten light years away from it you will never get out.

Bravo Lima Two. I don't really believe all that crap. I am sure Starbase Eternity will beam me out. After all, I am one of their real good guys.

Bravo Zulu One. Surely, by now you know that reality is intolerant. It doesn't matter what you think you are doing or how good you think you are, you have got to come to grips with the facts of eternal forces.

11. THE ETHICAL THERAPIST

We require all Hope Alive counsellees to make a signed and public declaration to professional conduct. Regardless of previous training or other professional associations, it is important to adhere to these professional practices, manners and ethics. Since this basic theory and practical program have a fundamentally different basis, the *Commitment to Professional Conduct* and ethics are also essentially different.

COMMITMENT TO PROFESSIONAL CONDUCT AS AN IIPLCARR GROUP COUNSELLOR

As an IIPLCARR group counselor, I solemnly commit myself to the following Code of Ethics:

1) I will promote the health and freedom of each person with whom I have an actual or implied agreement to counsel. My aim is to help restore as much as possible the individual to their original God-given design and purpose. Thus I must promote health, freedom and love. I must avoid creating dependencies. I must encourage each person to continue knowing and growing and using what they have learned for the benefit of others.

2) I will adhere to the *My Declaration for Life* statement of ethics or approved alternative ethical statement. I will display my ethics prominently for counsellees to see. I must live a life that is consistent with these ethics.

3) Before proceeding, I will obtain informed consent, carefully providing each counselee with the knowledge of the process, hazards and benefits of Hope Alive group counselling.

4) I will make a commitment to each counselee to continue working with them until they are healthier, are deceased, have voluntarily withdrawn themselves from counselling, have moved away or have been referred elsewhere.

5) I will adhere to the principles of the laws in my country regarding confidentiality and the reporting of abuse, neglect, potential homicide and possible suicide.

6) Together with my facilitators and counsellees, I will sign *the Principles of Commitment to Hope Alive Treatment and Training* and adhere to each provision, noting and discussing any exceptions.

7) I will carefully evaluate each potential counselee and form an independent opinion of each referral based on the damage, difficulties and needs of the individual, not being influenced by what is politically correct or socially approved or family coerced.

8) With the consent of the individual 1 assessed, I will report to the professional person who made the referral a summary of my findings.

9) I will maintain contact with and/or form a network of professionals from whom I can seek assistance or advice for any difficulties that arise in group counseling and after I have first spoken to my supervisor (except in emergent situations).

10) Before beginning group counseling, I will obtain a physician's opinion to determine whether my counselee's have an illness or condition that is inappropriate or incompatible with this type of counseling.

11) I will constantly evaluate the results of my counseling with interviews, questionnaires and as many objective measures as possible and be prepared to allow others to examine these results.

12) Not attempting to counsel people beyond my capabilities, I will readily refer to or consult with somebody who is more expert than I am, whenever it is required.

13) I will avoid counseling people beyond my competence and training.

14) I will improve my scientific understanding and treatment techniques with continued training, reading, experience and corrective feedback.

15) I will help further the science of treatment and, with the consent of my counselees, collect research data, both clinical and research.

16) I will accept supervision and corrective feedback and seek these from appropriate sources.

17) I will avoid treating family or friends or more than two people at any time from the same church or congregation.

18) I will honor my mentors in word and deed.

19) I will support my colleagues, providing encouragement, information and corrective feedback when necessary.

20) I will expect appropriate remunerations according to guidelines established by IIPLCARR or associates in my area and, if necessary, arrange for deferred payment, depending on my client's ability to pay.

21) I will control my group counseling by ethics, rules, and tasks rather than by personal influence, coercion, or manipulation and concentrate the counseling process in the group.

22) I will use the best IIPLCARR techniques available, ensuring they are always backed by good science, sound theory and Christian principles.

23) I will follow the Hope Alive Manual to direct my counseling.

24) I will maintain safe working conditions and protect co-workers and myself with liability and errors and omissions or malpractice insurance.

25) I will make and keep secure, proper clinical records.

26) I will not misrepresent my qualifications or advertise services I am not qualified to perform. I understand IIPLCARR certifies me solely to do group counseling for adults injured by childhood mistreatment and pregnancy loss.

27) Acknowledging that health and healing come from God, I will give credit where credit is due.

My DECLARATION FOR LIFE

Therapists must keep on learning and listening carefully to their patients so that they do not impose a treatment that tries to distort the patient's Blueprint.

The ethical therapist should display his/her ethics prominently and hold to them. The ethical standards for Hope Alive counselors can be summarized in the following statement:

MY DECLARATION FOR LIFE

REASONS

Almighty God, With You all life begins and ends.
I know my life entirely depends on You.
By You, all human life is loaned for a season.
I cannot give life to, or take life from anyone.

For You, I must hold in careful stewardship
My life, and the lives of all my neighbors.
You created mankind a little lower than the angels
And have given me Your life and love giving Spirit.
Through Jesus Christ, You have made me Your child,
Now my first priority is to show people their hope is in You.
You have honored me with Your challenging friendship
Thus, what I am becoming is more important than what I achieve.

You have conquered death and will soon destroy it.
Since I am Your servant, Your enemy is my enemy.
It is Your creation but death is seeking to ruin it.
I must fight death on its doorstep or it will attack me on mine.
There are no innocent bystanders in matters of life and death.
Unless I am fighting death, I am aiding and abetting its terror.
Without forgiveness and reconciliation between those who injure and are injured,
The triangles of tragedy must be re-enacted from generation to generation.
Unresolved bitterness will kill us and those we hate.
Unless forgiving and forgiven, our sins and illness will remain.

With love, You are always healing the weak and wounded,
By helping the smallest and weakest I learn to love like You.
Every person was wonderfully made in Your image,
So how could I ever benefit at the expense of another.
No, I benefit when I give my neighbors what they need,
For we are intrinsically bound together in the bundle of life.

COMMITMENT

I will love You more than my life; as long as I live I will always promote and enhance life for everyone,
Not regarding their wealth or rank, sex or race, ability or disability, Their size or completeness, I will love them as myself.
I will seek my neighbors' physical, mental and spiritual wholeness. Treating them equally, I will help distribute
Health and life, maintaining resources equally throughout the world.

I will help each one to the limit of my abilities and resources.

If, because of circumstances, I must choose who I will treat first,
I will treat those who most likely will benefit from what I can offer.
I will seek to know all the needs of all my neighbors And help find and apply new remedies.
I will try to untangle the tragic triangles that injure and kill.

Starting with myself I will exemplify and promote reconciliation.
I will not kill or hasten death or just let anyone die,
But will seek to remedy all factors that lead to the destruction of life.
I will oppose abortion, euthanasia, murder and genocide
And help heal all those affected by these tragedies.
I will fight death in all its guises
And avoid compromise with any form of evil.

PRAYER

Please Lord, help me to do what I say I believe.
Give me the courage to love life and live it fully.
Remind me that my struggle is but for a short time.
Forgive me for vanity and pride in my accomplishments.

Remind me You alone heal and I am privileged to be your helper. Keep me from fearing death or the consequences of serving You. Grant me sufficient strength to bring hope, healing and joy to others. Make me determined to loan my life without interest for The most complete life of each and all of my neighbors.

NOTES: 6 THE HEALING PROCESS

'John 9.

[2]Ney, P.G. &Ney, P.M. (1986). Our patient's seven unspoken questions. Canadian Medical Association Journal. 35. 879-880.

'John 7.

'*11 Corinthians 4:18.

international Copyright. Philip G. Ney. Used by author's permission.

7

THE USE OF EARLY HYPOTHESIS TESTING IN THERAPY

Deeply Damaged is designed to guide a reasonably competent counselor into developing a unique therapy, but not to teach basic skills. We have frequently found that even experienced counselors make basic mistakes. An especially common one is by trying with a series of leading questions to make the counselee guess what the counselor is thinking. Anyone who has ever received this kind of interview knows just how much it feels like either being taught by a poor teacher or being interrogated by a clumsy police officer. It seems unbelievable, but a counselor can conduct very good counseling sessions without asking one question. The following section was originally written for family physicians, and attempts to make counseling more efficient by getting the counselee to work hard at putting together the pieces of the subconscious puzzle.

All psychotherapists and counselors hope that they can find some method that will make them more effective and efficient in the analysis of illness and the formulation of good management plans. Because the human mind is so complex, attempting to determine what is really troubling an emotionally disturbed counselee often takes a lot of time and effort. This section attempts to describe one method that might make counselors more efficient in their interviews.

1. PRESUPPOSITIONS

Every counselor enters an interview with a host of assumptions that prejudice his/her capacity to observe. Although physics, existentialism, behaviorism, Freudianism and transactionalism teach us that it is impossible to separate the observed from the observer, there is a practical advantage for counselors in understanding their own assumptions. These assumptions are often components of their early experience with life and they are not easily detected.

In psychoanalysis, it is assumed that you will not see in counselees what you cannot see in yourself. The counselor must therefore be aware of his/her defense mechanisms. The counselor's own disinclination to work may be projected onto a counselee ("you are not really working at your problem"). Alternatively, the counselor may deny stresses he/she is feeling ("you don't really have a problem"), engage in reaction formation ("don't worry, I will fix

everything"), displace conflicts from his/her own home ("it sounds like your wife is really getting to you"), or identify with the counselee's suffering ("that must have been terribly painful").

Counselors tend to identify with the person who appears to be suffering most. This is usually the counselee they have engaged in treatment. This means they tend to see the world through the counselee's eyes. It is small wonder, for example, that male counselors who more frequently see women than men, tend to see men through women's eyes and often may not understand that men suffer as much as women.

2. OBSERVATION

The counselor must question why he/she observes a counselee in a particular way. The first answer is, "Because of me, my abilities and prejudices." The next is, "Because it is really there. I see that the counselee is relatively slow in responding, pale looking, teary eyed and preoccupied." The counselor must then ask, "Why is the counselee this way?" Very little information can be acquired before the counselor begins hypothesis testing.

3. HYPOTHESES

A counselor's hypotheses are seen in the directions of his/her questioning. As soon as more interest has been generated in one aspect of a problem than another, a simple hypothesis can be formulated and put forward tentatively. It is even better to suggest more than one possibility, e.g. "I suspect the root of the problem can be found in the type of relationship this counselee has with the spouse and mother." It is more efficient to make careful observations, formulate early hypotheses and test them with statements that both the counselor and the counselee can examine, e.g. "Hello Mr. Jones, I am Dr. White. I want to help you, so please tell me what brings you here and how you think I can help. You look pretty unhappy." is preferred over "Hello, what is your name and your age? Now, what is your problem and how long have you had it?"

Once the hypothesis is declared, the counselee is free to respond, "No, Dr. White, you are quite wrong. Although I look pale, sad and preoccupied, actually I am much more anxious than depressed. I think I have cancer." Even if the counselee is not obviously trying to be helpful, the counselor can assume that the first response to the hypothesis is additional useful information. The counselor then has a choice to collect more information or pursue the hypothesis. "No, Mr. Jones, I think I was right the first time. You are looking depressed and I really need to know why. From what I know about your family, I believe it has something to do with your father's recent death. Maybe, you are afraid to tell me more because it might overwhelm you with grief." The counselor is now not only hypothesizing about why the counselee is looking sad, but also about why the counselee denies something that is very apparent to them both. As in psychoanalysis, the inquiring counselor must tackle any resistance in communicating.

4. TEST

A good counselor, like a good scientist, will observe, hypothesize and test. The test is to see how counselees will respond to various possible hypotheses. The hypothesis is stated as a partial and tentative explanation. The counselee is invited to consider it and elaborate on it if possible. Usually, the counselor is on target if either a strong affirmative or negative response is obtained, and probably wrong if the counselee looks puzzled. If the hypothesis fits and makes sense, the counselee usually feels vastly relieved and grateful that at last someone understands what she or he has been trying to say. In my experience, counselees will definitely let you know if they think you are trying to put some idea into their head that does not belong there. When a counselee protests too much you are probably right.

5. COMPONENTS OF AN INTERVIEW

The efficient interview should be made up of the following components and in the following order of frequency *(viz.* the counselor should be requesting information much more frequently than asking questions):

Request for information. "Please tell me how it all began", or "I need to know what you think is the cause of all your trouble." Requests are more polite, less restricting and less demanding for the counselee.

Empathetic statements. "That must have been an awful time for you", or "I can understand why you might feel like giving up." If you have observed well and expressed an un-stated feeling, there is often a cascade of emotions. The therapeutic relationship will quickly intensify because the counselee no longer feels alone or alienated when his/her counselor has sufficient understanding to put the right words to a deep feeling.

Observations. "You have described a very sad event, but I noticed while you were talking about it that you were smiling." "It appears that each time your wife mentions going dancing you start talking about your back ache." People are not as aware of themselves as you might think. Your quietly spoken observations can have startling effects.

Reassurance. "Don't worry. I don't think you are crazy even though I can see you have had some very peculiar mental experiences." "1 am not here to tell you what to do." You can probably guess what is worrying your counselee. Do not wait for reassurance to be sought by the counselee.

Questions. "How old were you when that happened?" "Why did you say that just now?" The more questions you use, the more your counselee will feel he/she is being interrogated rather than interviewed. Yet, occasionally a question is the most efficient way of getting a particular piece of information.

Explanations. "If 1 understand you correctly, there is a connection between your anger at your wife and the experience you had as a child with your mother." "I suggest your depression began shortly after your first-born arrived. You seemed to have been very disappointed he wasn't a girl." An interpretation is a type of explanation and should tie together the impulse, anxiety, and defense from the past, present and from transference. Your explanation should be put forward tentatively as a hypothesis.

Advice. The usual rule is "If you feel like giving advice, don't." This is not because you are not wise and helpful; it is because they have probably heard it before. The counselee probably knows what to do, but he/she is unable to follow through. More advice only makes him/her feel more inadequate. So only give advice when you are reluctant to do so and then only if you are paid for it.

Confrontations. "Quite frankly, I don't believe you." Or "This is the third time in a row you have been late for your appointment." Some people need a straight, hard statement before they will take what you say seriously.

Once you get used to this method of interviewing, you will find very little need for questions. When people feel you are on their wavelength, they will readily talk. Use your requests and explanations to guide the communication when it is necessary.

6. FOCUS

The important things to focus on in an interview are:

- those themes that are often repeated.
- those statements that are loaded with feeling.
- obvious blanks.

Remember that the counselee's behavior is distorted by the interaction with you and your prejudices. Yet counselees, although changed by the setting in which they are interviewed and sometimes by your tentative hypotheses, are themselves and usually cannot lie. Eventually, they will disclose themselves by how they describe things. Like criminals, no matter how much they are stretching the truth, they leave a characteristic trail.

During the interview the counselor is the instrument of observation and his/her most finely tuned senses are those of emotions; unfortunately, emotions can get the counselor into trouble and are easily distorted. Thus, the counselor must have a high degree of self-knowledge. Once the counselor understands why he/she has a certain emotional response to a counselee's communication, his/her own feelings can be used to clarify many other observations.

It is important that counselors realize their main functions are to empathize, encourage and explain. To reiterate, if they feel like giving advice, that is usually when they should not. Very seldom is it possible to give advice that the person can use. Counselees have usually heard all the advice before. The difficulty is that they lack the skills or strength to do what they know they should. If, by dint of great wisdom, you give advice that a person is able to carry out, it is very affirming to you and the counselee.

Psychotherapy is the fine clinical skill of moving puzzle pieces of the mind together so the counselee can see how they fit. They are encouraged to keep working on the puzzles in their minds by the wonderful satisfaction they gain from piecing together elements of important conflicts and feeling they made the discovery themselves. Psychotherapy is not either waiting indefinitely for the counselee to stumble on a solution, or completing the puzzle yourself. When counselees are helped in their natural quest to understand complicated conflicts, they have gained insight that will be useful and stay with them. This process of guided self-discovery also motivates them to continue the struggle to understand the roots of the difficulty for the rest of their life.

It is very important that the group counseling keep from being sidetracked from a discussion of "rights." The object of this therapy is to be as human as possible and to make it possible for others to be as human as possible. If counselees are striving to find and defend their "rights," then they will also have to find some authority to enforce those rights. There are plenty of situations where there are no "rights" or no one to enforce them. The only thing that will always work is being fully human.

7. SUMMARY

It is virtually impossible for a counselor to be completely objective about a counselee but, the more self-knowledge the counselor has, the less likely is he/she to distort communication. If the counselor observes, then tentatively states an early hypothesis, both counselor and counselee can test it. The net effect is that both parties, instead of playing the time wasting game of "What's on my mind?" can work more co-operatively and efficiently.

8

REQUIREMENTS FOR THE GROUP TREATMENT OF ABORTION WOUNDED PEOPLE

1. WHY CHRISTIANS SHOULD BE BETTER SCIENTISTS AND THERAPISTS

At one time, psychotherapy was greatly influenced by existentialism. The existentialists were determined to ask the fundamental questions about existence. They could ask those questions of their counselees only if they had some answers for themselves. They had to be able to know why people existed, when they began and where they were going. Obviously, this required knowing God. As therapy became increasingly anti-theistic, people lost the ability to answer existential questions for themselves and for their patients. Eventually they disregarded the need to seek solutions to existential questions. Thus, the pursuit of the knowledge of humans has become increasingly materialistic and dehumanizing. At the same time, astrophysicists, in their pursuit of truth about the universe, have been prepared to seek answers to the questions of origins, meanings and endings, and their science has blossomed. If people are prepared to address existential questions, God-loving counselors have been able to discover many things that psychologists and psychiatrists never could.

Christians should be better scientists for the following reasons:

- There are no questions that they are afraid to ask. There is no truth that is too embarrassing or uncomfortable. At best, we are all sinners saved by grace.
- Christians do not need to be afraid to face human chaos. Knowing God means that there is always an ultimate answer, even if the present ones do not seem to make sense. There is no chance they will have to deal with a deep anxiety that springs from realizing parents; scientists and teachers do not know answers to the ultimate questions.
- There is no fear of being abandoned if they err or stray from the truth. As long as they persist and they honestly seek the truth, they will find truth. God has sworn by Himself never to forget or forsake His own.
- Because truth is self-revealing, they are not afraid of distorting observations by observing. They do not need to be so anxious in collecting and analyzing data as long as they are prepared to accept corrections.
- They know truth is self-correcting. If they honestly persist, mistakes that they make will be revealed. They will be brought to understand where they are wrong or pursuing research in the wrong direction.

- They have the assurance that truth will triumph. This will enable scientists and therapists to be both gentle and persistently persuasive. Knowing you are on the winning side helps you always to put the person before the principle.

2. REQUIREMENTS FOR COUNSELLEES

Individuals who become counselees in the Hope Alive post-pregnancy loss and/or child abuse and neglect counseling group must meet the following requirements. They:

- have no major psychiatric or physical illnesses.
- have a reasonably stable home and work situation.
- have at least one mature, supportive person (spouse, relative or good friend) willing to stick with them for the duration of counseling.
- are able to commit themselves to staying with the group until its completion.
- are capable of tolerating high levels of stress without acting out or becoming seriously unwell.
- are suffering and genuinely seeking healing for themselves, and not just to please someone else.
- have a sponsor assigned to them.

Those who do not meet these criteria should be referred to, or provided with, other appropriate treatment.

Until or unless they have appropriate professional training, Hope Alive counselors should not treat the following:

- those who have an important relationship with somebody who is very obstructive to their doing Hope Alive.
- those who are on psychotropic medication, e.g. chlorpromazine, or major antidepressants.
- those who have had previous psychiatric hospitalizations.
- those who are being treated by another counselor.
- those who have had treatment by a number of other counselors.
- those who are epileptic, psychotic, anorexic, suicidal, hypochondriac, sociopathic, etc.
- those who have had more than two abortions.
- those who have had a combination of adoption, abortion and being an abortion survivor.
- those who have recently dropped out of a previous group.

- those who are involved in the occult.
- anyone who is losing a struggle with alcohol or drug addiction.
- those who decompensate (fall apart) or act out under stress.

Experience has shown these people need expert treatment and/or very experienced group counsellors.

3. REQUIREMENTS OF THE GROUP

The Group Should:

- consist of four to seven women and/or men. Mixed groups work well, but it is wise not to have one woman or one man in a group where all other members are of the same sex.
- have one counsellor (or two co-counsellors), one trainee or cocounsellor, one facilitator.
- meet in a secure, private, comfortable place where refreshments can be made available.
- continue for no less than two hours per session. A three or four hour session is more effective (with breaks).
- usually do one manual described session for each meeting. On an outpatient basis, it is difficult to handle more than two group sessions per week.

4. FIVE HARSH REALITIES

People committing themselves to the group process must recognize five harsh facts about themselves:

1. Many important changes in the way they think and act are possible, but the person they should have been is not alive and they will never become in this life what God had originally planned for them.

2. A helpless child has died *in utero*. Therefore there must be deep and difficult mourning because that child cannot be replaced.

3. They have been deeply wounded by early mistreatment and by an abortion and they require extensive healing, but some damage cannot be healed.

4. There are many broken relationships that need the hard work of real reconciliation, but some relationships cannot be mended.

5. One of God's most beautiful paintings, a beautifully constructed, unique

baby, was wantonly cut to pieces and He is hurt and angry about it. Thus, there is need for repentance, forgiveness, and for reinstatement of a relationship with

the Lord. He is ready to receive anyone who calls to Him and, through Christ, forgive them, but He does not break His own rules and there are painful consequences to face.

5. THE VALUE OF GROUP COUNSELING

For the following reasons, group counseling facilitates the efficient and effective healing of adults who were abused or neglected as children and/or have had abortions or are abortion survivors:

- Hearing others emote encourages the expression of a wide range of feelings. When one counselee identifies with the feelings of another, she vicariously experiences emotions she might not have otherwise allowed herself to feel or express.
- Counselees gain insight from each other's hard won understanding.
- The empathetic expressions by other group members about the effects of abortion and mistreatment tend to validate how a person felt. As a child, his/her loneliness, pain and hopelessness were seldom communicated. When it was, it was often denied or denigrated by the adults.
- The group produces a sense of cohesiveness that diminishes the loneliness of their suffering.
- The group exercises and role-plays require the participation of a group of people. Often they do role-plays in pairs. Sometimes the group takes one side of the issue, while the one person being focused on, takes the other.
- Group counseling is efficient and egalitarian. It makes treatment of more people possible and spreads the scarce resource of competent counselors more equitably among so many wounded people.
- Any insights and explanations provided by the counselor tend to be received differently by each member of the group. The variety of reactions helps the counselor clarify his/her statements.
- Groups are good opportunities to collect clinical information and train additional counselors.
- Being in a group encourages people to muster courage and more freely express their feelings and their opinions. As they watch others, each small expression encourages a larger or different expression from another counselee.
- Each person represents a potential 'transference object.' Thus there is an increased opportunity to interpret various defense mechanisms.

- People in the group are representative of many others in the world. Counselees will interact with them as such.
- Many people who have been mistreated become isolated, even though they appear to be popular. The group provides an opportunity to gain acceptance for the person they are; wounds, warts, weariness and all. It provides the realization that they can always find acceptance somewhere.
- Hope Alive group counseling is an opportunity for people to become honest and hear the honest expression of other people, so that they gradually drop various aspects of their facade and look deeper into themselves. Their ability to see the worst aspect of themselves gives them the courage to look into any truth and have sensitivity to falseness.
- This group is a very good place to learn and practice new communication and social skills.
- It is a good, and usually honest, sounding board for thoughts and ideas they have long suppressed, whether they be philosophical, theological, etc. Counselees very seldom find that anyone thinks they, or their ideas, are foolish. In the healing process, you will often realize that an explanation given by yourself as a counselor is less well heard than if it was given by somebody else in the group.
- The group provides an opportunity to attempt to re-enact tragic triangles in a controlled fashion.
- Each group member triggers in others strong emotions that can be traced to their origins and understood.

6. THE VALUE OF ROLE PLAYS, PSYCHODRAMAS AND OTHER GROUP EXERCISES

The psychological exercises in the Hope Alive group counseling process are both real and metaphorical. They are particular, but with wide application. They begin a process that most people have been putting off. They teach skills people can use for the rest of their lives. These exercises illustrate the nature of that process, give people a real taste of what it is like, and teaches them new communicating and self problem-solving techniques.

Role plays are used in this counseling process because they:

- provide an opportunity to practice a new skill, e.g. assertion.
- dramatically highlight aspects of some interpersonal conflict from the person's earlier life.
- show aspects of an intra psychic conflict by having one person play one side of the debate in one's head, while another person plays the other side.
- Illustrate part of the explanation or interpretation that is being developed.

- Externalize an internal conflict so it is easier to identify both sides.
- demonstrate how having someone lake another's part helps the other to see him/herself.
- help them recognize how easy it is to take opposite sides of almost any conflict and recognize their deeply ingrained ambivalence.
- practice a new behavior or way of communicating. If it is practiced often enough, this produces neural connections, i.e. a type of neurolinguistic programming.

The purposes of the rehabilitation projects to prevent abortion and abuses are:

- to decrease the chances of harm happening to children.
- to stop the persons from being self centered. Counseling of necessity encourages people to focus on themselves. At the end of the counseling they must turn outward and become loving to complete the healing.
- to stop re-enacting cycles of tragedy with a practical, approved project.
- to teach people to be loving. It is healthy to be loving, both physically and psychologically. It brings the right mix of neuron-transmitters. It lowers pulse and blood pressure.
- to put to good use hard won lessons from life so that though their painful experience was tragic, it can also be helpful to others.
- to use residual anger and pain only to enhance and try to protect scapegoats.

7. THE NEW COUNSELOR

We recommend that anyone who has just completed the training course and is embarking on their first few groups carefully follow the directions in the Hope Alive manual and make sure their counselees do all the recommended exercises. These are well-tested techniques and are supported by a reasonably well-proven therapeutic outcome. After a counselor has done a few groups he/ she can innovate, adding some original ideas and adapting the treatment to her/ his own style. No matter how experienced the counselor, it is important to follow the sequence of phases and do the critical exercises if one is to expect a reasonable outcome.

The dangers of trying to treat before being healed are:

- The person who is trying to treat before they are healed will not let the counselee grow past them, or become any more mature than they are, just as immature parents cannot encourage their child to greater maturity.
- One will not see in others what one will not see in oneself. One will tend to re-enact unresolved problems from one's own past in the group and

recruit the counselees to assist him/herself in the re-enactment.

Long ago, Jesus asked a very frightened lady (Luke 8:42-48), who was trying to hide the fact that she had a very embarrassing menstrual problem, to talk in front of a noisy, skeptical crowd. This was good for her and good for them.

She was taught not to be ashamed of her humanity, e.g. menorrhagia. The crowd was taught to listen, to hear her distress and see how sympathetically but adroitly Jesus dealt with the essential issue. It is also important to note that Jesus felt power going out of Him, something like two photons leaving the sun. It took energy to heal, and this immense power resource, Jesus, felt it. It is both because He was so sensitive and because healing, or, more precisely, facilitating healing, is time and energy consuming. It is too power draining to be in the healing profession unless a person stays tapped into God's infinite source of power. If anyone tries to heal with their own strength, they become tired, cynical, mechanistic and eventually dehumanizing. That process is often seen in idealistic, newly trained people. They too soon become quick pill or quick advice 'pushers.'

8. HEALING THE WHOLE PERSON

The physician's first intent should be to prevent illness. For CAN, PLS, PAS, PLSS and PASS, among many other preventative measures, this involves ensuring that:

- all babies (from conception) are welcomed and preparations are made to protect, nurture and guide each child.
- there is sufficient support for husbands and wives anticipating pregnancy.
- maturity is promoted so that children are not bearing children.
- the myth of overpopulation is exposed and the value of children is increased.
- sexual titillation is decreased.
- marital fidelity is promoted by the media and 'sex education' programs.
- marriage partners and young parents are given insight and wisdom about what and why their experience is so challenging.

Once a pregnancy has occurred, health-care professionals must:

- help resolve any ambivalence about changing and maturing.
- help each couple through their Crisis of Incorporation.
- nurture every pregnant mother.
- support every expectant father.
- help prohibit abortion by providing a wide range of alternatives and accurately informing everyone of the consequences.

- help resolve conflicts from early mistreatment in each parent.

Conflicts arising from abortion, child abuse and neglect are often passed on despite a person's determination to be a better parent. Children are preoccupied with surviving and with developing. Seldom there are qualified people to counsel them. Intense, early conflicts are seldom resolved by children. The conflict stays with them as adults. Because it is not understood through either introspection or communication, it has a high chance of being re-enacted. When these tragic triangles are well treated, they do not cycle from one generation to the next.

9. PREVENTION BETTER THAN CURE

I contend that abortion is the most destructive force within humanity. It destroys millions of babies, deeply damages millions of parents, grandparents and siblings, and undermines the basic structures of society and civilization. Although it is vitally important to treat those who are damaged, obviously it would be much more effective to stop abortions from occurring. It is very important that everyone involved with treatment spend as much time in preventing the disorders they treat, otherwise they could subtly promote problems in order to financially gain. I suggest all the following principles apply in preventing abortion:

PRIMUM NON NOCERE

It is a physician's first duty not to do harm. Anybody engaged in health care must realize that, unless they are absolutely convinced they are doing good, they must do nothing - regardless of how much pressure or persuasion is placed upon them. This is especially true for a natural, self-limiting condition like pregnancy.

BURDEN OF PROOF

The burden of proof lies with those who provide or promote any procedure to show beyond reasonable doubt that it is both safe and effective. It is not the responsibility of pro-lifers to show that abortion is harmful. It is the responsibility of those who are so-called pro-choice and anyone who supports the idea of freely available abortions to show beyond any reasonable doubt that abortion is effective treatment for some kind of conditions and safe for the patient and that the reported hazards are not true. To date, no one has shown that abortion is safe or effective for any medical, surgical, psychiatric or social condition.

Humans are tightly bound in the bundle of life. What one does to others, one does to oneself. When a person loves others, he/she loves him/herself. One cannot benefit at the expense of others. If a person harms others, he/she is harming him/herself. Killing unborn babies harms everyone, even those observers who could and should do something.

BEST EVIDENCE

Medicine has always worked on the basis of the best evidence. With respect to abortion, the best evidence is that there is no benefit and that there is much harm. According to this principle, abortion should not be done.

POLITICAL POSITION.

Although many good politicians feel that they have to provide abortion because that is what is demanded, they do not seem to understand that what they should be saying is, "Of course, we are happy to provide abortions, once it has been conclusively demonstrated they are beneficial and safe."

INCONSISTENCY WEAKENS DETERMINATION

Many Christians and others, who should be strongly pro-life are soft on abortion because:

- they may need to have one for their daughter if she becomes pregnant at an early stage of life or out of wedlock.
- they are implicated in causing abortions by not trying hard to stop them.
- they, or some member of their family, have had an abortion and have not yet dealt with it in sufficient depth.
- they are afraid of facing the rejection or loss of job if they are strongly pro-life.
- they think that God does not care because he is not doing anything visible to stop abortions.
- they have counseled or referred somebody for an abortion or are implicated in such a way that until they are clear of their part of contributing to abortion they cannot, in all good conscience, speak to stop abortions.

The inconsistency of Christians being soft on abortion creates an enormous problem because now 60-70% of women in the United States and Canada, by the age of 45, have had an abortion. There are a vast number of people who are implicated and cannot speak out against abortion until they have dealt with their problems. Unfortunately, there are very few people available or interested in healing those damaged by child abuse and abortion.

Some of the required healing is summarized in Table 8.1 on the following pages. It is easy to see that, before all the core conflicts are dealt with, there are processes to be completed that are not part of this book. We hope this group counseling will achieve enough healing and teach enough skills that counselees will be able to complete the rest. It may take the rest of their lives.

CORE CONFLICT	COMPLETE CARE (Well. Almost)
1. **Unresolved Griefs** "I know I must, but I cannot let go." Most complicated griefs for 8 reasons: ▪ fetus de-humanized ▪ no one listens ▪ loss of person I was ▪ loss of person 1 could have been ▪ loss of childhood I never had ▪ is easily delayed ▪ pathological depression ▪ dysfunctional immune system, poor health	▪ Prevent losses, stop abortions, life and sex are sacred ▪ Foster parents for mother and child as long as needed ▪ Welcome, incorporate and grieve dead child ▪ Acknowledge and grieve the death of the PISHB ▪ Relinquish and commit Blueprint to God ▪ Welcome and establish Pilgrim ▪ Grieve aborted siblings
2. **Anger at Perpetrator, Victim, Observer and Self "What do I do with all this bate?"** ▪ pain of physical, verbal, sexual abuse and/or neglect ▪ afraid will hurt as hurt • lack of support ▪ pass on scapegoating to child ▪ being abandoned	▪ Accept Christ as scapegoat ▪ Accept role as surrogate scapegoat [a] realize permanent damage ▪ Reconciliation with Perpetrators, Observers and victims ▪ Learn to assert Pilgrim ▪ Identify and desensitize triggers ▪ Learn when and how to flee

Table 8.1 Summary of Treatment

CORE CONFLICT	COMPLETE CARE (Well. Almost)
3. **Worthlessness** **"I want to be loved, but how could anybody love me?"** • not welcomed • neglected as worthless person • ontological guilt - did not achieve potential • damaged by criticism • not given what needed, so nobody • series of damaging relationships • punished as bad person, so no body	• welcomed into existence as priceless, • unique person • allow Pilgrim to be loved and to love • discard False Faces • redefine authentic self • negotiate realistic expectations . • define and affirm Pilgrim
4. **Death Desires** **"There is always one way out of this pain and confusion, but I do not really want to be dead."** • survivor guilt • murderous anger turned inwards • destroyed own helpless child • real guilt and unreal guilt from abuse • desire for reunion with lost loved ones	• welcomed by Jesus, family and friends • welcome aborted siblings • face criminal charges, confess, and • accept pardon • face hate in self and world • reconciliation with P,V,0
5. **Self-Doubt 1** **"It seems I can make only bad choices, but I cannot procrastinate any longer." "** • my decisions were destructive • always told to be careful • my desires are misleading • frequent criticism • destructive relationships	• learn to listen to your body • care for dependent creatures • safe, holding environment • test in-built limits

Table 8.1 Summary of Treatment

CORE CONFLICT	COMPLETE CARE (Well. Almost)
6 . Anxious Attachment **"I feel I need him/her, but I should say good-bye."** • parent always was not there • fear to commit and be committed • fear of rejection confirmed • parents aborted sibling • early day care •	• held while holding • detach, then reattach comfortably • face good-byes and parents' destructiveness • trustworthy commitment • fulfilled commitment of group
7. Collusion of Pseudo-Secrets **"There is so much I need to know, but I am afraid to ask."** • abortion or abuse in family • need to explore, but afraid • fear of destroying family • fragile parents • questioning suppressed • Cain syndrome •	• discard False Faces • face truth and consequences • accept parents' limitations • all questions answered • push through resistance to knowing
8. Distrust **"Who can I trust? - not even myself."** • do not believe in love and parents • cannot accept feedback • self-serving parents • parents abort but avow love	• grieve loss of parents I should have had • truthful expression of love • parents admissions of limitations • take risks loving others • given meaningful responsibilities

Table 8.1 Summary of Treatment

CORE CONFLICT	COMPLETE CARE (Well. Almost)
9. Fears **"There are many dangers. I cannot keep hiding from them."** • illogical punishment • death sentence is passed on siblings • existential anxiety • replacement child • not welcomed, but wanted - therefore cannot exist • threats of abandonment	• assert welcomeness • eternal security in Christ • commitment by parents, spouse and families • face unwelcomeness • confront evil
10. Desperate Guilt **"I made so many mistakes I cannot correct."** • contribute to abortion or abuse • confession obstructed • being an abortion survivor • ignore or tempt God • Jacob complex	• reconciliation with Perpetrator, Victim and Observers • know and accept God's mercy • rejoice in forgiveness • forgive others as is forgiven • realize given goodness

Table 8.1 Summary of Treatment

CORE CONFLICT	COMPLETE CARE (Well. Almost)
11. Loveless, self-centered **"I want to love and be loved, but I know 1 am not capable Of either."** • selfish or immature parents • feel unlovable because not loved • loving attempts have been rejected • taught to be selfish • pointless counseling	• assert welcomeness • eternal security in Christ • commitment by parents, spouse and families • face unwelcomeness • confront evil
12. Joyless **"There are many reasons to be joyful, but I do not know how. I just cannot feel it."** • feel deserve sad life and pain as punishment • do not know what joy is • believe the joy would soon fade • no real celebrations in past • resist being thankful • no models for joy • do not know or credit God	• reconciliation with Perpetrator, Victim and Observers • know and accept God's mercy • rejoice in forgiveness • forgive others as is forgiven • realize given goodness

Table 8.1 Summary of Treatment

6. OUTLINE OF THERAPEUTIC PHASES

The eleven phases outlined on the following pages (Table 8.2) have thirty sessions that would ideally require one group each, i.e. 30 x 2 hours. Because of the variability in amount of damage and composition of groups, the complete process may require five to eight additional group sessions.

Phase	SESSION	OBJECT
I. COMMITMENT	**1: Informed Consent**	Describe the process, collect data, each give a brief history and obtain informed consent. Deal with issues of trust.
	2: Defences & Excuses Denial & Resistance	Assign role-play partners. Get and give a solemn commitment. Lay excuses on table.
II..REALIZING MISTREATMENT	**3: Remembering the Pain, Fear and Confusion**	Remembering abuse, abortion and neglect in a controlled way.
	4: Recognising the Damage	Recognizing the damage caused to individuals and relationships from abuse, neglect and abortion.
	5: Reconstructing the Tragic Triangles	Understanding who played the three parts of the tragic triangle and why.
	6: Training triggers, breaking barriers.	Finding the roots to strong reactions, then overcoming the internal and external resistance to the natural healthy responses.
III. CHANGING ANGER AND WITHDRAWAL	**7: Assertion Against Assault**	Training in assertion and desensitization to deal with the real and implied threats.
	8: Flight when necessary	When and how to run away from danger and traps.
	9: Resisting Manipulation	Learning to resist guilt induction and subtle manipulation, yours and theirs.

Table 8.2 Outline of Therapeutic Phases

Phase	SESSION	OBJECT
IV.. DEALING WITH GUILT	**10: Accepting Partial Responsibility**	Assessing and accepting a portion of the contribution and responsibility of the tragedies.
	11: Facing Existential Guilt	Learning to accept your right to exist and need to mature.
V. REMOVING FALSE FACES	**12: Describing the False Faces**	Describing and owning the Dancer and Urchin
	13: Discarding Dancer and Urchin	Laying to rest False Faces that frustrate the Pilgrim.
VI. PASSING THROUGH DESPAIR TO HOPE ALIVE	**14: Rediscovering My Blueprint**	A close and careful examination of the Person I Should Have Become
	15: Needs that Were Never Met	Recognizing and mourning the loss of a reasonable childhood and family.
	16: Mourning the Person I Should Have Become	Recognizing and grieving the loss of what 1 could have been
VII.. GRIEVING MY LOSSES	**17: Remembering the Forgotten**	Humanize and name the children of pregnancy losses.
	18: Welcoming Lost Children into the Family	Remembering the events surrounding the pregnancy loss, feel the pain, and know what happened to the infant. Welcome them into the family.
	19: Relinquishing Lost Babies and Committing Their Spirits to God	Lay to rest and grieve the miscarried, stillborn and aborted children. Committing their spirit into God's hands.

Table 8.2 Outline of Therapeutic Phases

Phase	SESSION	OBJECT
VII. RECONCILIATION	**120: Forgiving Myself**	Forgiving all those who should have done something.
	21: Reconciliation with Perpetrators and Observers	Forgiving and being forgiven by my Victims
	22: Reconciliation with Those I Have Injured	Forgiving and being forgiven by God.
IX. RECONSIDERING RELATIONSHIPS	**23: Reconciliation with God.**	Getting others to help me know my real authentic Pilgrim.
	24: Redefining Myself	
	25: Negotiating Realistic Expectations with Adults and Children	Learning ways to establish reasonable expectations of myself and others.
X. REHABILITATION AND REJOICING	**26: Attenuating Pair Bonds**	Loosening bonded ties to previous and pathological relationships.
	27: Learning to Love	Defending and helping children with a specific rehabilitation prevention project.
XL FUTURE AND BEYOND	**28: Celebrating Life, The Alternative Plan**	Sharing the Blueprint with God and planning a full life. Making some practical rearrangements in my life to create order and direction.

Table 8.2 Outline of Therapeutic Phases

1. THERAPY AS UNDERSTANDING, UNLOCKING AND LEARNING

THERAPY AS UNDERSTANDING

Loved. People need to be understood. Until they are understood, no one knows what they need and they cannot be loved. Being understood will help them realize they are not alone and they are not crazy.

Hope. Being understood creates hope. If one is understood, then one believes that one's needs are understood and those needs now have a better chance of being met.

Efficiency. Metaphorically, to understand oneself makes it possible to be a better "driver of the machine.'' Those who understand transmissions, compression, timing, etc. can drive cars more effectively and efficiently. When we understand ourselves - our mind, body and spirit - we are better able to organize and program ourselves.

Continuing insight. To learn how to learn about oneself is a useful skill that promotes self-directed insight. For example, one can use an understanding of dream analysis or trigger tracing learned in group, for the rest of one's life.

Puzzle-solving. Humans are intrinsically curious about themselves, more curious about themselves than anything else. They see the content of their mind as a gigantic puzzle. It is possible, as a counselor, to put the right pieces together - but that would not be appreciated, or to wait indefinitely, but that would take enormous time.

Alternative plan. The blueprint is permanent, an eternal, God-given direction for oneself. It must be dusted off so that people can better see and understand their Alternative Plan. The Alternative Plan is a more painful route, but in time and by God's grace, it results in the same fulfillment.

Knowing others. People need to know themselves so that they can know others. They need to know others so that it is easier to be known by others.

Discovering past. Solutions are hidden in the experiences of the painful past. One needs a route to that invaluable information.

My contribution. There are deep fears of unearthing information from the painful past, partly because people know that they are implicated in creating that painful past. They need help in understanding how to acknowledge their contribution and resolve their guilt.

THERAPY AS UNLOCKING

With words. Humans were designed to communicate. In fact, they are unable not to communicate. If communicating with words and emotions is blocked, the communication will come out in some other way - often misdirected, muted or confusing. Often it comes out as painful problems.

Distrust. Communication is aided when the counselee first deals with the feelings and appeals that the individual is most preoccupied with, namely communicating their pain and distrust.

Flooding. Once a person feels that he/she is understood, there is often a great unlocking of communication resulting in a flood of thoughts and emotions. One has to be careful not to let people communicate faster than they feel they can deal with the implications. Otherwise their defenses are undermined and they become anxious and, subsequently, more resistant.

Energy release. There is immense pressure in everybody to communicate. Therefore there is an equal amount of energy used to block that communication. Those two countervailing forces result in fatigue and inefficiency.

Specific help. People need to express their needs and ask for help. They need to have words for their emotions and be able to be specific about their needs before they can ask for specific help.

THERAPY AS LEARNING

Recovering. The brain of a child is incredibly plastic. Most of the plasticity is lost by the first two years of life. However, people can still lay down new axonal connections from learned experience. Therapy is, in many respects, re-wiring the brain.

Relearning. Counselees need to learn new ways of problem-solving, new ways of communicating and new attitudes about life and recover lost childlike ways of experiencing joy.

Feedback. Counselees need to learn new ways of unlocking communication and expressing clearly their emotions and thoughts. This is partly done by listening to others and giving them

Mirror. In role-play, people have an opportunity to hear both sides of the conflicts in their minds. This is the best kind of mirror for their thoughts and behaviors. Gradually they learn to see and accept who they are.

7. DISCUSSIONS WITH A POTENTIAL COUNSELLEE

In an attempt to help people realize that they should have group counseling, with the Hope Alive method if it is indicated, you can suggest the following:

"Your distress will not get better with time. It can be suppressed, but at any point in your life when you become weak, tired, depressed or discouraged, pain you experienced long ago often comes rushing to your awareness, and then there may be nobody to help you."

"You will have to deal with the conflicts, e.g. grief, sooner or later. The sooner the better for your health, maturity and joy. Until you grieve pregnancy losses, it is hard to bond to other babies."

"You do not want to pass on your problems to the next generation. You must know that, until the conflicts are resolved, they will recur in your life. If you do not resolve them, you will probably pass them on to the next generation, e.g. frequently abortion is repeated in the next generation. You do not want your children to endure the same kind of experience as you."

"You are in no position to help others as a counselor until your own conflicts are resolved. You will often re-enact your unresolved conflicts in your counselees, and this is to their great detriment. You cannot see in others what you cannot see in yourself. You will not hear the sensitive nuances of their communication until you are able to accept the quiet communication from inside yourself."

"Until you are able to recognize and express your own needs, others cannot really love you and you cannot grow. Until you deal with your own pain and conflicts, your internal computer will be preoccupied with your own problem-solving and you will be inefficient in enjoying, inventing or helping others grows."

"Your mind will keep alive unresolved problems. This requires the utilization of energy you could use for other purposes and brain space you could use for other benefit."

"Until you know how you have been hurt and damaged, you cannot accurately ask for apologies. Until you understand when, how and why you have hurt or allowed others to be hurt, it is impossible to seek forgiveness and forgive. Until you forgive, you will not forget. Until you forgive, you cannot be forgiven."

8. GETTING STARTED

We strongly recommend that counselors conduct themselves in a very professional manner. This means keeping clear lines of communication with anyone who refers people to them, and with the counselee, and with significant others. It is wise to ensure that each counselee has been assessed by a physician prior to beginning a group. This is to ensure they are sufficiently healthy, have no significant psychiatric disease and are able to sustain the stress. It is also wise to see each counselee for two or three sessions prior to beginning the group. This provides them with the opportunity to gain trust in the counselor and learn to talk about certain issues that they would have difficulty expressing.

9. NECESSITY OF COMPLETION

The group counseling of individuals damaged by abuse and abortion is difficult. It is essential that each part and the whole process be accomplished. Experience shows that those who drop out of counseling are sometimes worse off than if they had never begun the treatment. For these and other reasons, a solemn commitment is needed (*Principles of Commitment to Hope Alive Treatment and Training).*

In addition, the *Informed Consent* to group counseling must be attained from each group member. Anyone who misses more than two consecutive sessions, except for valid reasons, should be dropped from the group but encouraged to return when he/she is able to finish.

There is an unfortunate cycle between trust and talking. People may leave the group because they cannot speak fully and honestly. They do this because they do not trust the group. They cannot trust the group because they cannot talk and analyze the reasons why they are unable to trust people. Even though we try very hard to increase the confidence within the groups by the imposition of strict rules, to trust others with one's honest expression of pain, hopes, fears, hopes and despair is always a leap of faith. We have been complemented by how well people trust us.

This program, like life, is cyclic.

1. "I must know the truth." returns to "I must know more about the truth."
2. "You hurt me" in role-play, returns to letters of reconciliation. "You hurt me when..."
3. "Please listen to me" goes back to "I have something to tell you, world," a rehabilitation project to stop happening to children the kinds of painful experience that happened to them.

10. OUTCOME MEASURES

Each counselor must obtain corrective feedback using a variety of objective measures, follow up sessions, and reports by other people, such as spouses. Being rigorous about follow up helps compensate for any inadequacy of supervision and evaluation as groups in your area are getting started. Just trying to obtain outcome measures increases one's credibility. There is no excuse for saying "It is O.K. I know they are getting better. God is guiding me." Working with God should make one more rigorous scientifically, not less.

9

SOME KEY CONCEPTS OF THE TREATMENT PROGRAM

The treatment manual, Hope Alive, contains a detailed description of each step in the program treatment methodology, both theoretical and practical. A brief summary of some key components follows. We do not allow people to purchase the Hope Alive treatment manual for fear that some will attempt to use it without training or understanding the essential concepts. It is dangerous to use only parts of Hope Alive. It is like trying to use parts of a total operation such as cardiac surgery. It will not work and will leave more wounds, scars and dysfunction than if it had never been tried. The Hope Alive program is one complete operation and has to be used as such.

1. COMMITMENT

Before anybody feels safe to know and be known, a thorough commitment must be made to the group as a whole and to each individual within the group. This means making a commitment to confidentiality, to change, to honesty, willingness to change, etc.

The commitment to confidentiality is life-long. People must take to the grave what personal information they learn in the group. Once a commitment is made, counsellees feel reasonably safe to let others in the group know them. They can reveal experiences, no matter how sordid and sorrowful they may be. The commitment is both spoken and written. All retain a copy of the commitment to remind them. By repeatedly saying the details of the commitment to each of the individuals, they learn not only to communicate to the individual directly, but they better remember the components of that commitment.

2. I MUST KNOW

Every real change must begin with a determination to know the truth. The truth will set us free; all of the truth, not just some of the truth some of the time. You must know the truth in order to understand yourself. The most useful truth is the most painful truth. The most painful truth is the most deeply buried truth, whether it is with individuals or nations. The best way to stop history from repeating itself is to uncover and know the truth, but the painful truth is deeply hidden.

Individuals and nations have well-guarded, deep, dark vaults full of valuable, but painful, records. In a huge vault under a park outside Moscow the KGB has accurate records of the people they killed or exiled. It is possible, though difficult, to gain access to those records. It seems few people really want to know what happened to their relatives and neighbors. Is it because they are too often implicated? They feel they did not defend their neighbors and friends when arrested and tried because they were afraid of being taken into custody themselves.

Solzhenitsyn[1] uncovered the fact that in the Bolshevik constitution there is a provision that when someone is arrested, neighbors or friends have a constitutional right to question the police. The reason for it is that the Cheka, the secret police of the czars, used night arrest as a favorite technique. The Bolsheviks carefully wrote into the constitution a provision that would restrain this practice because they were so abhorred by it. Of course, the KGB used the same tactics and the Communists never let anybody know they had a right to ask what was going on, where was the person being taken, etc.

In the deep recesses of the human brain, just as in the vaults of the nations, there is valuable information that all must know if they wish to be free of the dreary cycle of repetitious tragedy. Not only must they reach into their minds to recover memories of experiences and thoughts, but they must also question their family about the past. They will soon realize that as they question their family there are many objections stated and defenses erected, e.g. "Not now. We should forget it and talk about pleasant things. You are going to upset the whole family. Can't you see I am an old man? Who put you up to this?" etc. These resistances have to be overcome in the family and by the counselee. The resistances inside the person are similar to those in the family. The Hope Alive treatment program uses a number of techniques to understand and overcome those resistances.

Each person must be able to say; "I must know the truth regardless of the consequences to me." One must know the truth regardless of the pain of remembering past trauma or becoming disillusioned with others. Others must know the truth about you and about themselves, but timing is very important. Jesus demonstrated that a progressive but persistent revelation of the truth is necessary so people do not become too uncomfortable or too defensive.

3. YOU MUST KNOW

Not only is it important that a person understands him/herself, but it is vitally important that he/she be understood by others. Humans are created to communicate. If they do not communicate with words, their bodies express it in psychosomatic symptoms. Children have to express their feelings and their needs in order to be properly cared for. Unfortunately, they learn to suppress their desires to be heard and understood very early in their experience. They quickly realize mummy is busy, daddy is in a bad mood and sister is not interested, just from the looks of these people. They anticipate being told to shut up, and so they stop themselves even before they start. What is initially an external resistance becomes an internal resistance to being known.

To overcome the resistance, it is important to:

- recover memories of how their communication was first repressed.
- resolve the conflicts surrounding communicating.
- practice pushing through the resistance, e.g. "Please listen to me. You must hear what I have to say."

Many people who have been badly neglected and abused deeply fear going insane. Losing contact with his/ her parents through abandonment is losing contact with reality. To remain in contact with reality, many children hurt themselves. In effect, they say, "I am because I am hurt." The child should be able to say, "I am because I am welcome. I am welcome because they know me and accept me as I am. I am loved because my needs are met."

Counselees must learn to be very insistent with "please listen to me." If you can be persistent with direct communication, then you will not resent it when others, i.e. counselees, say to you "you must listen to me." Otherwise, you are likely to say to yourself, "This isn't fair. I listen to others all day long, but there is no one who listens to me."

If a mother can listen to the subtle changes and stirring within her, then she is more likely to sense the coming of the child as a new presence into her that occurs with conception. Psalm 139:16 states, "Your eyes saw my unformed body." This implies one fertilized cell was "my body" at one time. Our earthly life is only the adding or later subtracting of cells. It is amazing to think a whole person could be contained in one cell, yet in the fullness of God, the amazing, magnificent God of the universe was embodied in Jesus.

Building the wall of silence occurs when an individual debates in her own mind, "I must tell. I can't tell." This may be debated many thousands of times in her head. The wall becomes higher and thicker, e.g. a child who has been molested goes to bed at night saying to herself, "I must tell my mother. No, I can't. It will upset everybody." Many years later she is still debating whether she should, or should not, speak to anyone about what happened to her.

The Hope Alive program is equally determined to provide an individual with insight and to teach new skills. Insight is the understanding of oneself - why we think and act as we do. Insight is gained from:

- improved thinking that comes from clear self-talk and self-listening, which is partly gained from role-plays in the Hope Alive program.
- observations on how one effects others.
- explanations of conflicts, dreams, emotional triggers, behavioral patterns and ambivalent emotions provided by other group members, facilitator and counselor.
- realizing the outcome of the tendency to re-enact in the group, tragedies from one's past.

Humans are much more interested in themselves than anything else in the universe. This is a natural tendency because when we understand ourselves we can better regulate, program and direct our own conversation and behavior. With insight, our chances of surviving are vastly increased. Insight needs to be gained into the origins of the conflict that distort or frustrate our attempts to be the person God designed us to be.

The basic conflict is a frustration in our attempts to construct the person God designed us to become. Those frustrations come from neglect, i.e. not getting the right building materials, in the right amounts, in the right order, at the right time, and abuse, which is partly destroying the person as they are in the process of construction.

These frustrations result in:

- confusion. "Now what am I supposed to do?"
- doubts. "I thought I knew who I was. I thought I knew somebody loved me."
- despair. "I am inclined to give up. There is no hope."
- an increase in the tendencies to both fight and flight, therefore a polarization of the characteristics in oneself.
- an internal disequilibrium so that we inefficiently use our energy and the building materials that we are given.
- external disharmonies so we are not effective in gaining what we need.

This results in increased desperation in attempts to search for and use maladaptive mechanisms to gain the materials we need by:

- constructing false faces and interacting with people in false ways.
- ruminating, attempting to think one's way through.
- self-centered conversation in which people try to obtain insight from

others.

- re-enacting the tragedy until one learns from it.

4. THE SURROGATE SCAPEGOAT

The people who need and accept an offer of counseling are usually those who are most affected by the family conflicts that may have been handed down for many generations. Often they are the most sensitive and intelligent members of that family. Often they are the most vulnerable. They have been subconsciously selected to express the symptoms of family conflict. In this way they are scapegoats. They must realize this and temporarily allow themselves to be the family's scapegoat. Later they must be willing to stand in society in place of other little people, most particularly pre-born children, who are generally scapegoated. In this way, they are most likely to accomplish their healing.

5. RE-HUMANISE PRIOR TO GRIEVING

To properly grieve the loss of a baby who died *in utero*, it is important that he/she be re-humanized. The baby was an individual with physical and personality characteristics that the parents subconsciously knew quite well. To abort the baby, the parents first had to dehumanize him/her. Dehumanizing their baby was not as hard as it might be for others because the parents themselves had been frequently dehumanized by childhood experiences of abuse and neglect, or were survivors of an abortion in their family.

The Hope Alive program is thus designed to re-humanize the parents by helping them deal with their early damaging experiences. Although some of these damages cannot be repaired, parents can at least become more human. When re-humanized, they are much better able to re-humanize the baby, and therefore better able to mourn his/her loss.

6. I MUST GROW

Although people realize that they want to be without the symptoms of depression, tension and self-injury following abuse and abortion, they often do not realize they must change and become more mature. Although almost everybody would say, "of course I want to be mature," he/she might find considerable internal resistance and resistance from friends and family. To overcome the resistance, he/she must assert him/herself. "I am going to change." Often this is met with such resistances from spouse and family as, "No, you are fine the way you are." "If you change and I do not, that will produce real strains in our marriage." "What is this silly nonsense about group therapy? You are fine." "I'm okay. You're okay." "Let's just live and let live."

Counselees must understand the roots of the resistance to change and reassure their friends and family they will not desert or deride them. Because they are becoming more mature, they will be more loving and accepting, not less. One aspect of the Hope Alive program includes a meeting with spouses of group counselees to explain the program (without divulging any information about the other individuals in the spouse's group) and answer a wide range of questions.

7. UNDERSTANDING THE TRAGIC TRIANGLE

Almost all tragedies, personal, interpersonal or international, are composed of a Perpetrator, Victim and Observer whom all contribute to the problem and suffer from its consequences. Observers are best able to stop the tragedy, but will not because they want to appear innocent. There are no innocent bystanders, Observers protest, "I wasn't there. I didn't see it and, besides, I could not have done anything about it. This tragic triangle rotates with time and circumstance so that in time any individual could be all three.

8. RE-ENACTING TRAGIC HISTORY

Humans are constructed to be efficient. With the efficient use of energy, they are more likely to survive privation. To be efficient, the body must maintain internal harmony, homeostasis. Internal and interpersonal conflict causes inefficient use of energy. Therefore, humans must, and will, try a wide variety of mechanisms to resolve the conflicts within them. They may quietly think and discover, "Oh, now I realize why I do that." They may talk to a friend, "Please tell me. Why do I keep doing this stupid thing?" But, for major problems, they will attempt to understand the critical conflicts by re-enacting them.

Conflicts engendered during childhood are not resolved because children do not have time and energy. They are much more interested in developing. Besides, there is no one who is interested in helping them resolve their major conflicts, partly because many people believe small people have only small conflicts. The destabilizing conflicts from childhood become embedded in their minds and are re-enacted in their adult life. Too frequently, people re-create the conflicts without understanding what is happening. The Hope Alive program is an attempt to help people uncover the roots of these conflicts and to re-enact them in a controlled environment where counselees can learn from them.

9. PROTEST (FIGHT)

Children are naturally protective of themselves. If offered medicine on a spoon, almost every child will push it away. They are naturally suspicious of people they do not know. When hurt, like every mammal their psycho-biological response is to fight or flight. Unfortunately, children realize their survival is endangered by either fighting or fleeing so they remain immobile, almost as if waiting for the worst but hoping for the best. It is essential that people learn how to resist, assert their humanity and protest, not only for themselves, but for others. Since verbal abuse is so damaging, it is very important that they learn how to resist, protest and assert themselves against verbal abuse. The Hope Alive techniques teach them to:

- defuse a potentially tragic situation.
- affirm themselves.
- treat themselves and the other Perpetrators, Victims or Observers as a human.
- desensitize themselves to some previous verbal abuse that still has a major effect on their lives.

10. WITHDRAWAL (FLIGHT)

There are times in one's life when it is wise to run away. Too often, people have been badly damaged or killed because they did not recognize the time and an opportunity to flee a dangerous situation. People who have been damaged by child abuse and abortion often feel trapped by fear and conditioned passivity, or they do not know there are other options. They are afraid to stay, but even more afraid to leave. The Hope Alive techniques help them assess situations realistically, break out of that immobility and run in the right direction at the right speed.

Too often people have said and are told: "Once you have made your bed, you must lie in it." This makes it difficult for people to be wise and spontaneous in knowing when to run away. People also get stuck when they try so hard to show that the second marriage was not the same mistake as the first. It is sad to see people re-living history without even knowing they are doing it.

"Giants" grow from a child's fantasies arising from flight. As you run away, the pursuer grows larger and larger in your mind. "Dwarfs" grow from a child's fantasies of revenge. Both these fantasies are behind many of the fears in writing letters to the Perpetrator.

11. PARTIAL CONTRIBUTION AND RESPONSIBILITY

There is plenty of experimental and clinical evidence to show that victims may subconsciously contribute to their own victimisation.[2] The most tragic expression of this is that children who were mistreated may tend to behave in such a way that they may initiate, precipitate or prolong abuse and neglect. Children who have been physically abused, even in the most benign foster homes, may be provocatively aggressive. Verbally abused children may be verbally provocative and sexually abused children may be sexually provocative. This fact does nothing to lessen the Perpetrator's responsibility. Children who were neglected may become so demanding that they are neglected even more.

One foster child I knew, having come out of a physically abusive home, went to live in a beautiful foster home. In time he settled in and behaved much more naturally. However, on one occasion when the foster mother told him to finish something he did not care to do, he disappeared. After half an hour of quietness, the foster mother investigated to find that he had lined up all the shoes of the family and urinated in each one of them.

It is very important that the Perpetrator, the Victim, and the Observer in the tragic triangle learn what part they contributed to the tragic event. In the Hope Alive program, people are helped to unravel the difference between real and unreal guilt. When they have done so, they must estimate the different percentages apportioned to all those who contribute to an event. The people who contribute to a particular abortion include the mother, the father, maternal and paternal grandparents, physician, nurse, media, government, pastors, siblings, friends and many others. Each of them has a portion of the contribution. Even if their contribution was small, it often makes the difference whether a tragedy will occur. To use a metaphor, it is a little bit like adding one chemical to another. Often, two drops of one reagent (two words by a particular individual) can result in the flash (the anger) that kills the baby *in utero.*

The contribution is a realistic assessment of how much people's activity or lack of activity result in a particular tragedy. Their responsibility (0-100% of their contribution) is their ability to freely choose whether to be involved or not. Their responsibility is often curtailed by their experiences in life, intelligence, education, hormones, lack of sleep, etc. This is hard to ascertain. In a sense, only they and God know how much responsibility for abuse or abortion is theirs.

The Hope Alive program is not involved in any kind of legal assessment, blame or culpability. Therefore, it is possible to be more objective about one's contribution and one's responsibility. It is to that extent one should feel guilty. Unfortunately, children too often feel either no guilt or all the guilt. As adults in group counseling, people must learn to realistically reassess their responsibility as a proportion of their contribution (which is a proportion of the overall tragedy). On that basis, they must know that they are guilty and feel guilty to that extent. Far too often, one individual is blamed and punished as if he/she were the only one who is responsible. That is scapegoating.

12. DISCARDING FALSE FACES

In the face of neglect, children will do anything they must in order to survive and to grow. The little carpenter is a determined builder. If he cannot get his building materials upon reasonable request, he will perform or beg for those materials. Out of the tendency to perform, children develop the false face of a Dancer. A Dancer is apparently happy, agreeable, helpful and malleable, but underneath there is bitterness, anger and manipulation. The child's tendency to beg results in the Urchin mask. This is a pitiable, sad, withdrawing person, but underneath there is also anger, manipulation and despair. Children learn to develop these masks spontaneously. Because they are reasonably effective in getting at least some of the building materials, the masks are well established and difficult to dispense with. The Hope Alive program uses a number of techniques to help people discard their masks and re-discover the Blueprint-carrying Pilgrim.

13. DISCOVERING AND ASSERTING THE PILGRIM

In a desperate attempt to get their needs met and to defend their core self, those who are injured by child abuse and abortions wear the False Faces (or masks) of the Dancer and the Urchin and elaborate their modes of thinking and behavior. They must learn to identify their masks, why they wear them, what occasions bring them out, and then how to discard them. Once they are able to stop wearing false faces and after they have mourned the loss of the PISHB, their Pilgrim gradually begins to emerge. Hope Alive techniques help people identify and assert their Pilgrim, with all their accompanying talents, warts and wounds. Since there is strong opposition to being an honest, authentic person, people need to be constantly reminded when they wear False Faces, and helped to assert and exercise their Pilgrim.

Their Pilgrim carries the Blueprint God designed for them. They must now gradually realize what can still be realistically achieved in building the beautiful castle God intended them to be. They can be assured that when they arrive in Heaven they will be able to finish the construction of the person they have been developing on earth. God, recognizing that person, will give them a new name, written on a white stone - a name known only to the one who receives it.[3] This name will be only theirs, not shared by anybody else in the universe, and will accurately encapsulate who they are.

14. THE LOSS OF THE PERSON I SHOULD HAVE BECOME (PISHB)

Certain requirements for a child's development must be filled at specific ages and stages of development; much like building a house. You need the re enforced concrete for the foundation at the very beginning. There is no point in getting the material for the foundation after the walls are up and the roof is on. In this way, children at a very early age need a great deal of touch, comfort, security, affection, affirmation, regularity and critical nutrients. For example, babies need their mother's milk with critical ingredients of essential fatty acids (EFA). Although some milk supplements now provide EFA's, breast milk is still the best source. Essential fatty acids are necessary for the formation of the white matter of the brain and myelin sheaths. Children who are not breast fed do not have the quality of brain and peripheral nerves they were designed to have. They are not as smart and as quick as they should be.

It is now apparent that early experience not only produces a memory trace and a mindset for further learning, it actually determines the hard wiring of the brain. Traumatic experiences for infants literally cannot be undone or re-wired. Thus, it is very important to provide the necessary nutrients and experiences to babies before and after birth in the right amounts and in the correct sequence. Brain plasticity diminishes with age. Thus, although it may be possible to discover some of the roots of conflicts from early experiences of neglect and abuse, it may not be possible to treat these. The sad result is that beautiful little person God designed cannot develop, no matter how good the later environment or how good the treatment of traumatic experience.

In the Hope Alive treatment program, a fundamental part of the process is mourning the loss of the PISHB. Since it is not possible to recover or reconstruct that person, one must discover what he/she has lost, grieve that person, and then find the person he/she really is. There are many benefits to mourning the PISHB. It:

- enables one to see and accept the person one really is, the Pilgrim.
- enables one to see and accept other people as they really are.
- enables one to understand one's children, clearly see their Blueprints, and encourage them to be the persons they were designed to be (instead to trying to fulfill one's own Blueprint through them).
- encourages contentment and gratitude. Instead of being dissatisfied with what one is getting from other people because it is such a small portion of what one needs, one becomes grateful for every small gift or help.
- promotes giving and receiving. When one is grateful it is easier for

people to give and therefore one gets more. When one gets more of one's needs met, one becomes a more mature person, more grateful, appreciative and praising, which makes it easier to graciously give and to receive from others.

- stabilizes relationships. Because one is less disappointed in what other people give, relationships are more likely to stay together.
- one can better use the time, opportunities and talents one still has instead of wasting time searching in vain for experiences one should have had in childhood.
- allow real grieving. Once one is able to grieve the loss of the PISHB, it is possible to humanize babies who died *in utero* and much easier to accomplish these other griefs.

15. GRIEVING PREGNANCY LOSSES

For the reasons described in this book, it appears that grief following an abortion is the most complicated and difficult kind of grief. To initiate any grief, it is normally important to see and/or hold the body of the deceased person. It is the usual practice in helping people mourn a stillborn baby to allow the parents as much time as they need to examine, hold, cuddle, name, welcome, bury and grieve the child. Since it was not possible to do this for an aborted baby, we use techniques that help people remember, humanize, welcome, hold, lose and then grieve miscarried and aborted babies.

Since attachment always occurs, grief is inevitable. It is vital that the baby has a family and that he/she be welcomed into it. Every human needs a name. The child, welcomed in the name of Jesus, individualized, humanized and given a name, is then welcomed just as he/she is, in the family's name. It is then important to commit the spirit of the dead baby to Christ. Nobody knows for certain what happens to the spirit of the aborted and miscarried babies, but, from time immemorial, Christians have always felt it was necessary to commit the spirit of the departed to God, asking Him to welcome that child. They can be sure God welcomes everybody who comes to Him.

16. GRIEVING ABORTED SIBLINGS, THEN CHILDREN

Although it might seem most urgent to grieve the loss of an unborn baby, many people find they cannot do that until they have grieved the loss of an aborted, miscarried or stillborn sibling. Once that is accomplished, they are in a better position to remember and visualize their unborn baby. At times when people have attempted to visualize their own baby, their mind suddenly sees the person who could only be a sibling. Since there is often a number of griefs to deal with, we concentrate on teaching a technique that people can then use by themselves, in their own time, in a quiet place.

17. VISUAL PARABLES

A number of the processes in Hope Alive healing use a technique denoted as Visual Parables. When Jesus told stories to His disciples, He told them in a basic form that could be understood in every culture, in every age. In the minds of some Africans, when Jesus said "the sower went out to sow," this means taking a bag of seed, walking across a prepared field and scattering the seed by hand. To a Canadian farmer this means getting up at four o'clock in the morning, drinking a couple of mugs of coffee, climbing into the Massey Ferguson, starting the engine, putting on the stereo music headphones, turning on the air conditioner, putting the huge tractor into gear and rolling across the prairie with the seed drill behind. In a similar manner, we tell a skeletal story and ask people to use their memories and imaginations to fill in the details. There is enormous variety in the detailed stories that follow. This is convincing evidence that we are not introducing ideas, manipulating people or hypnotising them. What the technique does is to engage the mind in a critical task that it has avoided until now. In this way, the mind is able to recapture the memory of the aborted child, visualise what he/she would look like at this point in life (had he/she lived), picture his/her death, burial and then engage in various steps necessary for a grief that is long overdue.

18. ATTENUATING PAIR BONDS

Men and women become bonded as pairs with whomever they have an intimate sexual relationship. These bonds are inevitable to some degree, even when it is an adult-child or same-sex relationship. In all those pair bonded, there is part of the person and part of each mate. Thus, pair bonding can be a great blessing or a great curse. Those who have had sexual relationships with many others find that they are struggling to recapture lost parts of themselves and fighting to determine their own identity. This scientific view of mating, now termed serial polygamy, accords with Scripture[4] and the oft-repeated phrase in a marriage ceremony "until death do you part."

To re-gain one's identity and the ability to have an intimate relationship with the committed husband and wife, it is necessary to attenuate these bonds. I use the term attenuate because "what God has joined together, no one can separate." Yet the force and effect of these bonds can be lessened. A number of techniques in Hope Alive are used to help people attenuate pathological and unnecessary bonds so they can recover parts of themselves and re-gain an ability to have a committed relationship.

Pair bonds (mating) occur because of:

1. Imprinting. As adolescents develop, so their hormone-determined sexual tension increases. They then become infatuated with an individual, and that sexual tension rises steeply. When they have sex, that tension suddenly diminishes, creating an imprint onto the person with whomever they have sex. As a gosling becomes imprinted to the first moving object it sees as its mother, so humans become imprinted to each other the first time they have intercourse, and, to a lesser extent, the first time they have intercourse with a new partner. Thus they can be imprinted on a number of people.

1. Intravaginal absorption of hormones. The male seminal plasma is full of powerful hormones (estradiol, estrone, DSS, TSH, androgen, prostaglandin, etc.) that are quickly absorbed through an active transfer mechanism in the vagina.[5] Thus the woman takes on the male hormones and probably the male absorbs hormones from female vaginal secretions. Thus they take on each other's hormonal profile. Those hormones, absorbed into the biological system, create an antigen-antibody reaction. For that reason, the immune system makes a permanent record of the hormones of the partner. They literally become one flesh for life.

2. Conditioning. When an individual has an orgasm, there is a sudden release of endorphins, naturally producing morphine-like substances. Those substances produce an extraordinary sense of pleasure. The pleasure reinforces (strengthens) any activity that occurs immediately before and during. Thus people are conditioned by the pleasure of orgasm and seek further sexual activity of the same kind and especially with the same partner.

3. Rescuing. As in the trenches or on mountain climbs, anybody that rescues a person from a desperate or life-threatening situation becomes your buddy for life. Sexual partners often rescue each other from despair, boredom, meaninglessness, etc. In so doing, they become "good buddies" for life.

4. Childbearing and rearing. The whole process of childbearing further bonds the partners together, if they allow the natural process to occur. In the intense emotional atmosphere of giving birth, men and women become strongly bonded to each other. Later, as they struggle together to raise a family, that bond is enhanced.

The first three aspects of pair bonding always take place. This makes it difficult for people who have been involved in sexual intimacies that did not accord with their Blueprint. These bonds were made to last for a lifetime. It should be clear from a study of human physiology and psychology that the penis and vagina were made for each other. Thus, people's Blueprint drives them toward a committed, intimate relationship with one person of the opposite sex.

Commitment allows true intimacy. Commitment to a wife or husband makes true intimacy possible. They can truly get to know the other person. All other kinds of sexual relationships are damaging.

18. RECONCILIATION

Until there is reconciliation, tragic history must and will be repeated. The process of reconciliation is necessary, but usually difficult, sometimes dangerous, and not always successful. The first part of reconciliation involves forgiveness. Christians are taught that they must forgive in order to be forgiven.[6] Christ is stating a universal law. Counselees must recognize that they are partly contributing to the things that happen to them. If they do not forgive the obvious perpetrator, how can they forgive themselves? Therefore they are not forgiven. Forgiveness is necessary for many reasons:

- If you do not forgive you become bitter and bitterness increases the risk of cancer. For what is bound in earth is bound in heaven.[7]
- Forgiveness sets people free who are imprisoned in a dungeon of guilt so they can mature and love others.
- Forgiving frees a person's mind to stop retaining problems and get on with more inventive activity.
- Forgiveness is beneficial for others, but just as beneficial for oneself, for we are tightly bound together in this bundle of life.
- Once a person has forgiven and there is reconciliation, one's mind does not constantly have to remember the event. Nor does it so readily respond to triggers that propel him/her into dealing with the underlying problem.
- When people forgive, they gradually forget.

The Bible teaches that people are not to keep waiting for the Perpetrators and Observers to initiate reconciliation.[8] When the counselee goes to Perpetrators and Observers, he/she should remind them of what harm they have done to him/her, and ask for an apology. If a Perpetrator repents, he/she must be forgiven. Forgiveness cannot be imposed. It is a gift that one offers. It can be freely accepted only when the one who perpetrates or observes acknowledges their contribution to the hurt, apologizes, promises not to repeat the hurt, seeks to change and tries to repair the damage or compensate for it. Receiving the gift of forgiveness obviously implies you are accepting your contribution and responsibility to any tragic event.

Some may contend a general forgiveness of other people is sufficient. On the other hand, consider loaning your house to a friend while you are away for a week. On your return you find that they have had a long, wild party and spoiled and broken a number of treasured items. A general apology is not very satisfactory for the hurt and damage. Each damaged item is like an insult that bangs about in one's head. An itemized rebuke allows your friend to be specific in his/her apology and to compensate you for each item.

The Hope Alive treatment program uses the model from the Bible regarding reconciliation, starting with "if your brother sins, rebuke him." It starts with the writing of a letter. The letter is addressed first to oneself, then to Perpetrators, Observers, Victims and God as Perpetrator, Observer and Victim. These are hard letters to write. People suddenly realize that they must be accurate and courageous. They have to overcome all of their inhibitions in talking to somebody who has badly hurt them, and break through the self and other imposed "sound barriers" that restrict all kinds of communication.

In the Bible, it is clear that rebuking, repenting, forgiving and healing are associated. One lead to the other in that order. That is the way God deals with humans, so it is a model of how we should interact with each other. Once forgiveness is given and accepted, the relationship, and consequently the person, can heal. It will involve further communication, learning to trust, struggling to love each other by meeting each other's needs, then engaging in fellowship while together they praise and thank the Lord before full reconciliation takes place.

God is reconciling the world to Himself through Christ,[9] but He gives everyone the opportunity to say yes or no to His free gift of salvation. Humans, likewise, can offer reconciliation and forgiveness, but they must leave the other person opportunity to decline. Clinical experience has shown that about 30% of the Perpetrators to whom people in Hope Alive group counseling write are able to recognize their responsibility, apologize, and seek reconciliation. About 20% of the Observers do so. About 30% of the Perpetrators and 50% of the Observers want to debate the details, but still are interested in communicating. Approximately 30% of the Perpetrators, and larger proportion of Observers, continually deny that they have any responsibility that they have done no harm and are very angry about being confronted.

In the event that a person does not reply satisfactorily to the first letter, we encourage as many letters as the counselee feels he/she can. Often the second, third, fourth or fifth letter has a much different response from the first one.

Letters to victims are much more successful. Letters to God are always answered, if only people will read and listen. We have witnessed some remarkable changes in people's attitudes to God, many of them beginning to communicate honestly with Him at this point. Thus, though counselees often recognize their need for Christ as their Savior and become one of His children, in Hope Alive we do not pray or read Scripture.

We define reconciliation as forgiving and establishing adult communication when necessary, but not always having an ongoing relationship. When reconciliation is not successful, people are advised to write a goodbye letter. It is better to have no relationship than a dishonest one that traps a person into false expectations, limited communication and dishonesty with others and with themselves. The goodbye letter always has a stipulation that the other may initiate the reconciliation process, and the writer is always ready to hear from them and respond.

19. NEGOTIATING REALISTIC EXPECTATIONS

In many human relationships, there is often much conflict stemming from the unrealistic expectations people have of each other. Having discovered and asserted the Pilgrim, set aside false faces, mourned the loss of the PISHB, initiated the difficult process of reconciliation, counselees are now in a position to negotiate realistic expectations with the important people in their lives. One Hope Alive technique requires realistically recognizing one's capabilities and disabilities, then negotiating and holding firm, or compromising when necessary. People report that there have been remarkable exchanges and beneficial changes when they engage in this process with a mate, employee/employer or child.

20. REHABILITATION THROUGH LEARNING TO LOVE OTHERS

Counseling, of necessity, requires people to focus intensely on themselves. Unfortunately, most counseling procedures leave people in a very self-centered, often narcissistic state. As such, they are vulnerable to all sorts of minimal slights and are frequently very boring in conversation. It is necessary to turn people's thoughts outward to the needs and hurts of others. To do that we ask each person to initiate a project that they can do by themselves with the resources at hand and right away; no waiting for group support or money. Before they conclude Hope Alive counseling, they must present a reasonably formal outline of their proposal and defend it against their skeptical peers.

The project is not only an attempt to prevent happening to others what happened to counselees when they were children, but it is to help them realize that their tragic experiences can be used to help facilitate human understand. Therefore, in a paradoxical way, their tragedy is beneficial. During follow-up, people are asked to report on their projects. Unquestionably, those who take their projects seriously and work at helping others by preventing problems, do better in the long run.

During counseling, people perforce think intensely about themselves. They become increasingly self-preoccupied. To leave them in that state is to leave them in a vulnerable condition. It is important to turn their thoughts outward by helping them to realize they can make a significant difference in the world. With the time, talent, money and opportunity they have at present and, if necessary, quite alone, they can formulate a project that could help protect others from the trauma they experienced as children. In doing so, they turn outwards and begin to love others.

Research has demonstrated that when a person is concentrating on another, blood pressure, pulse rate, etc. drop. It is literally healthy to love. Christ commands us to love, not just for the benefit of others, but for our own physical and mental health. Christ's spirit in people gives them the natural desire and ability to love. Therefore He can command them to do what they would be inclined to do anyway. But still they have a choice. Counselees need to learn why it is important to love and practical ways they can do it. They love by meeting each other's needs. Since needs are definable, love is measurable and doable.

21. DECISIONS

Part of the original commitment was to not make any major decisions during the counseling process. Now it is time for people to carefully look at the decisions they must make and order their lives in such a way that they have the best opportunity of utilizing their alternative plan. The decisions are not just an evaluation of the pros and cons, but an examination of the underlying conflicts. People also need to learn how to ask for help, to whom to turn for advice and how much initiative they should take. They are now better able to make wise judgments about relationships so that sad history will not repeat.

22. GOOD GOOD-BYES

Too frequently, people who have been damaged by child abuse and abortion have experienced many bad good-byes. A good good-bye means:

- there is no unfinished business so that he or she does not feel someday

they must meet again to deal with some unresolved issue.

- the good-bye is mutual, not “good-bye” and “please don’t leave me.”
- they are able to give a blessing.

From ancient times, when people parted they gave each other a formal, loving blessing. This includes recognizing who the person is, what they still need and a promise to think about them, love them in any way possible, bless them and pray for them. Then it is possible to say a good good-bye. The blessings are usually epitomized by giving a small gift, flower, poem or Scripture.

24. HOPE

People can live only if they have hope. It is a terrible thing to take away a child’s hope. Much of hope arises from the joy of having someone who listens and understands. A great deal of hope comes from the satisfaction of having needs met. Yet, persistent, often unrealistic, hope may arise in situations of deprivation and occasioned need-meeting.

Children must keep hoping so that they keep seeking, find what they need and become the person they were designed to be. To keep hoping, they must keep shining the tarnished image of their parents. To acknowledge they have hopeless parents makes children give up. It is small wonder that they keep hoping someday their parents will change and they will be given what they need to become the person God designed them to be. When neglected, most children will first blame themselves, “I’m unworthy of their love.” Thus, neglected children have low self-esteem and will tend not to express disappointment in their parents.

NOTES: 9 SOME KEY CONCEPTS OF THE TREATMENT PROGRAM

'Solzhenitsyn, A. (1975). The Calf and the Oak. New York: Harper & Row.

-Ney, P. G., Moore, C., McPhee, J. & Trought, P. (1986). Child abuse: A study of the child's perspective. Child Abuse and Neglect. 10. 511-518.

'Revelation 2.

[J]Matthew 19:4-6.

'Ney, P.G. (1986). The intravaginal absorption of male generated hormones. Med Hypotheses. 20. 221-231.

''Matthew 6: 14-15.
'Matthew 18:18.
"Luke 17: 3-4.
[M]II Corinthians 5:16-20.

10

SUMMARY OF CLINICAL AND RESEARCH FINDINGS, PUBLISHED AND UNPUBLISHED

1. Child Abuse and Neglect (1978 -1997)

SAMPLE

1. High school students
2. Inmates in a Young Offenders Centre
3. Patients in two child and adolescent psychiatric units
4. Child and adolescent patients in two child psychiatric practices
5. Parents of referred children

Approximate sample size: 600 (numbers are approximate because this is an ongoing study)

MEASURE

1. Clinical interviews
2. Rating scale and (5 point) visual analogue scales
3. Parent Experience Questionnaire
4. Child Experience Questionnaire
5. Staff Questionnaire

Measures were checked for reliability and validity and were satisfactory.

A visual analogue scale made it possible to include the whole range of effect; frequency, intensity, duration, etc. Therefore, all types and all ranges of abuse and neglect are included. This also meant that we could avoid the awkward problem of defining child abuse or neglect.

Measured duration, frequency, severity, impact and amount of self-blame for 5 types of abuse and neglect:

1) Physical abuse; hits, shakes, etc.
2) Verbal abuse; demeaning, criticizing, etc.
3) Sexual abuse; fondling, intercourse, etc.
4) Physical neglect; lack of food, medical care, etc.
5) Emotional and Intellectual Neglect; lack of affection, education, etc.

DATA ANALYSIS

Analogue readings digitized, coded and analyzed with the assistance of the University Computing Centre, University of Calgary, Calgary, Alberta, Canada.

RESULTS

Staff ratings of abuse and neglect tended to be the highest, then children, and then parents.

Abuse and neglect occur in combinations in 95% of participants. The worst effect on a child's self esteem and future orientation is a combination of physical abuse, physical neglect and verbal abuse. Neglect shows in 9 of the 10 most damaging combinations.

The angry types of abuse, verbal and physical abuse, tend to go together. Sexual abuse tends to correlate highly with emotional neglect.

There are significant correlations between a previous abortion and the severity of verbal abuse by mother, severity of physical abuse by mother, severity of emotional neglect by mother, severity of emotional neglect by father and severity of sexual abuse by father.

Children who have been mistreated expect to die an early death. The greater the severity of the mistreatment, the earlier they expect to die.

There are a number of significant correlations between the ways in which children expect to die and the type of mistreatment. Physically abused, physically neglected, verbally abused and emotionally neglected children have a higher expectation of dying violently by accident, war, murder or suicide. A disproportionate number of sexually abused children expect to be murdered. Interestingly, sexually abused children are the highest percentage of people who expect to die in old age.

Children who are physically abused tend to blame themselves if it is light abuse, and the other person/parent etc. if it is severe. If the child is verbally or sexually abused, they blame themselves more if it is light and if it is greater. In between, there is the tendency to blame the other.

The impact of abuse and neglect is greater if it begins at an earlier age. This is supported by recent research that shows the brain is hard-wired by early experience.

From a child's point of view, the most frequent causes of being mistreated are (1) parent immaturity, then (2) marital disharmony, and then (3) poverty.

In this study, psychiatric illness did not seem to be a major cause of abuse and neglect.

There is no evidence that an unwanted child is more likely to be abused and neglected. In fact, there is evidence that wanted children are more likely to be abused in some ways.

Characteristics of the child seem to contribute to abuse and neglect. Children who were active, non-cuddly and demanding appear to be more frequently abused. There is a strong correlation between sexual abuse and accident proneness.

There are strong correlations between the types of child abuse and neglect and the mother's response to the child's helpless cry. Mothers who respond with feelings of anger are more likely to verbally or physically abuse their children. Those who respond with feelings of anxiety and helplessness are more likely to neglect their children.

Wantedness varies throughout the pregnancy, being lowest in the first trimester and gradually increasing as the pregnancy proceeds.

What pleased parents about a child the most, is the child being helpful and, secondly, being affectionate.

From a step-wise regressive analysis on the 66 factors that might contribute to child abuse and neglect, we found lack of partner support, less breast feeding and previous pregnancy losses were the most important factors

CONCLUSIONS

Children are neglected and abused by parents almost always in combinations. This means that anybody doing research and writing scientific articles on children as if they had only one type of abuse, e.g. sexual abuse, are not considering all the factors that are involved. Any article not considering combinations is probably not worth reading.

On children, the damaging effect of neglect is greater than that of abuse. If abuse is preceded by neglect, the impact of abuse is greater.

The greater effect of neglect over abuse tends to be seldom investigated and is under-reported, possibly because those who should be studying the impact of neglect are themselves neglecting their children, i.e. doing research or professional work while putting their children in day-care. Neglect appears to make a child both more vulnerable and susceptible to abuse. Neglected children tend to blame themselves and, because of the ensuing low self esteem and because they are contributing to a re-enactment of early unresolved conflicts, they look for what they need in the wrong places. Literally and figuratively, starved children look for food in garbage dumps rather than asking at the doors of rich people.

Child abuse and neglect significantly damage children's self-image and their ability to enjoy living. It also results in lack of purpose in life, poor future orientation of the world, poor future for him/herself, poor chances of getting a good job, poor chance of having a happy marriage, poor chance of having happy children and a poor chance of being a good parent.

The correlation between the way in which children expect to die and the type of mistreatment they experience is important because even children tend to live out their lives as they expect them to run. Approximately 15% of abused and neglected children expect to kill themselves.

There are a number of significant correlations between the ways parents abuse their children and the ways they were abused as children. This is particularly true for verbal abuse, i.e. verbal abuse is more likely to be trans generational. There are even larger numbers of significant correlations between the ways the spouse abused the child and how they were abused by their spouse.

The high number of correlations between how people are abused by their spouse and how they were abused as children seem to indicate that people tend to be treated by their spouse as they were treated as children, prompting one to wonder why people do not learn from experience. This finding initiated a series of studies by us into trans generational child abuse.

There are close correlations between mistreatment and bad early child-hood experiences, including moving, family splits, etc.

Because a child is so determined to find the materials for his own development, if neglected, he will use any scrap material he can get his hands on. Because this determination persists into adulthood, a person will accept damaging situations and pathological relationships if they appear to offer any possibility of help and support for growth and maturity. Thus they become vulnerable to materialism, cults, and narcissism.

Traumatic early experience, to some extent, cannot be undone because experience helps hard-wire the child's brain, and plasticity diminishes with increasing age.

It appears that wanted children are wanted to provide help or affection for their parents. It is small wonder wanted children feel used. It is so much easier for them to be themselves when they are welcomed.

2. Pregnancy Outcome Study I. & II. (1991 -1997)

This study was initially done in conjunction with the College of Family Physicians in British Columbia, Canada. It was expanded to include samples from other countries, now totaling approximately 4,000 participants.

Sample

1. Victoria: 1430.
2. Christian Medical and Dental Society (Canada wide): 660.
3. China: 1205.
4. Other countries: approximately 705 (ongoing study).

The Victoria sample is representative of the general population. We have checked demographic characteristics against Statistics Canada data and found that the sample was typical of women across Canada. The sample was taken from those waiting in their family physician's office. They filled in the questionnaire and then returned it to the receptionist before leaving.

The sample size is growing and the study is ongoing. The questionnaire has been translated into a number of different languages.

Measures

Self-Report Questionnaire. With visual analogue scales questioning attitudes and assessment of health. A grid provided an opportunity to indicate the outcomes of all pregnancies and assessing amount of partner support, breast-feeding, etc. These were checked against other assessments: a) assessment of patient health - done by the family physician and b) independent assessment - done by a research assistant, analyzing the patient's chart.

There was good agreement between the three measures.

Test-retest reliability and alternate form have been checked and found to be satisfactory.

RESULTS

In Victoria, first pregnancy outcomes indicate that teenagers had approximately 50% average weight, full term babies, 12% miscarriages and 27% abortions. Older groups showed an increase in the number of full term pregnancies, diminished abortions. Miscarriages gradually increased with the age after the first pregnancy. If abortions were subtracted from the teenage pregnancies, they had the same percentage of full term, normal birth weight babies as any other age group.

In all countries, the outcome of the first pregnancy is the best predictor of the outcome of the second pregnancy. If the baby was full term first pregnancy, there is 77% chance of a full term second pregnancy. The chance of a full term, normal birth weight baby in the second pregnancy is (a) 45% if the first pregnancy was premature, (b) 51% if miscarriage, and (c) 51.4% if a previous abortion. If there was a miscarriage in the first pregnancy, there is a 21% chance of a miscarriage in the second pregnancy. If there was an abortion in the first pregnancy, there is a 22% chance of having an abortion in the second pregnancy. If the baby was full term in the first pregnancy, there is a 9.3% chance of having a miscarriage in the second pregnancy, but, if the first pregnancy was aborted, there is a 14% chance of a miscarriage in the second pregnancy.

The three most important factors that determine the mother's health, considering the 44 factors that were analyzed by a multiple regression are (1) the quality of family life, (2) previous pregnancy losses and (3) the amount of support by a partner.

The quality of the mother's present physical health, as analyzed by a multiple regression of the first three pregnancies, appears to be determined by (1) family life, (2) age and (3) need for professional help to deal with loss of a child or pregnancy.

All kinds of losses have a negative effect on the mother's health. According to the Pearson's Correlation Coefficient, miscarriages g. < 0.04, abortions g. < ***0.000.***

The impact of abortion versus miscarriage indicates that abortions have a greater impact on "my health as affected by a previous loss" and this difference grows from the first to the second pregnancy.

The impact of a pregnancy loss is cumulative. The negative impact of two pregnancy losses is greater than one, and three greater than one or two.

The effect of the immediacy of the pregnancy loss on the mother's health indicates that a loss in the first pregnancy resulted in some effect 46.8% of the time, and a marked deleterious effect in 12.9% of the time. In the last pregnancy, a loss had some effect in 45.2% of the participants and affected 25.2% of participants a great deal.

When considering the impact of a full term outcome compared to abortion with the emotional health of a woman after her first pregnancy, both in China and Canada, the chi square is p. < 0.0001. When considering the differing effect of a full term versus an abortion outcome of the first pregnancy on the mother's emotional health during the second pregnancy: in Canada, p. < 0.02 and in China, p. < 0.001.

The effect of pregnancy outcome on the mother's emotional health, as indicated by a visual analogue scale, shows that a full term outcome has no effect in 77.1 %, miscarriage = 48.6%, abortion = 50.7%. For those outcomes that have a marked effect on the mother's emotional health, full term 5.4%, 5.7% miscarriage, abortion 10.3%.

The effect of the immediacy of a pregnancy loss on the mother's need for professional help also declines. However, in the first pregnancy, if there is a pregnancy loss, 10.4% of women indicate a strong need (5+ on VAS) for professional help after their first pregnancy loss, no matter how long ago it was, and 22.2% indicate a strong need for professional help if there was a baby lost in their most recent pregnancy.

At the time of this survey, 29.2% of women indicate some need for professional help following a loss in their last pregnancy.

The survival analysis of our data indicates that a miscarriage shortens the interval between pregnancies. Abortion lengthens the interval between pregnancies.

We compared the pregnancy outcomes of the patients for Victoria physicians and those of the Christian Medical and Dental Society (CMDS) across Canada. In the first pregnancy, the CMDS Doctors' miscarriage rate was 6.2, Victoria 12.5. The rate for abortions was CMDS, 10.7 compared to Victoria, 26.8. The full term rate was, CMDS 72.0, compared to Victoria, 50.4.

PREGNANCY OUTCOME	INCLUDING ABORTIONS		NOT INCLUDING ABORTIONS	
	VICTORIA DOCTORS	C.M.D.S. DOCTORS	VICTORIA DOCTORS	C.M.D.S. DOCTORS
Full term, normal birth weight	50.4	72.0	66.9	80.6
Full term, low birth weight	4.3	2.5	5.9	2.8
Premature	3.2	6.6	4.4	7.4
Miscarriage	12.5	6.2	17.1	6.9
Abortion	26.8	10.7	-	-
Stillborn	1.4	0.4	1.9	0.4
Early Infant Death	1.4	1.2	1.9	1.3
Ectopic	0.0	0.4	0.0	0.4
	100% N=280	100% N=243	100% N=280	100% N=243

Table 10.1 Outcomes of First Teenage Pregnancies: Victoria and C.M.D.S. Physicians' Patients

PARTNER SUPPORT FIRST

PREGNANCY OUTCOME	PRESENT AND SUPPORTIVE	PRESENT, NOT SUPPORTIVE	ABSENT	PRESENT AND SUPPORTIVE	PRESENT, NOT SUPPORTIVE	ABSENT
Full term, normal birth weight	76.3	47.1	55.3	78.6	62.7	46.8
Full term, low birth weight	4.0	8.8	1.6	5.4	6.7	9.7
Premature	4.7	6.9	7.3	5.3	8.0	12.7
Miscarriage	8.7	18.6	8.9	7.8	12.0	9.7
Abortion	4.0	16.7	25.2	1.1	8.0	19.4
Stillborn	1.1	1.0	0.8	0.5	0.0	1.6
Early Intent Death	0.8	0.0	0.0	1.0	2.7	0.0
Ectopic	0.3	1.0	0.8	0.3	0.0	0.0
	100%	100%	100%	100%	100%	100%
Combined abortion and miscarriage x^2 significance	12.7	35.3	34.1	8.9	20.0	29.1

Table 10.2 Effect of Partner's Presence and Support on the Outcome of the First and Second Pregnancies

It appears that the miscarriage, early infant death and ectopic pregnancy rates increase following an abortion.

In an analysis of the China data, there is obviously an increasing rate of abortions with diminishing age. The older age group of Chinese women have had eight or nine children, whereas the younger age group are regulated to one, possibly two. The data shows that with the older age group, 87% of children were breast fed, and with the younger age group, 18% breast fed their babies.

In the first pregnancy (Canadian sample), if the partner is present but not supportive, a woman has four times an increased chance of having an abortion; if absent, six times increased chance of abortion. If, in the first pregnancy, the partner is present but not supportive, the miscarriage rate is doubled but is the same rate in the second pregnancy. The effect of lack of partner support continues until the sixth pregnancy. During the second pregnancy, if the partner is present but not supportive, there is 700% increased chance of having an abortion, and if the partner is absent, an 1800% increased chance of having an abortion.

As determined by a multiple regression analysis, the most important factors related to a higher number of abortions are (1) less partner support, (2) higher number of pregnancies, (3) young age, and (4) general approval of having abortions.

The miscarriage rate appears to depend, to some extent, on whether women have a generally approving attitude toward abortions. Those who approve of abortions have 52.6% miscarriage rate, and those who disapprove of abortion have a 48.1% miscarriage rate. On a Pearson's Correlation Coefficient this is significant, $p. < 0.05$.

A step-wise regression analyses of various variables determining any relationship between the first pregnancy outcome and these variables indicates that present health, quality of family life, enjoying being a parent are not significant. What is important is the mother's attitude about having an abortion, whether the partner is supportive and whether the mother's health has been affected by a previous loss.

CONCLUSIONS

Teenagers are as capable as any other age group of having full term babies. Therefore, being young is no indication for abortion.

The outcome of the first pregnancy is the best predictor for the outcome of the second pregnancy, and therefore it is very important to make sure women receive good maternal care during the first pregnancy to increase the chance of their having a full term baby, subsequently. Abortions increase the chance of having a miscarriage by between 1.8 and 2.4 times.

It appears that well-known factors, such as the quality of family life, show as expected in our study. We also found that pregnancy losses have a major impact on a mother's emotional and physical health.

Even though the duration of the pregnancy with an abortion is, on average, shorter than that with a miscarriage, the abortion appears to have a greater negative effect on the mother's present health.

It appears that women do not adapt to pregnancy losses. The impact of abortions, in particular, appears to have a cumulative, increasing negative effect.

There is some diminishing impact of a pregnancy loss, but, when the first pregnancy is a loss, it still has a major impact many years later.

At any point in time, 25% - 30% of women who have had a pregnancy loss desire professional help. This is greatly ignored or underestimated by physicians and other caregivers. Women generally do not speak of a need to deal with their pregnancy loss, but try to obtain help by indicating they have headaches, backaches, menstrual problems, etc. Since approximately 60-70% of all women in North America by the age of 45 have had one or more abortions, and as many have had miscarriages, this seems to indicate there is a vast need for professional helpers in dealing with pregnancy losses. It should be remembered that we measured the need for professional help as a point estimate. Therefore, it is likely that a much higher percentage need help to deal with their pregnancy losses at some time.

Women who have had miscarriages are eager to quickly try pregnancy again. Women who have had abortions intuitively understand the grieving must be done first and, if they have not gone through the grief, they know there will be difficulty. They do not want to go through another pregnancy without resolving the underlying problems.

It appears that physicians who do not abort their patients also provide the emotional support that diminishes the number of miscarriages.

Although it is a controversial finding, the following abortion in rates of ectopic pregnancy, miscarriage and early infant death is supported by both aspects of our pregnancy outcome study. Other studies tend to report that, "all other factors being equal," ectopic pregnancies do not increase after an abortion. Unfortunately, all other factors are not equal because the abortion undermines many aspects of the mother's physical and emotional health.

It is apparent that some factor, quite likely an abortion, interferes with a mother's ability to breast feed her baby. After an abortion, women report that they have greater difficulty touching, holding and breast feeding their infants.

The need for partner support appears to be constant throughout a woman's pregnancy. The quality of partner support is vitally important and women (up to 6 pregnancies) do not appear to adapt to lack of a supportive partner.

Of all the factors we examined, the amount of partner support is the most important impact on the number of abortions and the number of miscarriages. People who have grown up on farms realize that if an animal is not supported during its pregnancy, it will spontaneously abort its young. There appears to be a sensitive neuro-hormonal, psychological mechanism operating to ensure babies are born into families. Without the husband's concern, care and encouragement, women get rid of unborn children. They reject, as they feel rejected.

It appears that younger women have more abortions because they have only a 50% chance of having a partner who is present and supportive. In an older age group, partner support is 70% to 90%. This indicates that the best way to prevent abortion in a young age group is to make sure that they have a present and supportive partner.

DISCUSSION

Is it possible that, in some way, the mother's attitude about abortion affects the pregnancy so that it is more likely to spontaneously abort? It seems so from our data.

It appears abortions are more likely to result in unresolved grief, which increases depression, which interferes with the immune system, which leaves women more vulnerable and susceptible to cancers and infections.

3. ABORTION RECOVERY CANADA (1994 -1995)

SUMMARY

An analysis of the data provided by Abortion Recovery Canada indicated that there is a fluctuation in the frequency of calls, depending on the duration of time between the abortion and the time of the call. The frequency of call is highest at 9 months, 12 months and 24 months. This indicates that women need help ail the time when the baby would have been born if it had not been aborted, and on the anniversary of the abortions. The stronger need for counseling 6 months after an abortion confirms the idea that a pregnancy is a long biorhythm, which, if truncated, leaves the woman in an unstable physical and emotional condition.

Approximately 80% of the sexual relationships broke up following an abortion.

20% of the callers were men. A significant number of callers were also grandparents.

4. POST ABORTION SURVIVOR SYNDROME (1979 -1997)

SAMPLE

100 (ongoing study)

MEASURES

Self-Report Questionnaire. With visual analogue scales questioning attitudes and assessment of health. Grids provide an opportunity to indicate the outcomes of all the mother's pregnancies and all of self or partner's pregnancies, assessing amount of partner support, breast-feeding, etc.

RESULTS

Preliminary data indicates that being an abortion survivor leaves deep and difficult conflicts.

Most people know, or strongly suspect, that they are abortion survivors.

When people are told explicitly about their parent's abortion, they are deeply upset. The upset is more easily resolved if they hear the news from their parents directly, than if they hear through some other source, e.g. gossip.

Of the abortion survivors, 27% felt their parents had considered aborting them, 47% felt their chances of survival were diminished by the situation in their country, 35% had aborted siblings.

Being an abortion survivor affected their lives in many ways; 23% felt that they did not deserve to be alive, 53% had difficulty knowing who they were.

In most countries, approximately one third of the pregnancies are aborted. In Washington, DC, one-half are aborted. In Russia, the abortion to a live birth ratio is three to one. In China, although the statistics are not easily available, it I likely that the abortion to live birth ratio is two or three to one.

CONCLUSIONS

In many places of the world, children's chances of surviving their intrauterine life may be as low as 10-20% and thus they are truly a survivor. World-wide, approximately 50% of children born into the world today have aborted siblings.

5. POST-ABORTION PROVIDERS SYNDROME (1993 -1997)

SAMPLE

27 men and women, mostly physicians

SUMMARY

The vast majority of those who perform abortions do it very reluctantly, and nobody we know who is doing abortion is happy doing it.

The majority of people doing abortions feel they are being used by society and by their colleagues. Partly for that reason, they feel very angry and uncomfortable among their peers.

The data we have suggests that the majority of abortion providers become enmeshed in a vicious cycle, but primarily begin because of a desire for money or power.

As the person becomes more enmeshed in providing abortions, he/she becomes increasingly unhappy with him/herself and very frequently depressed. Many abortion providers have family and marital problems.

GLOSSARY OF TERMS

The purpose of this glossary is to briefly define terms that appear throughout the text. All of these terms have detailed explanations, but they may not appear in the section where they are first used.

Abuse Any trauma or attack that partly destroys the person who is becoming whom God determined him/her to become. Used to include physical abuse (hitting, burning, shaking, etc.), verbal abuse (criticism, blaming, humiliating, etc.) and sexual abuse (pornography, fondling, intercourse, etc.). It is sometimes used to include all kinds of child mistreatment.

Acting Out Rather than deal with internal tensions and conflicts, the individual expresses his/her dilemmas by aggressive or self-destructive behavior.

Alternative Plan Not the second best, but the more painful route inaugurated by Christ in His suffering, death and resurrection, whereby people can still become whom God designed them to be.

Assertion Learning to proclaim and demonstrate one's full humanity in the face of threats or assault.

Blame The guilt and responsibility others attribute to a person for sins of omission or commission that they may or may not have done.

Blueprint This is the picture in each individual's mind of the person he/she should become (the building he/she is working on) Children see their Blueprint most clearly. It is expressed in their fantasy and play.

Builder Beginning during infancy, an individual seeks the materials and opportunity to develop the person he/she was designed to become.

Building Materials In a metaphor, these are the ingredients, food, affection, experiences, etc. necessary for the construction of the person he/she was designed to become.

Building Supplier Adults responsible (mostly parents) for providing the building materials quickly and advising on the construction of the castle.

Castle Metaphorically, this is the whole, authentic, integrated person the child is helping God construct; a sturdy, attractive, welcoming home.

Child Abuse and Neglect (CAN) A combination of not getting the proper building materials at the right time for the construction of the person according to his/her blueprint and the partial destruction of his/her person as the result of physical and/or verbal and/or sexual assault.

Co-Creation Working with God to develop the person he/she is designed to be.

Commitment At the beginning of the Hope Alive treatment program, counselees are asked to commit themselves to a number of important expectations that will keep them working with each other and finishing the program

Committing Spirits The ancient Christian practice of asking God to receive the spirits of those who have died.

Conflict The intra psychic memory and structure of opposing thoughts, feelings and impulses.

Contribution The percentage of input a person or people have in making some tragedy occur. In metaphor: the amount of each chemical reagent that resulted in an explosion.

Core Person We are essentially indestructible spirit. The core of our being centers on our spirit (see Pilgrim).

Created Humanity People did not evolve. They were purposely made, and those purposes are seen most clearly in the character and the intentions of the Great Designer, God Almighty.

Dancer The False Face, or Mask, used to attract things people need for their development, or to repel aggression, used in the face of neglect or abuse; almost invariably maladaptive.

Defense Psychological mechanisms people use to ward off threats of annihilation or psychosis.

Dehumanizing The net effect on an individual of abuse, neglect and bad choices, so they become less than fully human.

Evil Personified in the devil. A force that seeks to destroy God's creation and insult God.

Existential Anxiety Feeling that a person's life will be suddenly ended by forces that come out of nowhere and for no particular reason. Most frequently felt by abortion survivors.

False Faces Used interchangeably with Masks to indicate the false front one puts on while attempting to deal with adversity (neglect and abuse) in order to try and gain the essential ingredients for the development of the PISHB.

Family A mated man and woman, plus at least one child.

Fight (Protest') When attacked or threatened, the human responds with either fight or flight, depending on the relative size and nature of the threat. The physiological reactions of fight or flight and the mental states consequent to these reactions are quite different.

Flight (Withdrawal) If aggressed or threatened by someone or something for which there is no assertive defense, a person should flee. The difficult questions are when, how and where.

Guilt The sensation and the knowledge that you have: 1) made a bad mistake, 2) cannot completely undo it, 3) will soon feel the consequences of that bad mistake in yourself or in others.

I.P.P.F. International Planned Parenthood Federation. An almost ubiquitous organization well funded by western governments. Promotes "free choice" and "easy access to abortions."

Love The desire and action of meeting a person's needs. Because needs are definable, love is measurable.

Manipulation Attempting to get someone else to do what you want for your selfish purposes without overtly asking, but by maneuvering them to do it out of guilt, fear, etc.

Masks Used interchangeably with False Faces to indicate the false front one puts on in the face of adversity (neglect) in order to try and get the essential ingredients for the development of the PISHB.

My Name A term used in the Hope Alive treatment program to indicate the real, permanent, whole person. New body, mind and spirit, all three which have the impression and the ingredients from one's earthly life.

Needs Definable, measurable ingredients necessary for a person's full physical, psychological and spiritual development.

Neglect Used to include physical neglect (lack of food, shelter, proper medical care, etc.) and emotional and intellectual neglect (lack of affirmation, guidance, education, etc.).

Observer The third part of the tragic triangle. Composed of the person or people who knew or could have known, but did nothing or did little to prevent the tragedy from happening.

Ontological Guilt The sense and knowledge that one has not used talents and opportunities as well as he/she might have to become the person he/she was designed to be.

Original Plan God's initial project to create humans with whom He could have deep fellowship. Individuals who chose to know and love Him freely.

Perpetrator One of the three parts of a tragic triangle. The person who apparently contributes most to the tragedy and usually initiates it, although the major responsibility is often held by the Observer.

Person I Should Have Become (PISHB) The full human God designed a person to become, whose development was truncated or made impossible by the dehumanizing effects of abuse, neglect, abortion and bad choices.

Pilgrim The authentic, core person who has been able to survive, hope, dream and co-create, although he/she may have been wearing Masks. Every Pilgrim has considerable ability, but all have some disability, warts and wounds, and are often very weary.

Post-Abortion Survivor Syndrome (PASS) The effects of deep wounds and conflicts associated with being alive when others in the family, neighborhood or country were killed. This is one type of the larger category of Pregnancy Loss Survivor Syndrome.

Post-Abortion Syndrome (PAS) A constellation of signs and symptoms arising from conflicts engendered by the fact one has directly or indirectly contributed to the death of an unborn child. This is one type of the larger category of Pregnancy Loss Syndrome.

Pregnancy Loss Survivor Syndrome (PLSS) The effects of surviving when others in one's family or neighborhood were killed by abortion or died b> miscarriage, ectopic pregnancy, stillbirth, childbirth, or early infant death.

Pregnancy Loss Syndrome (PLS) The damaging effects of the death of a pre-born or newborn baby for all reasons, e.g. miscarriage, abortion, stillbirth, ectopic pregnancy, childbirth or sudden infant death. These damaging effects on women (PLS W) and on men (PLS M) result from not completing grief and not resolving the conflicts regarding the baby and family that occurred before, during and after the loss.

Primary Affect Those feelings that arise from basic anxieties or basic joys.

Psycho Drama A short, spontaneous play used to highlight the essential elements of some intra psychic and interpersonal conflict.

Realistic Expectations The hope that people will meet needs that they are capable of providing.

Reconciliation The process of re-establishing and improving a relationship broken or damaged by abortion, abuse and neglect. Usually initiated by the Victim and begins with forgiveness.

Re-enactment The tendency, on the part of all those who have unresolved conflicts arising from past trauma or bad choices, to re-stage a tragedy in an effort to learn the essential how and why of the early trauma.

Rehabilitation One of the final phases of counseling whereby the individual learns to love by attempting to prevent happening to others what happened to them. This facilitates the turn away from the necessary self-centeredness while in counseling towards a concern for other people.

Resistance A tendency to oppose knowing unwelcome truths and difficult growing toward the maturing possible for the Pilgrim.

Responsibility A portion of the contribution determined by one's ability to choose. It may be interfered with by previous neglect or abuse, or present handicaps, drugs, etc.

Role-play A pre-set series of interactions between two or more individuals. Used to externalize a conflict or to teach a new skill.

Royal Law of Love God's command to humans that they love Him and love one another. A law that is as firmly established, universal and powerful as gravity.

Scapegoat The person onto whom are attributed and imputed family and social mistakes, foibles, and foolishness of past and present generations. The unborn baby is most frequently chosen.

Scapegoating The tendency of all those with sins and omissions to place the blame on others, particularly those who are voteless, voiceless and innocent, in an effort to exchange their innocence for the individual's guilt.

Sound Barrier A metaphor to indicate one's very large difficulty in communicating that has grown since childhood.

Surrogate Scapegoat Someone who volunteers to take the place of the Scapegoat, and thus accept the anger, etc. that would have been directed at the Scapegoat in order to stop repetition of tragic history. This takes great courage.

Survivor Guilt The sensation and experience one has that he/she should not be alive when others near and dear to him/her have died. This is almost always true for abortion survivors.

Time Line A brief history of the sequence of events in a person's life. Used in Hope Alive counseling to help people understand the essential conflicts; the how and why of each tragedy.

Tragic Triangle A triangle composed of Perpetrator, Victim and Observer, who usually all contribute and are all partially responsible for some event that damages all three of them. Before the first tragedy, children do not contribute to their own victimization.

Trans generational Tragedy The re-creation of unresolved problems arising from abuse, neglect and abortion in one generation after the other.

Triggers Large or small events, gestures and communication that evoke a strong emotion and often point to an earlier trauma or neglect. They result in an unusually large emotional reaction.

Universal Ethic of Mutual Benefit (UEMB) An expression of the Royal Law of Love in which nobody can benefit at the expense of any other. One only benefits when one's neighbor, friend or family member also benefit.

Urchin The False Face, or Mask, an individual wears when he/she is unable to get what he/she needs as a Pilgrim or as a Dancer then tends to collapse in on him/herself. The Urchin attempts to get what he/she needs, or seeks protection by eliciting pity in others.

Victim That part of the tragic triangle where an individual or individuals are hurt as a result of some action by the Perpetrator and inaction by the Observer. Although unborn babies and small children are obviously innocent, many victims may contribute to their own victimization.

Visual Parables A Hope Alive technique used to help people imagine while they follow the skeleton of a story designed to highlight certain conflicts and engage the mind in completing the task of conflict resolution, e.g. grieving.

Warts The imperfections of the Pilgrim that limit him/her or the expression of his/her humanity.

Welcoming Applied in the Hope Alive program to a situation where the parents recognize and accept the arrival of each new baby, regardless of his/her size, shape or age (conception, gestation, birth) as he/she is, where he/she is and when he/she is.

Wounds The damage done to the Pilgrim from abuse, neglect, abortion and their own bad choices.

ADDITIONAL READINGS

Berkeley, D., Humphreys, P.L. & Davidson, D. (1984). Demands made on general practice by women before and after an abortion. Journal of the Royal College of General Practitioners. 34. 310-315.

Kent, I., Greenwood, R.D. & Nicholls, W. (1978). Emotional sequelae of elective abortion. British Columbia Medical Journal. 20 118-119.

LeJune, J., Rethore, M.O., deBlois, M.C., Peeters, M., Naffah, J., Megarbane, A., Cattaneo, F., Mircher, C., Rabier, D., Parvy, P., Bardet, J. & Kamoun, P. (1992). Acides amines et trisomie 21 (in French). Ann Genet. 35. 8-13.

Lenoski, E.F. (1976). Translating injury data into preventive health care services: Physical child abuse. Department of Paediatrics, University of Southern California, unpublished.

Ney, P.G. (1994). The universal ethic of mutual benefit. Turkish Journal of Medical Ethics. 2. 53-56.

Ney, P.G. (1993). Some real issues surrounding abortion. J Clin Ethics. 4. 179-180.

Ney, P.G. (1992). Transgenerational triangles of abuse: A model of family violence. In Intimate Violence: Interdisciplinary Perspectives. (Ed: Emilio C. Viano). Washington, USA: Hemisphere Publishing Corporation, pp. 15-25.

Ney, P.G. (1991). Existential questions for physics and psychiatry. Medicine and Mind. 1(1). 13-29.

Ney, P.G. (1990). Putting your ethics on display. Can Med Assoc J. 142. 752.

Ney, P.G. (1989). Child mistreatment: Possible reasons for its transgenerational transmission. Canadian Journal of Psychiatry. 34. 594-601.

Ney, P.G. (1988). Transgenerational child abuse. Child Psychiatry Hum Dev. 18. 151-168.

Ney, P.G. (1988). Triangles of child abuse: A model of maltreatment. Child Abuse Neel. 12. 363-373.

Ney, P.G. (1987). Does verbal abuse leave deeper scars: A study of children & parents. Canadian Journal of Psychiatry. 32. 371 -378.

Ney, P.G. (1987). Grief work for adolescents. Psychiatry in Canada. 1. 95-102.

Ney, P.G. (1987). Helping patients cope with pregnancy loss. Contemporary Ob/ Gvn. 29. 117-130.

Ney, P.G. (1987). The treatment of abused children: The natural sequence of events. American Journal of Psychotherapy. 46. 391-401.

Ney, P.G. (1986). The intravaginal absorption of male generated hormones. Med Hypotheses. 20. 221-231.

Ney, P.G. (1985). Early hypothesis testing in patient interviews. J Gen Pract (NZ). June. 20-21.

Ney, P.G. (1983). A consideration of abortion survivors. Child Psychiatry Hum Dev 13. 168-179.

Ney, P.G. (1983). Ethical dilemmas in psychiatry. NZ Med J. 96. 939-940.

Ney, P.G. (1979). A psychopathogenesis of autism. Child Psychiatry & Human Development. 9. 195-205.

Ney, P.G. (1979). The relationship between abortion and child abuse. Canadian Journal of Psychiatry. 24. 610-620.

Ney, P.G. (1977). Depression in children. Hong Kong J Mental Health. 6.21-25.

Ney, P.G. (1976). Combined approaches to treating families. Can Ment Health. 24,2-5.

Ney, P.G. (1974). Four types of hyperkinesis. Canadian Psychiatric Association Journal. 19. 543-550.

Ney, P.G. (1974). The Law and the Essence of Love. Victoria: Canada, Pioneer Publishing.

Ney, P.G. (1971). Quantitative measurement in psychiatry. Indonesian J Psvchiatr 2. 66-78.

Ney, P.G. (1967). Combined therapies in a family group. Can Psvchiatr

Assoc J. 12. 379-385.

Ney, P.G. (1968). Psychodynamics of behaviour therapies. Can Psvchiatr Assoc J. 13. 555-559.

Ney, P.G. & Barry, J.E. (1983). Children who survive. NZ Med J. 96. 127-129.

Ney, P.G & Herron, J.A. (1985). Children in crisis: To whom should they turn? NZ Med J. 98. 283-286.

Ney, P.G & Herron, J. (1985). Mandatory reporting. NZ Med J. 98. 703-705.

Ney, P.G. & Mills, W.A. (1979). A time limited treatment program for children and their families. Hosp Community Psychiatry. 27. 878-879.

Ney, P.G & Mulvihill, D. (1983). A case of parental abuse. J Victimology. 7. 194-198.

Ney, P.G & Mulvihill, D. (1985). Child Psychiatric Treatment: A Practical Guide. London: Croom Helm.

Ney, P.G & Ney, P.M. (1986). Our patients' seven unspoken questions. Can Med Assoc J. 35. 879-880.

Ney, P.G & Ney, P.M. (1972). How to Raise a Family for Fun and Profit (Yours and Theirs). Victoria, Canada: Pioneer Publishing.

Ney, P.G. & Peeters, M.A. (1995) Hope Alive. Victoria, Canada: Pioneer Publishing.

Ney, P.G. & Peters, A. (1995). Ending the Cvcle of Abuse. New York: Brunner/ Mazel.

Ney, P.G. & Wickett, A.R. (1989). Mental health and abortion: Review and analysis. Psvchiatr Univ Ott. 14. 506-516.

Ney, P.G., Collins, C. & Spenser, C. (1986). Double blind double talk. Med Hypotheses. 20. 119-126.

Ney, P.G., Fung, T. & Wickett, A.R. (1994). The worst combinations of child abuse and neglect. Child Abuse and Neglect. 18f9L 705-714.

Ney, P.G., Fung, T. & Wickett, A.R. (1993). Child neglect: The precursor to child abuse. Pre- and Perinatal Psychology J. 8(2). 95-112.

Ney, P.G., Fung, T. & Wickett, A.R. (1993). Relationship between induced abortion and child abuse and neglect: Four studies. Pre- and Perinatal Psychology J. 8. 43-63.

Ney, P.G., Johnson, I. & Herron, J. (1985). Social and legal ramifications of a child crisis line. Child Abuse & Neglect. 9. 47-55.

Ney, P.G., Mulhivill, D. & Hanna, R. (1984). The effectiveness of child psychiatry inpatient treatment. Can J Psychiatry. 29. 26-30.

Ney, P.G., Wickett, A.R. & Fung, T. (1992). Causes of child abuse and neglect. Can J Psychiatry. 37. 401 -405.

Ney, P.G., Adam, R.R., Hanton, B.R. & Brindad, E.S. (1988). The effectiveness of a child psychiatric unit: A follow-up study. Can J Psychiatry. 33. 793- 799.

Ney, P.G., Fung, T., Wickett, A.R. & Beaman-Dodd, C. (1994). The effects of pregnancy loss on women's health. Soc Sci Med. 38(91. 1193-1200.

Ney, P.G., McPhee, J., Moore, C. & Trought, P. (1986). Child abuse: A study of the child's perspective. Child Abuse Negl. 10. 511-518.

Peeters, M. (1995). Eugenics and the population control mentality. UN Social Summit. NGO Forum (Copenhagen. Denmark). March.

Peeters, M. (1995). Human and ethical aspects of genetic engineering. Hearth.(Winter) 8-12.

Peeters, M. (1994). Infections recidivantes chez l'enfant trisomique 21. Impact Medecin. Sept.

Peeters, M. (1994). The effects of eugenics on the self-perception of mentally handicapped persons. UN Conference. NGO Forum (Cairo. EvgpO. September.

Peeters, M. & Le Jeune, J. (1994). Desequilibres biochimiques biochimiques et manifestations neuro-psychiques chez les personnes porteuses de trisomie 21. Proceedings FAIT 21 (Nimes. France). 39-48.

Made in the USA
Charleston, SC
11 September 2016